# ISLAMIC ECUMENE

# ISLAMIC ECUMENE

Comparing Muslim Societies

**Edited by David S. Powers
and Eric Tagliacozzo**

CORNELL UNIVERSITY PRESS   ITHACA AND LONDON

First published 2023 by Cornell University Press

Library of Congress Cataloging-in-Publication Data

Names: Tagliacozzo, Eric, editor. | Powers, David Stephan, editor.
Title: Islamic ecumene : comparing Muslim societies / edited by
    David S. Powers and Eric Tagliacozzo.
Description: Ithaca [New York] : Cornell University Press, 2023. | Includes
    bibliographical references and index.
Identifiers: LCCN 2023022941 (print) | LCCN 2023022942 (ebook) |
    ISBN 9781501772382 (hardcover) | ISBN 9781501772399 (paperback) |
    ISBN 9781501772405 (epub) | ISBN 9781501772412 (pdf)
Subjects: LCSH: Muslims—Non-Islamic countries. | Islam—Social aspects. |
    Islam—Influence. | Islamic countries—Civilization.
Classification: LCC BP52 .I845 2023 (print) | LCC BP52 (ebook) |
    DDC 306.6/97—dc23/eng/20230522
LC record available at https://lccn.loc.gov/2023022941
LC ebook record available at https://lccn.loc.gov/2023022942

# Contents

# INTRODUCTION

*David S. Powers and Eric Tagliacozzo*

How unified is the Muslim world? In matters of culture and praxis, many answers might be given to this question. Several scholars have attempted to define the *umma* (global Muslim community) but have come up with different indices.[1] In seeking answers to this question, we took a broad approach: we invited twenty-two scholars to contribute chapters on Muslim societies that they know well. Together, these contributions suggest that there are, in fact, multiple "ways of being" in the Muslim world. By moving across time and space, as well as between a number of related disciplines, we hope to identify and problematize these "ways of being" in the pages that follow. We also hope to illustrate processes of negotiation—both internal and external—that help determine what it means for a particular society to be "Islamic." These processes, in our view, are dynamic and continually renegotiated by the members of any religion.

Making such large-scale identifications of what constitutes a Muslim society is not a simple task. More than one billion Muslims are living on the planet at present.[2] They do not perform the exact same practices, nor do they hold the exact same beliefs. But this book is not about Islamic practices or beliefs; rather, it is about Muslim societies. Certainly, Muslims think of themselves as members of a single faith. Almost all Muslims adhere to key doctrines, such as the oneness of God and the finality of Muhammad's prophecy. This is a near-universal fact. Many Muslims (in theory, but also in practice) perform five basic rituals: the testimony of faith, prayer, almsgiving, fasting, and pilgrimage. Ask almost any Muslim if he or she feels a kinship to other Muslims, a sense of belonging to a shared tradition, regardless of caste, creed, or color, and he or she will invariably respond yes.[3]

1

**FIGURE I.1.** Muslim Africa and the Middle East. Map courtesy of Bill Nelson.

However, Muslim societies are complex, as Clifford Geertz (1971) shows in his important monograph *Islam Observed*, published more than fifty years ago. Although many of Geertz's specific conclusions have been challenged over time, the value of analyzing Muslim societies comparatively has been demonstrated by scholars such as Janet Abu Lughod (1991), Juan Cole (1992), and Nile Green (2020). We have also engaged in comparison in our own scholarship, and we too acknowledge the value of such work (Masud, Messick, and Powers 1996; Powers 2002; Tagliacozzo 2009, 2013; Tagliacozzo and Toorawa 2016). In this book, building on Geertz and inspired by others following in his path, we analyze some of the similarities and differences across global Muslim communities.

In *Islamic Ecumene*, we study Muslim societies along an arc that stretches from the Western world to China, and from central Asia to sub-Saharan Africa (see figures I.1 and I.2). Our central argument is that "Islam" is in fact the sum

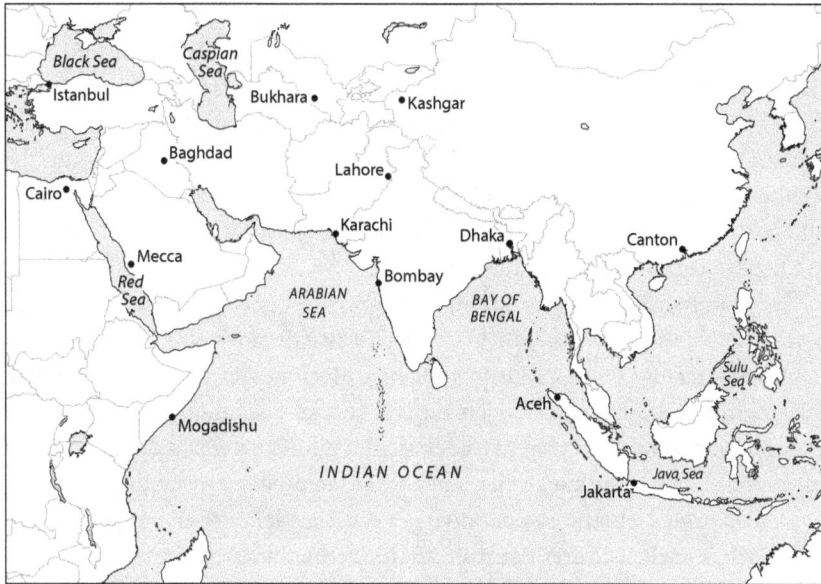

**FIGURE I.2.** Muslim Asia. Map courtesy of Bill Nelson.

of choices made by Muslims over time and space. We study those choices by grouping analyses of Muslim societies according to different rubrics. We argue that those choices tell us much about what a Muslim ecumene might mean. By using a perspective informed by Geertz—comparative and global—we shine a light on the diversity of Muslim societies and on their histories. The scholars who have contributed to this book represent the disciplines of anthropology, archaeology, architecture, art history, history, literature, and political science. The vision produced by their shared scholarship is nothing if not interdisciplinary, and interdisciplinarity is the beating heart of this book.

This book covers not only *dar al-Islam* or the Muslim world proper but also regions of the world in which Muslims are minority populations. Through the comparative treatment of these loosely connected communities across a range of topics, we are able to develop a better idea of what it means to think of the Muslim umma as a cultural community of common affiliation. The book also moves across temporal rubrics such as medieval, early modern, and modern. By transcending geographic and temporal boundaries, we hope to offer a longer and broader view of the ties that bind Muslim societies.

There are pressing reasons for undertaking such a comparative examination at this moment in history. The need to understand Muslims and their societies has never been more urgent. For the past twenty years, large parts of the Muslim world have been in a state of unrest, both internally, inside individual nation-states, and regionally, as in the lands once controlled by the Islamic State of Iraq and Syria (ISIS), which straddle a fair section of the heartland of the Middle East. In addition, the Arab Spring has drawn attention to social energies lying below the surface of Muslim societies that were on a low boil, chafing against coercive regimes. If one adds regional variants of disaffection and violence (e.g., western China, the southern Philippines, and coastal East Africa), it is readily apparent that a global and comparative understanding of the dynamics of Muslim cultures is overdue. We hope to contribute to this understanding.

The Comparative Muslim Societies Program at Cornell, which hosted talks by the contributors to this book over the past two decades, was inaugurated in 2001, a momentous year for Muslims and non-Muslims alike. Note, however, that the program began six months *before* the 9/11 attacks. The timing is important: the program's reasons for trying to understand the Muslim world did not emerge in response to 9/11, although the rapid spread of political instability after 9/11 has added urgency to the comparative project. The phenomenon of political instability has made it clearer than ever that a methodology of comparison in our understanding of the Muslim world is crucial. This book seeks to advance that comparative agenda.

How can we best understand these societies as part of something larger than the nation-state, the primary organizing unit of almost all human societies in the early twenty-first century? Which disciplines can be utilized to look for common themes across these cultures, and how can these disciplines be deployed as a group to elicit differences and commonalities? Which themes allow us to see the organizational matrices of common Muslim affiliation in societies scattered across the globe that have their own vernacular languages, folk traditions, and worldviews? How can we identify connections between people who regard themselves as members of a single community when the tools for doing so are so varied and require the interventions of specialists across a wide range of disciplines and approaches to knowledge? How does a book of this magnitude provide us with insights into the Muslim world that a single-authored monograph would not? Finally, what can we gain from an attempt to cross centuries and thousands of miles of geographic space in search of an answer to the question, What makes Muslim societies Muslim in the face of myriad differences?

The chapters in this book were solicited for the coverage that they provide across the span of the Muslim world. This is true both geographically, from Europe to Asia and from the central Asian steppe to sub-Saharan Africa, and temporally. The table of contents specifies the rubrics under which we have divided the chapters. Note, however, that we could have arranged the chapters differently. By design, the configuration we have chosen breaks up time and space so that a reader can see the comparisons on offer across Muslim communities wherever and whenever they exist. In other words, we want the comparisons to be the center of our story. As noted, this book is not about Islam but about Muslim societies and the ways in which these societies constitute a unity within their overall diversity. This is so even while the distinctiveness of Muslim peoples is clearly sketched out here, both as one travels across the globe and as one moves backward and forward in time.

We do not claim to have discovered the inner workings of Muslim societies or what makes them unique as a category of human organization. Rather, we attempt to show that these communities have certain shared features while retaining their individual specificities. By examining ethics, education, the experience of colonial subjugation, and postcolonial liberation, many of these nuances of the common and the particular rise to the surface. Manifestations of politics, race, and identity formation concretize these comparisons; so, too, do the vagaries of artistic renderings and the processes of translation across multiple societies. Even the ways in which Muslim communities commemorate and mark their dead both connect and separate them; this also emerges from the process of comparison across societies. We try to view these processes as if from an airplane, from the high vantage point of comparison. Some of the main lessons we have learned in placing these chapters in conversation with each other follow below.

Over the span of what historians call the long nineteenth century, the languages and technologies associated with educating the umma and furthering knowledge—a main concern of Muslim communities throughout Islamic history—changed profoundly. These changes are clearly evident in central and south Asia, though they take place wherever one might go in *dar al-Islam*. It is also clear that the colonial period and its aftermath were vital in orienting and reorienting Muslim societies in numerous ways. Between the nineteenth century and the first half of the twentieth, Muslim communities resisted external non-Muslim regimes, as in Algeria, where Algerians were eventually able to overthrow their Gallic overlords. The dynamism of Muslim societies during the colonial era is also reflected in how Muslims changed certain key practices, such as marriage, as in early twentieth-century British colonial Zanzibar. Coastal East Africa was a complicated zone in which non-Muslim majority populations in Kenya and Tanzania designated coastal Muslims as "foreign" and "other" despite the fact that these Swahili peoples had been Muslim and part of the shared history of these coasts for many centuries.

The relationship between colonialists and colons was unsettled by the institution of slavery, which was widely practiced throughout the Muslim world. Islamic notions of sovereignty differed from those of occupying Western powers, as in the

Sulu Archipelago of the southern Philippines, a seascape Islamized many centuries before the Spanish (and later the Americans) started planting flags in this part of the world. Muslims who lived at great distances from European metropoles could be linked to "great events" that were taking place across the globe. The French Revolution, for example, echoed in Anjouan, a small and otherwise insignificant Indian Ocean island whose story was folded into the narrative of global events. The melding of cultures under colonialism led to significant changes in the way in which members of the umma identified themselves as Muslims. In Ottoman Izmir in the eighteenth century and in Accra (contemporary Ghana) in the nineteenth, identity formation was significantly affected by economic interactions between Muslims and non-Muslims. In the twentieth century, the ramifications of interreligious contact extended as far as Tibet, where the invasion of Communist China in 1950, following the end of the Chinese civil war, had substantial adverse consequences on a centuries-old Muslim community in Lhasa. The same was true of the southern Philippines and Mindanao, where local Muslims resisted indigenous Catholic elites from Manila who usurped American rule when the Philippines became an independent republic after World War II.

Some of our authors engage with the concept of "othering." Just as Westerners use walls as a literary trope to marginalize Muslims (in the past and in the present), the Turkish regime under Erdogan used the built environment (actual physical space) to marginalize Turkey's Alevi minority. In both cases—one literary, the other physical—a powerful group uses the built environment to categorize and control the "other" in ways that support dominant power. These tropes are also invoked in an effort to repress the forces of resistance. We also look comparatively at the portrayal of Muslims in a range of media—for example, poetic representations of Muslim women in Britain in the age of Romanticism, a mid-twentieth-century film project jointly produced by Russians and Indians that tells the tale of a Muslim traveler, and newspaper coverage of Muslims in Germany and the United States.

We also examine art and its service in the formation of the nation. Muslim musicians, for example, have created novel musical genres that incorporate non-Muslim artistic forms, such as the Bengali Hindu *bhakti* genre, which was developed in West Bengal and what is now Bangladesh. Farther west in the Persian Gulf, tiny oil-rich emirates vie with each other to create hypermodern museums as public spaces in which modern art and ancient artifacts fashioned by Muslim artists are displayed and celebrated as part of the national patrimony. However, what is possessed must also be translated. Muslims have long been adept at translating and then incorporating external ideas. The Ottomans and post-Ottoman Turks were masters of such practices, blending into their societies "foreign" ideas that were considered useful. But the activity of "translation" sometimes proves difficult, as reflected in Arab American diasporic literature, which seeks to balance "Old World" culture and the newer cultural demands of American life.

Finally, the multivalent forces of comparison are manifest when Muslims find themselves in end-of-life situations in the process of remembering the dead. We see this in medieval Iberia and also in Yemen over a period of four centuries, from Yemen's "coffee age" to its violent and anarchic present. Decisions about how to mark off and signify the departed show us that Muslim societies are simultaneously local, regional, and global, often in overlapping ways. Muslim cultural practices relating to death are dizzyingly complicated. These practices manifest the same signs of local singularity and complexity found in many other aspects of life in the Muslim global community. Whether in medieval Iberia and the western Mediterranean or in Yemen at the present time, specific ways of saying goodbye to the departed—while simultaneously remembering their lives—echo across Muslim lands.

Is there an Islamic ecumene, as suggested by the title of this book? It is beyond doubt that most Muslims feel a sense of recognition in the practices and cultural expressions of their coreligionists, wherever they are located across the globe, and no matter the temporal epoch. In other ways, however, there is clearly a disconnect between the experiences of these societies, many but not all of which underwent painful periods of cultural subjugation by the West.[4] Choices about what to translate from the outside world, how to do this, and how much should be adopted distinguish one Muslim society from another in recognizable and less recognizable ways. Some of these differences developed slowly over long periods of time, with the result that some Muslim societies bear little resemblance to others.[5]

There is no way to avoid the fact that these societies manifest bonds of similarity that cross cultural boundaries. In this respect, the Muslim ecumene may be little different from, for example, Buddhist, Jewish, or Christian religious communities. Societies can be singular and corporate in cadence, while at the same time individual and communal in outlook. This book attests to that duality across time and space and through the assembled lenses of a multiplicity of disciplines. Through the work of historians, anthropologists, political scientists, and art historians, we can identify some of the key features of the Muslim ecumene: a broad sense of community; adherence to the five pillars of Islam; and a set of often (though not always) shared beliefs, both religious and secular. We can also see how these features are reinforced through social norms that cross time and space in the fabrication of the umma. The pages that follow illustrate these processes and the many ways to see both unity and diversity within the global Muslim community.

## NOTES

1. On the caliphate and what it has meant to believers over time, see Kennedy 2016 and Hassan 2017.

2. Almost two-thirds of all Muslims in the world live in Asia, and the number of Muslims living in the Middle East and North Africa (the historical heartland of Islam) is very close to the number of Muslims living in sub-Saharan Africa. The four largest Muslim nation-states in the world are all located outside of the Middle East, with only Egypt breaking into the top five, and then only a distant fifth. Clearly, there is no single model of a Muslim society.

3. The sense of communal identity is reflected in academic literature on the Hajj. During the pilgrimage to Mecca, Muslims repeatedly express their sense of attachment to the umma. See Kane 2015 on the Russian Hajj, Faroqhi 1994 on the Ottoman Hajj, and Can 2020 on the Hajj from central Asia.

4. One may compare the spread of Islam along East Africa's Swahili coast (see Campbell 2019) and its spread across eastern India to the "Bengal Frontier" (see Eaton 1993).

5. For example, for several centuries Muslim families from the Middle East have enjoyed significant prestige in Indonesia; an Arab lineage opens many doors in Muslim circles. Over the past several decades, however, as social and political unrest have spread through parts of the Middle East, increasing numbers of Indonesian Muslims are asking whether that prestige is justified. This is especially the case when such prestige is combined with derision of Indonesian Muslims as "Muslims in name only." In some circles, Southeast Asian Muslims have begun to see less continuity with their Middle Eastern coreligionists and have pointed this out in increasingly open and aggressive ways. Many Indonesians contrast their success with democratic elections in the past twenty years with the political repression prevalent in much of the Muslim Middle East. On these issues, see Hefner 2000 and Hefner and Bagir 2021.

## REFERENCES

Abu Lughod, Janet. 1991. *Before European Hegemony: The World System AD 1250–1350.* New York: Oxford University Press.

Campbell, Gwyn. 2019. *Africa and the Indian Ocean World from Early Times to Circa 1900.* Cambridge: Cambridge University Press.

Can, Lale. 2020. *Spiritual Subjects: Central Asian Pilgrims and Ottoman Hajj at the End of Empire.* Palo Alto, CA: Stanford University Press.

Cole, Juan, ed. 1992. *Comparing Muslim Societies: Knowledge and the State in a World Civilization.* Ann Arbor: University of Michigan Press.

Eaton, Richard. 1993. *The Rise of Islam and the Bengal Frontier.* Berkeley: University of California Press.

Faroqhi, Suraiya. 1994. *Pilgrims and Sultans: The Hajj under the Ottomans.* London: I.B. Tauris.

Geertz, Clifford. 1971. *Islam Observed: Religious Development in Morocco and Indonesia.* Chicago: University of Chicago Press.

Green, Nile. 2020. *Global Islam: A Very Short Introduction.* New York: Oxford University Press.

Hassan, Mona. 2017. *Longing for the Lost Caliphate: A Transregional History.* Princeton, NJ: Princeton University Press.

Hefner, Robert. 2000. *Civil Islam: Muslims and Democratization in Indonesia.* Princeton, NJ: Princeton University Press.

Hefner, Robert, and Zainal Abidin Bagir, eds. 2021. *Indonesian Pluralities: Islam, Democracy, Citizenship.* Notre Dame, IN: Notre Dame University Press.

Kane, Eileen. 2015. *Russian Hajj: Empire and the Pilgrimage to Mecca*. Ithaca, NY: Cornell University Press.

Kennedy, Hugh. 2016. *Caliphate: The History of an Idea*. New York: Basic Books.

Masud, M. Khalid, Brinkley Messick, and David S. Powers, eds. 1996. *Islamic Legal Interpretation: Muftis and Their Fatwas*. Cambridge, MA: Harvard University Press.

Powers, David S. 2002. *Law, Society and Culture in the Maghrib, 1300–1500*. New York: Cambridge University Press.

Tagliacozzo, Eric, ed. 2009. *Southeast Asia and the Middle East: Islam, Movement, and the Longue Durée*. Palo Alto, CA: Stanford University Press.

——. 2013. *The Longest Journey: Southeast Asians and the Pilgrimage to Mecca*. New York: Oxford University Press.

Tagliacozzo, Eric, and Shawkat Toorawa, eds. 2016. *Hajj: Pilgrimage in Islam*. New York: Cambridge University Press.

# Part 1
# ETHICS, MORAL RECTITUDE, AND EDUCATION

The two chapters in this part address the eastern flank of the Muslim cultural sphere: India and central Asia. In the first, Farina Mir examines the transmission of the Islamic literary genre known as *akhlāq* from central Islamic lands to India. This literary genre treats both personal ethics (moral rectitude and cultivation of the self) and the ethics of statecraft. The first *akhlāq* treatises appeared in Arabic in the tenth century and in Persian a century later. Subsequently, these treatises were transmitted to India, where Persian was the language of the Mughal court. Between the sixteenth and the eighteenth centuries, the Persian-language texts played an important role in shaping the political culture of the Mughal empire. At an undetermined date, these texts began to be translated into Urdu, the vernacular language of north India. In the nineteenth century, new technologies, especially the printing press, made it possible for laymen to purchase and read cheap copies of these Urdu texts. Mir discusses one of these texts, *Mehboob al-Akhlaq*, published in 1910 and sold for 1/64th of a rupee. She highlights the eclecticism of this text, which includes, in addition to classical Islamic materials, quotations from Benjamin Franklin, the *Bhagavad Gita*, *Ramayana*, Kabir, and more. The scholars who produced this new Islamic genre appropriated colonial knowledge and used it to their own ends. The genre attracted a large popular audience and was an important component of Urdu print literature.

In the second chapter, James Pickett treats the transmission of knowledge from the Arabic-speaking world to the Persian-speaking world by examining the curriculum of the madrasa, or law college. The starting point of his investigation is Bukhara, where there were more than 200 madrasas in the nineteenth century.

Pickett identifies a more or less standard curriculum that was composed of three parts: (1) a common core (grammar, syntax, logic, and theology); (2) electives (poetry, metaphysics, disputation, and substantive law); and (3) postgraduate disciplines (mysticism, the occult sciences, and philosophy). He argues that the madrasa was the fulcrum of multiple cultural vectors that facilitated the fusion of scholarly writings in Arabic and Persian. The Bukharan madrasa, Pickett concludes, may accurately be characterized as Persianate, albeit with two qualifications: the foundation of the educational system was Arabic, and, beginning in the nineteenth century, Persian disciplines were supplemented by Turkish vernacular disciplines.

These two scholars highlight the importance of Persian as an Islamicate language and the eclecticism and sophistication of Islamic knowledge.

# URDU ETHICS LITERATURE IN COLONIAL INDIA

## *Akhlāq* in the Vernacular

*Farina Mir*

In Islam, ethics in a broad sense—that is, as a set of moral principles—is derived from a number of sources, principally the Qur'an and hadith (traditions of Muhammad) but also "the works of theologians, philosophers, mystics, historians, political thinkers, and other writers" (*OEIW*, s.v. "Akhlāq" [I. Kalin]). As Fazlur Rahman suggests, however, a more specific tradition emerged in Islam as well: "The moral tradition that grew out of religion [principally the Qur'an and hadith] and further developed under the influence of philosophy," he writes, "was called *elm al-aklaq*" (*EIr*, s.v. "AKLĀQ" [F. Rahman]). This chapter is concerned with this latter, more specific tradition of ethics—identified in Islam by the term *akhlāq* (hereafter: akhlaq)—and its circulation in late-colonial India (1858–1947).[1]

Akhlaq is a polysemous term: it is the plural of the Arabic *khulq* (character, nature, and/or disposition). As a concept within Islam, however, akhlaq refers to ethics (*ODI*, s.vv. "Akhlaq," "Ethics"). Akhlaq is also a classical genre of Islamic literature. Ethical treatises that help define the genre emerge as early as the tenth century, and in the eleventh century the philosopher Ibn Miskawayh (932–1030) produced a more comprehensive work, *Tehzib ul-Akhlaq*, or *The Refinement of Character* (Miskawayh 1968; Leaman 1996), that, Peter Adamson argues, brought "together all of the themes . . . in ethical works up to this point" (*EI³*, s.v. "Ethics in Philosophy" [P. Adamson]). Akhlaq literature, as a genre and as represented in Miskawayh's text, is a specific Islamic tradition of philosophical ethics. One of its defining features is that this Muslim tradition is heavily influenced by Greek thought. Miskawayh's *Tehzib ul-Akhlaq*, for example, is marked by an insistence "on the agreement of Greek moral philosophy with the basic tenets of Islam" and an "attempt to reconcile revealed and philosophical truth on the basis of rational thought" (*EI²*, s.v. "Akhlāk̲" [R. Walzer]). While *Tehzib ul-Akhlaq* "separated personal ethics from the public realm" (*ODI*, s.v. "Ibn Miskawayh"), Miskawayh was clearly concerned with ethical statecraft. This latter emphasis became central as akhlaq literature entered the Persian world of letters.

Nasir al-Din al-Tusi (1201–1274) was not the first Persian to embrace the genre (Miskawayh, too, was Persian, though his renown rests on his Arabic compositions), but Tusi's Persian *Akhlaq-i Nasiri*, or *The Nasirean Ethics*, is undoubtedly the genre's most celebrated Persian text, and one that circulated widely. Tusi is today remembered as an important astronomer, mathematician, philosopher, and scientific and political adviser to both the Ismaili and Mongol rulers of his age. Hamid Dabashi, who places him alongside al-Farabi and Ibn Sina in terms of his significance to classical Islamic thought, argues that Tusi's vast corpus, on an array of subjects, is "among the finest achievements of medieval learning" (Dabashi 1996, 580). The *Akhlaq-i Nasiri*, composed in 1235 and named for and dedicated to an Ismaili governor (Nasir al-Din Abd al-Rahim, governor of Quhistan), relates directly to Miskawayh's text; the first of its three parts is a Persian translation and reworking of the latter, while its second and third parts relate to domestic economy and politics, respectively. Often referred to as a "mirror for princes," Tusi's text was influential both in his time and subsequently as a manual for ethical governance. The *Akhlaq-i Nasiri*—along with other akhlaq texts—circulated throughout the Persianate world, which from the turn of the second millennium extended from Iran northwest to the Caucasus, northeast to central Asia, and east to India.

Little is known about the precise chains of transmission that brought Arabic and Persian akhlaq literature to India. What is known, however, is that by the sixteenth century akhlaq literature had a significant cultural and political impact there. Mughal courtier and chronicler Abul Fazl records that Emperor Akbar (r. 1556–1605) wanted the *Akhlaq-i Nasiri* read to him regularly and that it was among the favored texts of Mughal political elites (Alam 2003, 61). Muzaffar Alam argues that the *Akhlaq-i Nasiri* was the most important intellectual influence at Akbar's court and that it shaped the political culture of the Mughal empire from Akbar's reign to at least the early eighteenth century, when the empire went into decline (Alam 2000, 2003). While not all scholars share this opinion (Khan 2009, 52), two things are indisputable: (1) based on extant manuscripts, Tusi's text—as well as other Persian akhlaq literature—was circulating in India, and in decidedly influential circles, from the sixteenth century and (2) Persian-language akhlaq manuscripts continued to be produced in India throughout the seventeenth and eighteenth centuries and into the nineteenth century, even as Persian was increasingly being replaced by vernacular languages in India's literate and government circles (Mir 2006).[2]

Like other Arabic and Persian genres that circulated in India, akhlaq literature was absorbed into Indian vernacular-language literatures, among them
Urdu. Urdu is a vernacular language that can be dated to as early as eleventh-
century north India; it was cultivated in Gujarat and the Deccan sultanates in
the fourteenth through sixteenth centuries and became a popular medium of
literary expression, particularly in north India, from the eighteenth century onward (Faruqi 2003). Alas, little is known about when, precisely, akhlaq literature began to be produced in Urdu, whether in translation (of Persian and Arabic
antecedents) or as original compositions. But even a cursory analysis of Urdu
print culture, which exploded in the nineteenth century owing to the ease and
affordability of lithography, suggests that akhlaq literature was an important
genre of late-colonial India's Urdu print culture.

It should perhaps be of little surprise that akhlaq, a literature about moral
comportment and a genre of classical Islamic literature, was one of the genres to
enter Urdu print culture from its nineteenth-century inception. An important
body of scholarship has shown that ulama, Sufi brotherhoods, and religious reformers alike used vernacular print as an effective medium for the wide propagation of their religious messages in colonial India (Green 2005; Ingram 2013; Jones
1990; Metcalf 1982, 2002; Robinson 1993). Religion—and related questions of
proper comportment and moral rectitude—was very much a part of the public
sphere in colonial India, and print publics were important arenas of debate and
contestation (Reetz 2006). The historiography that has alerted us to the use of
print for religious purposes in colonial India has at the same time, however, focused almost entirely on elite actors, organizations, and movements—reformist,
revivalist, and educational—and on their impact on the lives of South Asian
Muslims. While elite actors, organizations, and movements played an important
role in the history of Islam in late-colonial India, the role of nonelite actors and
noninstitutional formations in the vibrant public sphere and religious debates of
the age has been significantly harder to gauge. Similarly, the historiography has
struggled to understand religious concerns that emanated from middle- and/or
lower-class Muslims, as opposed to the concerns of elites, religious or otherwise, who often spoke for—or have been taken by scholars to represent—Indian
Muslims.

Urdu akhlaq literature affords an opportunity to consider more popular concerns. To infer popular concerns from akhlaq literature may, at first, seem like an
odd choice. Akhlaq literature is, after all, fundamentally a philosophical endeavor
that normatively constitutes a "high" literature (which is certainly true of the Arabic and Persian texts highlighted above). And it is didactic: by its very nature—a
concern with proper conduct and the cultivation of the self—akhlaq literature is
trying to persuade its audience to take action. However, Urdu akhlaq literature

was not, by and large, produced by either recognized religious authorities or religious/reform institutions. Rather, it was largely sustained by market forces and was directed at a literate audience, but not necessarily an elite one. Akhlaq literature is akin to what has been described in the context of early modern Europe as "cheap print"—that is, books produced to be accessible to the nonelite (Raymond 2011). Colonial-era Urdu akhlaq texts circulated without the benefit of patronage and subsidy, relying instead on an emerging commercial book trade.[3] It is in this sense that akhlaq is analyzed here as a genre of Urdu popular print culture.

The analysis below focuses on a single text: Muhammad Farooq's 1910 publication, *Mehboob al-Akhlaq* (Beloved ethics), which I take to be emblematic. I aim to show how akhlaq literature can help reconstruct a more popular history of Islam in late-colonial India. Specifically, the analysis underscores the various ways in which *Mehboob al-Akhlaq* reflects the popular print culture of the era; I then consider the contents of the volume, arguing that the text is asking its readers to reconsider what knowledge is authoritative in the context of British colonial rule in India. The chapter closes with a consideration of how, in the context of popular Urdu akhlaq literature, Islamic and colonial knowledge production were coconstitutive.

## Urdu Akhlaq Literature

The discussion above treats akhlaq as a stable genre, moving from Arabic to Persian to Urdu, across time and space. This representation is too straightforward, however. The Urdu akhlaq tradition bears important hallmarks of its Arabic and Persian antecedents, and indeed, many authors cite these earlier texts as inspiration or source material for their Urdu renditions (Samadani 1894, for example, cites Miskawayh, Tusi, and Asad Jalal al-Din Dawani [1427–1502; author of *Akhlaq-i Jalali*] as inspiration [41] as well as additional sources in Arabic, Persian, and Urdu [141]). But there are also important divergences. Perhaps most important is the question of genre. When referring to akhlaq as a genre, the definition must rest more on content than on form. Indeed, with regard to form, Urdu akhlaq texts are fluid, with authors appropriating different literary forms to their desired ends. Thus, Urdu akhlaq literature comprises both poetry and prose; some texts are in narrative form, while others are compendiums of sayings and the wisdom of sages of the past. Some are more "traditional" in content, hewing closely to antecedents (Sarwar 1871, for example, is based on Hussain Vaiz Kashifi's late fifteenth-century Persian *Akhlaq-i Muhsini*), and some are translations.[4] Others are products of their age and context, reflecting the impact of new knowledge and its circulation in a colonial context.

Diversity notwithstanding, Urdu akhlaq literature coheres in the following ways: it draws on a particular, Islamic philosophical tradition; it remains attentive to its aims of self-cultivation; it exploits its history of engagement with other traditions (originally Greek philosophy) to expand a corpus of Islamic knowledge; and, finally, it coheres in having been a staple of late-colonial popular publishing.

The spread of Urdu print culture in India is crucial to the argument that akhlaq is a popular literature. This diffusion did not happen (in any language, vernacular or otherwise) until the nineteenth century, despite the availability of print technology in India from the sixteenth century and vibrant manuscript/book cultures there (Orsini 2013). Typeset printing, which was expensive, remained almost completely limited to missionary activity after its introduction by the Portuguese in 1556. It was only after the introduction of lithography, a technology transferred to India in 1822 (Shaw 2013), that print culture became widespread and powerful. The first commercial lithographic press was established in Calcutta in 1823 (Shaw 2013), and it would be twenty or so years before the establishment of a robust Urdu print culture.[5] From extant texts and records of publishing, we surmise that print culture began to emerge in earnest in the 1840s and that publishing boomed from the 1860s on.[6] Urdu was a significant language of vernacular print production, with texts produced across north India and in important centers of cultural production in other parts of the subcontinent, such as Calcutta, Bombay, Madras, and Hyderabad.

Akhlaq texts were among the earliest texts produced by commercial Urdu printing presses. In 1844, the Matba-i Jami al-Akhbar Press of Madras published *Tahsin-i Akhlaq*, an Urdu translation of excerpts from two classical Persian texts—Kashifi's *Akhlaq-i Muhsini* and Dawani's *Akhlaq-i Jalali* (both of which were in the tradition of Tusi's *Akhlaq-i Nasiri*).[7] In 1848, the Matba-i Ahmadi Press in Calcutta published *Jami-ul Akhlaq*, Amanat Allah's Urdu translation of Dawani's *Akhlaq-i Jalali*.[8] By the 1870s, Urdu translations of these Persian classics were being published in Kanpur, Lucknow, and Lahore, and by the 1880s, in Bombay.[9]

These early texts tie Urdu akhlaq literature to the classical Persian tradition. But the subsequent history of Urdu akhlaq literature suggests broader horizons. In the late nineteenth and early twentieth centuries, a range of Urdu texts were published under what we might call the sign of akhlaq. All were about ethics, but they varied immensely in style and content. Focusing on printed books, and not serials and journals,[10] one can divide them into two discrete categories: translations and original compositions. Among translations, many were of classical Persian originals, principally those by Tusi, Dawani, and Kashifi. Some of these were translations of entire works, sometimes with the original Persian included; others were amalgams of a few closely related works, such as *Tahsin-i Akhlaq*, mentioned above, or *Iksir-i 'Azam*, published in Lahore in the 1870s, which excerpted and published together sections of Tusi's *Akhlaq-i Nasiri*, Dawani's *Akhlaq-i Jalali*, and Rumi's *masnavi*s (a genre of Persian poetry), translated by Karim Baksh of Rahimabad (about whom nothing else is known).[11] These translations into Urdu point to the continued currency of the classical Persian tradition in colonial India. But they are not the only indication of the vitality of the classical tradition.

Alongside translations, a number of original Urdu akhlaq texts were produced in the late nineteenth and early twentieth centuries. A notable few were written by men of great social standing, such as the eminent educationist Maulvi Mohammad Zaka Ullah (1832–1910), who published three akhlaq volumes in the 1890s—*Tehzib ul-akhlaq Arya-e Hind, Mahasin ul-akhlaq* and *Makarim ul-akhlaq*—texts that have been the subject of important study (Hasan 2008, chap. 5; Pernau 2011). Most, however, have remained largely unremarked upon and have had little bearing on the historiography of Islam in late-colonial India. As an important element of the popular print culture of their day, these texts deserve to be examined for the insights they can provide into contemporary Muslim ethical concerns and schema.

## *Mehboob al-Akhlaq* (Beloved Ethics)

*Mehboob al-Akhlaq* (hereafter *Mehboob*) is emblematic of popular Urdu akhlaq publishing in the late colonial period. An eighty-two-page lithograph, *Mehboob* was published in 1910 by the Khadim-ul Talim Steam Press, Lahore, owned by *Paisa Akhbar*, an inexpensive daily newspaper that, as its name suggests, was sold for one paisa (1/64th of a rupee). *Paisa Akhbar* was an extremely successful commercial endeavor, and its ownership of the Khadim-ul Talim Steam Press makes clear that *Paisa Akhbar* was a broader enterprise, involved in the commercial book trade. *Mehboob* was inexpensive, with a list price of 7 annas, or just less than half a rupee (7/16th). Both the book's price and the press that published it suggest a book produced for the commercial book market, as do indications from the title page.

Unlike many of the printed books produced for the commercial market, which employed floral or geometric-patterned borders mimicking refined manuscripts on their cover/title pages, or pictorial representations of their contents, *Mehboob*'s cover/title page has no decoration or embellishment; it is composed entirely of text. Imitating the refinement of manuscripts in printed books was about continuity with manuscript traditions as well as a means of summoning the attention of potential readers/buyers. *Mehboob* did the same, though through other means. Its title page was printed in red ink, for example, perhaps to distinguish it from other lithographs, most of which were monochromatic. *Mehboob*'s title page includes a short description of the work:

> *Mehboob al-Akhlaq*
>
> Or, an interesting and appropriate compilation [*majmu'a*] of the sayings of Muslim, Christian, and Hindu famous and eminent persons, and Greek philosophers

This description provides the potential reader/buyer with more precise information than is included in the title. At the same time, the inclusion of Greek philosophers confirms that the text continues the tradition of akhlaq outlined above.

The title page also includes information about the author: "his honor [*janaab*] *Maulvi* [cleric] Syed Muhammad Farooq *Sahib* [a title of courtesy] / translator of '*Phoolon ki Tokri*,' etc." The four honorifics—*janaab, maulvi, syed,* and *sahib*—suggest that the author was a man of learning and high social standing. *Janaab* (from Arabic), which can be attached to any name, denotes honor. *Maulvi* (from Arabic) is the Urdu term for one learned in Islamic law (i.e., a cleric). *Syed* denotes descent from the prophet Muhammad. And *sahib* (from Arabic), like *janaab*, denotes honor or references a great man. Together, this name with its honorifics underscores for the reader/buyer the author's authority to compile a book on ethics. The title also references his prior endeavors as the translator of *Phoolon ki Tokri* (literally "a basket of flowers"; flowers and gardens were significant literary motifs for poetry and literature on morals, as in the eminent poet Sadi's seminal Persian works, *Bustan* [Orchard] and *Gulistan* [Rose garden]). Because this is the single reference (beyond his title, *maulvi*) to the author's accomplishments, we may assume two things: (1) that *Phoolon ki Tokri* was likely well known at the time (it is not today) and (2) that the highlighting of Farooq's role in its publication, and that of similar texts, was meant to recommend *Mehboob* to potential purchasers/readers.

If the cover/title page of *Mehboob* was an attempt to make the book appealing in a competitive commercial book market, then one additional feature is also noticeable: the choice of script. Most of the title page and the text that follows is written in standard *nastaliq*, the calligraphic style commonly used for Urdu (and Persian and Punjabi) printed texts at the time. One line, however, is visibly different. The penultimate line of text, which bears the publishing information, is in *naskh*, which was used specifically for the Qur'an throughout the early modern Persianate world, including India. The Qur'an written in *naskh* is replete with the various short vowel markers and other diacritics that Indian Muslims—the vast majority of whom had no facility with Arabic—need to recite the text correctly. Unlike Arabic, written Urdu does not include short vowel markers and only rarely uses other diacritics; readers are expected to know correct pronunciation based on linguistic knowledge or context. Why might the calligrapher have used a different style here? Was it to invoke the authority of the Qur'an through an aesthetic style that would have been familiar to any reader of the Qur'an—a text that was circulating more widely at the time through commercial publishing? Taken together, the textual and visual cues of *Mehboob*'s cover/ title page may be read as forms of persuasion, which was perhaps required in the context of a competitive market. Put another way, *Mehboob*'s cover/title page provides a strong indication that this was a book produced for the burgeoning arena of Urdu popular print culture.

*Mehboob* brought to the arena of Urdu popular print culture an akhlaq text that was in continuity with the classical tradition, even as it used the form of the *majmu'a* (or compilation) and drew on a wide array of sources for its moral teachings. The *majmu'a* is a textual form that has a long history in Muslim societies and has long been related to issues of self-comportment (Babayan 2021, introduction and chap. 2). The *Mehboob*, in Farooq's words, is a compilation of sayings of "elders and philosophers" (1910, 1). Composed in prose, with some poetry interspersed, the language of the text is highly accessible. Sentence constructions are simple, and Farooq avoids ornate language. Its opening section (*fasl*) is in some ways predictable, given akhlaq's embrace of Greek philosophy. It contains the sayings of Muhammad, Umar (the second caliph), Sadi (a thirteenth-century Persian poet), al-Ghazali (the late eleventh-century jurist and Sufi), Aristotle, Socrates, and Plato (3–20, 23–28). The sayings are basic moral maxims, such as "In the final judgment, God will assign he who has two tongues in this world (that is, someone who sometimes says one thing, sometimes another) to the infidels" (attributed to Muhammad) (4); "Individuals who are able to keep their secrets to themselves keep their welfare in their own hands" (attributed to Umar) (7); "One should never break an agreement, and one should not take oaths; he who commits to a promise [verbally] should fulfill that promise" (attributed to Aristotle) (19); and "One should help the weak and indigent" (attributed to Plato) (27).

Where *Mehboob* differs from the classical akhlaq tradition is in the inclusion of Benjamin Franklin (20–23), though the pithy aphorisms included in the text are of much the same sort: "God helps those who help themselves" (22). Similarly, it veers from the classical tradition with a subsequent subsection of quotes from famous Hindus and their texts (23–33). This subsection has a part A (*alif*), on Bhartrihari, a famous Sanskrit scholar, and a part B (*bey*), titled "*Mahabharata, etc. . . ,*" with quotes drawn not only from the *Mahabharata* but also from the *Bhagavad Gita*, *Ramayana*, Kabir, Tulsidas, and Guru Nanak.

Section two (34–63) is even more eclectic. It is divided into three parts, the first of which opens with the sayings of Suleiman (Solomon), Abu Bakr (the first caliph), and Ali (the fourth caliph and first imam of Shiism). It goes on to include sayings attributed to a diverse array of people, including (in order) Saint Augustine, Isaac Newton, Thomas Babington Macaulay, Ben Johnson, John Milton, Abu Hanifa, Luqman, Francis Bacon, Mansur al-Hallaj, Thales (of Miletus), Pythagoras, Napoleon Bonaparte, Buddha, [George] Herbert, Erasmus Darwin, Saint Anthony, Jesus, Charles Darwin, (Qazi) ibn Ma'ruf, Hasan al-Basri, Galen, Martin Luther, Fariduddin Attar, Ptolemy, Augustus, Charles Cornwallis, Sayyid Ahmad Khan, Oliver Goldsmith, Robert Hall, and Edward Gibbon, among others. Then come Turkish, English, and Chinese parables, before the section closes with Confucius, the Duke of Wellington, and Alexander Pope. Despite this dizzying diversity of religious figures, classical philosophers, and a range of European writers, the text is all of a piece: pithy maxims of advice on good, moral conduct.

The text continues with Persian couplets by the fifteenth-century poet Jami under the heading "Advice for Children," followed by Persian couplets by the twelfth-century poet and Sufi Fariduddin Attar and by Omar Khayyam (d. 1131) under the heading "Selections of Religious Counsel, and Maxims." The second part of the section contains maxims without attribution. It concludes with Urdu couplets from the early nineteenth-century poet Zauk (d. 1854).

The third and last section of the book (63–82) contains more maxims, some with attribution, but most without. Like those earlier in the book, the maxims are straightforward and written in an accessible prose: "Prevailing over anger is the most significant aspect of manliness" (63); "Aristotle said: 'Man's greatest enemy is a shameful deed, and his greatest friend is good action'" (64); "The most unfortunate person in the world is he who finds faults with his elders" (66); "The just and the unjust individual are both famous. But people take the name of the just with respect, and they loathe the name of the unjust" (71). Overall, the language and content of this section, and that of the book as a whole, are remarkably consistent. The *Mehboob* is an accessible text for the common person on good and reputable conduct, articulated in an Islamic idiom (references to Allah, love for the prophet Muhammad, etc.), drawing on a range of authorities, with a message relevant for all, irrespective of their religion.

That Farooq identified the "public" as the target audience for the book (what we might consider a reading public) might go some way in explaining the broadranging sources upon which he drew (1). Using Urdu, Persian, Arabic, and English books as sources for his material, he thought of himself as performing a task "in service to the country" (2). Be that as it may, Farooq was making an argument to his audience about the proper sources for knowledge on good conduct. His decision to embrace the akhlaq genre anchored the *Mehboob* in a genre that from its inception was capacious in defining Islamic knowledge; in akhlaq,

Greek philosophy does not stand outside Islamic knowledge but is incorporated within it. Much the same seems to happen in *Mehboob* vis-à-vis colonial knowledge. In this text, Islamic and colonial knowledge are not distinct entities. Rather, colonial knowledge is appropriated in this Islamic genre to *its* ends. Indeed, rather than treating this akhlaq text as an example of the "watering down" of a classical genre or as an akhlaq text in name only, I see it as an evolution of the genre—one very much in keeping with the genre's foundations—in which Islamic and colonial knowledge become coconstitutive.

In recent years, popular print culture in South Asia has become a site of scholarly interest because it is an interactive arena in which authorial intent meets commercial interests and both, in turn, meet audience desires. In newspaper publishing, it has in some cases been possible to document this reflexive relationship by tracing the impact of reader response, through letters, on production (an excellent example is Dubrow 2018, chap. 4). With printed books, this process becomes more opaque. The prevalence of akhlaq as a genre in Urdu publishing, however, from the very foundations of Urdu print culture through its rise in the late nineteenth and early twentieth centuries, is one important indication that there was a popular audience for these texts. The content of the texts, in turn, provides insights about ideas that resonated with a print public.

*Mehboob al-Akhlaq* points to forms of Islamic knowledge in colonial India that were capacious. Akhlaq is a form of Islamic knowledge that appropriates other forms of knowledge (religious and secular) to its own ends. Further study of the genre in its Urdu context is necessary. Hopefully, *Mehboob al-Akhlaq* provides a compelling case that such study will increase our understanding of Urdu print culture and the insights it can provide about Islam in late-colonial India.

## NOTES

1. This chapter incorporates some material that first appeared in my much longer piece, "Urdu Ethics Literature and the Diversity of Muslim Thought in Colonial India," *American Historical Review* 127, no. 3 (2022): 1162–1189.

2. Manuscript collections in the Indian subcontinent and beyond hold numerous Persian manuscripts of *Akhlaq-i Nasiri* that were produced in India. Interestingly, along with *Akhlaq-i Nasiri* manuscripts, commentaries and glossaries also circulated in India. See, for example, references to manuscript no. 940, *Sharh-i Akhlaq-i Nasiri* (commentary), and manuscript no. 941, *Hadiqat-ul Luqat*, described as a glossary for the *Akhlaq-i Nasiri*, in Muqtadir 1925. Both of these manuscripts were produced in the nineteenth century.

3. On the vernacular book trade, see the following: for Bengali, Ghosh 2006; for Hindi and Urdu, Stark 2007; for Punjabi, Mir 2010; for Tamil, Venkatachalapathy 2012 and Blackburn 2003. On the commercial book trade, also see Orsini 2009.

4. On the *Akhlaq-i Muhsini*, see Subtelny 2003.

5. We still await a comprehensive study of Urdu print culture, comparable to Francesca Orsini's pathbreaking work on Hindi (Orsini 2002). Stark 2007 and Dubrow 2018 provide important histories of the broader story of Urdu print culture.

6. In 1867, the colonial state began to surveil publishing in India and to produce quarterly reports on publishing activity, by province. These quarterly reports provide a vivid portrait of print culture in India, even if the majority of printed texts have not survived. See Darnton 2001 and 2002.

7. British Library, Oriental and India Office Collection, VT 134.

8. Library of Congress, MLCSA 94/2497 (B) So Asia Cage.

9. See, for example, *Akhlaq-i Jalali* (1872 and h. 1292 [Hijri Islamic calendar] [1875–1876]), published in Kanpur, British Library, Oriental and India Office Collection, VT 844; *Iksir-i 'Azam* (which contains portions of Tusi's and Dawani's texts), published in Lahore, British Library, Oriental and India Office Collection, VT 637.

10. My decision to focus on book publishing, to the exclusion of journals, is dictated by the fact that late colonial book publishing requires different analytics than serial and journal publishing. The former was often a commercial venture, while the latter either was tied to organizations/institutions or enjoyed the patronage of the colonial state. One consequence of limiting my discussion to printed books is that I will not here consider the most famous colonial-era publication that invokes akhlaq, Sayyid Ahmad Khan's journal, *Tehzib ul-Akhlaq*.

11. Published in 1872 and 1875 by the Koh-i-Nur Press, Lahore, and the Muhammadi Press, Lahore, respectively.

## REFERENCES

Alam, Muzaffar. 2000. "Akhlaqi Norms and Mughal Governance." In *The Making of Indo-Persian Culture: Indian and French Studies*, edited by Muzaffar Alam, Francoise Delvoye, and Marc Gaborieau, 67–95. New Delhi: Manohar.

——. 2003. *The Languages of Political Islam: India 1200–1800*. London: C. Hurst.

Babayan, Kathryn. 2021. *The City as Anthology: Eroticism and Urbanity in Early Modern Isfahan*. Stanford, CA: Stanford University Press.

Blackburn, Stuart. 2003. *Print, Folklore, and Nationalism in Colonial South India*. Delhi: Permanent Black.

Dabashi, Hamid. 1996. "Khwajah Nasir al-Din al-Tusi: The Philosopher/Vizier and the Intellectual Climate of His Times." In *History of Islamic Philosophy, Part I*, edited by Seyyed Hossein Nasr and Oliver Leaman, 527–84. New York: Routledge.

Darnton, Robert. 2001. "Literary Surveillance in the British Raj: The Contradictions of Liberal Imperialism." *Book History* 4 (1): 133–76.

——. 2002. "Book Production in British India, 1850–1900." *Book History* 5 (1): 239–62.

Dubrow, Jennifer. 2018. *Cosmopolitan Dreams: The Making of Modern Urdu Literary Culture in Colonial South Asia*. Honolulu: University of Hawaii Press.

*EIr* (*Encyclopedia Iranica*). 1982–. London: Encyclopaedia Iranica Foundation.

*EI²* (*Encyclopedia of Islam*, Second Edition). 1960–2007. Edited by P. Bearman et al. Leiden: Brill.

*EI³* (*Encyclopedia of Islam, THREE*). 2007–2023. Edited by Kate Fleet et al. Leiden: Brill.

Farooq, Syed Muhammad. 1910. *Mehboob al-Akhlaq*. Lahore: Khadim-ul Talim Steam Press.

Faruqi, Shamsur Rahman. 2003. "A Long History of Urdu Literary Culture, Part I: Naming and Placing a Literary Culture." In *Literary Cultures in History: Reconstructions from South Asia*, edited by Sheldon Pollock, 805–63. Berkeley: University of California Press.

Ghosh, Anindita. 2006. *Power in Print: Popular Publishing and the Politics of Language and Culture in a Colonial Society, 1778–1905*. New Delhi: Oxford University Press.

Green, Nile. 2005. "Making a 'Muslim' Saint: Writing Customary Religion in an Indian Princely State." *Comparative Studies of South Asia, Africa, and the Middle East* 25 (3): 617–33.

Hasan, Mushirul. 2008. *A Moral Reckoning: Muslim Intellectuals in Nineteenth-Century Delhi*. Delhi: Oxford University Press.

Ingram, Bannon. 2013. "The Portable Madrasa: Print, Publics, and the Authority of the Deobandi Ulama." *Modern Asian Studies* 48 (4): 845–71.

Jones, Kenneth. 1990. *Socio-religious Reform Movements in British India*. Cambridge: Cambridge University Press.

Khan, Iqtidar Alam. 2009. "Tracing Sources of Principles of Mughal Governance: A Critique of Recent Historiography." *Social Scientist* 37 (5/6): 45–54.

Leaman, Oliver. 1996. "Ibn Miskawayh." In *History of Islamic Philosophy, Part I*, edited by Seyyed Hossein Nasr and Oliver Leaman, 252–57. New York: Routledge.

Metcalf, Barbara. 1982. *Islamic Revival in British India: Deoband, 1860–1900*. Princeton, NJ: Princeton University Press.

——. 2002. *Perfecting Women: Maulana Ashraf Ali Thanawi's Bihishti Zewar*. Berkeley: University of California Press.

Mir, Farina. 2006. "Imperial Policy, Provincial Practices: Colonial Language Policy in Nineteenth-Century India." *Indian Economic and Social History Review* 43 (4): 395–427.

——. 2010. *The Social Space of Language: Vernacular Culture in British Colonial Punjab*. Berkeley: University of California Press.

Miskawayh, Ahmad Ibn. 1968. *The Refinement of Character: A Translation from the Arabic of Ahmad Ibn-Muhammad Miskawayh's "Tahdhīb al-Akhlāq."* Translated by Constantine K. Zurayk. Beirut: American University of Beirut.

Muqtadir, Maulavi Abdul. 1925. *Catalogue of the Arabic and Persian Manuscripts in the Oriental Library at Bankipore*. Vol. 9. Patna: Superintendent, Government Printing, Bihar and Orissa.

*ODI (Oxford Dictionary of Islam)*. 2003. Edited by John L. Esposito. Oxford: Oxford University Press.

*OEIW (Oxford Encyclopedia of the Islamic World)*. 1995. Edited by John L. Esposito. Oxford: Oxford University Press.

Orsini, Francesca. 2002. *The Hindi Public Sphere 1920–1940: Language and Literature in the Age of Nationalism*. New York: Oxford University Press.

——. 2009. *Print and Pleasure: Popular Literature and Entertaining Fictions in Colonial North India*. Ranikhet: Permanent Back.

——, ed. 2013. "Introduction." In *The History of the Book in South Asia*, edited by Francesca Orsini, xi–xxxix. Burlington, VT: Ashgate.

Pernau, Margrit. 2011. "Teaching Emotions: The Encounter between Victorian Values and Indo-Persian Concepts of Civility in Nineteenth-Century Delhi." In *Knowledge Production, Pedagogy, and Institutions in Colonial India*, edited by Indra Sengupta and Daud Ali, 227–47. New York: Palgrave Macmillan.

Raymond, Joad. 2011. "Introduction." In *The Oxford History of Popular Print Culture*. Vol. 1, *Cheap Print in Britain and Ireland to 1660*, edited by Joad Raymond, 1–14. Oxford: Oxford University Press.

Reetz, Dietrich, ed. 2006. *Islam in the Public Sphere: Religious Groups in India, 1900–1947*. New York: Oxford University Press.

Robinson, Francis. 1993. "Technology and Religious Change: Islam and the Impact of Print." *Modern Asian Studies* 27 (1): 229–51.

Samadani, Aziz. 1894. *Aziz al Aafaq fi Masail al Akhlaq*. Allahabad: Namoor Press.

Sarwar, Mufti Ghulam. 1871. *Akhlaq-i Sarwari*. Lahore: Koh-i-Nur.

Shaw, Graham. 2013. "Calcutta: Birthplace of the Indian Lithographed Book." In *The History of the Book in South Asia*, edited by Francesca Orsini, 159–81. Burlington, VT: Ashgate.

Stark, Ulrike. 2007. *An Empire of Books: The Naval Kishore Press and the Diffusion of the Printed Word in Colonial India*. Ranikhet: Permanent Black.

Subtelny, Maria. 2003. "A Late Medieval Persian *Summa* on Ethics: Kashifi's *Akhlāq-i Muhsinī*." *Iranian Studies* 36 (4): 601–14.

Venkatachalapathy, A. R. 2012. *The Province of the Book: Scholars, Scribes and Scribblers in Colonial Tamilnadu*. Ranikhet: Permanent Black.

# EDUCATING MUSLIM INTELLECTUALS

Was There a "Persianate" Madrasa in Central
Asia in the Nineteenth Century?

*James Pickett*

Pick up nearly any book on Islam, and the ulama, or Muslim scholars, will feature prominently. This was an elite group that spanned the Islamic world, from Morocco to Indonesia, and in many countries their influence persists to the present day. In principle, the power of the ulama rested solely on knowledge, not bloodline or wealth (though neither hurt, of course). This knowledge, in turn, rested on a rigorous training regime: the madrasa, or Islamic college.

The core innovations of the madrasa, which crystallized in eleventh-century Baghdad, were an institutional setting that provides students and instructors with the necessities for sustained learning—stipends, lodging, space for study circles—along with a pedagogical method that very likely precipitated scholasticism in Europe (Makdisi 1981, 32, 286). This basic format had legs: it spread to most parts of the Islamic world and flourished well into the modern period.[1] Unsurprisingly, the predominant emphasis in scholarship has been on the madrasa's status as an *Islamic* institution, with a curriculum emphasizing scriptural and legal knowledge above all else (Moosa 2015, 2).

From another direction, an emergent field of scholarship on the Persianate world has traced a cohesive sphere of literary culture stretching from the Balkans to Bengal.[2] The forms of learning in this cultural continuum—from poetry to ethics to the occult—were every bit as involved and rigorous as the Arabic-medium sciences of the eleventh-century madrasa in Baghdad, all of which circulated in various forms within the emergent Persian domain. What, then, was the relationship between Islamic and Persianate forms of knowledge? Was there a Persianate madrasa?

Nineteenth-century central Asia was a bastion of both Islamic learning and Persianate high culture. The educational center of the region—Bukhara—boasted over two hundred madrasas that produced a vast cadre of ulama for the region as a whole. This moment in Islamic history is ideally suited for the task of exploring not only the connection between Arabic-medium and Persian-medium forms of learning but also their connection to a nascent Turkic literary sphere.

Rhetorical questions in academic chapter titles are generally answered in the affirmative. In this case, however, the answer is a shrug: "sort of." In fact, the question "Was there a Persianate madrasa?" is itself a misdirect, intended to focus our intention on the meaning of not only neologisms such as "Persianate" but also more widespread terms such as "Islamic" and seemingly ethnic categories such as "Turkic." As will be seen, the madrasa environment was saturated with Persian literature, so treating the central Asian madrasa as a "Persianate" institution is not off base. However, the caveats to such a contention are perhaps even more telling than the assertion itself. Persianate knowledge assumed prior mastery of Arabic-medium sciences; many of the students in central Asian madrasas were of Turkic origin and increasingly carved out a Turkic literary sphere grounded within the Persianate one (which, in turn, was grounded in the Arabic one) (Sartori 2021). Thus, the madrasa must be understood as the fulcrum of multiple cultural vectors, no matter what term is used to characterize it.

More important than the retrospective qualifier appended to "madrasa" is the ecology of knowledge underlying it. Although the madrasa became a symbol of backwardness in the eyes of modernizers, it produced intellectuals who were capable of engaging across myriad disciplines and cultural registers. The suitability of the madrasa for its environment explains its remarkable endurance.

## The Core Curriculum

No state dictated a set of textbooks for madrasas in Bukhara or anywhere else in central Asia.[3] Nevertheless, with caution and a few important caveats, one can speak of a loosely standardized madrasa "curriculum" in Bukhara.[4] Surviving lists of texts taught in the madrasas (a) overlap a great deal and (b) are consistent in excluding certain forms of knowledge from the "formal" madrasa curriculum, thereby approximating an internal understanding of curricular versus elective/postgraduate learning.[5] Let us first consider the curricular side of that equation.

The "core" madrasa curriculum taught students how to teach themselves and how to continue their intellectual journey under new mentors in other disciplines. It inculcated the fundamental skills necessary for mastering a much larger array of interrelated fields *after* "graduation," or at least after meaningful progress in the core sequence. Before beginning madrasa study, students achieved basic literacy through Qur'anic recitation in primary school (*dabiristan*, or, more commonly, *maktab*). Primary schooling was open to both boys and girls, though only boys continued their formal training beyond the *maktab*. Early schooling was generally segregated by gender, but there is some evidence of female scholars instructing male students as well, and some female students continued their studies outside of the madrasa.[6]

At the initial stage of madrasa training, students were introduced to basic Arabic grammar and syntax through Persian-medium primers, which accounted for around 30 percent of the curriculum.[7] Next came logic (*mantiq*) (studied for at least five years and, similarly, making up around 30 percent of the listed texts) and rhetoric (*balagha*) (accounting for approximately 7 percent of the texts) (Kuhn, no. 144).[8] Philosophy (*hikmat*, around 7 percent of the texts) and theology (*kalam*, close to 20 percent of the texts) were covered in the final six years of study (Kuhn, no. 144). In total, this core sequence of texts usually took around a decade to complete, though especially esteemed scholars sometimes boasted of having finished it in as few as six years (Musayyab Bukhari, f. 678a).[9]

The madrasas of central Asia cultivated *intellectuals* who were capable of grasping the underlying principles of their subject matter. When students studied law, the emphasis was initially on jurisprudence (*usul al-fiqh*), the science of deriving substantive law, rather than on memorizing content.[10] Despite this theoretical training, independent reasoning for the purpose of deriving law (*ijtihad*) was not, in fact, something that many scholars of the long nineteenth century would claim to do, the canonical Hanafi interpretations having been consolidated many centuries prior.[11] Thus students who received a diploma (*ijaza*) for completing this course of study were not qualified to perform *any* of the most prestigious social roles of the ulama, not even that of the jurist—at least not yet.[12] (Of course, many graduates went on to become local mosque imams, but it is not clear how logic or *usul al-fiqh*, for instance, would be crucial for that task.) Rather, the diploma marked them as worthy of continuing their pursuit of knowledge across diverse disciplines, either through self-study or in apprenticeship to new mentors.

This common core of grammar, syntax, logic, theology, and—slightly more inconsistently—rhetoric and principles of jurisprudence is well substantiated in surviving reading lists and was common throughout much of the Islamic world. Over 40 percent of the titles on a 1909 Samarqand reading list can also be found in the "Dars-i Nizami" curriculum of the late Mughal Empire.[13] Overlap with the Ottoman curriculum was about the same (Ahmed and Filipovic 2004; Robinson 2001), and even the Safavid curriculum overlapped with that of Bukhara by at least 30 percent (Robinson 2001, 244–48). A core layer of grammar, syntax, logic, and rhetoric was quite similar throughout the Islamic world, whereas sectarian differences manifested most acutely in exegetical, theological, and legal texts, which accounts for the lower percentage of common texts in the Safavid sequence of core texts.[14]

The curriculum was remarkably stable over time.[15] The average date of writing of works appearing on madrasa reading lists was sometime in the fifteenth century.[16] Yet this curriculum stability did not mean that the curriculum was static, even though it was certainly conservative. For instance, Muhammad al-Mubarak Lahuri's commentary on Muhibballah Bihari's (d. 1707) *Sullam al-ulum* was listed as one of the core texts on logic, likely illustrating the direct influence of the Indian Dars-i Nizami curriculum (of which Bihari's work was a constituent element) on central Asia (Kuhn, no. 144).[17] Moreover, Bukharan scholars likewise continued to write updated commentaries of older works: Ata'allah Khwaja wrote a commentary on Mulla Yusuf al-Qarabaghi's theological work, which appears as a core madrasa text in its original form (Mu'azi 1908, 17; Ziya, f. 43a).[18] Similarly, Sayyid Alim Khwaja "Hatif" (d. 1852–1853) wrote a commentary on the *Tafsir-i bayzawi*, which was frequently studied in madrasas (appearing in Ottoman and Indian curricula as well) (Wazih, 241–42). Muhammad Sharif ibn Ata'allah would scribe hadiths into the margins of philosophy texts, relating them to the principle at hand (Musayyab Bukhari, f. 811a). Even if these newer texts were not adopted into the core curriculum, at least not immediately, they were undoubtedly important resources for students and point to continued intellectual engagement with an enduring canon.[19]

These core subjects in the madrasa curriculum may seem far removed from the practical concerns of the day, but they were essential for central Asian society. Much of what Anthony Grafton and Lisa Jardine argue about the displacement of European scholasticism in favor of humanism might equally be asserted about the madrasa system vis-à-vis the new method schooling of the Islamic modernists (the Jadids): "The triumph of humanist [or Jadidi] education cannot simply be explained by reference to its intrinsic worth or practical utility. On the contrary, the literary education of the humanists [or Jadids] displaced a system far better adapted to many of the traditional intellectual and practical needs of European [or pre-Soviet central Asian] society" (1986, xii).[20] To continue the interpolation: "At the level of the school [or *maktab*], it offered literacy in Latin [/ Arabic and Persian] of a sort to thousands of boys. At the higher level of the university arts course [/ madrasa], it [i.e., scholasticism] provided a lively and rigorous training in logic and semantics. At the higher level still of the professional faculties of law, medicine and theology [mostly pursued in postgraduate study after making significant progress in the core madrasa curriculum], it trained men for employment in powerful and lucrative occupations" (xii–xiii).

# Extracurricular and Postgraduate Learning

What is to be made, however, of the conspicuous absences? If not in the madrasa, where did scholars learn to quote hadiths from memory, compose Persian couplets on the fly, debate Sufi metaphysics, and adjudicate law? These subjects were studied simultaneously with the madrasa curriculum (and often physically within the walls of the madrasa as "electives" of sorts) and then mastered afterward. Where there are differences between the attested lists of central Asian madrasa texts, it is often in precisely these areas—particularly hadith, Qur'anic exegesis, and legal topics. That such electives were absent from most lists of core texts does not mean that they were unimportant, nor does it suggest that they were rarely studied. Rather, they were absent from most core sequences of texts because the core was necessary to access the electives in the first place.

Substantive law (*furu' al-fiqh*, literally "branches of law") is in some ways the trickiest subject to pin down in relation to the standard madrasa curriculum. Substantive legal texts do appear as part of the core on some reading lists, but the genre is conspicuously absent on others.[21] In Alexander Kuhn's commissioned list of madrasa texts, *furu' al-fiqh* texts are included but are separate from the main sequence.[22] It seems that in central Asia, substantive law was often considered separate from the core—perhaps "elective," in a sense—but because so many career paths revolved around it, a large proportion of students studied it both simultaneously with the core curriculum and after graduation.[23]

What is indisputable is that even students destined for modest imamships studied some amount of substantive law, either on the side or integrated into the curriculum. For instance, when a local *qazi* was faced with the minor administrative hiccup of the mosque's imam abruptly skipping town to return to his home province, his replacement was required to read eleven lines from a section of the *Hidaya* (the paramount Hanafi legal manual throughout Eurasia that, according to one list, was studied for five years in the madrasa ["Madrasy . . . v gorode Samarkanda," 138–51]) on prayers according to the rules of Arabic grammar, translate the meaning, and correctly expound on the issues contained therein (*Tetrad' s razlichnymi zapisiami*, f. 26b). Another account depicts a candidate for local imamship botching his explanation of the Hajj section of the *Hidaya* and subsequently losing favor (*Tetrad's razlichnymi zapisiami*, f. 27b). The core madrasa curriculum provided students with the requisite tools for pursuing more specialized fields, such as *furu' al-fiqh*, which were essential for even a relatively humble position such as that of imam.

Considering substantive law as an elective, layered on top of a core of grammar, syntax, logic, rhetoric, and theology, provides a model for understanding other forms of knowledge as well. Much like *furu' al-fiqh*, hadith and *tafsir* (Qur'anic exegesis) appear on reading lists elsewhere in the Islamic world but inconsistently in central Asian curricula.[24] Yet Ata'allah Khwaja received separate diplomas (*ijazas*) for mastering hadith and Qur'anic exegesis (tafsir) as part of his madrasa study (Musayyab Bukhari, f. 678a). And Ata'allah's son, Rahmatallah, taught a famous thirteenth-century tafsir by Nasir al-Din Bayzawi (the aforementioned tafsir on which Hatif would later write an original commentary) to students studying in the Muhammad Sharif madrasa—which was the very same text included on Ottoman and Mughal reading lists (Rizawi, f. 64b).[25] Rahmatallah's brother was known to recite from memory pages of tafsir at a time during madrasa lessons, from both Bayzawi and lesser-known commentators (Musayyab Bukhari, f. 815a).

That the author felt the need to draw special attention to Rahmatallah's instruction of tafsir may point to its quasi-extracurricular status (i.e., not part of the core but nevertheless widely studied). Similarly, an east Turkestani student from Khotan (a city in what is now western China) named Muhammad Ibrahim began madrasa study in Kashgar (where he remained only eight months) and then received diplomas from numerous instructors in Bukhara after spending many years there.[26] After Bukhara, Muhammad Ibrahim traveled to Tashkent, where he received separate diplomas for hadith and tafsir, and to Andijan, where he received yet another diploma for Qur'anic recitation (Fazli 1993, 15). Again, the core subjects were bundled together in a diploma (*ijaza*) separate from the elective and postgraduate disciplines (in this case, tafsir).

To this point, we have considered only Arabic disciplines. Yet the categories, technical terms, and symbols permeating those disciplines also infused Persian writing (and, by extension, Turkic as well). If there is some ambiguity as to whether substantive law was part of the core curriculum, it is eminently clear that Persian literature (e.g., poetry, Sufi treatises) generally was not—in central Asia or anywhere else.[27] And yet training in Persian literature may be less categorically distinct from substantive law than initially meets the eye. Kuhn's commissioned list of madrasa texts also included a list of the most important works of Persian literature, such as the *Shah-nama* and the poetry of Hafez (Kuhn, no. 144, f. 3a).[28] Like substantive law (*furu' al-fiqh*), literature appears alongside the core madrasa texts as the common domain of madrasa students, even if studied outside of formal study circles (as implied by their being listed separately from the core madrasa texts).[29]

Muhammad Karim al-Bulghari's trilingual Arabic-Persian-Turkic dictionary provides a striking illustration of the integration of core and extracurricular curricula. Al-Bulghari's dictionary was expressly aimed at conveying wisdom necessary to Tatars who hoped to study in Bukhara, where they would be required to know not only Arabic and Persian but also the dialectical idiosyncrasies of central Asian colloquial Turkic (al-Bulghari, f. 1b); after all, core texts were in Arabic, and supplementary lessons were in Persian, but many Bukharans spoke Turkic.[30] Before addressing grammatical and lexical points, the introduction to al-Bulghari's lexicon explains the importance of the Persian language in terms of the fusion of Islamic and Persian history. First, al-Bulghari proffers an unsound hadith to the effect that "the language of heaven is Arabic and Persian."[31] Then—in mixed Turkic and Arabic—the author attributes to the Persian language a divine (*ilahi*) provenance as the language spoken by sons of Noah and the legendary kings of Iran alike.[32]

The integration of Persian into the madrasa environment is illustrated by other texts. Abd al-Wahid Sadr Sarir Balkhi (d. 1885/1886) had little to say in his personal notebook (*jung*) about his formal schooling but waxed nostalgic about his schooldays in Bukhara's Tursunjan madrasa. He portrayed the informal nocturnal gatherings convened by the students as a magical time, especially one particular night in 1838/1839 when he discovered the famous Indo-Persian poet Abd al-Qadir "Bedil."[33] After studying Bedil's poetry, Abd al-Wahid and his friends composed their own verses in the style of the great poet and took turns reciting them in the madrasa after hours by candlelight. The core courses by day were a necessity, but poetry was a pursuit of passion (*Jung-i 'Abd al-Wahid Sadr Sarir Balkhi*, f. 102a).

Sufism has been aptly described as "the post-graduate creed of Islam"—that is, a body of knowledge and practices pursued in addition to the madrasa curriculum, not so different from poetry or (sometimes) even substantive law (Jafri 2006, 74). After receiving a madrasa diploma, and not infrequently additional diplomas for collateral subjects, students continued their course of study under the tutelage of a sheikh in a Sufi lodge (*khanaqah*), which was frequently part of the same complex as the madrasa.[34] However, tutelage in Sufism did not necessarily begin after graduation. There is some evidence that Sufi forms of knowledge were taught already at the madrasa stage, albeit separately from the formal lessons. For instance, a short biography of the Dahbidi sheikh Tash Muhammad (d. 1815/1816) states, "The habit of the *akhund* [i.e., Tash Muhammad] was to have his students spend four days of the week studying the traditional Islamic sciences (*ilm-i qal*) [likely referring to the core madrasa curriculum][35] and during the three days off engage in mystical exercises (*ilm-i hal*)" (Musayyab Bukhari, 659a). Similarly, Qari Mir Muhsin's biographer wrote that as a young boy he came to Bukhara and completed the madrasa curriculum (*ilm-i qal*) and also studied *ilm-i hal* under Sufi teachers until he himself became a Sufi deputy (*khalifa*) (Muḥtaram, f. 148a).

A scholar named Khuday-berdi began studying under Sufi sheikhs at several shrines in Bukhara before he was old enough to begin formal madrasa study; at these shrines he would study both silent and vocal *zikr* (trance-inducing ritual chanting) and engage in fasting (Saʿadatallah, 25a).[36] After beginning his madrasa study, Khuday-berdi would often spend all night studying his madrasa texts at shrines situated beyond the city limits, making it back to the madrasa at daybreak just before class. The hagiography's author seems to imply that the otherworldly presence of Amir Kulal, a famous Sufi sheikh, aided Khuday-berdi in his study: "Beneath the standard of Amir Kulal I practiced my lessons, weeping" (Saʿadatallah, ff. 25a–25b). At these Sufi shrines the madrasa core blended into mystical practices as Khuday-berdi engaged in discussions (*munazara*) with custodians of the holy sites (Saʿadatallah, f. 26a).[37]

Conceptualizing the madrasa experience in terms of "core curriculum" versus "elective" and "postgraduate" study can take us only so far. As we have seen, students pursued fields of study far beyond the scope of the putative core curriculum, both within the walls of the madrasa and without. Different madrasa instructors integrated different extracurricular disciplines into the core: some drilled hadith study from a very early age, and others emphasized substantive law. Students did not necessarily regard any of those subjects as more authentically part of a "standard" curriculum than others, even if there are observable patterns in terms of which disciplines were most consistently included and expected to be mastered in advance of others.

The fact that the concept of ulama remained a flexible category—one without a specific legal or theological definition—did not stop a central Asian scholar from writing the following: "By the Sharia, a scholar (*ʿalim*, sg. of *"ulama"*) is one who is characterized by the quality of [knowing] the religious sciences, [including] law (*fiqh*), *tafsir*, Hadith, and jurisprudence (*usul al-fiqh*)."[38] The fact that this minimum résumé of a bona fide scholar *mostly* lists fields beyond those emphasized in madrasa curricula suggests that the examples recounted above, in which extracurricular study coincides with the core curriculum, followed by postgraduate study, constituted the norm rather than the exception.

Although there were discrepancies between broadly overlapping curriculum lists, those disparities were not a product of institutional differences between madrasas. Madrasas did not have corporate identities, and in that sense "college" is slightly misleading as a translation. Students were not limited to attending lessons at the same madrasa as their *hujra* ("cell," effectively a dorm room funded by a modest stipend) but rather mixed and matched study circles throughout the city. The aforementioned Khuday-berdi shared a room at the celebrated Diwan-begi madrasa, where he would spend several days studying, before rotating to lessons at the Qushbegi and Kokaltash madrasas (Saʿadatallah, ff. 36b–37a). Certainly, some madrasas were more prestigious than others (especially Mir-i Arab and Kokaltash), but when it came to study circles, the emphasis was on the individual teacher rather than the institution.[39] A scholar named Dam-ulla Hasan Akhund turned his own home into a madrasa, dividing and expand-ing a portion of it to house students ("Soobshchenie o prepodavatel'iakh bukharskikh medrese," f. 10b). Thus, the nature of the madrasa is best conveyed by the literal definition of the Arabic term: a "place of learning," any place in which a student could find a teacher (*mudarris*).

In theory, if a willing teacher could be found, and an endowed cell with a sti-pend could be secured, *anyone* could become a scholar, regardless of economic background. Of course, reputation and resources helped, and some families managed to ensure access to the best training for their children for generations. But the system was *relatively* open to students from modest backgrounds. Sources do not allow easy assessment of social mobility in any systematic fashion, but rags-to-riches stories are common in biographies of prominent scholars, and stu-dents from diverse economic backgrounds mixed together in the *maktab*s and madrasas.

What might the evidence presented above tell us about the extent to which we may consider the madrasa curriculum of Bukhara to be meaningfully *Persianate*?

Persian-medium disciplines and genres were indispensable to Islamic scholars and permeated their world. Moreover, the madrasa was the foundation of a broader educational environment within which the ulama cultivated Persianate forms of knowledge. Even if Persian texts were not central to the core curriculum, that curriculum was the price of entry to the Persian-medium textual sphere: in central Asia, at least, few scholars lacked a madrasa education, and all scholars had some connection with Persianate forms of knowledge. Thus, the Bukharan madrasa might indeed be characterized as "Persianate," so long as one bears in mind that Arabic—not Persian—was the bedrock of the knowledge system and that by the nineteenth century Persian disciplines shared space with emergent Turkic vernacular forms as well. By the same logic, one might characterize the fin de siècle Bukharan madrasa as "Turkic," so long as one bears in mind that even students of Turkic origin (by one definition or another) were taught in Persian and that Persian terminology permeated the literary register of Turkic. For these reasons, perhaps one might reach for the more conventional designation of "Is-lamic" to describe these educational institutions. But even that seemingly safe characterization elides the fact that for any scholar worth his salt, the Arabic-medium "core" was merely a launching pad for continued scholarship in Persian-ate disciplines (which were every bit as Islamic as the Arabic-medium ones).

Ultimately, the label is much less interesting or important than the ecologies of knowledge that underpinned the madrasa system. It is no coincidence that the core fields that show up on nearly every reading list—grammar, syntax, logic, rhetoric—are also some of the earliest to emerge in Islamic history and, consequently, the ones with the most consistent overlap throughout the larger Islamic world. Many of the extracurricular and postgraduate disciplines—Sufism, Persian poetry, occult sciences—were the product of canonization processes that crystallized several centuries later than the core disciplines and were often more geographically constrained to the Persianate territories. This is why African, Ottoman, and Bukharan students all read some of the same works of logic, but only Ottoman and Bukharan ones memorized Rumi's Persian poetry. By the nineteenth century, history was repeating itself, as works were increasingly composed in eastern Turkic (Chaghatay), which remained in symbiosis with Persian and Arabic and began to set the knowledge ecology in central Asia apart from the rest of the Islamic world.

The broader madrasa environment was hardly a calcified edifice and drew strength from deep continuities in Islamic history reaching back over a thousand years. The madrasa at twilight buttressed a complex knowledge system that integrated languages, cultures, and disciplines and produced a powerful transregional social milieu.

## NOTES

1. Madrasas still exist, and in some places are even expanding. However, most modern madrasas (e.g., the famous Deobandi madrasa system) have updated their pedagogical style (e.g., professional staff, desks, and the inclusion of Western sciences) (Metcalf 2004, 92–93; Tasar 2016).

2. There are several ways to conceptualize the term "Persianate" (Amanat 2018; Green 2019; Hodgson 1974, 2:293), and a number of other terms capture something similar, such as the "Persian cosmopolis" (Pollock 2006; Beecroft 2015, chap. 3), "Turko-Persia" (Canfield 1991), and the "Balkans-to-Bengal complex" (Ahmed 2015). All these terms signal interactions with Persian language and literature.

3. Bukharan rulers did, however, specify reading lists in *waqf*s that they established in their capacity as individuals (Liechti 2008, 304–405). Unless otherwise stated, this chapter treats the period from 1747 to 1920, although many of the observations may be applied to previous centuries as well.

4. In part because of variations in extant book lists, even in the highly systematized Ottoman case, historians have been reluctant to fully embrace the term "curriculum" along with its modern connotations of standardization and systemization. Nevertheless, I use the terms "curriculum," "diploma," "graduation," and "extracurricular" as a heuristic—with occasional scare quotes to emphasize that these concepts are inevitably a loose fit. These terms also serve to underscore close parallels with European scholasticism.

5. For instance, over 60 percent of the twenty titles listed in a 1909 Russian report on madrasas in Samarqand ("Madrasy . . . v gorode Samarkanda") overlapped with those listed in Sadriddin Ayni's autobiography (Ayni 2009, 135). Every one of the titles on Ayni's much shorter list of fourteen texts is accounted for in the 1909 Samarqand report and in Alexander Kuhn's commissioned list (Kuhn, no. 144). Some sources mention a "Bukharan curriculum"—for instance, one student is described as studying in the city of Guzar, but according to the "Bukharan method" (*manhaj al-ta'līm fī Bukhārā*) (Akrām, 159). This chapter will not list specific titles in the usual sequence; on which see Khan 2013, chap. 1

6. One source praises a female instructor (*bībī khalīfa*) not only for her teaching but also for her scholarly acumen in many of the same disciplines studied in the madrasa system (Musayyab Bukhārī, f. 792a-b). The *bībī khalīfa* figure is similar to that of the *otin* (Fathi 1997). Female scholars are largely absent in Bukharan sources, aside from rare references to *bībī khalīfa*s or female instructors. More sources for the lives of female ulama have survived for the Farghana Valley (Kılıç-Schubel 2011).

7. This figure is out of thirty-one texts listed in Kuhn. Of course, not all texts were studied for the same amount of time. However, in a reading list that stipulates months and years devoted to each text, students studied grammar (*naḥw*) and syntax (*ṣarf*) for around 30 percent of the total time they were in the madrasa ("Madrasy . . . v gorode Samarkanda").

8. Again, the percentage of texts is based on Kuhn's list, and the duration comes from "Madrasy . . . v gorode Samarkanda." Students in modern Iran study some of the same texts taught in Bukhara and in a similar style of engagement (Mottahedeh 2008, 71–75). The 1909 Samarqand report does not include rhetoric. However, there is ample evidence, including Bukharan book endowment lists, that Taftāzānī's treatise on rhetoric, *al-Muṭawwal*, was a core part of the Bukharan curriculum; the work also appears in Safavid, Ottoman, and Indian curricula (Liechti 2008, 403; Robinson 2001, 48–52, 240–51).

9. Raḥmatāllāh ibn ʿAtāʾallāh Khwāja spent twelve years completing the core texts (*jamʿ-i kutūb-i mutadāwila*) (Musayyab Bukhārī, f. 729a). From the very beginning of the madrasa system, there was no set duration, and different students spent different amounts of time mastering the texts (Makdisi 1981, 96).

10. The pattern and sequence of study—an initial focus on jurisprudence (*uṣūl al-fiqh*) followed, as a postgraduate discipline, by substantive law (*furūʿ al-fiqh*)—is not so different from the sequence of study in US law schools, where, only after three years studying legal theory and jurisprudence do students take the bar exam in substantive law.

11. This statement is not meant to rekindle the debate over the "closing of the gates of *ijtihād*"; there were indeed some scholars who claimed to be *mujtahid*s (Mīr Muḥammad Siddīq, f. 151b). Rather, I seek to emphasize that for most scholars of the long nineteenth century, such a claim would amount to the height of arrogance, placing the scholar on seemingly equal footing with the scholars who first formulated the Sharia.

12. I have not seen many original, handwritten *ijāza*s in central Asian collections. However, published exemplars identify the student's teacher and his respective teacher, as far back as possible (*Ijāzat al-Imām Muḥammad Zāhid al-Kawsarī*).

13. The Dars-i Niẓāmī list (which contains approximately forty separate works) is longer than most of the central Asian lists (which contain twenty to just over thirty works). Nevertheless, nearly 20 percent of the Dars-i Niẓāmī titles can be found in the central Asian exemplars (i.e., Kuhn, Ayni, and the 1909 Russian report). If one (a) includes works known to have been read in Bukharan madrasas based on endowment deeds and (b) counts commentaries mentioned on central Asian lists in addition to the original works, then nearly 50 percent of the Dars-i Niẓāmī curriculum coincided with that of central Asia. A major source of discrepancy is the fact that the Indian system included mathematics, a subject absent from the central Asia core (and one that does not appear in the supplementary book lists reported by Kuhn, although mathematical texts certainly circulated in Bukhara).

14. Indeed, this foundation was common as far away as West Africa (Hall and Stewart 2011, 118–28).

15. For instance, more than 70 percent of the texts found in nineteenth-century curricula are also found in book endowments from the sixteenth century, as evidenced by surviving endowment lists (Liechti 2008).

16. This chronological trend coincides with findings in a statistical survey of the West African curriculum, for which texts produced in these centuries formed the foundation (Hall and Stewart 2011, 144).

17. It is perhaps not a coincidence that the development of the Dars-i Niẓāmī in the eighteenth century coincided with the influx of Naqshbandī-Mujaddidī scholars into central Asia.

18. This would make ʿAtāʾallāh's work a commentary on a commentary on a commentary: al-Qarabāghī's work is a commentary on al-Dawwānī's *Kitāb-i Mullā Jalāl* (ubiquitous on central Asian reading lists), which is a commentary on Aẓud al-Dīn al-ʿĪjī's *al-ʿAqāʾid*.

19. As Wael Hallaq points out, commentaries may appear at first glance to merely explain an older, more authoritative work but in fact depart radically from that text (2002, 321, passim).

20. Jadids (literally "new" in Arabic) were a group of central Asian modernizers whose reformist program had much in common with Islamic modernists elsewhere (Khalid 1998).

21. According to the 1909 Russian Samarqand madrasa report, students spent four years studying the *Mukhtaṣar al-wiqāya* already in the first level ("Madrasy . . . v gorode Samarkanda," f. 139a). According to Ayni, however, students in Bukhara received their diplomas (*ijāzas*) without ever touching such texts; although Ayni was indignant at the absence of *tafsīr* (Qurʾanic exegesis) in the core curriculum, his list of texts lacks any references to *furūʿ al-fiqh* (2009, 135–36).

22. The following is written above the list of *furūʿ al-fiqh* texts: "Studying [legal] issues is in the following manner" (*taḥṣīl-i masʾala bar ēn rawīsh* [sic]) (Kuhn, no. 144).

23. This understanding helps reconcile a debate in the literature (Frank 2012, 120–21; Khalid 1998, 33) over whether *furūʿ al-fiqh* was taught in central Asian madrasas: it was indeed taught inside the madrasas (along with a number of other subjects outside the core curriculum, as will be discussed) but outside of some (though perhaps not all) incarnations of the standard reading list. In the Ottoman realm, madrasas were organized into beginning and advanced institutions. The curriculum of one of the advanced institutions focuses nearly exclusively on subjects I have characterized, in the central Asian case, as "extracurricular"/"postgraduate," such as substantive law, hadith, and *tafsīr* (Ahmed and Filipovic 2004, 207).

24. The fourteenth-century hadith collection *Mishkāt al-maṣābīḥ* appears as the capstone of the reading list commissioned by Kuhn on madrasa endowment lists (along with associated commentaries), and on Indian and Ottoman lists as well. This curriculum apparently differed significantly from that of the first madrasas in the eleventh century, which started with the study of scripture (Makdisi 1981, 80).

25. Nāṣir al-Dīn al-Bayẓāwī's *tafsīr* appears frequently in Bukharan madrasa book endowment lists (Liechti 2008, 404), and Ṣadr-i Żiyāʾ's personal library contained two copies (Vohidov and Erkinov 1999).

26. Muḥammad Ibrāhīm's son and biographer states that he received *ijāzas* in Bukhara for "completing his study," a statement that supports the notion of a less standard core curriculum; moreover, the texts that he began to study in Kashgar (and presumably finished in Bukhara) are well represented on central Asian curriculum lists, such as Taftāzānī's commentary on Nasafī's *ʿAqāʾid* (theology), and Taftāzānī's commentary on Qazwīnī's *Talkhīṣ al-miftāḥ* (rhetoric) (Fażlī 1993, 12–14).

27. There are exceptions to the absence of Persian poetry in madrasa curricula: Rumi's *Masnawī* was apparently taught in some Ottoman madrasas in the nineteenth century (Akgündüz 2004, 156). In premodern Persian, there is no emic category of "literature"

(*adabiyyat* is a neologism) (Utas 2006, 199–200); here I use "literature" to refer casually and broadly to any work that was copied and recopied.

28. Literary works such as the *Dīwān* of Hafez and Attar's *Conference of the Birds* appear on Bukharan madrasa book endowment lists (Liechti 2008, 404). More recent works, such as those composed by the eighteenth-century poets Bedil and Mashrab, are also included, as are the Turkic works of Alisher Navoi—even though these "literary" materials are sometimes collectively glossed as *Fārsī*.

29. On another list (also commissioned by Kuhn), Persian poetry, *tafsīr*, and substantive law texts are combined into a common list of "texts we study" (Kuhn, no. 150).

30. Al-Bulghārī distinguishes between central Asian and Tatar Turkic dialects (*al-lughāt al-Turkīya al-ghayr al-Bulghārī*). As in this phrase, the text is predominantly Tatar-inflected Turkic, but the author shifts in and out of Arabic.

31. The text specifies *al-Fārsī al-Darī*, referring to the late antique language, not the modern language of Afghanistan, as the text clarifies elsewhere (Muḥammad Karīm al-Bulghārī, "Sabab-i taqwiyat," f. 3a). Elsewhere, al-Bulghārī provides a remarkably detailed typology of Persian dialects, delineating seven types of Persian, including four "archaic"/"abandoned" (*mahjūr*) ones (the only western Iranian languages in the group)—Harawī, Shikrī (perhaps Sagzi), Zāwulī (Zabuli), Sogdian—as well as three still in use (*mustaʿmal wa mashhūr*): Pahlavi (likely here referring to Parthian), Dari, and Farsi. Al-Bulghārī seems to be building on models from classical Arabic literature (e.g., Ibn al-Muqaffaʿ), though the origin of this particular seven-part sequence is unclear (Bulghārī, f. 4a).

32. Al-Bulghārī builds on the work of early Arabic-medium historians to connect the Persian language to a grandson of the prophet Noah, to the legendary Kayanian kings of Iran, and to Jamshid (Bulghārī, ff. 3a–3b).

33. Bedil is included on Kuhn's list of madrasa texts.

34. The term *ijāza* (diploma) is also used to indicate completion of Sufi training and license to train others.

35. Direct equation between ʿilm-i qāl and the madrasa curriculum is made by Ḥiṣārī, who wrote that he spent ten years pursuing ʿilm-i qāl after procuring a cell at the ʿAbdallāh Khān madrasa (Ḥiṣārī, ff. 13a–13b).

36. Since *zikr* can induce an ecstatic state (*ḥāl*) of proximity to God, it may be that this is exactly what other authors had in mind by ʿilm-i ḥāl. The term *taṣawwuf*, which is synonymous with ʿilm-i ḥāl, tends to be associated with senior scholars—perhaps more of a postgraduate field of study.

37. Khudāy-berdi's biographer wrote that he was often only one step ahead of the night watchman (*mīrshab*) during his nocturnal peregrinations, and that his classmates tried to scare him by telling him stories of ferocious dogs roaming the streets (Saʿādatallāh, f. 26a).

38. "Bi-sharīʿat ʿālim kas-ē bāshad kih mutaṣṣaf bi-ṣifat-i ʿulūm-i dīnī . . . wa ʿilm-i fiqh ū tafsīr ū ḥadīṣ ū uṣūl-i fiqh bāshad" (Ḥusaynī, f. 225a).

39. These madrasas provided larger salaries for instructors and larger stipends for students (Zhumanazar 2017, 94–104). *Ijāzas*, or diplomas, list the entire chain of teachers by name, sometimes stretching back hundreds of years, but are often silent on the venue of study. The concept of *khizmat* (service) frequently describes the relationship between teacher and student, suggesting the centrality of the individual relationship compared with association with the institution.

## REFERENCES

Ahmed, Shahab. 2015. *What Is Islam? The Importance of Being Islamic*. Princeton, NJ: Princeton University Press.

Ahmed, Shahab, and Nenad Filipovic. 2004. "The Sultan's Syllabus: A Curriculum for the Ottoman Imperial Medreses Prescribed in a Fermān of Qānūnī I Süleymān, Dated 973 (1565)." *Studia Islamica* 98/99:183–218.

Akgündüz, Murat. 2004. *Osmanlı Medreseleri XIX. Asır.* Istanbul: Beyan Yayınları.

Akrām, ʿAbd al-Muʾmin ibn Sayyid. ca. 1975. *Ażwāʿ ʿalā tārīkh Tūrān.* N.p.

Amanat, Abbas. 2018. "Remembering the Persianate." In *The Persianate World: Rethinking a Shared Sphere*, edited by Abbas Amanat and Assef Ashraf, 15–62. Leiden: Brill. https://brill.com/view/title/39353.

Ayni, Sadriddin. 2009. *Yāddāsht-hā.* Dushanbe: Sarredaksiiai ilmii ensiklopediaii millii tojik.

Beecroft, Alexander. 2015. *An Ecology of World Literature: From Antiquity to the Present Day.* New York: Verso.

Bulghārī, Muḥammad Karīm al-. "Sabab-i taqwiyat al-taḥṣīl wa najāt-i taṣnīʿal-waqt" ms. BL no. Or. 11042.

Canfield, Robert L. 1991. "Introduction: The Turko-Persian Tradition." In *Turko-Persia in Historical Perspective*, edited by Robert L. Canfield, 1–34. Cambridge: Cambridge University Press.

Fathi, Habiba. 1997. "Otines: The Unknown Women Clerics of Central Asian Islam." *Central Asian Survey* 16 (1): 27–43.

Fażlī, Muhammad Yaḥyā al-. 1993. *Tarjimat wālidī al-Shaykh Muḥammad Ibrāhīm al-Fażlī al-Khutanī al-Madanī.* Riyadh: Fihrisat Maktabat al-Malik Fahd al-Waṭaniyya Aṣnāʾ al-Nashr.

Frank, Allen J. 2012. *Bukhara and the Muslims of Russia: Sufism, Education, and the Paradox of Islamic Prestige.* Leiden: Brill.

Grafton, Anthony, and Lisa Jardine. 1986. *From Humanism to the Humanities.* Cambridge, MA: Harvard University Press.

Green, Nile. 2019. "Introduction: The Frontiers of the Persianate World (ca. 800–1900)." In *The Persianate World: The Frontiers of a Eurasian Lingua Franca*, edited by Nile Green, 1–74. Oakland: University of California Press.

Hall, Bruce Stewart, and Charles C. Stewart. 2011. "The Historic 'Core Curriculum' and the Book Market in Islamic West Africa." In *The Trans-Saharan Book Trade: Manuscript Culture, Arabic Literacy and Intellectual History in Muslim Africa*, edited by Graziano Krätli and Ghislaine Lydon, 109–74. Leiden: Brill.

Hallaq, Wael B. 2002. "*Takhrij* and the Construction of Juristic Authority." In *Studies in Islamic Legal Theory*, edited by Bernard G. Weiss, 317–36. Leiden: Brill.

Ḥiṣārī, Mīrzā Bābā bin Dāmullā Ṣafar Muḥammad. *Yāddāsht-hā* ms. Rudaki Institute of Language, Literature, Oriental and Written Heritage, Academy of Sciences, Tajikistan (Institut iazyka, literatury, vostokovedeniia i pisʾmennogo naslediia imeni Rudaki Akademii nauk Tadzhikistana) no. 1428/1.

Hodgson, Marshall G. S. 1974. *The Venture of Islam: The Expansion of Islam in the Middle Periods.* Vol. 2. Chicago: University of Chicago Press.

Ḥusaynī, Ḥabīballah ibn Jalāl al-. *Jung-i majmūʿa-i riwāyāt* ms. Al-Biruni Institute of Oriental Studies, Academy of Sciences, Uzbekistan (Institut vostokovedeniia imeni Abu Raikhana Beruni Akademii Nauk Respubliki Uzbekistana) no. 2802.

*Ijāzat al-Imām Muḥammad Zāhid al-Kawsarī li-l-Shaykh Muḥammad Ibrāhīm al-Khutanī.* 2012. Edited by Muḥammad ibn ʿAbdallāh Āl Rashīd. Amman: Dār al-Fatḥ li-l-Dirāsāt wa-l-Nashr.

Jafri, Saiyid Zaheer Husain. 2006. "*Madrasa* and *Khānaqāh*, or *Madrasa* in *Khānaqāh*? Education and Sufi Establishments in Northern India." In *Islamic Education, Diversity and National Identity: Dīnī Madāris in India Post 9/11*, edited by Jan-Peter Hartung and Helmut Reifeld, 73–103. New Delhi: SAGE Publications.

*Jung-i ʿAbd al-Wāḥid Ṣadr Ṣarīr Balkhī* ms. Al-Biruni Institute of Oriental Studies, Academy of Sciences, Uzbekistan (Institut vostokovedeniia imeni Abu Raikhana Beruni Akademii Nauk Respubliki Uzbekistana) no. 2260.

Khalid, Adeeb. 1998. *The Politics of Muslim Cultural Reform: Jadidism in Central Asia*. Berkeley: University of California Press.

Khan, Sarfraz. 2013. *Muslim Reformist Political Thought: Revivalists, Modernists and Free Will*. New York: Routledge.

Kılıç-Schubel, Nurten. 2011. "Writing Women: Women's Poetry and Literary Networks in Nineteenth-Century Central Asia." In *Horizons of the World: Festschrift for İsenbike Togan*, edited by İlker Evrim Binbaş and Nurten Kılıç-Schubel, 405–40. Istanbul: İthaki.

Kuhn, Rare Books Collection of the National Library of Russia, F 940, no. 144.

——. Rare Books Collection of the National Library of Russia, no. 150.

Liechti, Stacy. 2008. "Books, Book Endowments, and Communities of Knowledge in the Bukharan Khanate." Diss., New York University.

"Madrasy . . . v gorode Samarkanda." 1911. Russian State Historical Archive (Rossiiskii Gosudarstvennyi Istoricheskii Arkhiv). F 1396 O 1 D 342, ff. 138–51.

Makdisi, George. 1981. *The Rise of the Colleges: Institutions of Learning in Islam and the West*. Edinburgh: Edinburgh University Press.

Metcalf, Barbara Daly. 2004. *Islamic Revival in British India: Deoband, 1860–1900*. New York: Oxford University Press.

Moosa, Ebrahim. 2015. *What Is a Madrasa?* Chapel Hill: University of North Carolina Press.

Mottahedeh, Roy. 2008. *The Mantle of the Prophet*. London: Oneworld Publications.

Muʿaẓī, Muḥammad ʿĀrif al-. 1908. *Tārīkh-i Bukhārā wa-tarjumat al-ʿulamā' (Tārīkh-i Muʿaziyya)*. Orenburg, Russia: Dīn u Maʿīshat.

Muḥtaram, Ḥājjī Niʿmatallāh. *Taẕkirat al-shuʿarā-yi Muḥtaram* ms. Al-Biruni Institute of Oriental Studies, Academy of Sciences, Uzbekistan (Institut vostokovedeniia imeni Abu Raikhana Beruni Akademii Nauk Respubliki Uzbekistana) no. 2252/II.

Musayyab Bukhārī, Mīr. *Kitāb-i maqāmāt-i mashāyikh* ms. Manuscripts and Rare Books section of Kazan State University (Nauchnoi biblioteki imeni N.I. Lobachevskogo Kazanskogo Gosudarstvennogo Universiteta, Otdel' Rukopisei i Redkikh Knig) no. 854.

Pollock, Sheldon. 2006. *The Language of the Gods in the World of Men: Sanskrit, Culture, and Power in Premodern India*. Berkeley: University of California Press.

Riżawī, Abū al-Barakāt al-mulaqqab bi-Pādishāh ʿAzīz Khwāja Mirghānī. *Manāqib wa maqāmāt-i Sayyid Muḥammad ʿAṭā'allāh Shaykh al-Islām* ms. Rare Books Collection of the National Library of Russia no. P.n.s. 200.

Robinson, Francis. 2001. *The ʿUlama of Farangi Mahall and Islamic Culture in South Asia*. New Delhi: Permanent Black.

Saʿādatallāh. *Luṭf-i buzūrg* ms. IVR RAN, no. B 1932.

Sartori, Paolo. 2021. "From the Demotic to the Literary: The Ascendance of the Vernacular Turkic in Central Asia (Eighteenth–Nineteenth Centuries)." *Eurasian Studies* 18, no. 2 (March): 213–54.

Siddīq, Mīr Muḥammad. *Zhizneopisanie bukharskogo uchionnogo sheikha* (Untitled biography of Muḥammad ʿAṭā'allāh Khwā) ms. Al-Biruni Institute of Oriental Studies, Academy of Sciences, Uzbekistan (Institut vostokovedeniia imeni Abu Raikhana Beruni Akademii Nauk Respubliki Uzbekistana) no. 79/XII.

"Soobshcheniia o prepodavateliakh bukharskikh medrese" ms. State Archive of Uzbekistan (Tsentral'nyi Arkhiv Respubliki Uzbekistana), Tashkent, R-2678.

Tasar, Eren. 2016. "The Official Madrasas of Soviet Uzbekistan." *Journal of the Economic and Social History of the Orient* 59 (1–2): 265–302.

*Tetrad's razlichnymi zapisiami* (Untitled ms.). Rare Books Collection of the National Library of Russia F 924 no. 561.

Utas, Bo. 2006. "'Genres' in Persian Literature 900–1900." In *Literary Genres: An Intercultural Approach*. Literary History: Towards a Global Perspective 2. New York: Walter de Gruyter.

Vohidov, Šodmon, and Aftandil Erkinov. 1999. "Le *fihrist* (catalogue) de la bibliothèque de Ṣadr-i Żiyâ'." Translated by Maria Szuppe and Alié Akimova. *Cahiers d'Asie centrale*, no. 7 (July): 141–73.

Wāżiḥ, Qārī Raḥmatallāh ibn ʿĀshūr Muḥammad al-Bukhārī. *Tuḥfat al-aḥbāb fī tazkirat al-aṣḥāb* ms. Rudaki Institute of Language, Literature, Oriental and Written Heritage, Academy of Sciences, Tajikistan (Institut iazyka, literatury, vostokovedeniia i pis'mennogo naslediia imeni Rudaki Akademii nauk Tadzhikistana) no. 483.

Zhumanazar, Abdusattor. 2017. *Buxoro ta'lim tizimi tarikhi*. Tashkent: Akademnashr.

Żiyā, Sharīf-jān Makhdūm Ṣadr-i. *Nawādir-i żiyā'īy* ms. Al-Biruni Institute of Oriental Studies, Academy of Sciences, Uzbekistan (Institut vostokovedeniia imeni Abu Raikhana Beruni Akademii Nauk Respubliki Uzbekistana) no. 1304-II.

# Part 2

# COLONIAL ENCOUNTERS AND POSTCOLONIAL AFTERMATHS

In the first of three chapters in this part, Benjamin Claude Brower analyzes the *état civil* in colonial Algeria, a register that recorded the names and professions of the colony's French citizens and Muslim residents, as well as information relating to births, marriages, children, and deaths. Unlike Jews, Muslims in Algeria were not citizens of France. Beginning in 1882, however, the French state required them to register in the *état civil* in an effort to render them visible for military conscription, taxation, and the registration and sale of land. One aspect of the new registration process involved the conversion of the names of Muslims to a form recognizable to French administrators who spoke no Arabic. For example, Aḥmad ben Sālim al-Ḥājj al-Tamīmī Bū Maʿaza became Aḥmad Bensalam. The replacement of traditional naming practices with names that facilitated the colonial state's identification of its subjects, Brower argues, was a form of symbolic violence and an assertion of French power.

In the second chapter, Mandana Limbert examines British attempts to regulate Muslim marriage in colonial Zanzibar, an island off the coast of East Africa. In 1912, concern over "lawless promiscuous cohabitation between the sexes" caused British officials to pay close attention to Islamic law and its rules on marriage. As in Algeria, so too in Zanzibar, the key issue for the British was control and logistics: they divided the island into marriage districts, appointed marriage officials in villages, and instructed these officials to collect fees for registering marriages. The new marriage registration system brought British officials into contact with local ideas about race and social status. For Muslims, the key issue was the rule of *kafāʾa*, or marriage equality. According to this rule, a Muslim woman may marry a man of equal or higher status but may not marry a man of lower social status—for example, an "Arab" woman may marry an "Arab" man of equal or higher status but may not marry a non-Muslim Indian or a Muslim of Indian or Iranian descent. The British, of course, had their own, very different, ideas about race and social status. Be that as it may, in the new marriage registration system, local categories ("native" and "nonnative") were replaced by new categories ("African," "Indian," "European"). These colonial period categories, Limbert argues, created social tensions and divisions that contributed to the massacre of thousands of Arabs in the years leading up to, and during, the 1964 Zanzibar revolution.

The colonial need to control its subjects is also the focus of Jeremy Prestholdt's chapter on race, identity, and space in coastal Kenya. In the colonial period, British policymakers introduced legal categories based on race that reinforced connections between identity, prestige, and space. Following the withdrawal of the British in 1963, ethnicity and religion became important measures of identity. According to the standard postindependence narrative, coastal Muslims are not "native" Africans but rather immigrants from Arabia, Oman, and India. They are "other": not sons of the soil. In this process of othering, the sea became a key marker of "foreign" identity. In the middle of the twentieth century, the state began to marginalize Muslim communities living along the coast, communities that previously had regarded themselves as members of an Afro-Arab Swahili civilization whose roots reach back to the first millennium CE.

# 3

# ALGERIAN PERSONAL NAMES AND THE COLONIAL *ÉTAT CIVIL*, 1850–1900

*Benjamin Claude Brower*

In 1882 a new law required Algerians to register in the *état civil*. This collection of vital statistics contained records of major life events like birth, marriage, children, and death for each French citizen, as well as their profession and personal name. As an administrative and legal institution, the état civil represented a key tool of the modern French state. It served as the means both to produce the individual rights-bearing citizen and to interpolate and define individuals (Noiriel 2001). The état civil was nearly a century old, established in the early years of the French Revolution, but it had not extended to France's Algerian subjects, except in incomplete or haphazard ways for record keeping of births and deaths. This changed for Algerian Jews in 1870 when a decree extended them French citizenship. As citizens, they entered the état civil registers more or less regularly from this point forward. Algerian Muslims had a different status (Amara 2019). An 1865 law recognized them as having French nationality, but citizenship remained barred to most based on what was known as their *statut personnel*—that is, their ability to settle questions of family and inheritance according to confessional law. While Algerians generally welcomed having access to these legal forums, they came at the price of a separate juridical status that the French government used to bar them from the basic rights of citizenship. Thus, authorities in Algiers and Paris did not look to the état civil as a mechanism of Muslims' emancipation. Instead, lawmakers and administrators recognized the power of the état civil to bring individual Algerian Muslims into the state's legal and administrative records. In particular, it made colonial subjects available for new duties, such as military service and taxation, as well as establishing their legal identity as property owners and as debtors who could be called before the courts. In this respect, the success of the état civil depended on introducing new types of names, particularly the patronym (Scott 1998, 64–71). Inasmuch as these names used European norms, a linguistic and cultural gap had to be crossed. Algerian names had to be converted to a form understandable to French administrators with no knowledge of local languages. This chapter examines questions in the decades surrounding the 1882 law, a period when names underwent significant transformation, yielding a personal name that some in Algeria today call an *onomacide* (Benramdane 2000).

Between the fourteenth and eighteenth centuries modern French naming practices took shape, a shift marked in particular by the use of hereditary family surnames that spread from a small group of elites to the rest of society (Lefebvre-Teillard 1990; Lapierre 1995). During the French Revolution the state claimed expansive powers over names, including answering questions that had previously fallen to the church and custom, such as deciding what was an appropriate type of name and standardizing its overall form. An 1803 law stated that "only the names used in various calendars and those of figures known in ancient history can be accepted as first names in the registers used for recording children's births" (Lefebvre-Teillard 1990, 129). This law set the rule that names must reflect prevailing French cultural norms, centered at this time on a Christian and classical Greco-Roman heritage. Such norms extended to minorities. An 1808 decree obliged some Jews to adopt a patronym while prohibiting that this name be taken from the Old Testament.[1] Beyond deciding cultural resonance, the state also fixed names at birth, establishing the immutability of names. In previous eras, names might evolve over time with nicknames and pseudonyms added to birth names during the course of one's life, but now it required a court order to change one's name (Lefebvre-Teillard 1990, 122). Thus, the era yielded a fixed two-part name: a given name (or names) conferred at birth, called the *prénom*, and a fixed family name inherited from the father, the patronym or *nom patronymique*.

Algerian Muslims did not have to adopt culturally French names, but their names did have to be technically French (i.e., responsive to the techniques of government record keeping). Their names departed considerably from the modern French model. In Algeria, people used variations on the classical Arabo-Islamic five-part name: a given birth name known as the *ism*; a patrilineal genealogical name called the *nasab*; an honorific name, the *kunya*; the *nisba*, which might reference origin, tribe, or distinctive physical characteristics; and the *laqab*, a nickname that might be honorific, prophylactic, or pejorative (Schimmel 1989, 1–13; Sublet 1991). These names contextualized individuals, making them distinct and identifiable but also socially legible, marking associations, networks, ties, and hierarchies. Depending on social rank and the circumstances of a name's iteration, Algerian names included up to the five classical components. These names were not generic but expressed locality, ethnicity, language, status, and religion (Yermeche 2002). Even the ism might do this work. A baby received an ism within a week of birth and at the same time inherited the patronymic nasab, the genealogical name formed by adding *ibn/bin* (son of) or *bint* (daughter of) before the ism of the child's father. The ism and nasab drew from common names, most frequently that of the prophet Muhammed and the noble names (*al-asmā' al-sharīfa*) used for him, as well as the names of celebrated early Muslims (Schimmel 1985, 105–122).[2] A popular name for a firstborn boy in Algeria was "Muḥammad" and for a firstborn girl, "Fāṭima" or "Fāṭima al-Zahrā'," after the Prophet's daughter Fāṭima, known as "al-Zahrā'" or "The Splendid One" (Desparmet 1948, 20). While these names drew on a common heritage, usage ensured that they marked family and regional particularities. Locally venerated saints provided a good source of regionally specific names. "'Abd al-Raḥmān" was a popular ism for boys in Algiers, commemorating the patron saint of the city, the scholar Sīdī 'Abd al-Raḥmān b. al-Tha'ālibī (d. 1468); "al-Hūwārī" frequently served as an ism in Oran and in other parts of western Algeria, after Oran's patron saint, Sīdī Muḥammad al-Hūwārī (d. 1439); and "al-Ghawthī" in Tlemcen after the Sufi sheikh Sīdī Abū Madīn (d. 1198) (known as "al-Ghawth" for his "succor"), buried in Tlemcen. In other cases, common names had regionally specific pronunciation and spelling. For example, "Aḥmad" had at least twenty-six variations in nineteenth-century Algeria, some of which reflected local preferences (Beaussier 1887, 139). In Oran, "Aḥmad" often became "Ḥammū," while "Ḥamī" was typical to Tlemcen, "Ḥamūda" in the east, and "Ḥamīdūsh" in the center of the country (Ould-Ennebia 2009, 11). "'Umar" also had two different forms: the standard spelling "'Umar" and "'Amr," with the former prevailing in cities and the latter in the countryside (Fleisch 1961, 271–73; Bresnier 1855, 281; Lacheraf, 1998, 150). A special case was the Prophet's name, which had different forms depending on the vowels. The standard "Muḥammad" existed alongside the variants "Maḥammad" and "M'ḥammad," each a separate name (Bresnier 1857, 480; Socin 1898, 487). The recording of these variations posed challenges. Written names customarily were left unvocalized (i.e., with the short vowels unmarked by diacritics), but in this case the short vowels served to distinguish the three different names. Some scriveners solved the problem by writing "Muḥammad with the *ḍamma*" (short *u*) and "Muḥammad with the *fatḥa*" (short *a*), preserving the name's integrity while not contravening the orthodox spelling (Doutté 1903, 62). Religious and linguistic minorities also revealed themselves in their names, even as these names reflected classical standards. The Amazigh or Berber-speaking people used many of their own words as names, but they also used many of the same Arabic names as other Muslims. These Arabic names could be Berberized, as with using "Muḥend" for "Muḥammad" (Chaker 2013, 5767). Given the region's linguistic complexity, having Arabic and Berber versions of the same name offered the important possibility of going back and forth between languages, as was necessary for Berberophone scholars working in Arabic (Chachoua 2001, 101, 159–60).

Algerian names provided precise information, holding true to the saying "Nomen est omen" (The name is a sign). When the ism was combined with the kunya, nisba, and laqab, a name might serve as a mini biography or a "cornucopia of information," as they do for scholars working in other periods (Bulliet 1993, 125). Indeed, these names communicated a far more robust array of details—family ties, locality, class, ethnicity, and gender—than the two-part French name, which, to make sense, required ancillary information, date and place of birth, names of parents, and so on. Facing the Algerian naming project, some administrators argued that they should use current names for the état civil, asking why they did not "complete and improve what already existed" (Mercier 1891, 42). But Algerian onomastics stood at counter purposes to the état civil: modern names fix individual identities rather than giving expression to them (Bruck and Bodenhorn 2006, 3–4, 26). Thus, part of France's project meant ending the fluidity of names, standardizing their information, and ending their change over time and context (Geertz 1976, 231–33). Moreover, the état civil needed to serve nonspecialists, including administrators with no training in Arabic and Berber who had to alphabetize Algerian names, make them fit within the columns of preprinted forms, and write them in approved handwriting styles (Cornu 1889, 70).

The French project required exogenous concepts, goals, and languages. It first took aim at narrowing the name to two parts, then fixing patronyms according to the model of the *nom patronymique*. Nasabs, of course, established relations between fathers and children, but they changed every generation and did not easily mark specific groups of related people. There were exceptions, such as powerful families that shared a name in common which they maintained over the generations. This was the case of the ben Ḥasīn of Constantine, a lineage of military administrators and landowners that dated back to the sixteenth century, and an Ottoman officer known as Ḥasīn al-Tūrkī (Grangaud 2004, 210–22). (A kunya or other type of name might also serve this function.) Algerians used an ism + nasab combination in everyday public iteration, like signatures, but how many "Aḥmad ben Ḥamūd-s" or "Yūsuf ben ʿAmmār-s" existed, and how to distinguish these two people, notables from Algiers and signatories to an 1831 petition, from the hundreds more in the city of Algiers or even in the same family who had the same name?[3]

In response to these questions, administrators decided that they needed classes of first names and patronyms that were easily distinguishable. In 1873 a new law introduced a new patronym as part of a project to register individual landowners and promote land sales. These rules followed the example of the *nom à particule*, a name formed from the preposition *de* (from) followed by the name of the family's landed estate.[4] In France the *particule* marked nobility, and despite attempts to abolish it during the French Revolution, it resurfaced as a way to elevate a family's cultural capital. In Algeria, however, the *nom à particule* worked in the opposite sense. Algerian personal names, at least the ism and nasab, were quite distinct from the names of farmland. People typically named a field after its physical features, the color of the soil, or animals that frequented the area. Some of these might strike us as inoffensive, like a parcel of farmland named Ḍabbābīa (Foggy) or Blad ʿAin al-Bayḍāʾ (Land of the White Fountain) or Muqsam al-Qanṭara (Portion of the Bridge). In France, any of these might have served as a patronym; no one would complain about a name like "Delafontaine" (From the Fountain). However, Algerians did not use these types of words for the ism, even if they might figure in the kunya or as sobriquets. Moreover, some field names contained culturally abject notions, such as a property named Muqsam al-Ḥalālīf (Plot of the Wild Pigs) or Raqāʿa Umm al-Aṣnām (Parcels of the Mother of the Idols). An officer in the indigenous affairs office clarified the problem: "Few natives would accept willingly to leave their traditional Muslim names and take new ones coined from the plants, beasts, or accidents of geography that name their property. What luck would one have to see a native named after the Prophet and one of the leaders of Islam . . . accept a sobriquet taken from his field."[5]

In an attempt to make these types of names acceptable to Algerians, one administrator proposed adding prefixes like the kunya "Abū/Bū," "Mawlay" (master), or "Ahl" (people of) to establish a buffer between the field's name and the person.[6] But while respected men had kunyas like Bū Maʿaza (Man with a Goat) and Bū ʿAmāma (Man with a Turban), it is doubtful that a family forced to call themselves the "Ahl al-Ḥallūf" (People of the Wild Pig) or the "Mawlay al-Aṣnām" (Master of the Idols) would appreciate such names, especially when conferred by a French administrator. Nevertheless, French commentators argued that over time Algerians (and more critically disposed Arabists in the administration) would accommodate themselves to whatever new names they received. As one report put it, "It is not a question of finding names so pure that they satisfy the Arabists, we need only find names such that one gets used to their apparent strangeness."[7] This mentality opened the door to the sort of abuses that plagued the Algerians' état civil throughout the colonial era, when civil servants entered pejorative names into its registers (Bénet 1937, 117). Infamous today, these practices are poorly documented in the archives, testimony to the fact that the rules later used for the état civil itself expressly barred pejorative names. One anecdote from the 1870s, however, recounts how an administrator maliciously translated farmland names into French and then presented them to unsuspecting Algerians (Mercier 1891, 41). While extant sources in the archives do not give specifics, such a linguistic maneuver conceivably meant converting something like "*ahl al-ḥallūf*" into "*les gens du cochon*" and then phonetically writing it in Arabic as the name "Lizjun du Kūshun." While an attentive Francophone might recognize the original on hearing it, the name would sound like gibberish to an untrained ear, and the words meant nothing in written Arabic. Moreover, if this Arabized expression were converted into French letters for use in official documents as "Lisjoun du Koushoun," the origins would further conceal themselves. We know little about Algerian reactions to the *nom à particule*. But the absence of petitions to change names suggests that they did not place much stock in them, using them only for administrative purposes and keeping their original names (Ageron 1968, 1:181).

Officials quickly scrapped this approach to the patronym. Recognizing that success depended on Algerian willingness to embrace and use the new names as their own, those responsible for writing procedures for the actual état civil in the 1880s reflected the consensus that Algerians should choose their names. The head of the family would receive a summons to present himself before an officer of the état civil and record an official patronym, along with *prénoms* and ages for all family members. The patriarch could select a new-style patronym, designated "*al-ism al-nisba*" (a neologism that attempted a literal translation of "*nom de famille*"), from a kunya, laqab, or nisba that circulated in the family.[8] A nasab was also acceptable, on the condition that the "*ben*" be joined to the progenitor's ism, as in "Bensalem." (More typically the French recorded the nasab along with the ism as a person's *prénom*, as in "Safia Bentchabane," the *prénom* for a woman from Constantine whom the clerk entered into the état civil in 1893 under the patronym "Bouhabik.")[9] If the family's leader could not decide on a patronym from the family's existing names, he could choose from a list of suitable names selected by the administration (Cornu 1889, 33–38). This project enjoyed important successes, and three million names were enrolled in the état civil's registers between the 1880s and the mid-1890s (Kehl 1931, 200).

Conventionally understood, proper nouns are untranslatable because they establish the unique relationship of "a pure signifier to a single being" (Derrida 2007, 192). France's second attempt to impose a French-style patronym, albeit using Algerian names, had to be "written in French" and in a way "that a French mouth can pronounce" (Mac Guckin de Slane and Gabeau 1868, 1, iii). Finding a method by which an Algerian name can be written in French letters poses considerable structural challenges, and contemporary specialists continue to seek solutions for the Algerian republic's état civil, which uses both Arabic and French (Amorouayach 2017, 228–29; Yermeche 2005, 25–27). Arabic can be converted to French letters through either phonetic transcription (writing what one hears) or orthographic transliteration (focusing on the written language and equivalences between letters). Even if one puts aside the unique aspects of the Arabic alphabet (such as the hamza) and considers only letters and phonemes, a basic problem emerges: the shortage of letters. The French alphabet has six basic vowels that can be expanded with diacritics to produce nearly two dozen different letters; however, it had only nineteen consonant letters at this time, not counting *w*, which had not officially entered the French alphabet, or the diacritically marked *c* or *cédille*, avoided for Arabic because it printed erratically (Mac Guckin de Slane and Gabeau 1868, vi). By contrast, the Arabic alphabet has twenty-eight consonants in all, three of which (*alif*, *wāw*, and *yā'*) serve for long vowels in certain words. In the simplest terms, the French alphabet is several sizes too small for Arabic, lacking some eight or nine letters (Mac Guckin de Slane and Gabeau 1868, iii). By the mid-nineteenth century, French Arabists had developed a diacritically marked French alphabet to transcribe Arabic (Carette 1853), but this alphabet worked imperfectly, even crudely. It combined transliteration and transcription, privileging phonetic equivalences as a workaround for the French alphabet's shortage of consonant letters with respect to Arabic. A single French letter served to represent two different Arabic consonants: the د and ذ were reduced to the French letter *d*, the ث and ت were combined into a single *t*, and the otherwise distinct letters ط and ض were combined into a diacritically marked letter *d'*. The rationale was that these letters were "purely conventional," as measured by the fact that North African pronunciation made no distinction between them. To drive this point home, the scholar working on the project called North Africans the "Barbaresques," using an old name for the region's people from the Greek *barbarous* or "those who stammered 'bar-bar' in incomprehensible and base tongues" (Carette 1853, n.p.).

While French Arabists turned up their noses at this system for their own work, using only Arabic script, the logic of expediency carried over into transcribing names (Messaoudi 316, 2015). This was the most delicate of tasks, given both the name's resistance to translation and the need for an exact spelling for identification purposes. An 1865 order clearly spelled the primacy of the second problem: "writing them as one thinks one hears them pronounced, not everyone spells them the same way" (Mac Guckin de Slane and Gabeau 1868, i). The project enlisted William Mac Guckin de Slane, an Arabist famous for his translations of Ibn Khaldun, as its leader. Mac Guckin de Slane could not use any diacritical marks, which resulted in an even more radical consolidation of letters. The separate Arabic letters ت and ط became *t*, ه and ح were rendered as *h*, س and ص as *s*, ر and غ as r, and ك and ق as *k*. Finally, in the case of ض, ذ, د, and ظ, Mac Guckin de Slane consolidated the four separate Arabic letters into the single

French *d* (Mac Guckin de Slane and Gabeau 1868, iv–ix). In sum, fourteen Arabic consonants shared six French letters. This consolidation helped Mac Guckin de Slane alphabetize his list of some 4,500 names, with "Ahmed" in the A's and "Zinet" at the end with the Z's, where the French user expected them. Readers also did not have to contend with prefixes and the like because Mac Guckin de Slane's team stripped names of definite articles, along with titles like "al-Ḥājj" (masc.) / "al-Ḥājja" (fem.) enjoyed by pilgrims to Mecca. But simplification for the sake of technical efficiency produced many inaccuracies. For example, while they all begin with the French letter *d*, the French adaptations "Daïd" (ذايد) and "Daud" (دواد) do not begin with the same letter in Arabic; and the *d* in "Demria" (ظمرية) is from an unrelated family of letters. Mac Guckin de Slane cited local pronunciation to justify this consolidation, an argument that might have worked for ذ and د, pronounced similarly in Algeria, but other letters had no relationship to each other than how they sounded to a French ear. While he recognized that these changes swept aside the possibility of returning to Arabic for some names, he reasoned that an "approximative painting of the sound" would suffice for government agents (Mac Guckin de Slane and Gabeau 1868, vi). Here, while the project otherwise showed sensitivity, it lost sight of the fact that the names belonged to the Algerians, not to the French administration. Moreover, Algerians bore them in both French and Arabic, and in oral and written forms.

The question of rendering names phonetically merits attention because the French specialists gave it precedence when converting names. Throughout the nineteenth century and beyond, Arabists struggled to negotiate the differences between spoken (*vulgaire*) and written (*littéraire*) Arabic. Some thought that spoken, dialectical Arabic should have priority in official situations and in teaching, while others scorned the *vulgaire* as debased and irrational, arguing that the written language alone is suitable for modern usage (Messaoudi 2015). Beyond these debates, as a general rule, the written form of any language does not correspond letter-by-letter with pronunciation; and when spoken language is spelled out phonetically, the results can look ridiculous. The French Arabist Louis Jacques Bresnier recognized as much in an instruction book in which he signaled the problems of writing out Arabic in French letters based on the spoken word. To show the effects of phonetic transcription, he gave examples from French in which the word *monsieur* written out phonetically becomes *mocieu*, *ils disent* becomes *il dize*, and *nous aimons* becomes *nou zêmon* (Bresnier 1855, 19). "In what method of learning *French* would one teach the *orthography* and the *syntax* of the coarse and colorful French of the rabble of Paris or Marseille?" he asked (518). He did not insist on the point, but his readers would have grasped the pejorative connotations of these examples. French texts often reproduced nonstandard pronunciations of the lower classes phonetically to ironic effect, with the most famous case at this time being Molière's *Don Juan,* which parodied the *patois* of the peasantry. In the language politics of later colonial contexts, this sort of language prejudice gave itself over to full-blown racialized caricatures of the French spoken by colonial subjects known as *"parler petit nègre."*

Franz Fanon wrote at length about the alienating effects of the French language, especially how it split into a high orthodox version used by metropolitan speakers, on the one hand, and a lesser pidgin language used by colonial subjects, on the other. The distance between the two racialized the colonized, "classifying him, imprisoning him, primitivizing him, decivilizing him" (Fanon 1967, 32). Fanon's observation is pertinent to names. The system of transcription used in the état civil produced a French version of the name arguably analogous to *"parler petit nègre."*[10] To cross a divide that could not be bridged simply by words and letters, administrators used sounds, particularly the limited repertoire available to their alien ears. This, then, was not a translation, nor did it pretend to convey what was "proper" in a name. How to measure the significance of all this? It might be read as the crowning example of Arabic's colonization, exposing French contempt for the language of a subjected people. The alienation effect of seeing what one hears redoubled itself in something like the name with its specific claims on one's being. This would be yet another example of the strong imposing on the weak. However, in the case of Algerian names converted to French and the problems of phonetic writing, French administrators played the role of Moliere's peasants, using the most subsidiary, lowest, and irrational forms of language in their own voice. If *"parler petit nègre"* revealed an essential lack of education, culture, and even humanity, as Fanon explained the colonial politics of language, what might it mean when colonizers used their strange approximation of Arabic with people who were, linguistically speaking, Arabic's true masters? Naming a colonized person in the equivalent of *"parler petit nègre"* might simply show contempt, but did it not also signal the failures of the colonizer?

Before this question can be answered, a host of subsidiary questions must be addressed (including the fact that parts of the état civil were in Arabic and written in Arabic script). Limited space precludes this project here. One can conclude, however, that the French conversion of Algerian names made a tabula rasa of them. The names it yielded did not designate Algerians *in se* but for the French state itself, with the name serving as a way of asserting power, even a primary form of symbolic violence (Siblot 1997, 52). Algerians recognized as much, calling their new patronyms by a neologism, either *naqma* or *naqwa,* which today refers both to the family name and, metonymically, to an ID card. The etymology of these words is unknown and remains a topic of debate, with some saying that *naqwa* used in this context is an Arabization of the French expression *"tu es né quoi"* (you were born [with] what [name]?).[11] But an interesting hypothesis suggests itself in the fact that in standard usage the Arabic word *naqma* means "vengeance" (Beaussier 1887, 689; Wehr 1994, 1168).

## NOTES

1. Decret of July 20, 1808, *Bulletin des lois de la République française*, 4th ser., vol. 9: 1808 (Paris: Imprimerie impérial, 1809), 27–28.

2. To protect children, parents sometimes included negative words in names as prophylactic devices that would turn away a malevolent or envious eye. In Kabylia, the Berberism Akli, or "Black/Slave," served this purpose (Chaker 2013, 5768).

3. Petition dated 15 Sha'bān 1246, Archives nationale d'outre mer (hereafter ANOM) 1H. My thanks to Estefanía Valenzuela Mochón, postdoctoral researcher at the Escuela de Estudios Árabes, Granada, for her painstaking transcription and paleographic analysis of the names appearing in this document.

4. J. B. Duvergier, *Collection complète des lois, décrets, ordonnances, règlements, et avis du Conseil d'Etat*, vol. 73, *année 1873* (Paris: A. Guyot et Scribe, 1873), 295.

5. "Affaires indigènes to Gouverner Général de l'Algérie," October 18, 1875, no. 770, ANOM 12h51.

6. "Note; noms patronymiques (loi du 26 Juillet 1873)," signed: Devaouly. n.d. (ca. 1874–75), ANOM 12h53.

7. "Note; noms patronymiques (loi du 26 Juillet 1873)," signed: Devaouly. n.d. (ca. 1874–75), ANOM 12h53.

8. "Procès-Verbal de la séance de 12 juin 1888," ANOM 12h52.

9. "Extrait du registre matrice de l'État Civil Musulman de la Commune de Constantine," ANOM 12h65.

10. *Vocabulaire destiné à la transcription en Français des noms des Indigènes* (Algiers: Adolphe Jourdan, 1885).

11. Kehl 1931, 181–82; Benam, "Expressions à l'algérienne IX," Forum Algérie, accessed June 14, 2019, http://www.algerie-dz.com/forums/archive/index.php/t-223718 .html; A. Giménez Reíllo, "Uso de alcuñas," Anís del moro, accessed June 14, 2019, https:// anisdelmoro.blogspot.com/2014/04/uso-de-alcunas.html.

## REFERENCES

Ageron, Charles-Robert. 1968. *Les Algériens musulmans et la France (1871–1919)*. 2 vols. Paris: Presses universitaires de France.

Amara, Noureddine. 2019. "Faire la France en Algérie: Émigration algérienne, mésusage du nom et conflits de nationalités dans le monde, de la chute d'Alger aux années 1930." PhD diss., Université Paris I Panthéon-Sorbonne.

Amorouayach, Essafia. 2017. "Adaptation d'anthroponymes algériens à l'orthographe française." *Synergies Algérie*, no. 24, 225–34.

Beaussier, Marcelin. 1887. *Dictionnaire pratique arabe-français*. Algiers: Jourdan.

Bénet, Henri. 1937. *L'état civil en Algérie: Traité théorique et pratique de la constitution de l'état civil des Indigènes algériens*. Algiers: Minerva.

Benramdane, Farid. 2000. "Qui es-tu? J'ai été dit: De la destruction de la filiation dans l'état civil d'Algérie, ou éléments d'un onomacide sémantique." *Insaniyat* 10 (January–April): 79–87.

Bresnier, Louis-Jacques. 1855. *Cours pratique et théorique de langue arabe*. Algiers: Bastide.

——. 1857. *Chrestomathie arabe: Lettres, actes et pièces diverses*. Algiers: Bastide.

Bruck, Gabriele vom, and Barbara Bodenhorn. 2006. "'Entangled in Histories': An Introduction to the Anthropology of Names and Naming." In *The Anthropology of*

*Names and Naming*, edited by Gabriele vom Bruck and Barbara Bodenhorn, 1–30. Cambridge: Cambridge University Press.

Bulliet, Richard W. 1993. Review of *Le Voile de nom*, by Jacqueline Sublet. *Journal of the American Oriental Society* 113, no. 1 (January–March): 125.

Carette, Ernest. 1853. *Exploration scientifique de l'Algérie*. Vol. 3, *Recherches sur l'origine et les migrations des principales tribus de l'Afrique septentrionale et particulière-ment de l'Algérie*. Paris: Imprimerie impérial.

Chachoua, Kamel. 2001. *L'Islam kabyle (XVIIIe-XXe siècles): Religion, État, et société en Algérie*. Paris: Maisonneuve et Larose.

Chaker, Salem. 2013. "Onomastique libyco-berbère (Anthroponymie)." In *Encyclopédie berbère*. Vol. 35, edited by Salem Chaker, 5760–79. Louvain: Peeters.

Cornu, E. 1889. *Guide pratique pour la constitution de l'état civil des indigènes*. Algiers: Jourdan.

Derrida, Jacques. 2007. "Des tours de Babel." Chap. 8 in *Psyche: Inventions of the Other*. Vol. 1, edited by Peggy Kamuf and Elizabeth Rottenberg, 191–225. Stanford, CA: Stanford University Press.

Desparmet, Joseph. 1948. *Coutumes, institutions, croyances des indigènes de l'Algérie*. Vol. 1, *L'enfance, le mariage et la famille*. 2nd ed. Algiers: Carbonel.

Doutté, Edmond. 1903. *Un texte arabe en dialecte oranais*. Paris: Imprimerie nationale.

Fanon, Franz. 1967. *Black Skins, White Masks*. Translated by Charles Lam Markmann. New York: Grove Press.

Fleisch, Henri. 1961. *Traité de philologie arabe*. Vol. 1, *Préliminaires, phonétique, mor-phologie nominale*. Beirut: Imprimerie Catholique.

Geertz, Clifford. 1976. "'From the Native's Point of View': On the Nature of Anthropo-logical Understanding." In *Meaning in Anthropology*, edited by Keith Basso and Henry A. Selby, 221–37. Albuquerque: University of New Mexico Press.

Grangaud, Isabelle. 2004. *La ville imprenable: Une histoire sociale de Constantine au 18e siècle*. Constantine: Éditions Média-Plus.

Kehl, C. 1931. "L'état civil des indigènes en Algérie." *Bulletin trimestriel de la Société de géographie et d'archéologie d'Oran* 52 (March): 173–212.

Lacheraf, Mostefa. 1998. *Des noms et des lieux: Mémoires d'une Algérie oubliée*. Algiers: Casbah Éditions.

Lapierre, Nicole. 1995. *Changer de nom*. Paris: Stock.

Lefebvre-Teillard, Anne. 1990. *Le nom droit et histoire*. Paris: Presses universitaires de France.

Mac Guckin de Slane, William, and Charles Gabeau. 1868. *Vocabulaire destine à fixer la transcription en français des noms de personnes et de lieux usités chez les indigènes de l'Algérie*. Paris: Imprimerie impériale.

Mercier, Ernest. 1891. *La propriété foncière chez les musulmans d'Algérie: Ses lois sous la domination française, constitution de l'état civil musulman*. Paris: Leroux.

Messaoudi, Alain. 2015. *Les arabisants et la France colonial, 1780–1930: Savants, con-seillers, médiateurs*. Lyon: ENS Éditions.

Noiriel, Gérard. 2001. "The Identification of the Citizen: The Birth of Republican Civil Status in France." In *Documenting Individual Identity: The Development of State Practices in the Modern World*, edited by Jane Caplan and John Torpey, 28–48. Princeton, NJ: Princeton University Press.

Ould-Ennebia, Karim. 2009. "Histoire de l'état civil des Algériens: Patronymie et ac-culturation." *Revue maghrébine des études historiques et sociales*, no. 1 (Septem-ber): 5–24.

Schimmel, Annemarie. 1985. *And Muhammad Is His Messenger: The Veneration of the Prophet in Islamic Piety*. Chapel Hill: University of North Carolina Press.

———. 1989. *Islamic Names.* Edinburgh: Edinburgh University Press.

Scott, James C. 1998. *Seeing Like a State: How Certain Schemes to Improve the Human Condition Have Failed.* New Haven, CT: Yale University Press.

Siblot, Paul. 1997. "Nomination et production de sens: Le praxème." *Langages* 31 (127): 38–55.

Socin, Albert. 1898. "Die arabischen Eigennamen in Algier." *Zeitschrift der Deutschen Morgenländischen Gesellschaft* 52 (3): 471–500.

Sublet, Jacqueline. 1991. *Le voile du nom: Essai sur le nom propre arabe.* Paris: Presses universitaires de France.

Wehr, Hans. 1994. *A Dictionary of Modern Written Arabic (Arabic-English).* 4th ed. Edited by J. Milton Cowan. Urbana, IL: Spoken Language Services.

Yermeche, Ouerdia. 2002. "Le sobriquet algérien: Une pratique langagière et sociale." *Insaniyat* 6 (17–18): 97–110.

———. 2005. "L'état civil algérien: Genèse d'un processus redénominatif." *Publications PNR du CRASC*: 19–29. https://pnr.crasc.dz/pdfs/des%20noms-yermeche-pnr -2005.pdf.

# 4

# BRITISH RULE AND OMANI MARRIAGE IN COLONIAL ZANZIBAR

*Mandana Limbert*

On October 15, 1912, a little over twenty years after Zanzibar was declared a British protectorate, Theodore Burtt, a Christian missionary in Pemba, a sister island to Zanzibar, sent a letter to the British consul general in Stone Town, Zanzibar's capital. The letter addressed two concerns: how to manage marriage among "native" Christian converts and whether the marriages conducted by the mission were valid under "Mohammedan law" (ZNA AB 30/7). But the main concern of the mission, according to the letter writer, was that the "present lawless promiscuous cohabitation between the sexes, and separation again, often for trifling causes and without any time for consideration, is a chief source of the continued unhappy and degraded condition of the people" (ZNA AB 30/7). It soon became evident that there was no "formal" marriage legislation on the island, something many officials believed needed to be remedied, if not to quell promiscuous behavior, at least to establish the institutions they believed were necessary for a responsible colonial government.

One British official, Judge Lindsey Smith, dissented: "I do not agree with the opinions put forward in some of the minutes that there is no marriage law in Zanzibar. The same marriage law exists here as has existed for thousands of years [*sic*] in all Mahomedan countries" (ZNA AB 30/7). This view of an established and unchanging Islamic law did not satisfy other officials who believed that it was necessary to create—with "Muslim" approval, of course—a procedure for marriage registration. What constituted "Muslim law," and perhaps "marriage," was clearly up for debate.

Responding in part to Burtt's letter, British officials formulated and reformulated marriage policy, producing four different decrees over the next fifty years. In 1962, when the protectorate administration decided to streamline and consolidate these four decrees, they needed a chart to help them sort out the different revisions and amendments. "This will show us what legislation we have in which Decree," one official noted (ZNA AH 46/8). But as the same official became ill and was hospitalized, and as independence was looming, the project was never completed.

The significance of marriage for the history and eventual violence of the revolution cannot be overestimated. While racialized violence in Zanzibar's history and its bloody revolution have long attracted considerable scholarly attention, and rightly so, some of the most visceral tensions about race revolved around marriage and sex. Indeed, marriage became a fraught and highly charged issue in the years leading up to the 1964 revolution, which erupted immediately after Zanzibar's independence from England in 1963. One goal of the revolution was to rid the island of Omani "Arabs," who had established themselves as the island's rulers and, subsequently, as a protected elite under British rule. It is this realm of intimate life that ultimately came to represent for many people in Zanzibar the greatest injustices and racisms of the prerevolutionary era, especially between what came to be known as "Africans" and "Arabs," as well as the greatest atrocities of the 1964 revolution, during which thousands of Arabs were massacred. Subsequently, in the late twentieth century, both the sexual violence of the revolution and the policies of forced marriage implemented by the Zanzibari revolutionary state after the revolution, whereby Arab women who had remained on the island after 1964 were married to non-Arab men, helped shape the sense of shared, national victimhood in Oman, to which many Arabs traced their origins and returned after the revolution.

As the discussions about establishing marriage registration policies on Zanzibar unfolded after 1912, a number of issues arose for British officials: To whom should a registration policy apply? Would the political elite accept registration? How could one identify to whom the policy should apply? And how could marriage legislation—and the officials, records, and payments—be managed as people moved between the outlying districts and the capital, Stone Town? Complicating these questions were the changing demographics of the island, the changing ways that people identified themselves, and the fact that British policy rested on establishing particular laws for particular populations, based on notions of race that were anything but clear.[1]

This chapter focuses on and explores policy debates in the first decades of the twentieth century in Zanzibar that gravitated in particular toward marriage registration and descent categories. On the one hand, these discussions illustrate what scholars of East Africa have long argued: that the British protectorate administration appeased the Arab population in particular, as they were the island's "protected" people. At the same time, these discussions also suggest how British officials noted practices and notions of marriage and status that appeared different from their own and were significant to some Omanis. As British officials sought to garner approval from religious scholars or attempted to remain politic, they acknowledged variation in understandings of and approaches to identity. Such an acknowledgment enabled officials to establish policy that they understood would be acceptable but that never required them to fully question their own racial thinking and logic.

Indeed, racial thinking among European colonial officials, as Frederick Cooper and Ann Stoler (1997) have argued, had remarkable "sustaining power in the face of such obvious hybridity and variation." In Zanzibar, such sustaining power was made possible through the acceptance of practices that officials did not believe were true reflections of how people's identities should be understood and classified. In other words, even though British officials accepted that Arab marriage practices were not determined by racial categories, they did so only because it was politically exigent and because such variation did not shake their own beliefs.

# Marriage Registration Policy and Marriage Equality

The concern expressed by Theodore Burtt in 1912 about marriage policy among "native" Christians soon expanded to include other sections of Zanzibar's population, raising questions about what was acceptable practice among specific groups and how those populations were to be defined. Letters were sent to the leaders of the most important recognized Arab and Muslim communities, including the Shafi'i and Ibadi chief judges (qadis), Ahmed bin Sumayt al-Alawi and Ali bin Mohammad al-Munthery. As representatives of the two branches of Islam that were dominant in Zanzibar (there were others), these were the most important scholars to contact.

While neither qadi objected to the registration of marriages, other issues came to the fore (ZNA AB 30/7). The primary issue for British officials was whether the subjects of a decree being drafted should be "native Muslims" or the "sultan's subjects" and what these categories actually meant. Some officials argued that "native" included mainland Africans as well as Comorans, even though there was doubt whether Comorans were of African "extraction" because "they are said to have Malay blood." At the same time, not all Muslims on Zanzibar were the sultan's subjects. Many Muslims hailed from British India, Iran, or parts of Arabia not under the dominion of the sultan of Zanzibar or his family. After much back-and-forth, it was finally decided that the word "native" would be removed entirely from the decree since it seemed to cause more confusion than it solved, and that the legislation would apply to "all persons professing the Mohamedan Faith other than British Indian subjects."

At the same time that discussion of marriage legislation began to circulate, the British resident Sinclair received several petitions from Arabs insisting that marriages performed among Muslims be in accordance with Islamic law.[2] The petitioners were not primarily concerned with whether the decree applied to them or whether they were subjects (they assumed it would and that they were not British Indian subjects); their main concern was that the policies be in accordance with religious law, Sharia. Most importantly for these petitioners, accordance with Sharia meant not only that an appropriate guardian (*walī*) must consent to the marriage but also that women must be married to men who were "sufficient" or their "equals." All three petitions received by the British resident in 1916 made clear that status position was critical for any legitimate marriage law and was the primary concern of these petition signers. In September 1916, for example, we read: "We beg most respectfully to lay before Your Honour two affairs . . . and trust that you will take them into your favourable consideration. We beg to state that ceremonies of marriage contracts are frequently performed by unauthorized persons between Arab women of better birth to husbands who are not their equal. This thing besides being contrary to the Sheria and to the Arab customs and usage is considered extremely loathsome by us" (ZNA AB 30/1).[3] In a note from Sayf bin Said bin Majid, dated October 12, 1916, we read:

> (1) No woman should be married except with the conformity of the Sheria. If the Sheria is averse to such woman's marriage she should not be married. (2) The Government may authorize certain persons to the number of the Muslim sects existing in Zanzibar to perform the ceremonies of marriage contracts of the members of their sects. (3) No woman should be allowed to marry except with the consent of her guardian. (4) If a guardian refuses to consent to his adult ward being married to a certain husband and such refusal is found to be in conformity with the Sheria it must be entertained. (5) The Court may authorize the marriage of a woman who has no natural guardian to a husband who is her equal. (ZNA AB 30/1)[4]

It is not clear from these passages what equality meant to the scholars. Nevertheless, in their view, the equal status of women and men was more important than whether a marriage registration was acceptable or a person was labeled "native" or "African."

A brief comment on the side of these memos—"Sheria?"—suggests that whoever read these petitions was interested in the degree to which these were legitimate religious legal matters and, perhaps, what Qur'anic verses or hadith these notions reflected. There was no immediate answer to this side note and question, but certainly someone wondered whether the notions about status distinctions that were central to the concerns of the petitioners were understood along pious lines.

Unbeknownst to the officials who read these petitions in 1916, the stipulation that women marry their equals clearly refers to the concept of sufficiency in marriage (*kafā'a*), a rule of "hypergyny" that was significant to religious scholars and the pious. According to this concept, women must marry men who are either of equal or, possibly, higher status, and they may not marry men of lower status. The petitions do not specify what determines equality or status, nor do the petitioners, at this time, identify the men who were marrying Arab women of higher birth. One possibility is that elite Arab women were marrying less elite men from Oman, considered Arab by the British but perhaps not by Omanis. In 1942, Arab Association members again complained that marriages were not in conformity with the Sharia and, specifically, that Arab women were marrying non-Muslim Indian men.

In the 1920s and 1930s, the concern about marriage sufficiency disappears in these files. Instead, British officials increasingly focused on negotiating the logistics of assigning marriage officials and determining the fees and payment allocations for these activities. Eventually, the island was divided into marriage districts, and a series of marriage officials were appointed in different villages throughout the island and given letterhead, receipts, and payment collection procedures. Logistics became more important than concerns about local custom. The files on marriage and divorce registration are filled with references to government officials who struggled to figure out how to phrase marriage registration legislation and how to manage marriage officials and the payments they were supposed to collect.

Similar attention to status in marriage appears at the same time in scholarly work across the Indian Ocean, in Oman as well as in the East Indies. For example, the most important twentieth-century Omani and Ibadi scholar, Nūr al-Dīn al-Sālimī (whose work was known to scholars in Zanzibar), addressed the issue in his *Jawhar al-Niẓām* (*Gem of the system*) ([1925] 1989, 2:250), a two-volume compendium of Ibadi law written in rhymed prose. It is the most popular and frequently referenced book in contemporary Oman. If Ibadis (or even Sunnis) had one book in addition to the Qur'an at home, it was likely *Jawhar al-Niẓām*. Nūr al-Dīn al-Sālimī writes: "Therefore, the person responsible for a woman must not (*lam yalzam*) marry her [off] if he [the potential groom] is not satisfactory (*marḍiyan*), such as a grocer, a cupper, a tailor or servant (*mawlā*) in Islam and others. Each of them has his assigned social status (*akfāʾ*), until he attains quality in his *nasab* and *ḥasab* and state."[5]

Grocers, cuppers, tailors, and servants were said to have their "positions," which were determined by their acquired status (*ḥasab*) or occupations as well as their genealogies (*nasab*).[6] Neither religion nor race (*jins*) is mentioned. Whereas religion was probably taken for granted, al-Sālimī did not, as British officials had, employ race as an operative category for distinguishing between, and ranking, distinct groups of people.

Although there is no direct evidence of a connection, it is important to remember that across the Indian Ocean in the Dutch East Indies as well as in Egypt a similar debate was unfolding at a much more intense level. In 1905 Mohammad Rashid Rida (1865–1935), an Egyptian scholar and modernist reformer, issued a controversial *fatwa* in which he criticized the rule of *kafāʾa* as outdated.[7] For Rashid Rida, and those in the East Indies who followed the *fatwa*, however, the issue was primarily about marriage between female descendants of the prophet Muhammad and men who were not descendants. Among Ibadis, unlike adherents of other branches of Islam, this distinction was irrelevant because, in theory, prophetic descent has little meaning for potential political status or role. Nevertheless, while different groups argued for and against the *fatwa* in the East Indies and Egypt, the leading scholars in Zanzibar and Oman clearly supported the practice of *kafāʾa*. Although it is possible that the Zanzibari petition writers were concerned that Arab women of "higher birth" were marrying men of "lower birth" who were Indian or African (and, in fact, there is some evidence that Arab women were marrying non-Muslim Indian men), it is also possible that women of higher birth were marrying men of lower birth who were considered—by the British—as Arab but who were not considered Arab by other Omanis because of their presumed patrilineal ancestry. This is exactly what I was told during fieldwork in 2015. Be that as it may, status clearly was of paramount importance to some Omani religious scholars. British officials, on the other hand, were especially and resiliently concerned with race, as also became apparent in debates about descent.

## Half Castes

Whereas British marriage registration policies eventually distinguished between "Muslims" and "British Indians," and Omanis focused on hypergyny and the guardianship of women, colonial officials discussing how to implement marriage policies acknowledged intermarriage among Omanis.

In a series of debates about native half castes that took place among British colonial officials throughout the East African territories in the 1930s, twenty years after Burtt's letter, questions about how to categorize different populations in East Africa and Zanzibar again became central to the legal system (ZNA AB 30/?).[8] Spurred on by a case in Nyasaland (present-day Malawi) that found its way to the highest authorities in England, judges and other British officials considered whether native half castes were, in fact, native or not. Although the defendant in this case refused to declare whether he was native or nonnative, the judge felt it necessary to rule on this issue, which would determine what law would apply. Over the next five years, as different authorities discussed the case, the defendant was said to be nonnative, native, and then nonnative again. Officials in London and in the East African Dependencies painstakingly considered whether nativeness was a matter of blood or circumstance, the same throughout East Africa or different in each state, with multiple views and arguments for each position.

In Zanzibar, British officials argued that questions about the status of half castes raised potentially "impolitic" problems, especially among the Arab elite. As a result, the Zanzibar government appealed for the exclusion of Arab half castes from the ultimate decision of the East African Dependencies. In a message to the secretary of state, the Zanzibar attorney general explains that in Zanzibar, beginning in 1925, the term "native" had been replaced by "African," because the category of "native" was not viable in Zanzibar in the same ways as it was elsewhere. It made more sense in Zanzibar to consider those who might be understood as native in other African contexts as Africans, along with mainland Africans (including former slaves). This was, in part, because Arabs might consider themselves (differently) as natives, solidifying their roles as settlers and subjects of the Arab sultan of Zanzibar and, thus, the island's elite (ZNA AB 30/?).[9] The protectorate administration clearly had difficulty grappling with a non-European elite colonial society that did not conform to ideas of hypodescent.

In Zanzibar, British officials concluded, half castes could not be either native or African. The memo continues:

> I am opposed to a strict definition of "African" being formulated which would include half castes, for the reason that in Zanzibar the number of Euro-Africans and Indo-Africans is negligible, while the number of persons with mixed Arab and African blood is considerable.
>
> I consider that, even with a provision enabling a person who is by definition an African to "contract out" of the definition (so to speak) by proof of better education or a higher standard of living, any legislation

which puts the onus of avoiding the definition of "African" upon a person of mixed Arab and African blood would be most unpopular and be liable to cause considerable heart-burning.

At the present time, the Arab community decides for itself and I do not think that any interference by legislation is desirable. . . . I would prefer, therefore, as far as Zanzibar is concerned, that persons of mixed African and other blood should be regarded in law as non-Africans as they are under the present law. (ZNA AB 30/?)

For the British, the children of a mixed marriage "by definition" (possibly a weak synonym for "truth") were African. In other words, notions of race (that might be organized around ideologies of hypodescent, though this is not mentioned here) were so resilient that British officials could accommodate them only by saying that Arab practices were different and that it would be impolitic to structure categories otherwise. Over the course of the early part of the twentieth century, as British officials tried to implement laws in Zanzibar, the distinction between native and nonnative was replaced by "Arab," "African," "Indian," and "European," with "half castes" not categorized for local, political reasons—even though in reality they would be African.

Clearly, while British officials understood that the practices of intermarriage and descent did not conform to their ideas about hierarchy and race, they held on to those ideas and argued that it was best not to enforce them. Indeed, it could have become possible to "contract out" of the conceived lower status through "better education" or a "higher standard of living," not through ideas of hypergyny (and patrilineality), as had been suggested in the earlier Arab petitions about marriage.

As Omanis traveled across the Indian Ocean to Zanzibar in the first half of the twentieth century, they encountered a legal regime and political order that continued to grapple with how to manage them and the various groups of people whose practices did not conform to British administrative logic. Clearly, British officials were sometimes also unsure about their own policies, often disagreeing among themselves. On some level, they attempted to garner approval from select members of the Arab elite in Zanzibar or to adjust their policies in response to what they understood would be impolitic. And yet, racial thinking, in the case of both marriage registration and half castes, seems to have been particularly resilient. Ultimately, the "glancing acknowledgment" of notions of identity different from their own enabled British officials to appease some of the Arab population without having to adjust their own presumptions.

Arabs, for their part, were hardly a homogenous group of elite compradors, though some of the Swahili-speaking Arab elite and many others from the Arabian Peninsula benefited from British policies that treated them as the island's protected community. They were thus empowered to insist on religiously sanctioned notions that proved to be among the most incendiary of the revolution.

## NOTES

1. As Jonathan Glassman (2000, 2011) has demonstrated, in the 1950s and 1960s, racial thinking was not limited to British officials. In response to the Arab-dominated Zanzibar Nationalist Party, some members of the Afro-Shirazi Party defined groups along explicitly racial lines and in ways that may have made British officials uncomfortable.

2. Zanzibar became a British residency in 1913.

3. This is the official British translation of the text. All translations from al-Sālimī are mine.

4. This is the official translation of the text, point number 5: *Al-imra'a allatī lā lahā walī bi-zawjihā al-shar' yakfū'hā.*

5. The two aspects of marriage equality are equality in descent (*kafā'a fi-l-nasab*) and equality in acquired status (*kafā'a fi-l-ḥasab*). See al-Sālimī (1925) 1989, 2:250.

6. Stefania Pandolfo (1997) analyzes the relationship between *ḥasab* and *nasab* as described to her during fieldwork in Morocco. This description is a partial inversion of understandings of the relationship in other contexts. In Oman, for example, *ḥasab* refers to acquired status (through marriage or work) rather than to patrilineal descent; and *nasab* refers to "natural" patrilineal genealogies, not to "synchronic acquired relationships."

7. The fatwa in question is titled *Tazwīj al-sharīfa bi-ghayr sharīf wa faḍl ahl al-bayt.* On this exchange, see Boxberger 2002 and Ho 2006.

8. For an account of this case as it unfolded in British Central Africa (contemporary Malawi, Zimbabwe, and Zambia), see Lee 2014.

9. In a later memorandum, the attorney general explains that before 1925, the term "native" also applied to those people "whose place of origin was the Protectorate of Aden or the Dominions of the Sultan of Muscat or the coastal strip within the sphere of British influences between Aden and Muscat. Thus, the term included Aden Somalis and all Arabs who were likely to visit Zanzibar" (ZNA AB30/?).

## REFERENCES

Boxberger, Linda. 2002. *On the Edge of Empire: Hadhramawt, Emigration, and the Indian Ocean, 1880s–1930s.* Albany: State University of New York Press.

Cooper, Frederick, and Ann Laura Stoler, eds. 1997. *Tensions of Empire: Colonial Cultures in a Bourgeois World.* Berkeley: University of California Press.

Glassman, Jonathan. 2000. "Sorting Out the Tribes: The Creation of Racial Identities in Colonial Zanzibar's Newspaper Wars." *Journal of African History* 41 (3): 395–428.

——. 2011. *War of Words, War of Stones: Racial Thought and Violence in Colonial Zanzibar.* Bloomington: Indiana University Press.

Ho, Engseng. 2006. *Graves of Tarim: Genealogy and Mobility across the Indian Ocean.* Berkeley: University of California Press.

Lee, Christopher. 2014. *Unreasonable Histories: Nativism, Multiracial Lives, and the Genealogical Imagination in British Africa.* Durham, NC: Duke University Press.

Pandolfo, Stefania. 1997. *Impasse of the Angels: Scenes from a Moroccan Space of Memory.* Chicago: University of Chicago Press.

Sālimī, Nūr al-Dīn al-. (1925) 1989. *Jawhar al-niẓām fī ʿilmay al-adyān wa-l-aḥkām.* 11th ed. Edited by Abū Isḥāq Aṭfiyyash and Ibrāhīm al-ʿAbrī. 2 vols. N.p.

ZNA (Zanzibar National Archive).

# 5

# KENYAN MUSLIMS AND THE POLITICAL IMAGINATION OF SPACE ON THE INDIAN OCEAN RIM

*Jeremy Prestholdt*

This chapter examines the political imagination of space as a response to questions of citizenship and belonging. Since the colonial era, the Muslim communities of Kenya's coastal region have experienced an acute feeling of alienation stemming from a sense of political marginality as well as economic and social grievances. This alienation has been heightened in recent decades as a result of international and domestic counterterrorism programs. Not only have coastal Muslims of diverse backgrounds suffered because of discriminatory state policies, but Kenyans of southern Arabian, Somali, and Swahili descent have also been denigrated as racial "foreigners," notably during moments of political tension. These and other developments have placed questions of belonging, social identity, and the rights of diverse Kenyan Muslims at the heart of regional political debates.

In coastal Kenya, alienation and historical injustices have engendered multiple political responses shaped by national and international interpretive frames. More precisely, demands for greater rights have contributed to forms of dissent and political organization that emphasize Muslim identity as a political catalyst, notably in coastal urban centers. The political strength of Muslim identity has, in fact, increased in recent decades, particularly around national legislative questions. However, ethnic, racial, and class divisions have limited the efficacy of Muslim identity as a political catalyst (Chome 2021; Elischer 2019; Ndzovu 2009, 2014). More precisely, while political thinkers have regularly emphasized Muslim identity, the cohesion of coalitions bound to ethnic, racial, or other social categories has often been significant. Yet, at many junctures the potency of each of these forms of political organization has hinged on their fusion with communal claims to physical space. Thus, a prominent recurring theme in the political history of Kenya's Indian Ocean rim is the interpretation of the coast as a discrete cultural entity typified by indigenes and "foreigners."

This interpretation of the coast as a discrete sphere has had several permutations. First, for many coastal Muslims, an emotive and historical connection to the wider Indian Ocean region has informed a discursive emphasis on the maritime essence of coastal society. This "basin consciousness," a mode of sociopolitical thought informed by historical linkages and perceptions of affinity across maritime space, was particularly evident in the late colonial era (Prestholdt 2015). A corollary emphasis has been on the Islamic historical profile of coastal urban centers and linkages with the wider Muslim world (Kresse 2007, 2018). Finally, claims of ethnic ownership of the coast, emphasizing either the region's continental or African orientation, have proved more attractive at unusually fraught junctures—for example, during the political turbulence of decolonization and the transition to multiparty democracy in the 1990s (Chome 2021; Prestholdt 2014). Indeed, Justin Willis and George Gona have suggested that the "politics of territoriality" in coastal Kenya have taken on greater significance during periods of political flux (Willis and Gona 2013; Medard 1996).

Since the colonial era, the concept of a discrete coastal sphere has acted as a powerful frame for mobilizing dissent and imagining alternative political futures. In this chapter I trace this politics of territoriality—the multiple catalytic uses of Muslim identity and related spatial imaginaries—across several periods of political tension to demonstrate not only its recurrence but also its flexibility. I place particular emphasis on articulations of autochthony, or the assertion of rights based on "original" habitation. Within this conceptual frame, diverse political thinkers have imagined entitlements to flow from historical, communal, and exclusive relationships to territory. In Kenya's coastal Muslim communities, the politics of territoriality linked to the notion of the coast as a clear and bounded entity has frequently represented certain groups, based on religious affiliation and ethnicity, as insiders with unique historical rights. Even as multiple ethnic and racial blocs have claimed exclusive, often conflicting autochthonous status, concepts of the coast as a discrete geography have served as a catalyst for political imagination and collective action.

# Decolonization between the Sea and the State

Kenya's Indian Ocean coast region has long been defined by mobility and heterogeneity. Coastal Kenya's position at the intersection of continental and maritime social imaginaries has also encouraged and complicated overlapping registers of nativism (Pouwels 2002; Willis 1993). As Ngala Chome (2021) has demonstrated, these contending perceptions of the coast as either essentially African or Indian Ocean in orientation have shaped and been shaped by a regional discourse of race that has long affected political tensions. In precolonial urban communities on the Swahili coast, social prestige and certain rights were denied to many "latecomers" or other outsiders, particularly migrants and enslaved people. Hierarchies of belonging accorded prestige to Muslims of local birth or patrician background, and elites often referenced distant, even mythic origins to justify exclusive rights. Among the coastal elite, narratives of historical migrations from southern Arabia or Persia as well as more immediate Arabian genealogies further cemented prestige claims. This was particularly evident in the nineteenth century, a period of Omani Busaidi political and economic dominance on the Swahili coast, which saw the significant expansion of plantation slavery (Glassman 1995; Pouwels 1987; Cooper 1977). British colonial administrative boundaries in late nineteenth- and twentieth-century Kenya reinforced conceptual links between social identity, prestige, and space. Administrators codified local social hierarchies and concretized inequalities by introducing racially defined legal categories rooted in a "native"/"nonnative" dyad. These, along with key privileges for nonnatives, such as land titles and better access to education, deepened socioeconomic divisions (Ng'weno 1997; Salim 1973, 1976). Complicating matters further, the language of race did not always follow official colonial categories. In the late colonial era, many non-Arabs commonly referred to Swahilis of mixed ancestry as Arabs, while both Swahilis and Arabs were often referred to as immigrant races, much like Asians and Europeans (Willis 1993; Salim 1973, 1976; Kindy 1972).

Across Indian Ocean Africa, decolonization created a conundrum for coastal groups, including those defined by diasporic or maritime identities (Brennan 2012; Glassman 2011; Gupta 2007). In Kenya, socioeconomic divisions, fortified by colonial categories and the greater rights of nonnatives, engendered explosive debates over the future of the coast region (Ndzovu 2009; Salim 1979). At the end of the 1950s, the future of the Protectorate of Kenya, a narrow coastal strip contiguous with Kenya Colony, became a political flashpoint. The sultan of Zanzibar retained titular sovereignty over the strip, and thus the drive toward independence raised the complicated question of how, and indeed whether, the protectorate would be integrated with Kenya. The ensuing debate within the protectorate exposed and encouraged divergent spatial imaginaries bound to social identity. Many coastal political thinkers feared that domination by an "up-country," majority Christian postcolonial government would prove disastrous for racial, ethnic, and religious minorities. Increased migration to the coast from other regions of Kenya exacerbated these concerns. Such fears led many Mijikenda, both Muslim and Christian, to support a form of federalism referred to as *majimboism*, which sought to check the political influence of larger ethnic voting blocs, such as Kikuyu and Luo. The most prominent proponent of *majimboism*, the Kenya African Democratic Union, enjoyed strong support at the coast (Chome 2021; Anderson 2005, 2010).

Many other movements emerged in response to questions over the coast's future. Some of the most influential were factions led by Muslim political thinkers of various backgrounds, including Swahili, Arab, Mijikenda, Bajuni, and Pokomo, who demanded complete autonomy for the coastal region. They argued that the protectorate gained little from British rule while up-country groups enjoyed superior economic and educational opportunities. Thus, they asserted that integration with independent Kenya would perpetuate disparities and even compromise Muslim social advancements. Many also claimed that integration would erode the coastal region's Muslim culture. Stressing this perceived existential threat, separatists argued that the departing colonial administration had an ethical obligation to grant full autonomy to the protectorate (Prestholdt 2014; Salim 1973).

Most coastal political thinkers also linked social identity to coastal geography in contentious claims of autochthony. This link reflected political trends in colonial Kenya and the wider decolonizing world (Weitzberg 2017; MacArthur 2016; Whittaker 2014). At the end of the 1950s, ethnic territoriality resonated strongly across Kenya since many saw decolonization as a zero-sum game in which the more advantaged ethnic groups would reap the future rewards of state power (Lynch 2011). Motivated by such anxieties, political thinkers across Kenya who represented less influential groups emphasized group solidarity and exclusive ethnic ownership of subnational territories, often articulated through metaphorical ties to "the soil": an emotive notion of historical connection to land, which for many Mijikenda likewise evoked land grievances (Prestholdt 2014; Lynch 2011, 17). In the coastal region, this politics of the soil and anxiety over the postcolonial future also dovetailed with a larger Muslim "cultural awakening," notably among urban Swahili speakers. For example, a number of social and culturally integrative programs, such as the Mombasa Institute of Muslim Education and the radio station Voice of Mombasa, contributed to a stronger feeling of commonality within Muslim communities in the protectorate (Brennan 2008, 2015; Salim 1970, 217; 1973, 216–17).

As numerous secessionist parties took shape in the early 1960s, fractures along racial and ethnic lines hindered any unified platform. For instance, the Coast African Political Union, a largely Mijikenda party that voiced concerns about up-country dominance as well as the perpetuation of racial inequalities, asserted the rights of coastal Africans over all others at the coast. They also championed the slogan "Upcountry people to their home areas" (*wabara kwao*) (Stren 1970, 40). Alternatively, the conservative, Arab-dominated Coastal League lobbied for reintegration with Zanzibar. Expressing a prominent form of late colonial basin consciousness, the league suggested that the coast had a uniquely maritime orientation and argued that separation from Kenya would allow coastal residents to "continue and expand our ancient relations with the Kingdoms, Sultanates and Sheikhdums [*sic*] of the Persian Gulf and Arabia" (National Archives of the United Kingdom and Ireland 1961a, 1961b). The more progressive Coast Peoples Party (CPP) similarly asserted the Kenyan coast's Indian Ocean essence but argued for complete autonomy from both Kenya and Zanzibar.

The CPP would emerge as the most influential separatist group, drawing support from those who decried the biases of ethnic-oriented parties such as the Coast African Political Union and the Coastal League. Under the leadership of the Swahili Member of the Legislative Council of Kenya for Mombasa, Sheikh Abdilahi Nassir, the CPP developed a pan-ethnic base that emphasized coastal Muslim identity. Party leaders asserted that the coast was defined by a history of Islamic praxis and maritime orientation, and they concluded that this underlying coherence of culture and origins was sufficient to constitute a coastal nation (National Archives of the United Kingdom and Ireland 1961c). However, nationalist leaders beyond the coast region charged that separatists had no right to demand autonomy. Referencing Nassir's partial Arab ancestry, one of Kenya's most important political figures, Tom Mboya of the Kenya African National Union (KANU), chided the CPP representative: "Go back to Arabia!"[1]

To safeguard Kenya's future economic interests, the Colonial Office and the sultan of Zanzibar resolved that the coastal strip would be joined with Kenya Colony before independence. As independence approached, however, many coastal political groups continued to lobby for autonomy, and the factional divides among coastal Muslims began to feel less consequential than dominance by Nairobi. Therefore, in the year preceding independence, two parties, Mwambao United Front and later the Coast United Front (CUF), drew erstwhile political opponents under an overarching banner of coastal nationalism to demand the separate independence of the coast. CUF, for instance, affirmed that all coastal people, regardless of race and ethnicity, were citizens of a discrete historical territory and bearers of a common identity. Though the protectorate was integrated with Kenya, diverse coastal political thinkers, by modifying their definitions of the autochthon to recognize each other as members of a common community, demonstrated that the concept of coastal autochthony could retain political value even as they redefined the "foreigner" (Prestholdt 2014).

Kenya gained independence in 1963, but questions of inclusion and coastal regional identity remained unresolved. Coastal Muslim communities occupied a "double periphery," as Kai Kresse (2009) suggested: on the margins of Kenyan national politics as well as on the periphery of the wider Muslim world. Among policymakers in Nairobi, suspicion of coastal Muslim communities lingered. Many at the coast charged that Muslim communities came under direct attack and also suffered from state neglect in the early postcolonial era (Ndzovu 2010; Kenya National Archives 1964). However, coastal Muslim engagement with domestic politics increased markedly in the late 1960s and 1970s, albeit in ways constricted by social and class divisions. An emergent identity as Kenyan encouraged many coastal Muslims to engage with the national political sphere. And after KANU became Kenya's only party in 1969, party politics became the sole means to affect national policies.

By the 1980s, many in the coastal region perceived the socioeconomic circumstances among Muslims to be in steep decline as compared with other groups in Kenya. In the era of President Daniel arap Moi, many coastal Muslims voiced particular alarm over increasing economic marginality, underrepresentation, discrimination in employment, and a repressive political environment (Kresse 2009). Moreover, Muslims' feelings of ambiguous citizenship were compounded by frequent discrimination and bribery when applying for essential documents such as national identity cards and passports. This sense of ambiguous citizenship, in turn, occasioned a resurgence of alternative sociogeographic political imaginations.

## Multiparty Politics and the Reimagination of the Coast

Political frustrations across Kenya engendered reforms in the early 1990s. These reforms culminated in multiparty elections in 1992, which had strong reverberations in Coast Province. In the context of democratic reforms, the notion of a coastal sociocultural sphere once again became a critical political lever. Longstanding economic, social, and political grievances, combined with a perceived potential for structural political change, produced a populist groundswell in coastal Kenya. One of the most consequential movements to emerge in this new environment was the Islamic Party of Kenya (IPK), an aspiring opposition party with roots in Mombasa. Its rise evidenced, among other things, a return to Muslim and coastal identity as catalysts for political action (Mazrui and Shariff 1994).

Conceived as a pan-ethnic party that sought a collective voice for the grievances of Muslims, the IPK became a popular platform for Muslim political engagement, particularly in Mombasa and other urban centers at the coast (Oded 2000; Wolf 2000; Bakari 1995, 2013). IPK leaders placed great emphasis on citizenship concerns shared by a cross-section of coastal Muslims, including discrimination in obtaining IDs and passports. They developed a political reformist agenda and a diffuse leadership structure while using Muslim identity to draw support among diverse urban youth. The IPK also drew inspiration from Islamic parties around the world, though the party was not Islamist per se. IPK supporters linked rights discourse in Kenya to a wider community of sentiment (Chome 2019). For example, they voiced solidarity with a global Muslim political "awakening" and embattled Muslim communities abroad. One graffito on a busy Mombasa thoroughfare emphasized the pluralism of this internationalist sentiment through a reference to a 1985 USA for Africa hit song: "We Are the World—IPK." Unlike earlier political movements at the coast, the IPK fused popular strains of Muslim internationalism with demands for greater rights within the secular Kenyan state.

As opposed to the coalition model of Kenyan political organization, in which multiple ethnically based political parties aligned under a broad tent, the IPK mobilized across social divides by emphasizing the common grievances of Muslims. In a return to the rhetoric of regional territoriality, some IPK members even declared Mombasa to be an "Islamic zone." This recasting of autochthony discourse in specifically religious terms, along with the IPK's provocative style of denouncing political elites at the coast and in Nairobi, incensed many political and religious leaders. Yet, the IPK's style of political engagement resonated strongly with young, urban Muslims, evidencing a generational divide around questions of political strategy (Wolf 2000; *East African Standard* 1992). The Moi administration and provincial leaders saw the IPK as a serious threat to KANU's power in Coast Province. Ahead of the 1992 elections, Kenya's attorney general denied the IPK registration, asserting that the constitution forbade parties oriented on religious lines. Police arrested party leaders and forced others into exile (Oded 2000; Mazrui 1993; *Weekly Review* 1992a, 1992b).

State and nonstate actors employed a variety of other means to silence the IPK. Notably, as party supporters were primarily young and urban, and many were Swahili, detractors used territoriality and race as wedges. Some attempted to delegitimize the IPK by claiming it was the party of wealthy, urban "Arabs." As the rhetoric of an Arab resurgence reached a fever pitch, a group called the United Muslims of Africa, which primarily recruited young Mijikenda men and purportedly received assistance from regional politicians, began to attack the IPK's base in the majority-Swahili neighborhoods of urban Mombasa. These attacks as well as other efforts to undermine the group, such as police harassment of IPK supporters and leaders, contributed to the collapse of the movement (Oded 2000). The IPK had used Muslim and coastal urban identity to build a political movement, but this orientation became the grounds on which the state denied it national legitimacy and detractors attacked its base.

Muslim identity, race, ethnicity, and concepts of coastal space continued to play a role in coastal political imaginations throughout the decade (Wolf 2000; Ndzovu 2012; Mghangha 2010; McIntosh 2009). The idea of *majimboism* began to resonate once again, but the election cycle of 1997 occasioned a particularly deadly return of autochthony discourse. Multiple KANU candidates, officials, and activists at the coast believed that up-country residents would vote for opposition candidates. Therefore, they aimed to force Kikuyu, Luo, and others of extracoastal origin out of the region before elections. To this end, political activists mobilized young Mijikenda, notably Digo men, with promises of land in return for attacking up-country residents. In early August, several months before the elections, Digo militias in suburban Mombasa and the south coast attacked and displaced those they deemed "foreign Kenyans." Specifically, militias killed or injured hundreds of people, almost exclusively Kikuyu and Luo. Leaflets distributed in mid-August entreated locals to "redeem your area against noncoastal people." One graffito in Likoni ominously warned up-country residents, "Three days to leave or you die" (Nduru 1997). As the violence spread across the coastal region, some Swahilis were also exhorted to leave (McIntosh 2009, 61). The militias thus reanimated and distilled the autochthony rhetoric of the 1960s, defining multiple ethnic groups and even some Muslims as "foreigners" (Mazrui 1997; *Nation* 1997).

The state's lingering mistrust of young coastal Muslims would have myriad repercussions when al-Qaeda operatives attacked the US embassy in Nairobi in 1998. Though the embassy bombers were mostly foreigners, the government of Kenya took a multifaceted approach to counterterrorism that disproportionately affected coastal and Somali communities. Security forces responded to the combined threat of terrorism and external pressure from the United States to act by developing a strategy that included mass arrests and detentions as well as intense scrutiny of passport applications (Prestholdt 2011; Salmon 2003; Kalyegira 2001; *Independent Online* 2000). Continued state suspicion of coastal Muslims, combined with long-standing Muslim grievances, created a generation of young people deeply resentful of Kenyan civil authorities (Mwakimako 2007; Maclean 2003). This resentment contributed to a form of popular rejection of mainstream politics that placed little faith in coastal elected leaders or in the political process generally. It also contributed to the elaboration of the idea of the coast as a discrete geographical entity. For instance, in the wake of the contested 2007 national elections, a group called the Mombasa Republican Council (MRC) began to gain attention. The MRC drew on strands of Indian Ocean basin consciousness, late colonial separatism, and autochthony rhetoric in their articulation of an interfaith discourse of dissent. Specifically, the MRC claimed that the Kenyan state had no legal right to the coast and resurrected the concept of coast regional secession, ostensibly along the lines of the early 1960s movement.

Under the banner "The coast is not Kenya" (*Pwani si Kenya*), MRC leaders, both Christian and Muslim, stressed exclusive rights to land and other regional resources (Willis and Gona 2013).[2] The MRC's rhetoric did not simply rehash 1960s nativism. Rather, its message represented an interlacing of 1960s, 1990s, and contemporaneous autochthony discourses in ways more inclusive of diverse racial, ethnic, and religious groups of the coastal region while maintaining a profoundly anti–up-country stance. By framing autochthony and the notion of a distinct coastal region in this way, the MRC by 2011 had crystallized what Paul Goldsmith called a "sense of unity" among many at the coast (2011, 4). This sense of common interest signaled a significant departure from the divisions that marred separatism in the years before independence. Given the political threat that the MRC posed, Kenyan authorities banned the organization, accusing its members of planning violence. Thus, while the MRC enjoyed significant support among Muslims and non-Muslims of diverse ethnic backgrounds, the group faced perennial legal battles and largely operated clandestinely.

State policies continued to exacerbate social and political tensions, which had multiple repercussions in the years after the 2007 elections (Kenya National Commission on Human Rights 2008). Most notably, Kenya's attempt in 2011 to neutralize the militant group al-Shabaab by sending troops to Somalia would add a layer of significant tension in relations between coastal Muslims and the state (Al-Bulushi 2021; Prestholdt 2019). It would also exacerbate divisions within the Muslim community, and it would see militants strategically develop exceedingly narrow formulations of coastal autochthony. Soon after the 2011 Kenyan invasion of Somalia, al-Shabaab and its affiliates launched a concerted campaign within Kenya that included scores of deadly attacks on civilian targets. This strategy was a calculated effort to weaken Kenya's resolve to pursue the war in Somalia (Anderson and McKnight 2015). Al-Shabaab likewise attempted to recruit Kenyans and paint itself as the champion of disaffected Kenyan Muslims. Al-Shabaab strategists wagered that by reciting Muslim grievances and evoking a transnational Muslim community they might pit Kenyan Muslims against the Kenyan state and thus create greater instability within Kenya (Jerejian 2017; Lowen 2014; Nzes 2012). To that end, al-Shabaab and its Kenyan affiliates appropriated strains of the autochthony rhetoric and claimed the coast as the sole preserve of Muslims.

Al-Shabaab's campaign of terror in Kenya prompted domestic demands for increased security. By 2012, counterterrorism efforts in Kenya focused intently on Muslim leaders and specific mosques believed to be centers of radicalism, including at the coast. Observers charged that the authorities subsequently killed several high-profile coastal Muslims (Haki Africa 2016; Open Society Justice Initiative and Muslims for Human Rights 2013). The 2012 murder of Aboud Rogo, a radical Mombasa-based preacher and outspoken supporter of al-Shabaab, was a case in point that proved a watershed. His death led to several days of rioting in Mombasa and drew condemnation from human rights groups and political leaders alike. Soon thereafter, several other preachers were murdered in what appeared to be a wider purge of al-Shabaab sympathizers (Goldsmith 2018; Horowitz 2012). As the violence escalated, radicals in Mombasa attempted to gain control of several important mosques (Mwakio 2013). Though young radicals were fewer in number, they began attacking moderates, including those who had been outspoken critics of the government's counterterrorism program. Several moderate coastal imams were also murdered, exacerbating the ideological rift within coastal Muslim communities (Ndzovu 2017).

Complicating matters further, in 2014 police raided multiple mosques, including Mombasa's Masjid Musa, where Aboud Rogo once preached. Seven young men were killed in the Masjid Musa raid and more than one hundred were arrested (Haki Africa 2016; Oketch, Kithi, and Mwakio 2014). Later that year, a multinational group of militants linked to al-Shabaab led a series of shockingly brutal attacks on towns in Lamu and Tana River Counties near the Somalia border. The militants killed Christian men, set buildings ablaze, and promoted the idea of the coast as a discrete Muslim territory. In a message left in the coastal town of Mpeketoni, the attackers claimed that the MRC was "sleeping" and charged Kenyan Muslims to "kick Christians out [of the] coast." "Muslims," an attacker hastily scrawled on a chalkboard, "this is your land" (Chome 2017; Harper 2014; Khalid 2014; Mwakimako and Willis 2014).

By restricting the definition of autochthony to Muslim coastal residents, al-Shabaab and its affiliates appropriated claims of historical propriety and labeled all non-Muslims interlopers in an unambiguous bid to win the support of Kenyan Muslims. In addition to subsequent violence against civilians, al-Shabaab used the internet and social media platforms to promote the idea that violence and the restoration of a global caliphate were the only effective response to state repression in Kenya. Though the envisioned support for al-Shabaab did not materialize, militants combined transnational rhetorics of radical Islamist thought with popular local discourses of autochthony and coastal space. In this way, their message appropriated wider discourses in coastal Kenya to service narrow strategic and transborder interests (Chome 2019; Anderson 2014; Ndzovu 2013–2014).

Long-standing economic, social, and political grievances have encouraged multiple—and often divergent—sociogeographic imaginings of Kenya's Indian Ocean rim. This chapter has traced recurring frames for mobilizing dissent since the late colonial era. Specifically, I have highlighted ways in which coastal Muslim political thinkers and others have promoted differing forms of solidarity and sought political leverage by asserting rights to physical space. By surveying several moments of heightened political tension, I have suggested that a significant and recurring catalyst for political organization has been communal claims to the "ownership" of the coast as a discrete sociocultural entity, one often imagined either to be continental in orientation or to evidence an Indian Ocean essence.

The history I have outlined here likewise demonstrates that this formulation of the past and the corresponding political imagination of the autochton have been not only contentious but also remarkably dynamic over time. Separatists, including former political adversaries, imagined and reimagined the "authentic" coastal resident in the waning days of colonial rule. Likewise, groups ranging from registered political parties to violent extremists have promoted various forms of religious territoriality, or the notion of Muslim "ownership" of the coast. But the political imagination of the coast has taken far less reductive forms as well, as evidenced in CUF's liberal definition of the coastal community on the eve of independence or the MRC's broadly similar formulation in recent years. Additionally, since the end of the 1990s, coastal political thinkers have placed less emphasis on race in their definitions of the "authentic local," though racial and ethnic tensions persist.

If, as I have outlined in this chapter, autochthony discourse and the imagination of a discrete coastal entity have retained political allure as tools to fortify sociopolitical communities and stimulate political action, this is at least in part because of their flexibility. When political thinkers have mobilized Muslim coastal identity for political action, they have often redefined the autochthon. Thus, while the politics of territoriality on Kenya's Indian Ocean rim may evoke deep histories, its malleability allows for the narration of regional pasts that at each juncture conform to contemporary interests and express shifting visions of the future.

## NOTES

1. Abdilahi Nassir, interview by the author, July 28, 2008, Mombasa; *Legislative Council Debates* 1961, 658–66.

2. Another refrain associated with the MRC was "Mombasa is ours; upcountry people go home!" (*Mombasa ni yetu wabara waende kwao*) (Van Metre 2018, 9, 15).

## REFERENCES

Al-Bulushi, S. 2021. "Citizen-Suspect: Navigating Surveillance and Policing in Urban Kenya." *American Anthropologist* 123 (4): 819–32.

Anderson, D. M. 2005. "'Yours in Struggle for Majimbo': Nationalism and the Party Politics of Decolonisation in Kenya, 1955 to 1964." *Journal of Contemporary History*, no. 39, 547–64.

——. 2010. "Majimboism: The Troubled History of an Idea." In *Our Turn to Eat! Politics in Kenya since 1950*, edited by D. Branch, N. Cheeseman, and L. Gardner, 17–43. Berlin: Lit Verlag.

——. 2014. "Why Mpeketoni Matters: Al Shabaab and Violence in Kenya." Norwegian Peacebuilding Resource Centre, September 2014. https://www.files.ethz.ch/isn/183993/cc2dacde481e24ca3ca5eaf60e974ee9.pdf.

Anderson, D. M., and J. McKnight. 2015. "Understanding al-Shabaab: Clan, Islam and Insurgency in Kenya." *Journal of Eastern African Studies* 9 (3): 536–57.

Bakari, M. 1995. "Muslims and the Politics of Change in Kenya." In *Islam in Kenya: Proceedings of the National Seminar on Contemporary Islam in Kenya*, edited by M. Bakari and S. Yahya, 234–51. Nairobi: Mewa.

——. 2013. "A Place at the Table: The Political Integration of Muslims in Kenya, 1963–2007." *Islamic Africa* 4 (1): 15–48.

Brennan, J. R. 2006. "Realizing Civilization through Patrilineal Descent: The Intellectual Making of an African Racial Nationalism in Tanzania, 1920–50." *Social Identities* 12 (4): 405–23.

——. 2008. "Lowering the Sultan's Flag: Sovereignty and Decolonization in Coastal Kenya." *Comparative Studies in Society and History* 50 (4): 831–61.

——. 2012. *Taifa: Making Nation and Race in Urban Tanzania*. Athens: Ohio University Press.

——. 2015. "A History of Sauti ya Mvita (Voice of Mombasa): Radio, Public Culture, and Islam in Coastal Kenya, 1947–1966." In *New Media and Religious Transformations in Africa*, edited by R. I. J. Hackett, B. F. Soares, and F. B. Nyamnjoh, 19–38. Bloomington: Indiana University Press.

Chome, N. 2017. "Why Raids Are a Cause for Worry as Al Shabaab Changes Face." *The Standard*, July 23, 2017. https://www.standardmedia.co.ke/counties/article/2001248735/why-raids-are-a-cause-for-worry-as-al-shabaab-changes-face.

——. 2019. "From Islamic Reform to Muslim Activism: The Evolution of an Islamist Ideology in Kenya." *African Affairs* 118 (472): 531–52.

——. 2021. "Uses of Race: Moral Debate and Political Action in Mombasa, 1895–1990." PhD diss., Durham University.

Cooper, F. 1977. *Plantation Slavery on the East Coast of Africa*. New Haven, CT: Yale University Press.

*East African Standard*. 1992. "Mombasa an 'Islamic zone'-IPK." September 6, 1992.

Elischer, S. 2019. "'Partisan Politics Was Making People Angry': The Rise and Fall of Political Salafism in Kenya." *Journal of the Middle East and Africa* 10 (2): 121–36.

Glassman, J. 1995. *Feasts and Riot: Revelry, Rebellion, and Popular Consciousness on the Swahili Coast, 1856–1888*. Portsmouth, NH: Heinemann.

——. 2011. *War of Words, War of Stones: Racial Thought and Violence in Colonial Zanzibar*. Bloomington: Indiana University Press.

Goldsmith, P. 2011. "The Mombasa Republican Council. Conflict Assessment: Threats and Opportunities for Engagement." Kenya Civil Society Strengthening Programme, November 2011.

——. 2018. "Comparative Perspectives on Islamic Radicalism in Kenya and the Horn of Africa." In *Confronting Violent Extremism in Kenya: Debates, Ideas and Challenges*, edited by M. Ruteere and P. Muthahi, 9–41. Nairobi: Centre for Human Rights and Policy Studies.

Gupta, P. 2007. "Mapping Portuguese Decolonisation in the Indian Ocean: A Research Agenda." *South African Historical Journal* 57 (1): 93–112.

Haki Africa. 2016. "What Do We Tell the Families? Killings and Disappearances in the Coastal Region of Kenya, 2012–2016." December 2016. https://hakiafrica.or.ke /wp-content/uploads/2019/01/HakiAfricaWDWTTF_V14.pdf.

Harper, M. 2014. "Kenyan Coastal Region of Lamu Hit by Deadly Attacks." *BBC News*, July 6, 2014. http://www.bbc.com/news/world-africa-28181246.

Horowitz, J. 2012. "Assassinations, Disappearances, and Riots: What's Happening in Mombasa?" Open Society Justice Initiative, August 29, 2012. http://www.soros.org /voices/assassinations-disappearances-and-riots-what-s-happening-mombasa.

*Independent Online* (South Africa). 2000. "FBI Interrogations Incur Muslim Wrath." May 30, 2000. http://www.iol.co.za/news/africa/fbi-interrogations-incur-muslim -wrath-39059.

Jerejian, T. E. 2017. "A Helping Hand? Recruitment of Kenyan Youth to al-Shabaab." MA thesis, University of Oslo.

Kalyegira, T. 2001. "Kenya's Muslims Protest New Passport Laws." United Press International, November 26, 2001.

Kenya National Archives. 1964. KA/6/35 Muhammad Hussein, Kenya Protectorate Nationalist Party, to Jomo Kenyatta. January 6, 1964.

Kenya National Commission on Human Rights. 2008. *"The Cry of Blood": Report on Extra-judicial Killings and Disappearances*. September 2008. http://file.wikileaks .org/file/kenya-the-cry-of-blood/crimes-against-humanity-extra-judicial -killings-by-kenya-police-exposed.pdf.

Khalid, H. 2014. *Mpeketoni Killings: Human Rights Fact Finding Report*. Haki Africa, July 2014. https://hakiafrica.or.ke/wp-content/uploads/2019/01/Haki-Africa -Mpeketoni-Booklet-FINAL.pdf.

Kindy, H. 1972. *Life and Politics in Mombasa*. Nairobi: East African Publishing House.

Kresse, K. 2007. *Philosophising in Mombasa: Knowledge, Islam and Intellectual Practice on the Swahili Coast*. Edinburgh: University of Edinburgh Press.

——. 2009. "Muslim Politics in Postcolonial Kenya: Negotiating Knowledge on the Double-Periphery." *Journal of the Royal Anthropological Institute* 15 (1): 76–94.

——. 2018. *Swahili Muslim Publics and Postcolonial Experience*. Bloomington: Indiana University Press.

*Legislative Council Debates: Official Report, Volume LXXXVII, May 1–Jul 21, 1961*. 1961. Nairobi.

Lowen, M. 2014. "Kenya al-Shabab Terror Recruits 'in It for the Money.'" *BBC News*, January 29, 2014.

Lynch, G. 2011. *I Say to You: Ethnic Politics and the Kalenjin in Kenya*. Chicago: University of Chicago Press.

MacArthur, J. 2016. *Cartography and the Political Imagination: Mapping Community in Colonial Kenya*. Athens: Ohio University Press.

Maclean, W. 2003. "Kenya Arabs Say Anti-terror Probe Hurts Muslims." Reuters, August 2, 2003.

Mazrui, A. 1997. *Kayas of Deprivation, Kayas of Blood: Violence, Ethnicity and the State in Coastal Kenya*. Nairobi: Kenya Human Rights Commission.

Mazrui, A. A. 1993. "The Black Intifadah? Religion and Rage at the Kenyan Coast." *Journal of Asian and African Affairs* 4:87–93.

Mazrui, A., and I. N. Shariff. 1994. *The Swahili: Idiom and Identity of an African People.* Trenton, NJ: Africa World Press.

McIntosh, J. 2009. *The Edge of Islam: Power, Personhood, and Ethnoreligious Boundaries on the Kenyan Coast.* Durham, NC: Duke University Press.

Medard, C. 1996. "Les conflits 'ethniques' au Kenya: Une question de votes ou de terres?" *Afrique contemporaine,* no. 180, 62–74.

Mghangha, M. 2010. *Usipoziba Ufa Utajenga Ukuta: Land, Elections, and Conflicts in Kenya's Coast Province.* Nairobi: Heinrich Böll Stiftung.

Mwakimako, H. 2007. "Christian-Muslim Relations in Kenya: A Catalogue of Events and Meanings." *Islam and Christian-Muslim Relations* 18 (2): 287–307.

Mwakimako, H., and J. Willis. 2014. *Islam, Politics, and Violence on the Kenyan Coast.* Nairobi: Observatoire des Enjeux Politiques et Sécuritaires dans la Corne de l'Afrique. https://shs.hal.science/halshs-02465228.

Mwakio, P. 2013. "Muslim Youth Extremism out of Hand, Warn Leaders." *The Standard,* December 24, 2013. http://www.standardmedia.co.ke/thecounties/article/2000100745/muslim-youth-extremism-out-of-hand-warn-leaders.

*The Nation.* 1997. "Six More Killed, Leaflet Target Groups." August 18, 1997.

National Archives of the United Kingdom. 1961a. CO822/2151. Memorandum Presented to the Right Honourable [R. Maulding] the Secretary of State for the Colonies on the Occasion of His Visit to Kenya in the Month of November, 1961, by the Coastal League, in Affiliation with the Central Bajun Association and the Coast African Political Union (ca. November 1961).

——. 1961b. CO822/2151. "Memorandum Re Constitutional Position of the Protectorate of Kenya Prepared by Representatives of the Coast Arabs" (ca. April 1961).

——. 1961c. CO894/13/2. Maalim Omar Rashid Bakuli, Memorandum on Coastal Strip Autonomy. October 20, 1961.

Nduru, M. 1997. "Kenya: Violence on Kenyan Coast." Inter Press Service, October 11, 1997.

Ndzovu, H. J. 2009. "Muslims and Party Politics and Electoral Campaigns in Kenya." Working Paper Series, n.09-001, Institute for the Study of Islamic Thought in Africa, Northwestern University, March 2009.

——. 2010. "Muslim Relations in the Politics of Nationalism and Secession in Kenya." Program of African Studies Working Papers, no. 18.

——. 2012. "The Politicization of Muslim Organizations and the Future of Islamic-Oriented Politics in Kenya." *Islamic Africa* 3 (1): 25–53.

——. 2013–2014. "The Prospects of Islamism in Kenya as Epitomized by Shaykh Aboud Rogo's Sermons." *Annual Review of Islam in Africa* 12 (2): 7–12.

——. 2014. *Muslims in Kenyan Politics: Political Involvement, Marginalization, and Minority Status.* Evanston, IL: Northwestern University Press.

——. 2017. "The Rise of Jihad, Killing of 'Apostate Imams' and Non-combatant Christian Civilians in Kenya: Al-Shabaab's Re-definition of the Enemy on Religious Lines." *Journal for the Study of the Religions of Africa and Its Diaspora* 3 (1): 4–20.

Ng'weno, B. 1997. "Inheriting Disputes: The Digo Negotiation of Meaning and Power through Land." *African Economic History* 25:59–77.

Nzes, F. 2012. "Terrorist Attacks in Kenya Reveal Domestic Radicalization." Combating Terrorism Center 5 (10): https://ctc.westpoint.edu/terrorist-attacks-in-kenya-reveal-domestic-radicalization/.

Oded, A. 2000. *Islam and Politics in Kenya.* Boulder, CO: Lynne Rienner.

Oketch, W., N. Kithi, and P. Mwakio. 2014. "Foreigners among Mombasa Mosque Chaos Suspects." *Standard,* February 6, 2014. http://www.standardmedia.co.ke/?articleID=2000104030&story_title=foreigners-among-mombasa-mosque-chaos-suspects&pageNo=2.

Open Society Justice Initiative and Muslims for Human Rights. 2013. *"We're Tired of Taking You to the Court"*: *Human Rights Abuses by Kenya's Anti-terrorism Police Unit*. New York: Open Society Foundations.

Pouwels, R. L. 1987. *Horn and Crescent: Cultural Change and Traditional Islam on the East African Coast, 800–1900*. Cambridge: Cambridge University Press.

——. 2002. "Eastern Africa and the Indian Ocean to 1800: Reviewing Relations in Historical Perspective." *International Journal of African Historical Studies* 35 (2/3): 411.

Prestholdt, J. 2011. "Kenya, the United States, and Counterterrorism." *Africa Today* 57 (4): 3–27.

——. 2014. "Politics of the Soil: Separatism, Autochthony, and Decolonization at the Kenyan Coast." *Journal of African History* 55 (2): 249–70.

——. 2015. "Locating the Indian Ocean: Notes on the Postcolonial Reconstitution of Space." *Journal of Eastern African Studies* 9 (3): 440–67.

——. 2019. "Counterterrorism in Kenya: Security Aid, Impunity and Muslim Alienation." In *Non-Western Approaches to Counterterrorism*, edited by M. J. Boyle. Manchester: Manchester University Press.

Salim, A. I. 1970. "The Movement of 'Mwambao' or Coast Autonomy in Kenya, 1956–1963." In *Hadith 2: Proceedings of the 1968 Conference of the Historical Association of Kenya*, edited by Bethwell A. Ogot, 212–28. Nairobi: East African Publishing House.

——. 1973. *The Swahili-Speaking Peoples of Kenya's Coast, 1895–1965*. Nairobi: East African Publishing House.

——. 1976. "Native or Non-Native? The Problem of Identity and the Social Stratification of the Arab-Swahili of Kenya." In *History and Social Change in East Africa: Proceedings of the 1974 Conference of the Historical Association of Kenya (Hadith 6)*, edited by Bethwell A. Ogot, 65–85. Nairobi: East African Publishing House.

——. 1979. "The Impact of Colonialism upon Muslim Life in Kenya." *Journal—The Institute of Muslim Minority Affairs* 1 (1): 60–66.

Salmon, K. 2003. "Muslims Say FBI Targets Them." Inter Press Service, March 6, 2003.

Stren, R. 1970. "Factional Politics and Central Control in Mombasa, 1960–1969." *Canadian Journal of African Studies / Revue Canadienne des Études Africaines* 4 (1): 33–56.

Van Metre, L. 2018. *Youth and Radicalisation in Mombasa: A Lexicon of Violent Extremist Language on Social Media*. Nairobi: PeaceTech.

*The Weekly Review*. 1992a. "Muslims Question Ban Decision." June 5, 1992, 22–23.

*The Weekly Review*. 1992b. "Second Wave of Coast Violence." July 24, 1992, 20–21.

Weitzberg, K. 2017. *We Do Not Have Borders: Greater Somalia and the Predicaments of Belonging in Kenya*. Athens, OH: Ohio University Press.

Whittaker, H. 2014. *Insurgency and Counter-insurgency in Kenya: A Social History of the Shifta Conflict, c. 1963–1968*. Leiden: Brill.

Willis, J. 1993. *Mombasa, the Swahili, and the Making of the Mijikenda*. Oxford: Clarendon Press.

Willis, J., and G. Gona. 2013. "*Pwani C Kenya*? Memory, Documents and Secessionist Politics in Coastal Kenya." *African Affairs* 112 (446): 48–71.

Wolf, T. P. 2000. "Contemporary Politics." In *Kenya Coast Handbook: Culture, Resources and Development in the East African Littoral*, ed. J. Hoorweg, D. Foeken, and R. A. Obudho. New Brunswick, NJ: Transaction Publishers.

# Part 3

# COLONIALISM AND SLAVERY

The *Umma* below the Winds

Like the chapters in part 2, those in part 3 deal with the colonial period, albeit in Southeast Asia, a part of the Muslim world known as "the *Umma* below the Winds." In the first chapter, Megan C. Thomas analyzes a colonial encounter with Muslims in the Sulu Archipelago in the southern Philippines, a conglomeration of islands that lies between the northern, Catholic parts of the archipelago and the Malay Peninsula and Borneo to the south. In the last decades of the eighteenth century, Spain, advancing south from Manila, and Britain, the most powerful European maritime power in Asia, collided in the Sulu Archipelago, where both encountered indigenous Muslim sultanates of long standing. Thomas explores the Muslim construction of "sovereignty" in the archipelago against the background of competition between Spain and Britain. The Sulu sultans, she explains, understood sovereignty primarily in terms of power over people and only secondarily in terms of control over territory. One important source of sultanic political power—and of sovereignty—was slaves. Whereas the British ignored the sultanate's engagement in slave trading, the Spanish sought to end the practice, which they regarded as a threat to their subjects and, thus, to the Spanish claim to sovereignty over the archipelago. Thomas analyzes an episode that took place in 1763: a conflict between British and Spanish authorities over the identity of the sultan, his power to authorize a treaty, and his status as a sovereign. She uses this episode to expose the different understandings of sovereignty held by the British, the Spanish, and the Muslims.

In the second chapter, Ian Coller tells the story of a remote Indian Ocean island that had an improbable connection to the French Revolution. Anjouan, a small island in the Mozambique Channel, was a sovereign Muslim state whose ruling elites were knowledgeable about the outside world and eager for news about wars in Europe, America, and Crimea. Slavers from Madagascar regularly targeted the island's inhabitants. In 1794, the French National Convention abolished slavery, but the practice continued in the colonies. Following the attempted assassination of Napoleon in 1800, the emperor deported seventy-one Frenchmen who purportedly had been involved in the plot. The dissidents were loaded onto ships and transported to Mahé in the Seychelles and then to Anjouan. Twenty-four of the deportees died shortly after their arrival and were buried on the island. The sultan's willingness to accept the deportees was driven by the dynamics of the slave trade. This episode, Coller argues, attests to the central role of slavery and its abolition in the revolutionary age, not only in the republic but also in its colonies around the globe.

# SOVEREIGNTY, SLAVERY, AND DIPLOMACY IN MID-EIGHTEENTH-CENTURY SULU

*Megan C. Thomas*

In 1763, the Spanish government of the Philippines and the British East India Company could not agree on the status of the sultan of Sulu: Was he an independent sovereign with the power and right to treat with other sovereigns or a vassal of the king of Spain?[1] For the sultan of Sulu, sovereignty was composed through a complex assemblage of alliances and patronage. The conflict between agents of British and Spanish sovereignty was one result of the complexity of how sovereignty was composed in Sulu.

This chapter treats the status of the sovereign in and of the sultanate of Sulu during a turbulent few years in the mid-eighteenth century, from different vantage points. British and Spanish officials sometimes understood the sultanate's sovereignty in different ways, as we will see from East India Company records of the period. From other scholars' accounts of eighteenth-century Sulu state structures and practices, we will see how power and authority operated in the sultanate. Those operations did not always meet with the expectations of European powers operating in the area, and the disconnect produced not only problems but also opportunities for various actors—of Europe and of Sulu.

Among the ways in which sovereignty operated differently across these state structures is the manner in which authority relied on and is reflected in documents, and where and how those documents traveled. British and Spanish sovereign structures, different as they were from each other, operated with a great deal of paper, collected and archived, and in some sense authority was created from these bureaucratic documents and the words they contained. In the sultanate, authority was produced differently. On the one hand, a closely guarded written genealogy provided a foundational part of the sultan's legitimacy, making the sultanate its own kind of literary and documentary state; on the other hand, authority was produced not through bureaucratic structures so much as through a series of nested, dyadic personal relationships. In this chapter, I reflect on these differences by considering the forms and practices through which sovereignty was produced in the Sulu sultanate.

These forms and practices of sovereign authority were on full display in the 1700s in a series of diplomatic negotiations and treaties between the sultanate of Sulu and Spain or the British East India Company. While sovereignty was asserted and produced internally, thereby expressing a relation between sovereign and subjects, it was also asserted and produced externally, in a sovereign's relation to other sovereigns and their mutual recognition. I begin by considering the internal production and operation of sovereignty in Sulu, using the accounts of other scholars, and then turn to a specific moment in 1763 when British and Spanish authorities argued about the sultan's status. This moment is one of conflicts over who was sultan, what he was empowered to delineate by treaty, and, ultimately, what his status was as a sovereign.

## Composing Sovereignty in Sulu

The sultanate of Sulu existed in relation to, and in tension with, other sultanates of maritime southeast Asia at the time, particularly those of Brunei, centered in northern Borneo, and Maguindanao, centered in Cotabato on Mindanao. The Sulu sultanate was centered in Jolo—the port on the island of the same name. (Contemporary Spanish and English sources also use "Xolo" or "Xola" to refer to port, island, and sultanate.) Jolo was a center for trade in maritime southeast Asia, connected to both Dutch Batavia and Spanish Manila, with Chinese junks among the trading vessels that regularly visited (Warren [1981] 1985, 5–10; Tarling 1978, 5; Saleeby 1963, 21). Enslaved people, pearls, birds' nests, tripang (sea cucumber), wax, and spices were among the commodities traded there (Warren [1981] 1985, 5–16).

Although the Sulu sultanate was centered in Jolo, it is best understood as an archipelagic state of patronage networks that extended across the sea, anchored at, and drawing from, various coastal settlements, but not well represented by identifying land territory under its sovereign control. James Warren has called the sultanate a "segmentary state" that "linked widely disparate communities and groups who were not organically united above the village level in a larger, complex, dynamic web of social and political loyalties" ([1981] 1985, xxiv). Muslim Tausugs occupied many positions of authority and power in the sultanate, and Tausug practices informed its structure, but it was a "plural polity embracing the entire Sulu archipelago and all its people," as Thomas Keifer has put it (1972, 23).

The sultanate's plurality was directly related to the slave trade (Warren [1981] 1985, 13–16, 198, 215–37). Many of the enslaved people who were traded in Jolo arrived there as the result of raids: surprise attacks, with the object of spiriting away human cargo along with any other valuables that could be quickly seized. Many of the communities that were the target of such raids were on the more accessible coastlines of the nearby Visayan Islands, communities of hispanized Catholics ostensibly under Spanish protection. Thus, many enslaved people were (formerly) Spanish subjects.

Some of the enslaved people traded at Jolo were destined for Batavia's larger market, but enslaved people were also part of the sultanate's political structures and contributed to the sultan's sovereign power. The sultan was not necessarily sultan for life, though many sultans did remain as such until their death, and primogeniture did not determine succession, though typically the position passed among male relations, as patrimony, particularly descent from the Prophet, strengthened a claim (Majul 1965, 38–39). Patrimony and lineages were recorded in *tarsilas*, which served, as Cesar Majul has explained, both as records and as a component of a sultan's claim to his position (1981, 167, 174). The sultan was not an absolute authority with control of those beneath him. Significantly, a sultan gained and held his position with the support of men of power and influence, recognized by their official title and status as *datu*. Some datus, like the sultan, could, on principle, trace their descent from the prophet Muhammad, and many were also descended from those whose local power predated Islam's arrival (Tarling 1978, 2; Majul 1965, 28). It was with the support of datus that the sultan gained and held his position (Majul 1965, 33–34). Yet the sultan was not "a mere rubber stamp of the principal *datus*" (Majul 1965, 26; quoted in Tarling 1978, 2). The sultan relied not only on the datus' continuing formal allegiance but also on their agreement and cooperation regarding any practical matter of rule (Majul 1965, 28–30).

Datus' power, in turn, depended only sometimes and in part on a hereditary claim. It also depended on the strength of their networks of patronage, which brought them recognition by the sultan. This power had to be continually exercised and renewed for them to retain their position, or, as Warren has put it, "a leader's power and status was based more on his control over personal dependents, either retainers or slaves, that he could mobilize at a given moment for what was deemed to be commercially or politically expedient, than on the formal state structure" ([1981] 1985, xxiv; see also Majul 1965, 35). Datus' retainers included people in various positions of unfreedom and slavery, whose military and economic labor collectively contributed to composing their datu's authority (Tarling

1878, 5; Majul 1965, 35–36). The slave trade, therefore, was not only a source of wealth but also a source of political power for the datus and for the sultan himself, both directly and indirectly, and if the sultan "made peace treaties with the state's opponents, particularly if such treaties prohibited piratical raids that provided slaves and booty," he risked losing the allegiance of datus (Tarling 1978, 2; cf. Majul 1965, 31–32, 40–41).

Therefore, in the Sulu sultanate, sovereignty was understood and practiced in terms of people and relationships, rather than area, as "power was always over men, and only secondarily over the territory on which they lived" (Keifer 1972, 26). Like other kinds of Tausug social formations, political groupings "were not bounded social units with the presumption of perpetuity, but rather fluid, ever-changing networks of personal ties which depended more upon the strength of the leader than any prior idea of the group as such" (23). There were structural inequalities, and status conferred power, but one's status—as sultan, datu, retainer, or enslaved—might change and was not understood in terms of membership in a class. Further, since Tausug groupings were organized in terms of the center—not their periphery or reach or even qualifications of membership—the "boundaries" of a polity were difficult to define and might in principle overlap with another (23, 25), though each man would only be part of one alliance at a time (28). Thus, "power remained diffuse . . . and governance in the traditional Taosug state was predicated on factional politics and revolved around highly variable leader-centred groups" (Warren [1981] 1985, xxiv). This arrangement of power, and the production and exercise of sovereignty, complicated diplomacy between the sultan and other sovereigns.

Anthony Reid has said of Sulu's plurality that it "baffled a succession of Spanish and American administrators" (1998, 31). Its plurality also composed its sovereignty, which, as we will see, baffled the British East India Company too. The fluidity of the sultanate's structures and unboundedness of its territory confused Spanish and British efforts to deal with the sultan as a sovereign ruler. Yet that confusion also created opportunities for diplomatic negotiations that otherwise might not have been possible.

## Whose Sovereignty?

The structures of labor and authority described above compose one very broad context of specific events to which we will now turn. These events also have more specific contexts that help to explain their contours, which have been the subject of previous research (Crailsheim 2013; de la Costa 1967; Tarling 1978, 10–20). However, for the purpose of thinking about sovereignty more broadly—how it was understood and misunderstood by British and Spanish agents, how it was produced, and what it in turn produced—we will try to read specific events into this very large and broad context.

Before turning to the documents of 1763, we need a provisional and brief account of the state of diplomacy among Sulu, Britain, and Spain at the time. In the 1700s, both the Spanish in Manila and the East India Company (extending from its base at Madras) sought to conclude treaties with the sultan of Sulu. For the Spanish, the object was to stem raids on coastal Visayan Catholic communities; for the British, the aim was to initiate a trade that would give the company access to the region's forest and sea products, highly valued in Canton. We will focus here on a moment in 1763, when the British and Spanish argued directly with each other about the sultan's status. The stage for this conflict had been set years prior, when Sultan Azim ud-Din (Alimudin, in British and Spanish sources) concluded an alliance with the Spanish, allowing Catholic missionaries into Jolo and prohibiting slave raids. This agreement precipitated tension among datus, between supporters of Sultan Azim ud-Din and supporters of his brother Bantilan, that eventually erupted into a threat to the sultan's life. The sultan fled to the nearby fort of his Spanish allies, Zamboanga, and from there to Manila, near which, in 1750, he converted to Catholicism, becoming the Catholic king Ferdinand I of Sulu. Meanwhile, in Jolo, his brother Bantilan assumed the title and name Sultan Muiz ud-Din. The Spanish were set to return King Ferdinand I (Azim ud-Din) to Jolo, in the hopes of reinstating him in power and thus putting a Catholic ally in the position of sovereign of Sulu, when the Spanish governor at Zamboanga discovered evidence of what he took to be a duplicitous plot. Thus, the sultan ended up not back in power in Jolo but back in Manila, this time a Spanish prisoner, where he remained, while his daughter Fatima and son Israel attended schools in Manila. The children's uncle, Sultan Muiz ud-Din (Bantilan), back in Jolo, had declared war on the Spanish; eventually Princess Fatima was able to broker a peace agreement, which promised among other results to welcome her father back to Jolo. In the meantime, Muiz ud-Din had concluded a treaty with the East India Company, which initiated a trade that the company hoped would allow it to exchange its British and Indian goods for products of maritime Southeast Asian seas and forests that were so valuable for Canton trade.[2]

The East India Company's desire for a trading factory somewhere in the realm of the sultan of Sulu also became a force propelling the British to try to occupy Manila, when Spain joined France in the war against Britain and its allies. When British forces, sent from India, attacked Manila in 1762, the Spanish governor-general Manuel Antonio Rojo surrendered relatively quickly, coming to terms with the British commanders to turn over Manila to them for the duration of the war, in exchange for a guarantee that the persons, religion, and property of

Spanish subjects would be preserved. Frustrating the British, however, was the military resistance they encountered in the countryside, headed by a high-ranking Spanish official. Throughout the occupation, Governor-General Rojo and the British commanders squabbled about the status of the resistance, whether it was under Rojo's authority and whether, according to the terms of the surrender, what had been ceded to the British was only the city of Manila (Rojo's position) or all of Spain's territories in the Philippines (Britain's position).[3]

This was the state of affairs in late 1762, when Sultan Azim ud-Din / King Ferdinand and his son, Prince Israel, were in the Spanish capital of Manila preparing to return to Jolo, the seat of the sultanate. Their plans were interrupted by the British attack on Manila, and when British forces encountered the sultan and his son, the latter were ready to negotiate with the new arrivals for their return to Sulu, this time with British support rather than Spanish. East India Company agents were eager to pursue such diplomacy, since the establishment of a trading base somewhere in the sultan's realms had been one of the initial aims of their participation in the venture.

The treaty between the East India Company and the sultan of Sulu was worked out, formalized, and ratified over the next several months (*MC* 3:36, 40; 6:24, 27–28). Its provisions included the right of the East India Company to establish a factory somewhere on Jolo or Borneo. The treaty also established a mutual military alliance, both offensive and defensive, according to which each side agreed to aid the other against the enemies of each (*MC* 3:40).

When the Spanish governor-general heard about the treaty concluded between the British and Sultan Azim ud-Din / King Ferdinand, he objected strongly, asserting that it violated the terms of the agreement that Britain and Spain had concluded upon Spain's surrender of Manila for the duration of the war. In words that might be an exaggerated performance of disbelief, Governor-General Rojo wrote to the East India Company board on March 19, 1763, "I cannot give credit to the News publickly reported that your Excellency . . . has concluded with [Prince Israel of Sulu] and the Sultan his Father a Treaty or League offensive and Defensive" (*MC* 6:58). Rojo's incredulity stemmed from what he characterized as an indisputable fact that such a treaty would violate the terms of the agreement that the British had signed with him five months prior. Rojo reminded the British that by signing the latter, the British had agreed to "look upon and attend to the preservation of these Islands, and maintain them in the same manner in which His Brittanick Majesty's Arms found them. . . . To this is to be added that the Life, liberty, and fortunes of these subjects should be preserved by the Articles of the Capitulation, and likewise the roman Catholick religion" (*MC* 6: 58). The integrity of the islands themselves, the "Life, liberty, and fortunes" of the Catholic king's subjects, and the Catholic religion were all threatened by the reported military alliance between the British and the sultan of Sulu; thus such an alliance was a violation of the capitulation treaty.

A military alliance between Britain and Sulu would violate the promises made by the former to preserve the Spanish islands, because, as Rojo explained, "the moors" of Sulu were an inherent threat to Catholic subjects of Spain in the Philippine Islands: "'Tis certain that to stir up the moors would be to occasion, the Destruction of all & raise inquietudes & disturbances in all the Islands since it is natural that the Inhabitants should defend themselves and much Blood be spilt, and many Lives Lost on both sides, with the Loss of the Villages and the Christian Instruction" (*MC* 6:58). Rojo's account posits "the moors" as inherent enemies of the inhabitants of the Philippine islands, who were Christian subjects of the Catholic king. By allying themselves with the sultan and his son, the British, Rojo charged, were allying themselves with Spain's enemy and inflicting harm on the lives, livelihoods, and religion of the Spanish sovereign's subjects.

However, Rojo further impugned the British treaty with Sulu by adding a note that invoked alliance between the sultan and the Spanish king, not enmity: "I also acquaint you that a preliminary treaty of peace and a voluntary cession both of the Sultan and his son towards an establishment of the Spaniards both in Xolo and Basilan with other priviledges in those Islands, have been made beforehand, preserving always those which his Catholick Majesty had over them these many years past, as the Sultan and the Prince can tell, and both, voluntarily and of their own accord presented them to me in Letters signed by them" (*MC* 6:58). Here Rojo invoked treaties and correspondence that had begun in 1737, though the letters to which he referred likely were written during more recent negotiations over the sultan's conversion and planned return to Jolo.

The British pushed back against Rojo's characterization of the situation, asserting that the sultan of Sulu was an independent sovereign and, as such, was not affected by the prior agreement between the British and the Spanish. The company noted, in its internal notes, that it had "an undoubted right to make Treaties or enter into Agreements with any Princes or people whatever," including the sultan of Sulu. The sultan was an independent sovereign, and so "the present [treaty] with Xolo cannot by any means infringe on the Articles of the capitulation as that Island [Xolo, or Jolo] never was included among the Philippines" (*MC* 6:58). In these deliberations, the board made a strong distinction between its dealings with the Spanish, on the one hand, and its dealings with the sultan of Sulu, on the other. The same principles would again be aired, in much the same terms, when the company referred to "our forming Alliances with the neighbouring Princes" in a letter to Rojo, asserting that the latter "cannot with any Property interfere therewith," again characterizing the sultan of Sulu as a sovereign independent of Spain (April 15, in *MC* 6:78).

When corresponding with Rojo, the company insisted that the sultan with whom they had concluded a treaty was the independent sovereign ruler of Sulu. But company agents clearly harbored doubts about whether this man would in fact be accepted as sultan upon his return to Jolo, the seat of the sultanate, and planned for the contingency that he might not be. It was with these hesitations in mind that the company proposed that Prince Israel should return first, without his father Ferdinand / Azim ud-Din, to prepare the way and test the waters. Though they had concluded the treaty with the sultan on the principle that he was the sovereign of Sulu, their action in first sending his son alone to the seat of the sultanate shows that they thought the father's sovereignty was not clearly established. The company hoped that Prince Israel's return would smooth the way for the reinstatement of their new ally; only after their ally had been reinstated as sultan could they hope to make good on the terms of the treaty that they had concluded. Yet the treaty had been concluded as if this man, who they hoped would again become sultan, were in fact already sultan.

The company council at Manila expressed its uncertainties about the sultan's prospects in a letter to their agent at Jolo in which they referred ambivalently to the status of the different claimants to the sultanate. On the one hand, the letter referred to "the King and Prince of Xola," Azim ud-Din / Alimudin / Ferdinand and Prince Israel, clearly referring to them as rightful sovereigns; consistent with this, it also referred to "the Sultan Bantilan" (Muiz ud-Din) as "the usurper" (April 11, in *MC* 6:79). Yet the letter's addressee, the company's agent in Jolo, had been operating under the presumption that Bantilan was not a usurper but rather a valid sovereign, and the letter reconciled the competing claims to the sultanate, all to the company's advantage. The letter began with the premise that when the British first arrived, "the King and Prince of Xola" were "tired of Spanish Controul," implicitly acknowledging that those two had been subject to Spanish sovereignty, a condition that validated Bantilan's claim to be sultan. But the letter immediately pivoted: the king and prince "threw of [*sic*] their yoke, and put themselves under our [British] Protection" (*MC* 6:79). In this narration, the moment in which they accepted British "Protection" was the moment in which they declared their independence from Spain by throwing off its yoke. This moment, then, simultaneously validated their claim to be (independent) sovereigns and proclaimed their alliance with, if not subjection to, Britain.

At this point, however, a dilemma emerged for the British agents: if they were to recognize the sovereignty of the king and the prince by contracting agreements with them as sovereigns of Sulu, then the British agents risked jeopardizing whatever prior agreements the British agent in Jolo had made with Bantilan (Muiz ud-Din) as sultan and sovereign of Sulu. The British in Manila therefore "declined accepting" the "very Considerable Offers" that the king and the prince had made to them, hoping first to find out the terms of whatever treaties their agent in Jolo had contracted with Bantilan as sovereign sultan (*MC* 6:79). The worries were eventually assuaged, however, and the conflict resolved because, as they explained, "the King offer[ed] to us Terms very advantageous to the Company, and such as would not interfere with, but rather confirm your Treaty with the Sultan Bantilan, and . . . also brought before us, the Embassader with a Letter from the usurper [Bantilan], & Dato's or Chiefs of the Island of Xolo, inviting either of them to the Governments" (*MC* 6:79). The result, they hoped, was that "a very extensive & Profitable Commerce will hereby be opened with the Adjacent Islands, and that many real and great Advantages, will here from result" for the company (*MC* 6:80).

The conflict between Spain and Britain over the sultan's status continued when, at the end of the war, they argued over whether the sultan was to stay in Manila until after the British withdrew or whether he would leave with them. The Spanish and British each wanted to be the ally that supported the sultan's return to Jolo; each wanted to claim the sultan as an ally, or even a vassal.

Internal struggles within the sultanate—between Azim ud-Din and his brother Bantilan / Muiz ud-Din—created the conditions in which the British and Spanish would each seek to leverage the sultan as an ally. The manner in which sovereignty was produced and exercised in Sulu contributed not only to uncertainty but also to possibilities for the British and Spanish.

Because sovereignty in Sulu was composed in part of slave raiding, the Spanish aim to quell that practice by negotiating and concluding treaties with the sultan contained an internal contradiction: the power of the sovereign whose authority could end slave raids was power to which slave raiding contributed. Spanish efforts to quell slave raiding through treaties with the sultan led in part to the unsettling of sovereignty within the sultanate, Azim ud-Din's exile, and the ascension of Bantilan as Sultan Muiz ud-Din. When the British arrived, then, the contradictions of Spanish strategy to contain Sulu slave raiding had led to conditions in which the British could pursue their objective with the sultan— namely, to initiate a trade relationship. British and Spanish aims differed fundamentally. The British cared not whether the sultanate engaged in slave raiding; indeed, insofar as it might strengthen an ally and contribute to robust trade, they stood to gain indirectly by its practice. For the Spanish, however, slave raiding threatened their subjects and thus the integrity of their claims to sovereignty of the islands.

## NOTES

1. I thank Eric Tagliacozzo and David Powers for inviting me to present at a Comparative Muslim Societies seminar in 2016 and to contribute to this book, and for carefully editing the chapter; and to Tony Rudyansiah, graduate student colleagues, and faculty colleagues of UCSC's Center for Southeast Asian Coastal Interactions who insightfully discussed a related piece. All errors are my own. The treaties mentioned here are among several of the period that merit fuller treatment but are beyond the scope of this chapter, which uses as a primary source a collection of eighteenth-century East India Company documents, transcribed and published under the title *Records of Fort St. George, Manilha Consultations* (hereafter *MC*) by the colonial government office in early twentieth-century Madras (now Chennai), India. These immensely useful and relatively accessible volumes are also partial, and quotations from them contain examples of idiosyncratic translation.

2. This account is greatly condensed and simplified; see further Crailsheim 2013; de la Costa 1967; Majul (1973) 1999, chaps. 6–7; and Tarling 1978, esp. pp. 13–14.

3. On the British occupation of Manila, see, in addition to the sources in the note above, Tracy 1995.

## REFERENCES

Crailsheim, Eberhard. 2013. "The Baptism of Sultan Azim ud-Din of Sulu: Festivities for the Consolidation of Spanish Power in the Philippines in the Middle of the Eighteenth Century." In *Image—Object—Performance: Mediality and Communication in Contact Zones of Colonial Latin America and the Philippines*, edited by Astrid Windus and Eberhard Crailsheim, 93–120. Münster: Waxmann Verlag.

De la Costa, H[oracio], SJ. 1967. "Muhammad Alimuddin I, Sultan of Sulu, 1735–1773." In *Asia and the Philippines*, 81–114. Manila: Solidaridad Publishing House.

Keifer, Thomas M. 1972. "The Tausug Polity and the Sultanate of Sulu: A Segmentary State in the Southern Philippines." *Sulu Studies* 1:19–64.

Majul, Cesar A. 1965. "Political and Historical Notes on the Old Sulu Sultanate." *Journal of the Malaysian Branch of the Royal Asiatic Society* 38 (pt. 1) (207): 23–42.

——. (1973) 1999. *Muslims in the Philippines*. Quezon City: University of the Philippines Press.

——. 1981. "An Analysis of the 'Genealogy of Sulu.'" *Archipel* 22:167–82. DOI: https://doi.org/10.3406/arch.1981.1677.

*MC (Manilha Consultations)*, Madras Presidency Records Office. 1940–1946. *Records of Fort St. George, Manilha Consultations*. 10 vols. Madras: Government Press.

Reid, Anthony. 1998. "Political 'Tradition' in Indonesia: The One and the Many." *Asian Studies Review* 22 (1): 23–38.

Saleeby, Najeeb M. 1963. *The History of Sulu*. Manila: Filipiniana Book Guild.

Tarling, Nicholas. 1978. *Sulu and Sabah: A Study of British Policy toward the Philippines and North Borneo from the Late Eighteenth Century*. Kuala Lampur: Oxford University Press.

Tracy, Nicholas. 1995. *Manila Ransomed: The British Assault on Manila in the Seven Years War*. Exeter, Devon: University of Exeter Press.

Warren, James F. (1981) 1985. *The Sulu Zone, 1768–1898: The Dynamics of External Trade, Slavery and Ethnicity in the Transformation of a Southeast Asian Maritime State*. Quezon City: New Day Publishers.

# THE FRENCH REVOLUTION COMES TO THE INDIAN OCEAN

Deportation, Slavery, and Empire in Anjouan

*Ian Coller*

Anjouan, or Nzwani, is a small Indian Ocean island of not much more than four hundred square kilometers located in the Mozambique Channel, part of the Comoros archipelago, equidistant from the coast of Africa and the island of Madagascar. Its sheer and heavily forested volcanic mountains present a striking backdrop to the capital, Mutsumudu. Fresh water streaming down to the shore of a well-sheltered bay first attracted Arab and Persian seafarers and, later, European ships as they passed around the Cape of Good Hope. Buried somewhere among the verdant foothills on the outskirts of the former capital, Domoni, on the eastern coast of the island lie the remains of more than two dozen French revolutionaries, among them men such as Jean-Antoine Rossignol, who participated in the seizure of the Bastille in Paris on July 14, 1789.[1]

This chapter began as a kind of thought experiment to discover what these forgotten bones and the story of their journey across two oceans might tell us about the wider world dynamics of the revolutionary age. To consider these bodies as a salient fact and not an exotic afterthought leads us to ask new questions about the global dynamics of the French Revolution. They mark the intersection of several phenomena: the closing of promises of equality opened by the French Revolution, the changing nature of global competition opened by the Revolutionary Wars, and indigenous struggles to forge new polities in the face of both imperial incursion and the emergence of new relations of power, violence, and resistance in the local arena. They remind us of the need to not only investigate more fully the implication of Indian Ocean spaces in an age of revolutions but also challenge our notions of how and where those revolutions operated. Above all, they lead us to the recognition that slavery and its abolition were more central to the revolutionary age than historians have sometimes suggested, and their implications concerned not only enslaved people and their masters but all categories of people.

# Ending the French Revolution in the Indian Ocean

On the evening of December 24, 1800, a powerful explosion rocked the area of Paris close to the Opéra-Comique, leaving seven people dead and dozens wounded. The improvised explosive device that came to be known as the "Infernal Machine" failed to kill the first consul, Napoleon Bonaparte, who had seized power in a coup d'état a year earlier (Thiry 1952). Bonaparte was informed by the police chief Joseph Fouché that the authors of the attack were royalist counterrevolutionaries, financed by Britain. The first consul, however, was determined to use this opportunity to purge his political opponents on the left. "Blood must flow," he insisted. "As many culprits must be shot as there were victims. Two hundred or more must be deported where they can do no further harm" (Woloch 2002, 74). Appealing to a "constant state of terror" posed by a "permanent conspiracy against society and its laws," Bonaparte bypassed elected representatives to use the newly created senate (not elected but appointed for life) to create a procedural mechanism that allowed him to alter the constitution at will. The "Senatus-consultum" of 14 Nivôse (January 4, 1801) designated 130 individuals for deportation without trial. Isser Woloch judged this "arbitrary and brutal repression" to be the "first truly transgressive act" of Bonaparte's dictatorship (80). It may also be considered a crucial step in creating the modern "terrorist"—a word Bonaparte used freely to vilify his Jacobin opponents.[2]

The idea of "saving the Republic" by expelling political undesirables had a longer genealogy: projects to expel priests, counterrevolutionaries, and even the indigent abounded throughout the Revolution. A number of these projects involved the southern coast of Africa or the spaces "beyond the Cape," including a project to settle beggars in Madagascar or one to send priests to Namibia (Decary 1964). If none of those projects came to fruition, they helped to shape the "fantasy of a clear, spatial separation between the free citizenry and their enemies," as Miranda Spieler (2012) has suggested. Geographical "separation" was the driving factor. Allyson Delnore (2004) has argued that these deportations had colonizing overtones, but the Directory showed little interest in the destination of deportees or how they would get there. However, the concentration of political dissidents in a single space, and the proximity of hostile groups, created new problems. Moreover, in the context of the global maritime war after Britain joined the coalition against France in 1793, there was no longer any space reliably "outside" the political sphere of the Revolution.

In the wake of the Nivôse decree, the minister of the marine, Denis Decrès, scrambled to find a location for these "scoundrels who never cease to menace the general security." In a note to Bonaparte he reviewed possible locations: Guiana, St-Louis in Senegal, Sodor and Galam on the coast of Guinea, the Seychelles, and Madagascar. He concluded that these far-flung spaces could be used to "establish different degrees of deportation according to the various advantages of the locations" (Destrem 1885, 23). This scheme of a carceral archipelago working to stabilize the space of metropolitan politics was another fantasy: the deportees were sent into an even more unstable colonial situation whose logic would ultimately cost them their lives.

Over half of the men named on the proscription lists were loaded onto ships without knowing their destination. The cramped and insalubrious conditions on board cost one deportee his life. When the seventy surviving prisoners arrived at Mahé Island, the principal port of the Seychelles, they were at first welcomed by a nonplussed population (Boulinier, Slezec, and Slezec 1996). The island's governor, Quéau de Quinssy, a former captain from the regiment of Pondicherry, sought to circumvent any hostile reactions and encouraged local families to house the new arrivals as an "act of humanity and benevolence" (Fauvel 1980, 180). Within days, most of the men had been lodged with families on the island.

The French captain who delivered the deportees to Mahé did them few favors when he declared that any settlers who feared their new neighbors should leave the island, fanning settler fears that the French authorities were planning to expropriate them and transform the island into a penal colony. The governor of Île-de-France, François Magallon, wrote to Bonaparte, claiming that since the colonial authorities in the Seychelles had signed a capitulation agreement with Britain (a detail Quinssy had failed to mention in his letter), the deportees could now, in theory, refuse their captivity and appeal for British protection (Destrem 1885, 72). Going further, he lamented that the deportees had "raised alarm in every mind, and re-opened the wounds that had begun to heal. The arrival of such men is seen to announce and provide a means for the execution of a principle which would mean an inevitable loss" (71). This "principle" was the abolition of slavery, decreed by the National Convention in France in April 1794, for application throughout the republic. Magallon's roundabout phraseology avoided directly mentioning the Colonial Assembly's refusal to implement this republican law in the Indian Ocean colonies. However, fears of a new challenge to the system of slavery were a powerful driver.

The campaign to vilify the new arrivals was led by the former commandant of the Seychelles, Louis Jean Baptiste Philogène de Malavois, who had been displaced under the revolutionary reforms of 1792. He declared to the other Seychellois that receiving the deportees was a violation of their capitulation and would soon be met with British reprisals. Moreover, he added, "the men that the French government are sending you are only deported as a pretext, and in reality they are charged with the horrifying mission to raise your slaves in revolt and seize your properties" (Rossignol and Barrucand 1896, 351–52). Malavois raised a panic around race and sex, liberally sprinkled with lurid descriptions of revolutionary violence. He announced that he was leaving the island—which he called a "new Gomorrah"—as a result of the putative domination by the deportees (353). In fact, he sailed only as far as Mauritius, where he agitated for further action against the deportees.

The real fear of the colonial authorities was that the arrival of these deportees would disrupt the mechanism by which the French Indian Ocean department had managed to remain within the French Republic while evading application of the 1794 decree abolishing slavery. The Colonial Assembly of the Île de France complained to Paris that the deportees had threatened to publicize the decree if they were not provided with adequate supplies. At Malavois's urging, the assembly undertook to prevent the "contagion" of these revolutionary monsters from reaching their coasts, pronouncing the deportees "*hors la loi*" (outlaws), and menacing them with death should they ever set foot on Mauritius or Réunion. This "death sentence" would ultimately be carried out in a different way.

The "radicalism" of the deportees was recontextualized and amplified by the colonial setting. Although they had little direct connection to slavery or abolition, they now represented a monstrous and threatening vision of equality and the rupture of the racial hierarchy. Some of the Seychellois began to murmur about relegating the deportees to a "desert island." This threat was realized when some of the deportees, ostracized by the white settler population, began to fraternize with the free people of color on the island. One of the new arrivals, Nicolas-Francois Serpolet, was arrested for attending a "ball" given by enslaved people. Malavois, chief enemy of the deportees, wrote to complain of "a horrible bacchanalia of negroes, presided over by a deportee," in which "the names of Liberty and Equality" were pronounced freely (Destrem 1885, 82). He represented this fraternization as "the beginning of a grand conspiracy to raise the blacks in revolt . . . to murder the whites and take over the island" (Rossignol and Barrucand 1896, 356–57). After meeting with the island's leaders, the chief deportees believed that they had allayed local concerns; however, a few days later they were surprised to discover that the Seychellois had drawn up an order to dispatch Serpolet along with four of the slaves who had associated with him to the Île-aux-Frégates, the uninhabited easternmost island of the archipelago. Soon afterward, the authorities in Île de France sent a ship, and its crew worked with Malavois's party to arrest the deportees and place them in chains. Although there was no evidence of any crime or disturbance beyond the simple fact of Serpolet's presence at the ball, thirty-three deportees were designated as "dangerous" and accused of "disorganizing" the colony. Along with three local men of color—innocent of any crime but unwitting association with the deportees—they were loaded onto the ship to be carried away from Mahé.

Although it appears that the original destination of these thirty-six men was to be Madagascar, they were taken to Anjouan. A Seychellois local was reported to have warned the commissioner that these men would not survive more than three months in Anjouan, owing to its "climate"—more likely the presence of diseases to which outsiders had little resistance. The deportees themselves begged to be deposited instead on one of the uninhabited islands of the Seychelles. It seems clear, however, that the colonial authorities did not intend for them to survive. If the purpose of the government in France was to suppress their revolutionary influence through geographical separation, in the Indian Ocean only their death could satisfy the fears of those seeking to prevent the "contagion" of liberty spreading to the enslaved.

Anjouan was not a colonial space or even a "desert island" but a sovereign Muslim state in the Indian Ocean. Why did the governors of this island accept the deportees from Mahé? This question is difficult to answer, as the sources are sparse and often contradictory. We must first trace how Anjouan became a crossing point of trade, empire, and slavery in the late eighteenth century.

## Anjouan in the Revolutionary Age

In 1783, a ship carrying the British orientalist William Jones—who had gained a long-awaited appointment in Bombay—made its first landfall beyond the Cape of Good Hope at Mutsamudu on the island of Anjouan. The canoes that surrounded the vessel were filled with English-speaking locals waving letters of recommendation and sporting what Jones considered "ridiculous titles" borrowed from English lords and dukes. Jones found more congenial company in the island's governor Abdullah and his erudite brother Alwi', who admired Jones's copies of the Qur'an and commented on another manuscript in unexpectedly accurate English. Jones confessed astonishment at the questions Alwi' put to him "concerning the late peace of America, the several powers and resources of Britain and France, Spain and Holland; the character and supposed views of the Emperor; the comparative strength of the Russian, Imperial and

Othman [Ottoman] armies, and their respective modes of bringing their forces to action" (Jones 1807, 90). Alwi's interests bore on two vital questions of the revolutionary age: the independence of America, and the Russian annexation of the Crimea, both concluded in that year. Jones answered all of Alwi's questions without reserve, "except on the state of our possessions in India" (90). Imperial information was a valuable resource to be traded with caution, as John McAleer observes (2016, 171).

Anjouan was legible to a visitor like Jones because, as Jean Martin suggests, it was a more developed state than other polities in the immediate area: "a kingdom with a sovereign flanked by a government whose authority extended to the whole island, an army and a treasury augmented by regular income" (1983, 51–52). Moreover, for more than a century Anjouan's development had been shaped in the nexus of the "distant sovereignty" between Britain and Bombay that Sudipta Sen (2002) has charted. A closer relationship to empires—the British, along with the Ottoman, Omani, or coastal Mozambican kingdoms—was attractive to the Anjouanais, and by the early nineteenth century the need for protection from rapacious neighbors provoked direct appeals for imperial protection. The East India Company's interests, however, were calculated by return on investment. With little to offer beyond provisions, Anjouan found itself relegated to the second or third tier of imperial spaces, a logistical node in the company's web. Yet its elites did not remain passive in an Indian Ocean theater of globalizing trade, revolutionary confrontation, and imperial rivalry.

Alwi' spoke lucidly about the shift that had taken place when monetary trade replaced the barter system in which locals had provided ships with supplies in exchange for guns, clothing, and other "playthings," as he called them. With money, he declared, the Anjouanais could "easily procure foreign commodities, and exchange them favorably with their neighbors in the islands and on the continent." They could then purchase "muskets, powder, balls, cutlasses, knives, cloths, raw cotton, and other articles brought from Bombay" and trade them for products from Madagascar. Admitted to an audience with the elderly sultan Ahmed, Jones observed the same "enlargement of mind, a desire of promoting the interest of his people, and a sense of the benefits arising from trade, that could hardly have been expected from a petty African chief" (Jones 1807, 101).[3]

Anjouan was a small island with big ambitions. In 1781 the English captain Henry Rooke reported that the sultan—armed with weapons purchased from visiting ships—was planning an expedition against the neighboring island of Mayotte, which it considered a rebellious dependency. According to Rooke, when asked about the causes of the war, the "natives" replied "Mayotta like America" (1784, 20). A decade later, in 1791, a French captain agreed to carry Anjouanais soldiers on his ship to subdue Mayotte in exchange for slaves that would be taken in battle. When the Anjouanais were caught in an ambush and forced to flee in disarray, the French crew were left without their promised payment. The sultan of Anjouan covered his debt by enslaving three hundred of the soldiers who had failed in their mission and giving them to the French along with fifty women (Péron and Brissot-Thivars 1824). Terrified, the men rose up in violent mutiny on board ship, leaving a dozen dead and many injured. Clare Anderson has drawn attention to such "maritime dimensions of the age of revolution" in seeking to broaden the scope of our understanding of what revolution entailed (2013, 231).[4] It is difficult to determine whether revolutionary contexts played any part in this mutiny by agents of imperial ambition suddenly transformed into its victims.

Anjouanais elites considered themselves participants in the revolutionary age as an aspiring imperial power. Yet that power was extremely fragile. The sultan's authority was "perpetually undermined by aristocratic greed and by the revolts of the rural populations of the interior," according to Jean Martin (1983, 53). These tensions came to a head in the mid-1770s. While the sultan was away on the Hajj pilgrimage, the ruling Arabo-Chirazian families of the coastal cities ramped up taxes on the inhabitants of the island. The revolt that followed was not just an economic protest: its leader, Tumpa, from the interior town of Bambao Mtuni, also claimed political legitimacy by ostensible descent from the earlier Fani rulers of the island. Tumpa took the city of Domoni in a surprise attack and sent messengers to Mutsamudu calling for the submission of the island. According to Said Ahmed Zaki's *Chronicle of Anjouan*, Tumpa declared, "If the Arabs are defeated, the Bushmen would be considered as their equals from every point of view, and would have the right to marry Arab women" (Allibert 2000, 25). Islamic law mandates inheritance by daughters as well as sons: by preventing intermarriage with other groups, the Arab "aristocracy" kept the wealth within their own families.

Tumpa's army besieged Mutsamudu, but the governor of the town sought the assistance of a British ship that happened to be in port at the time. Armed British sailors fired on the rebels, killing Tumpa and dispersing his followers. This was more than a local disturbance: one historian has suggested that "Tumpa's death ended a movement that could have had far-reaching consequences for Anjouan as well as for the other Comoros" (Kent 1992, 891). Moreover, Tumpa's resistance was ultimately effective in reducing the tax, according to an anonymous author who visited in 1784. "This is the age of successful rebellion," he said, evidently thinking of the Treaty of Paris, which had confirmed American independence a year earlier (*Letter* 1788, 8). The consequences of unequal integration into the growing world economy created conditions for rebellion in Anjouan as in America: contestation around equal taxation, social mobility, distribution of property, and political legitimacy seems to have been present in both cases.

Contemporary observers and the actors themselves noted the comparisons and connections between these simultaneous insurgencies at different points in the emergent British imperial network.

Christopher Bayly has argued that the language of revolution spread through Asia because it "made sense of deep conflicts which arose both from the expansion of the European world-system and attempts by indigenous institutions and ideologies to respond to these massive changes" (2010, 31). It is difficult to know what terms such as "equality" meant to the inhabitants of the interior and whether they themselves used any such term. They were certainly asserting their rights in some form, rather than simply seeking to raid or conquer the coast. Their revolt hinged—as was often the case elsewhere—on a charismatic leader whose death led to the fragmentation of the movement. Indigenous memory of these movements could survive far beyond the death of the leader and could grow stronger over time. Moreover, these revolts could push elites to seek new forms of power that could in turn breed different forms of resistance. In the Indian Ocean, as in the Caribbean, these local shifts were given shape and meaning by larger global phenomena of trade, empire, and slavery, particularly in the context of the growing confrontation between slaveholding societies—indigenous, Creole, and European—on the one hand, and revolutionary conceptions of liberty and equality, on the other.

## Slavery and Empire

As we have seen, slavery, and the anxieties around the threat of abolition, was at the heart of the impulse that sent the deportees of Nivôse to Anjouan. The slave trade also helps explain the sultan's willingness to accept men who were thrown onto his shores from a distant land. As a small but strategically located island with limited resources, Anjouan had long sought to enhance its position in the growing imperial networks of the Indian Ocean. However, in the period of the French Revolution, the set of power relations in the region changed radically. The intensified market for slaves in the Mascarene Islands helped push Anjouan from an aspiring local empire into a struggling and fragmented kingdom. The Anjouanais found themselves transformed from slave traders to victims desperately seeking protection.

The key event in this shift appears to have been the assassination circa 1792 of Cheikh Salim, son of Sultan Ahmed and leader of the unsuccessful expedition to Mayotte in 1791.[5] Salim began selling slaves to the burgeoning market in the Mascarenes but purportedly was induced to cease this "abominable traffic" by Abdallah, Ahmed's minister in Mutsamudu (Martin 1982, 116).[6] Salim was by most accounts a hated figure owing to his involvement in the slave trade and his assertion of arbitrary privileges. The motives given for his murder differ between accounts, but the outcome seems clear. Although Sultan Ahmed initially released the guilty parties to avoid warfare between clans, he later besieged Mutsamudu in order to secure the punishment of his son's killers. The army from Domoni, Ahmed's capital, was routed and Abdallah succeeded as "king" (despite his lack of legitimacy), moving the capital to Mutsamudu. A member of Salim's clan, seeking to avenge the murder, traveled to Madagascar to raise an army. He brought them back to attack Mutsamadu, but the siege failed to reduce the well-fortified citadel. The frustrated Malagasy then sacked the town of Ouani, killing or enslaving much of the population.

From this time forward, almost annually from the 1790s to the 1810s, large numbers of Malagasy warriors landed on the coast of Anjouan and other islands of the Comoros—and later on mainland Africa—where they killed, looted, and carried off the inhabitants as slaves to satisfy the "constant demand of the French" on the Mascarene islands (Allen 2008). Eugène de Froberville (1845, 197) estimated the numbers of attackers in these expeditions as reaching into the thousands, sailing in hundreds of pirogues carrying sixty men each. Jane Hooper (2017, 156) has emphasized the "almost unthinkable violence" of these raids, which produced a profound rupture in traditional commercial relations and energized the slave trade. One English observer marveled at a "nation of savages" producing fleets and armies capable of brutal slave raids that "attacked and ravaged distant islands." It was, he declared, "so strange an event in modern history as scarcely to be believed" (Prior 1819, 58). Although the raids have often been associated with the Sakalava kingdom in Madagascar, according to most historians they were organized by private initiative.

In 1796, ambassadors from Anjouan boarded a ship traveling to Bombay. Their petition to the East India Company declared that "people of Madagascar . . . have come to our country in boats under French colors and with powder, bullets and French muskets . . . carrying off the inhabitants and selling them for slaves to the French" (Dubins 1972, 65). The intention of the Malagasy, they claimed, was to subjugate the island and hand it over to the French. "Whenever you shall send troops to take possession of this island," the ambassadors declared to the company, "we shall reciprocally profit thereby . . . and we will live under British protection like the Muslims in India." Otherwise, they added, "the French will speedily come and will take possession of this island" (65). Although these threats appear little more than an astute manipulation of British fears, there is evidence that French influence in Madagascar was indeed strong: the French envoy Daniel Lescallier reported in 1792 that the French tricolor was fluttering over the Malagasy kingdom of the Betsimisaraka (Wanquet 2000, 93–94). By

1796, however, there were two distinct and contradictory versions of "France" in the Indian Ocean—the abolitionist republic and the slave-owning colonies.

The East India Company refused to make Anjouan a colony, "opt[ing] instead to treat the island as a satellite to which it would offer support and occasional resources, but no more" (Bowen 2018, 220). Nonetheless, the British sent a large consignment of muskets and powder and permitted the Anjouanais embassy to recruit sepoys from the local population in Bombay. This relative success set the scene for the Anjouanais agreement with Île de France to accept the deportees sent from the Seychelles. The French offered them cannons and insinuated that the military experience of the deportees—one of whom was a former general from the republican army—could assist the Anjouanais in resisting the Malagasy raiders. The French were careful not to inform the ruler of Anjouan of the reasons for the exile of their compatriots and advised the deportees not to breathe a word. The deportee Jean-Baptiste-André Lefranc, however, accused the officers who brought them to the island of divulging this information to the authorities: "They had doubtless painted us as born enemies of all governments and dangerous men, pursued by the law. It was not difficult to perceive the impression that this account had on the inhabitants of the island, as they refused to let us enter the town" (1816, 66). As we have seen, however, the Anjouanais were far better informed of local and global events than the French imagined. The deportees, according to Lefranc's account, set about constructing a residence and erecting a large obelisk in opposition to Bonaparte that attracted the admiration of the locals. Just as the deportees were beginning to accustom themselves to exile, however, the sudden appearance of an epidemic took a drastic toll.

Less than a month after their arrival, twenty-one of the deportees were dead. Later accounts suggested that they had been poisoned by the authorities on Anjouan (Repiquet 1901, 115), but Lefranc insisted that the epidemic was widespread and that the king and the governor sought to assist the survivors. Half of the remaining deportees left the island in a desperate attempt to seek passage to the mainland, but only three reached Europe. By 1804, when General Charles-Alexandre Linois visited the island—bringing with him the promised cannons—not a single Frenchman was left alive. A petition from the "people of Anjouan" to Bonaparte in 1803 declared their fervent wish "that these men had lived" and expressed their hopes that further associations with the French might help protect them from "a continual war that undermines our political existence." The Malagasy, they explained, "come every year to ravage our land, our houses, and we cannot combat them because we lack the means of defense" (Destrem 1885, 131–32).

This petition was carried to France by Lefranc, who survived the perils of the journey in part because of the courageous assistance of the enslaved men who accompanied him. The Napoleonic Empire had little interest in protecting the

Anjouanais, and British maritime supremacy quickly rendered the appeal futile. Lefranc's memoir, published during the Bourbon Restoration, sycophantically lauded the monarchy and appealed to the new interest in racial classification building in postrevolutionary France.[7] A competing version of the story was released by a journalist with whom Lefranc had spoken soon after arriving in France (Fescourt 1819). The fascination surrounding the fate of these revolutionaries was further demonstrated by the appearance in 1818 of a potboiler that recast the exiled General Rossignol as the "Robinson Crusoe of the Faubourg-Saint-Antoine" and described him leaving the island and establishing a new African kingdom (Ménégault 1818). This fantasy obscured the real ways in which the Indian Ocean islands, and even the mainland of Africa, had been drawn into the experience of revolution and its aftermath.

Ultimately, the bodies of French revolutionaries buried on the island of Anjouan speak to the centrality of enslavement and abolition as a dynamic of the revolutionary age in the Indian Ocean. Slavery lay at the heart of the struggles over freedom and equality. The French Revolution was a conflict with global stakes that enmeshed far greater parts of the world than just Europe and the Atlantic. Anjouan's willingness to become the prison and, ultimately, the graveyard for the deportees of Nivôse was driven by the consequences of the slave trade, just as the desire to preserve that trade—and the fear of what liberty had achieved on the French island of Saint Domingue—drove the French to dispatch their compatriots to an almost certain death.

## NOTES

1. In the 1820s an elderly sailor took B. F. Leguevel de la Combe to see the burial place in a "thicket" on the edge of the town of Domoni (Leguevel de la Combe 1840, 2:86). In 1927 local historian Said Ahmed Zaki wrote that he had "made every effort to find some trace of these Frenchmen" but could find no record in local writings, in oral traditions, or on the ground (Allibert 2000, 34).

2. The historian Georges Lenôtre (1932) called the deportees "the last terrorists"— that is, the last who were accused of participation in the state Terror of 1793–1794. However, their extrajudicial deportation, justified by a loose association with the attack on Bonaparte, made them the first "terrorists" to be targeted by the new security state.

3. The sultanate of Anjouan was founded by Arab Shirazians in flight from Shi'a domination in Iran. This may help explain their "elective monarchy" (Martin 1983, 50), following the Sunni tradition, but also the violent disputes between rival claimants.

4. A few months later, in Batavia, Péron encountered the survivors of the *Pandora*, the ship sent in search of the famous mutineers of the *Bounty*.

5. The date of Salim's assassination is unclear: Said Hamza el-Masela specifies 1794, while Dubins (1972, 74) says circa 1790. According to Péron and Brissot-Thivars (1824), Salim commanded the expedition of 1791. Most sources place the transition of power in 1792, so this appears a likely date. Froberville (1845) dates the beginning of the Malagasy raids to 1785, while Dubins (1972, 64) suggests that the first evidence of an attack dates from 1795. On problems relating to chronology, see Martin 1983, 86–87.

6. This story may be unreliable, since Said Hamza was a descendant of the el-Masela clan and thus related to Abdallah.

7. Fescourt (1819, viii) claimed that Lefranc's memoir was written by another author in an attempt to exculpate the former deportee for involvement in a new conspiracy against the monarchy.

## REFERENCES

Allen, Richard B. 2008. "The Constant Demand of the French: The Mascarene Slave Trade and the Worlds of the Indian Ocean and Atlantic during the Eighteenth and Nineteenth Centuries." *Journal of African History*, 49:43–72.

Allibert, C. 2000. "La chronique d'Anjouan par Said Ahmed Zaki (ancien cadi d'Anjouan)." In *Anjouan dans l'histoire*, edited by Claude Allibert, 9–47. Paris: Institut national des langues et civilisations orientales.

Anderson, Clare. 2013. "The Age of Revolution in the Indian Ocean, Bay of Bengal, and South China Sea: A Maritime Perspective." *International Review of Social History* 58:229–51.

Bayly, Christopher. 2010. "The Revolutionary Age in the Wider World c 1790–1830." In *War, Empire and Slavery, 1770–1830*, edited by Richard Bessel, Nicholas Guyatt, and Jane Rendall, 21–43. Basingstoke: Palgrave MacMillan.

Boulinier, Georges, Anne-Marie Slezec, and Casimir Slezec. 1996. "Des Seychelles aux Comores: Les déportés de nivôse An IX dans l'océan indien." In *Révolution française et Océan Indien. Prémices, paroxysmes, héritages et deviances*, edited by Claude Wanquet and Benoit Jullien, 195–206. Paris: Harmattan.

Bowen, H. V. 2018. "The East India Company and the Island of Johanna (Anjouan) during the Long Eighteenth Century." *International Journal of Maritime History* 30 (2): 218–33.

Decary, Raymond. 1964. "Un point d'histoire franco-malgache sous la Révolution." *Bulletin de Madagascar*, no. 216, 357–58.

Delnore, Allyson. 2004. "Political Convictions: French Deportation Projects in the Age of Revolutions, 1791–1854." PhD thesis, University of Virginia.

Destrem, Jean Marie. 1885. *Les déportations du Consulat & de l'Empire: Index biographique des déportés*. Paris: Jeanmaire.

Dubins, Barbara Dorothy. 1972. "A Political History of the Comoro Islands, 1795–1886." PhD thesis, Boston University.

Fauvel, A. A. 1980. *Unpublished Documents on the History of the Seychelles Islands Anterior to 1810*. Mahé, Seychelles: Government Printing Office.

Fescourt, M. 1819. *Histoire de la double conspiration de 1800: Contre le gouvernement consulaire, et de la déportation qui eut lieu dans la deuxième année du consulat*. Paris: Guillaume.

Froberville, Eugène de. 1845. "Historique des invasions madécasses aux îles Comores et à la côte orientale d'Afrique." *Annales des Voyages et de la Géographie* 2:194–208.

Hooper, Jane. 2017. *Feeding Globalization: Madagascar and the Provisioning Trade, 1600–1800*. Athens: Ohio University Press.

Jones, William. 1807. "Remarks on the Island of Hinzuan, or Johana." *Asiatick Researches* 2:77–108.

Kent, R. K. 1992. "Madagascar and the Islands of the Indian Ocean" in *General History of Africa* 5 (1992): 849–94.

Lefranc, Jean-Baptiste-André. 1816. *Les infortunes de plusieurs victimes de la tyrannie de Napoléon Buonaparte, ou, Tableau des malheurs de soixante-onze Français déportés sans jugement aux îles Séchelles: À l'occasion de l'affaire de la machine infernale, du 3 nivose an IX (24 décembre 1800)*. Paris: V. Lepetit.

Leguevel de la Combe, B. F. 1840. *Voyage à Madagascar et aux Iles Comores*. 2 vols. Paris: Louis Desessart.

Lenôtre, Georges. 1932. *Les Derniers Terroristes*. Paris: Firmin-Didot.

*A Letter from a Gentleman on board an Indiaman, to his Friend in London, giving an Account of the Island of Joanna, in the Year 1784*. 1788. London: Stockdale.

Martin, Jean. 1982. "Les mémoires de Saïd Hamza el Masela: Une relation de la vie politique anjouanaise de la fin du dix-huitième siècle à 1840." *Études océan Indien* 1:109–36.

———. 1983. *Comores: Quatre îles entre pirates et planteurs*. Paris: L'Harmattan.

McAleer, John. 2016. *Britain's Maritime Empire: Southern Africa, the South Atlantic and the Indian Ocean, 1763–1820*. Cambridge: Cambridge University Press.

Ménégault, A. P. F. 1818. *Le Robinson du faubourg Saint-Antoine: Ou, Relation des aventures du général Rossignol, et de M.A.C \*\*\*, son secrétaire. Déportés en Afrique à l'époque du 3 nivose*. Paris: Ménard et Desenne, fils.

Péron, Captain, and Louis Saturnin Brissot-Thivars. 1824. *Mémoires du Capitaine Péron: Sur ses voyages aux côtes d'Afrique, en Arabie, à l'île d'Amsterdam, aux îles d'Anjouan et de Mayotte, aux côtes nord-ouest de l'Amérique, aux îles Sandwich, à la Chine, etc*. Paris: Brissot-Thivars.

Prior, James. 1819. *Voyage along the Eastern Coast of Africa, to Mosambique, Johanna, and Quiloa; to St. Helena; to Rio de Janeiro, Bahia, and Pernambuco in Brazil, in the Nisus Frigate*. London: Phillips.

Repiquet, Jules. 1901. *Le sultanat d'Anjouan (îles Comores)*. Paris: Augustin Challamel.

Rooke, Henry. 1784. *Travels to the Coast of Arabia Felix: And from Thence by the Red-Sea and Egypt, to Europe. Containing a Short Account of an Expedition Undertaken Against the Cape of Good Hope*. London: R. Blamire.

Rossignol, Jean Antoine, and Victor Barrucand. 1896. *La vie véritable du citoyen Jean Rossignol: Vainqueur de la Bastille et général en chef des armées de la République dans la guerre de Vendée (1759–1802)*. Paris: E. Plon.

Sen, Sudipta. 2002. *Distant Sovereignty: National Imperialism and the Origins of British India*. New York: Routledge.

Spieler, Miranda. 2012. *Empire and Underworld: Captivity in French Guiana*. Boston: Harvard University Press.

Thiry, Jean. 1952. *La machine infernale*. Paris: Berger-Levrault.

Wanquet, Claude. 2000. "La première abolition française de l'esclavage et Madagascar: Une histoire fantasmée." *Revue des Mascareignes*, no. 2, 83–97.

Woloch, Isser. 2002. *Napoleon and His Collaborators: The Making of a Dictatorship*. New York: W. W. Norton.

# Part 4
# RELIGION, POLITICS, RACE, AND IDENTITY

In the first of four chapters in this part, Elena Frangakis-Syrett writes about Izmir at the end of the eighteenth century. At that time, Izmir was a heterogeneous, multiconfessional, and multilingual port city that linked the Ottoman Empire with markets in Europe, India, and the Far East. The residents of the city included Muslims, Christians, and Jews, and for most of the eighteenth century, relations between these communities were peaceful. However, on March 12, 1797, during a secular, public, open-air performance that featured inter alia Milanese trapeze artists, a fight broke out between intoxicated Greek Ionian sailors and Turkish Janissary guards. One of the sailors killed one of the guards, triggering a riot. Shortly thereafter, a fire broke out in the port, causing major property damage and resulting in the deaths of approximately 1,500 people, mostly Greeks. Although the rioters had no ideological agenda or political goal, Greek historians characterize the episode as a sectarian conflict between Muslims/Turks, on the one hand, and Christians/Greeks, on the other. In fact, Frangakis-Syrett argues, multiple factors contributed to the riot, including a global economic crisis and a political calculation by city authorities not to intervene in the initial altercation or to extinguish the fire. Religious zealotry and intolerance, she concludes, were not the cause of the riot.

In the second chapter, Carina Ray explores changing ideas about Islam in Accra in the Gold Coast (present-day Ghana). Whereas Islam was introduced to the northern part of the Gold Coast by North African traders and scholars, it was introduced to the south by the Tabon, recently enfranchised African Muslims who left Brazil and, in the 1830s, settled in West African cities on the Atlantic coast, including the port city of Accra. The Muslim immigrants possessed skills that were attractive to the original settlers of Accra, the Ga people, polytheists who practiced traditional African religion. The Ga gave the Tabon tracts of land and integrated them into their society. At that time, the association of Islam with Brazil conferred prestige on the religion. In the second half of the nineteenth century, however, as British control over West Africa expanded, the prestige of Islam in the Gold Coast declined, and the religion lost its reputation as a "linking faith." Over time, the Tabon adopted the religious practices of their Ga hosts. Islam now came to be associated with immigrants from the north, and many Christian African elites came to regard it as an inferior religion. Ray documents the changing perceptions of Islam in Ghana by focusing on Edward Blyden, a West Indian scholar and a champion of Pan-Africanism who promoted unity and cooperation between Muslims and Christians. Indeed, Blyden regarded Islam as the faith "best adapted to the Negro race." His writings stimulated a debate over the relative suitability of Islam, Christianity, and indigenous religions as a path to progress. Between 1903 and 1914, this debate played out on the pages of two of the leading African-owned newspapers in the colony: the *Gold Coast Leader* and the *Gold Coast Nation*. Ray concludes that the popular press positioned Islam in relation to Christianity and indigenous African religions as an alternative route to moral and spiritual progress.

In the third chapter, David G. Atwill examines the tense three-way relationship among Muslims and Buddhists in modern Tibet, on the one hand, and the country's overlord, the People's Republic of China (PRC), on the other. Muslims had been living in the capital city of Lhasa for approximately four hundred years, during which time relations with their Buddhist neighbors were peaceful. In 1959, the fourteenth Dalai Lama fled the country, sparking a massive uprising against the PRC during the course of which the Grand Mosque in Lhasa and much of the city's Muslim quarter burned to the ground. Nearly fifty years later, in 2008, on the eve of the Summer Olympic Games in Beijing, Buddhist Tibetans in Lhasa rioted against their Chinese overlords once again, targeting Chinese businesses, residences, and people. The rioters ransacked and looted Muslim shops and restaurants, attacked the Grand Mosque, and set its main gate on fire. Curiously, in the extensive media coverage of the uprising, one finds only a few references to the attacks on Muslims. One wonders why Buddhists targeted Muslims in 1959 and 2008 and why there is no mention of these attacks in the Tibetan historical narrative about the two uprisings. Atwill concludes that Buddhist violence against Muslims was a product of political alignments rather than religious antagonism and that the erasure of Muslims from the historical narrative is a product of the erroneous belief that Muslims were and continue to be outsiders, a foreign element in Tibetan society. He seeks to restore Muslims to their rightful place in the narrative of Tibetan history.

In the fourth chapter, Patricio N. Abinales examines the 2017 uprising in the southern Philippines in which "Moro" forces seized control of the city of Marawi on Mindanao, a large island on which Muslims began to settle at the end of the fourteenth century. More than one hundred thousand people fled the city, and thousands of militants, soldiers, and civilians died in the fighting. The 2017 Moro "invasion" of Marawi is generally associated with two brothers, Abdallah and Omar Maute, who, according to the standard narrative, wanted to establish a branch of the Islamic State of Iraq and Syria (ISIS) in the southern Philippines. Abinales reframes this narrative by focusing attention on Muslim *datus*, local political leaders who controlled cities located along the mouths of rivers and their hinterlands in Mindanao. Although Islamic fundamentalists who supported ISIS did participate in the siege of Marawi, Abinales argues that the siege was a product of a combination of factors that included Muslim separatist aspirations, religious zealotry, drug racketeering, political rivalries, and clan feuds.

# THE POLITICS OF IDENTITY AND RELIGION

Izmir in 1797

*Elena Frangakis-Syrett*

This chapter examines relations between Muslims and Christians in Izmir, a major Ottoman urban center, in the late eighteenth century. It is based on a case study of a riot and fire in 1797 that is commonly understood as a sectarian conflict but whose causes were multiple. In 1797 both the Ottoman Empire and Europe were undergoing fundamental political changes: radical ideology and rapid socioeconomic changes had widened the gap between the privileged and the less so. Ongoing military conflicts and a global economic crisis added to political uncertainties.

From its inception, the Ottoman Empire was a multiethnic, multiconfessional society in which all three monotheistic religions—Judaism, Christianity, and Islam—were represented. By the late eighteenth century, Izmir had become the premier port of the empire's export and import trade, landed and maritime, linking the empire with markets in Europe, India, and the Far East (Frangakis-Syrett 1992, 257–83). As a result, communities and individuals who were willing to cross both the socioeconomic and ethnoconfessional divides were in daily contact with one another in Izmir's harbor and nearby marketplace (Frangakis-Syrett 2017, 17–64). The city's identity was shaped by its status as a port city open to international commerce, by its marketplace, by the many languages spoken by its inhabitants, and by their respective religions (Frangakis-Syrett 2002, 183–89; Trivellato 2009, 70–101).

As an active commercial center, the city was socioeconomically stratified. Although all classes met and interacted daily in the marketplace, Izmir's mercantile bourgeoisie and administrative class had a so-called Casino—an exclusive club, in the European tradition (McCusker 1985). Beginning in the 1780s, Izmir had its own masonic lodge, the Saint-Jean-d'Écosse-des-Nations-Réunies, which accepted as Freemasons not only Europeans but also Ottomans. The European Freemasons, like the city's merchants, interacted with all nationalities, some of whom they initiated into the lodge (Beaurepaire 2006, 416–19). The city was open to the world, known for being so, and aware of its openness. Its cultural identity and self-awareness were reflected in the popularity of secular entertainment, which appealed to all ethnoreligious groups and classes, offered a welcome escape from the doldrums of everyday life, and had the potential to foster social cohesion (Artan 2011, 383–85; Faroqhi and Öztürkmen 2014, 5–8). In this chapter I examine the extent to which social cohesion was achieved through secular entertainment, taking into account the acute economic crisis and political turmoil in Izmir and in the eastern Mediterranean at the end of the eighteenth century.

The entertainment was a show by Milanese ropedancers or trapeze artists, a form of entertainment that was well known, appreciated, and much loved in the Ottoman world.[1] But public open-air entertainment shows could bring to the surface simmering tensions about social and economic status, gender relations, and public comportment. Indeed, a performance by ropedancers on Sunday, March 12, 1797, during Ramadan, triggered an urban riot unprecedented in scale, intensity, and loss of life.[2] As the last scheduled performance, it attracted a wide audience and much excitement. Before the show started, two sailors, possibly drunk, Zantiots or Cephaliniots (that is, Ionians under the protection of the Venetian consul), decided to watch the show by climbing a parapet to avoid paying for a ticket (Küçükkalay 2008).[3] Janissary guards, hired by the Venetian consul to safeguard the entrance, forced them to get off the parapet. The sailors left but returned shortly thereafter with more sailors. In the ensuing fray between sailors and Janissaries, one sailor mortally wounded a member of the Thirty-First Janissary Regiment garrisoned in Izmir. Following the stabbing of the soldier, the Janissaries carried the bloodstained shirt of their dead comrade through the city and demanded that the culprit be brought to justice (Clogg 1982). In the meantime, the show was terminated shortly after it had started, and everyone hurried home, apprehensive about what might happen next.

The regiment of the slain soldier, which was notorious for its radical political ideas and pro-French sentiments, had introduced what a British diplomat called "an obnoxious innovation"—namely, enrolling like-minded Frenchmen into their regiment as honorary members.[4] It was a regiment of "Candiote Turks": Cretan Janissaries who became Muslims when the Ottomans took control of Crete from the Venetians in 1669 (Greene 2000, 36–44). They were called Candiote Turks because of their association with the city of Candia or Kandiye (Iraklion). During the Ottoman takeover of Crete, the residents of Candia abandoned the city. It was repopulated by Greek Orthodox Cretans who had converted to Islam (Adıyeke 2005, 208–15; Kolovos 2008, 121). In Crete, these converts served as Janissaries and/or engaged in trade-related activities (Greene 2000, 39; Adıyeke 2008, 207–9). Over the course of the eighteenth century, Izmir developed close economic ties with Crete, acting as a commercial go-between, a banking center, and clearinghouse for French purchases of olive oil (Frangakis-Syrett 2016, 355–61).[5] As a result, many Cretan merchants resided in Izmir's Candiote Han. Cretan Muslims often remained in contact with their Christian relatives, kept their Greek family names, and continued to speak and write in Greek; they often collaborated in trading ventures with Cretans who had not converted and with Jews (Panzac 1996, 77–94).

The sailor who killed the Janissary was from Zante or Cephalonia, both of which were still ruled by Catholic Venice. Whereas the Ottoman state treated the sailors as Venetians, the inhabitants of Izmir, including the Janissaries, regarded them as Ottoman Greeks. Just as the Candiote Turks possessed multiple layers of identities, the sailors, as Greek-speaking Venetians, must have regarded the Candiote Turk Janissaries as Greeks with whom they shared a common language. Their ethnicity was clear to all: the British consul, Francis Werry, referred to them as Cretan Turks. Contemporary Ottoman Greek sources referred to them as Cretans, without necessarily implying inclusiveness. The opposite could be true: Christians in Izmir—both locals and sailors—disapproved of and at times manifested outright enmity toward Cretans who had converted to Islam.

On Sunday, March 12, following the killing of their comrade, the Janissaries, not without reason, turned to the city authorities to ask that the culprit, who had not been found, be caught and punished. They repeated this request for two successive days. It was suspected that the culprit was a Venetian, and the authorities asked the Venetian consul to hand him over. Lucca Cortazzi, who had been consul in Izmir since 1750, was the scion of an old Cretan Greek Orthodox aristocratic family with close relations to Venice.[6] Cortazzi claimed that the sailor in question was Russian, while the Russian consul claimed that he was Venetian. Neither consul was "willing" or able to find the culprit to hand him over to the Ottoman authorities. The city authorities, who were not prepared to confront or restrain the Janissaries, charged the entire European consular body with responsibility for finding the culprit. With Cortazzi absent, the consuls were unable to agree on a course of action. The decision of the city authorities not to confront the Janissaries may have been deliberate: the *voivode* (governor) of Izmir, Buldanlı Osman Efendi, apparently resented the growing presence of the Europeans and the Porte's policies, which sought to reduce the power of its provincial administrators (Laiou 2011, 6). By Tuesday evening, March 14, the impatient soldiers issued an ultimatum: hand over the culprit, or they would take matters into their own hands. The city authorities did nothing, making an escalation of the situation inevitable. The riot, widely known as the Smyrna Rebellion, broke out on Wednesday, March 15, 1797. Its scale and intensity were unprecedented and mark a sharp break from the generally peaceful intercommunal relations that had prevailed in Izmir over the course of the eighteenth century.

The riot took place in the marketplace near the Fasoulia and Chiotico Hans in which Ionian sailors, including Zantiots, usually stayed.[7] Both the sailors and the Janissaries were armed. According to contemporary accounts cited by Greek historians, upon entering the marketplace the Janissaries paused to discuss sending twenty of their most respected members to ask the authorities to punish the culprit. This opportunity to avert the riot was lost when a sailor, most likely a Slovenian Catholic of Venetian nationality, opened fire from the Chiotico Han, killing three Turks. Subsequently, Janissaries were seen firing from the walls of the nearby Candiote Han, a Cretan Muslim merchants' inn.[8] According to Ottoman sources, approximately 1,000 Venetian sailors were in the Chiotico Han, while the Janissaries who went to confront them numbered 1,000–1,500 (Laiou 2011, 3).[9] That part of the marketplace bore the brunt of the fighting (Kostis, 1901–1905, 4:358–72). It was a fire, however, that caused most of the fatalities and destroyed many buildings in the European quarter, especially the residences of British merchants situated adjacent to the marketplace. According to some sources, it was the Janissaries who set the Chiotico Han on fire (Tansuğ 2008, 46). A strong southern wind caused the fire to spread quickly and made it difficult to extinguish. The Janissaries did not let fire engines reach the area, and the Ottoman police refused to use their fire engines to put it out. Many Ottoman Greeks who lived or worked in that part of the market died or suffered property damage. According to initial estimates by European consuls, there were 2,000 fatalities, although the number was later reduced to 1,500. These estimates were repeated by the Greek Viennese-based newspaper, *Ephimeris*, which considered an earlier estimate of 3,000 to be an exaggeration.[10] An anonymous source estimated the fatalities at 1,256 (Laiou 2011, 4). According to the Ottoman central government, "Many Turks and *Rayas* [viz. non-Muslim Ottomans] died."[11] The government also held the Venetian sailors responsible for thirty to forty civilian deaths (Laiou 2011, 3).

Property damage varied according to proximity to the areas affected by the riot and the fire. After the riot began, more sailors came ashore, likely from ships anchored in the harbor waiting to load freight. These ships flew either Venetian or Russian flags. Joining fellow sailors already in the harbor, they headed to Frank Street, adjacent to the marketplace, to loot the warehouses of European merchants that contained valuable goods.[12] The brunt of the damage was borne by British merchants whose residences were on Frank Street. These residences were either looted by Janissaries and sailors or destroyed by the fire. On Wednesday morning, before the riot broke out, these merchants and their families had fled to ships anchored in the harbor, as did the British and most likely all other consuls.[13]

According to Werry, Frank Street may have been targeted for attack by the Janissaries, who resented the rising material prosperity of the Europeans.[14] Given the increasingly close relations between a reforming sultan and the Ottoman administrative elite who supported the reform and modernization of the armed forces, on the one hand, and France, on the other, the Thirty-First Regiment likely had adopted not only the reactionary ideas of the ulama—as is well known—but also the radical ideas of France (Yaycıoğlu 2016, 30–32). If Ottoman reformers supported modernization, the Janissaries arguably supported democratization—or, at least, they demanded that their voices be heard. This demand had its origins in the history of the contractual relationship between the Janissaries and the Ottoman state (Kafadar 2007, 129–31). Janissary regiments elsewhere in the Ottoman Empire, including the capital, professed similar ideas (Yaycıoğlu 2016, 40–44). Conversations in coffee shops and on the streets of Izmir following the riot reflected radical pro-French sentiments.[15]

The riot had no specific political goal or ideological agenda. Both Ottoman Greek and European eyewitness accounts noted that the substantial loss of life from the fire in the marketplace affected primarily Ottoman Greek civilians. Loss of life borne by one community turned the riot and fire in the Ottoman Greek sources into a Muslim attack on Christians and, especially, of Turks on Greeks, based on religious fanaticism and ethnic rivalry (Papayanopoulos 1938, 262–67). It is no accident that this is how the riot is remembered in the Greek historiography of the mid-nineteenth century (Philimon 1859, 3:249). The nascent Greek state was claiming the right to expand its territory to include Ottoman areas in which Greek speakers composed the majority of the population. This type of nationalism was current elsewhere in Europe in the middle decades of the nineteenth century.

Contemporary Greek sources identified the sailor who killed the Janissary and the sailors who looted the market as Slovenians, rather than Ionians, probably in an effort to blame non-Greeks for the events. However, no Greek source claimed that the Janissaries had planned the riot in advance. Had a sailor not killed a Janissary on March 12, the events that led to the riot and fire on March 15 likely would not have taken place. A French journalist, Charles Tricon, an eyewitness, recounted the role of the sailor, whom he identified as a Greek, in starting the chain of events, as well as the repeated attempts of the Janissaries to demand justice for the killing of their comrade from the city and/or the consular authorities.[16] Tricon also recounted how the Janissaries, faced with impending violence

on entering the marketplace, considered returning to the authorities before taking matters into their own hands. Twentieth-century historians, Greeks included,
offer scholarly accounts of the events (e.g., Veis 1948, 411–22; Solomonidis 1956;
Clogg 1982; Ülker 1984; Tansuğ 2008, 45–47; Laiou 2011, 1–15). Not only do they
identify the killer as a Greek islander, but they also recount the help that Turks
gave to Greeks by taking them into their homes to save them from danger (Veis
1948, 413–14). They also report that the imam of Izmir, Nadir Zabeth, went to the
marketplace to deter the Janissaries from killing innocent people in response to
the acts of a few. He reminded them how Turks and Greeks, Muslims and Christians, were all brothers. Upon his death in 1820, he was buried with great honors
(Solomonidis 1956, 184).

Reporting on the number of fatalities, Werry identified them as mostly Ottoman Greeks. Other consuls stationed in Izmir at the time issued reports in
which they too identified the victims as mostly Ottoman Greeks.[17] Werry regarded the looting and destruction of property on Frank Street by sailors and
Janissaries as the result of French revolutionary doctrine. As for the local authorities, they blamed both Janissaries and sailors for the events. It was only the
Porte that placed the blame squarely on local police and on city authorities who
allowed the fire and mayhem to continue as long as it did.[18] The Porte also blamed
the Venetian sailors for the looting.[19] On April 9, 1797, Hüseyin Ağa, a member
of the powerful and respected Karaosmanoğlu family and governor of the san-
cak of Aydın, accompanied by two other officials, was appointed by the Porte to
assume leadership of the local administration in order to lead the investigation
into the events and restore peace. Among the measures he took were the execu-
tions of "18 Turks and 3 Venetian subjects" and the expulsion of nineteen Ottoman officials.[20] Over time, Izmir would reestablish its acceptance, albeit limited
and fragile, of the ethnoconfessional *other*, in part due to economic growth in
the opening decades of the nineteenth century (Smyrnelis 2005, 46–57; Tansuğ
2008, 89–101).

The riot and the fire, unintended consequences of the trapeze artists' show, raise
a number of questions. Was it possible for public entertainment that did not have
any religious affiliation and appealed to a wide ethnoreligious and class audience to contribute to greater social cohesion in a multiethnic and multiconfessional Ottoman city? Was the shared experience of a popular form of entertainment
evidence of social cohesion? Were the riot and the fire caused by two groups of
men who knew that neither the Venetian consul nor the city authorities would
place any restraint on their actions? Did the apparent acceptance of religious differences hide the deep-seated anxieties and fears of Muslims, Christians, and

Jews? And was it dependent on economic prosperity? To what degree was the riot an intraethnic conflict resulting from religious conversion? To what degree did the growing lawlessness in the Ottoman provinces at the end of the eighteenth century make the riot and fire more likely to occur? Or was it the extreme uncertainty felt by the Janissaries about their future that made them more likely to riot? Was the considerable loss of life and property—an unintended consequence of a show— evidence that advances in social integration on the cultural sphere were limited and fragile? To what degree did the enormity of transformative socioeconomic and political changes in the late eighteenth century contribute to a riot and fire on a scale unprecedented in Izmir?

By all accounts, 1797 was a tumultuous year. Izmir suffered from widespread economic distress that affected the city's inhabitants. Shipping in the Mediterranean was in a dire state. Between 1795 and 1801, the British navy blockaded Dutch ports, making it impossible for Dutch ships to venture out. High insurance rates made it difficult for British ships to sail to the Mediterranean and to Izmir. Between 1797 and 1799, trade between the Ottoman Empire and Great Britain declined dramatically.[21] In an effort to attract silver to the treasury's mint, the Porte intervened in the financial and commodities markets, making matters worse (Pamuk 2000, 170–71; Frangakis-Syrett 2006, 23–27, 85). In the 1790s, the cost of basic commodities, including food and housing, rose in the empire's urban centers, affecting people from Izmir to Alexandria and beyond.[22] Economic distress was a global phenomenon. On February 26, 1797, following a run on the Bank of England, the bank suspended all payments in specie (Duryea 2010, 5–7, 9, 11). On March 2, it printed paper currency for the first time, a low denomination pound that was not convertible into gold or silver coinage. On May 3, 1797, Parliament passed the Bank Restriction Act, which remained in force until 1821, freeing the Bank of England from converting bank notes into gold (Anonymous 1867, 397–99, 410–11).[23]

In March 1797 space was being shared by too many actors in the city who had been affected by, and had an impact on, political and ideological changes. With crises taking place on multiple levels, events easily might get out of hand, even in a city whose inhabitants had experienced peaceful community relations for most of the eighteenth century. Although the casualties were borne by one community, the riot was not a primordial clash between two religions and ethnic groups. By most accounts, the city's Armenians and Jews were not affected, no doubt because they resided farther away from the marketplace and the conflagration.[24] Why didn't the Janissaries pursue members of these two communities? If religious fervor was the primary motivation for the riot, why did the sailors loot shops and warehouses belonging to fellow Christians? The material gains from the growth of Izmir's commercial sector in the last quarter of the eighteenth century were certainly distributed unevenly. Harsh economic conditions in 1797 created widespread uncertainty for all, especially for those who had been left behind by the earlier prosperity.

In May 1797, Selim III increased the insecurity of the Janissaries by establishing a new corps of infantry troops, the Nizam-i Cedid, recruited from Anatolian Turkish youth. On May 16, 1797, Napoleon's army ended Venetian rule in the Ionian Islands and brought radical ideologies close to home. The impending end of Venetian rule in the Ionian Islands made it less likely that Cortazzi, whose diplomatic appointment was about to end, would cooperate by delivering the culprit, thus increasing the ongoing tensions between Janissaries and sailors. The decision by city authorities not to intervene left a power vacuum at a crucial moment when intervention to stop the riot and put out the fire was most needed. All these factors, taken together, help explain the breakdown in communal relations. Giving due weight to these factors may also help move the narrative beyond the age-old interpretation of the Muslim-Christian conflict.

### NOTES

1. The troupe had been performing in Izmir since mid-February 1797. Ominously, on Sunday, March 5, 1797, a brawl between "Candiote Turks and some Zantiots" erupted outside the gates where the troupe was performing. The brawl was quelled before it escalated. Consul Francis Werry, Izmir, to Levant Company Directors, London, April 2, 1797, The National Archives: United Kingdom, London, SP 105/126 (hereafter TNA).

2. Spencer Smith, Chargé d'Affaires, British Embassy, Istanbul, to Lord Grenville, Foreign Office, London, April 16, 1797, TNA, FO 78/16; account based on British consul Francis Werry's dispatches sent from Izmir to Spencer Smith in Istanbul.

3. Although many ships in Izmir's harbor flew Venetian flags in the late eighteenth century, no Venetian ships visited Izmir in 1796 and 1797. Ionian sailors who had arrived in Izmir aboard Venetian ships and chose not to make the journey back were left stranded and without any clear prospects for employment.

4. Smith to Grenville, April 16, 1797, TNA, FO 78/16.

5. États de marchandises dans le Levant (1756–1787), Archives Nationales de France, Paris, AE Biii, 271–77. États de marchandises envoyées en Levant, 1748–1769 . . . 1786–1787, Archives de la Chambre du Commerce de Marseille, I, 19–20 (hereafter ACCM). États de marchandises venant du Levant 1700–1759 . . . 1786–1789, ACCM, I, 26–28.

6. Cortazzi may have had little sympathy for the victim, a Cretan convert to Islam. To be fair, however, he may have chosen not to cooperate in an effort to shield Venice from responsibility for monetary compensation to the Porte for damages caused by the sailors.

7. British Factory Meeting, Izmir, March 25, 1797, TNA, SP 105/126.

8. Werry, Izmir, to Levant Company, London, April 8, 1797, TNA, SP 105/126.

9. According to Werry, on Tuesday evening, between six hundred and seven hundred Janissaries gathered outside the house of the mullah to press their case. Werry, Izmir, to Levant Company, London, April 2, 1797, TNA, SP 105/126.

10. Ephimeris, April 17, 1797, 352, 354–57, quoted in Veis 1948, 419–22.

11. Imperial Edict addressed to the city's local authorities and transcribed for communication to the Foreign Ministers residing at the Sublime Porte, Istanbul, April 1797, TNA, SP 105/126. European sources use the word raya to refer to Ottoman non-Muslims (from Ar. ra'īya, i.e., subject, referring to both Muslims and non-Muslims).

12. Werry, Izmir, to Levant Company, London, "On board *The Withywood*, Izmir Bay," March 17, 1797, TNA, SP 105/126.

13. British material losses were considerable. Diplomatic efforts by the British diplomatic corps to receive compensation from the Ottoman government lasted for at least five years. It is not clear whether or how the matter was settled. "List of the loss sustained by Joseph Franel in the fire & rebellion of the 15th March 1797," submitted by Franel and attested by George Boddington, Treasurer, British Factory in Izmir and forwarded to Werry, Izmir, April 20, 1797, TNA, SP/105, 127; Werry, Izmir, to Smith, Istanbul, April 24, 1797, TNA, SP/105, 127; Werry, Izmir, Levant Company, London, September 1, 1799, TNA, SP 105/127; and Werry and the British Factory, Izmir, to Levant Company, London, February 1, 1802, SP 105/128.

14. Werry to Smith, April 24, 1797, TNA, SP 105/126.

15. Werry, Izmir, to Levant Company, London, April 24, 1797, TNA, SP 105/126.

16. On March 14, 1823, Charles Tricon published his account of the events in *Le Spectateur Oriental*, a respected Francophone newspaper published in Izmir. Excerpts and/or the entire text appeared in subsequent Greek and French publications.

17. Austrian Consul General Cramer, Izmir, to Baron de Herbert Rathkeal, *Internuncio*, Austrian Embassy, Istanbul, March 17, 1797, TNA, SP 105/126; Russian Vice-Consul Joseph Franceschi, Izmir, to Russian Ambassador M. de Köçübey, Istanbul, March 17, 1797, TNA, SP 105/126; and Werry to Levant Company, April 2, 1797, SP 105/126.

18. Imperial Edict addressed to local authorities in the city, TNA, SP 105/126; Franceschi to Koçübey, March 17, 1797, TNA, SP 105/126.

19. The Sublime Porte to the Chargés d'Affaires of the European Missions, May 15, 1797, TNA, SP 105/126.

20. Werry, Izmir, to Smith, Istanbul, June 2, 1797, TNA, SP 105/126.

21. In 1797 a temporary relaxation of British navigation laws made it possible for "foreigners" to sail their ships to London. This was an effort to appease British manufacturers who could not send their textiles to Ottoman markets or receive raw materials from them. Ottoman ships from Izmir reached British ports for the first time in January 1798. Werry, Izmir, to Levant Company, London, July 17, 1797, TNA, SP 105/126; and Levant Company, London, to Werry, Izmir, January 30, 1798, SP 105/122.

22. British Factory Meeting, Izmir, to Levant Company, London, January 15, 1798, TNA, SP 105/126; Werry and Factory, Izmir, to Levant Company, London, September 17, 1799, SP 105/127.

23. On April 2, 1797, Napoleon began his campaign to take northern Italy from the Austrians. On May 12, 1797, the Venetian Republic fell to Napoleon's army. With the conquest of Venice, the Ionian Islands became French.

24. Apparently, wind caused fire damage to the Armenian quarter as well (Laiou 2011, 3). On the duration of the fire, see Imperial Edict . . . , TNA, SP 105/126, and Franceschi, Izmir, TNA, SP 105/126.

## REFERENCES

Adıyeke, Nükhet Ayşe. 2005. "Crete in the Ottoman Administration before the Population Exchange." In *Common Cultural Heritage, the Foundation of Lausanne Treaty Emigrants*, 208–15. Crete: LMV.

Adıyeke, Nuri. 2008. "Multi-dimensional Complications of Conversion to Islam in Ottoman Crete." In *The Eastern Mediterranean under Ottoman Rule: Crete, 1645–1840*, edited by A. Anastasopoulos. Rethymno, 203–9. Crete: Crete University Press.

Anonymous. 1867. "The Bank of England Restriction, 1797–1821." *North American Review* 105 (217): 393–434.

Artan, Tülay. 2011. "Forms and Forums of Expression, Istanbul and beyond, 1600–1800." In *The Ottoman World*, edited by Christine Woodhead, 378–405. London: Routledge.

Beaurepaire, Pierre Yves. 2006. "The Universal Republic of the Freemasons and the Culture of Mobility in the Enlightenment." *French Historical Studies* 29 (3): 407–31.

Clogg, Richard. 1982. "The Smyrna 'Rebellion of 1797': Some Documents from the British Archives." Δελτίο Κέντρου Μικρασιατικών Σπουδών [*Deltio Kentrou Mikrasiatikon Spoudon*] [*Asia Minor Studies Centre Bulletin*] 3:71–126.

Duryea, N. Scott. 2010. "William Pitt, the Bank of England, and the 1797 Suspension of Specie Payments: Central Bank War Finance during the Napoleonic Wars." *Libertarian Papers* 2 (15): 1–17.

Faroqhi, Suraiya, and Arzu Öztürkmen, eds. 2014. *Celebration, Entertainment and Theatre in the Ottoman World*. Chicago: University of Chicago Press.

Frangakis-Syrett, Elena. 1992. *The Commerce of Smyrna in the Eighteenth Century (1700–1820)*. Athens: Centre for Asia Minor Studies.

——. 2002. "Networks of Friendship, Networks of Kinship: Eighteenth-Century Levant Merchants." *Eurasian Studies* 2 (1): 183–206.

——. 2006. *Trade and Money: The Ottoman Economy in the Eighteenth and Early Nineteenth Centuries*. Istanbul: Isis Press.

——. 2016. "Evolution du commerce maritime en Méditerranée orientale au XVIII\* siècle." In *La Maritimisation du Monde*, edited by Groupement d'intérêt scientifique d'histoire maritime, 355–62. Paris: Presses de l'Université Paris-Sorbonne.

——. 2017. *The Port-City in the Ottoman Middle East in the Age of Imperialism*. Istanbul: Isis Press.

Greene, Molly. 2000. *A Shared World*. Princeton, NJ: Princeton University Press.

Kafadar, Cemal. 2007. "Janissaries and Other Riffraff of Ottoman Istanbul: Rebels without a Cause?" *International Journal of Turkish Studies* 13 (1–2): 113–32.

Kolovos, Elias. 2008. "A Town for the Besiegers: Social Life and Marriage in the Ottoman Candia outside Candia (1650–1669)." In *The Eastern Mediterranean under Ottoman Rule: Crete, 1645–1840*, edited by A. Anastasopoulos, 103–76. Rethymno, Crete: Crete University Press.

Kostis, N. K. 1901–1905. "Σμυρναϊκά Ανάλεκτα. Τό εν Σμύρνη ρεμπελλιόν του έτους 1797 κατά νέας ανεκδότους πηγάς" [Smyrnaika Analecta. To en Smyrni rebellion tou etous 1797 kata neas anekthotous pigas] [Smyrna's 1797 rebellion according to new unpublished sources]. Δελτίον της Ιστορικής και Εθνολογικής Εταιρείας της Ελλάδος [*Deltion tis Istorikis ke Ethnologikis Etairias tis Ellathos*] [*Historical and Ethnological Association of Greece Bulletin*] 4:358–72.

Küçükkalay, A. Mesud. 2008. "Imports to Smyrna between 1794 and 1802: New Statistics from the Ottoman Sources." *Journal of the Economic and Social History of the Orient* 51:487–512.

Laiou, Sophia. 2011. "Τό ρεμπελιό της Σμύρνης (1797)" [To rebelio tis Smyrnis, (1797)] [The rebellion of Smyrna, 1797]. In Ιστορία της Μικράς Ασίας. Οθωμανική κυριαρχία [*I Istoria tis Mikras Asias. Othomaniki Kyriarhia*] [*Asia Minor history: The Ottoman period*], 4:1–15. Athens: Eleftherotypia Press. https://www.academia.edu (typed version).

McCusker, J. John. 1985. *European Bills of Entry and Marine Lists*. Cambridge, MA: Harvard University Library.

Pamuk, Şevket. 2000. *A Monetary History of the Ottoman Empire*. Cambridge: Cambridge University Press.

Panzac, Daniel. 1996. *Commerce et navigation dans l'Empire ottoman au XVIII\* siècle*. Istanbul: Isis Press.

Papayanopoulos, I. 1938. "Νέο φως στο ρεμπελιό της Σμύρνης" [Neo fos sto rebelio tis Smyrnis] [New insights into the rebellion of Smyrna]. *Μικρασιατικά Χρωνικά* [*Mikrasiatika Chronika*] [*Asia Minor Chronicles*] 1:261–67.

Philimon, Ioannis. 1859. *Δοκίμιον περί της Ελληνικής Επαναστάσεως* [*Dokimion peri tis Ellinikis Epanastasis*] [*Treatise on the Greek war of independence*]. 3 vols. Athens.

Smyrnelis, Marie-Carmen. 2005. *Une société hors de soi: Identités et relations sociales à Smyrne aux XVIIIᵉ et XIXᵉ siècles*. Paris: Peeters.

Solomonidis, Ch. 1956. "Το ρεμπελιό της Σμύρνης" [To rebelio tis Smyrnis] [The rebellion of Smyrna]. In *Ύμνοι και Θρήνος της Σμύρνης* [*Ymnoi ke Thrinos tis Smyrnis*] [*Hymns and lament of Smyrna*], 182–99. Athens: publisher unidentified.

Tansuğ, Feyral. 2008. "Communal Relations in Izmir/Smyrna, 1826–1864: As Seen through the Prism of Greek-Turkish Relations." PhD thesis, University of Toronto.

Trivellato, Francesca. 2009. *The Familiarity of Strangers*. New Haven, CT: Yale University Press.

Ülker, N. 1984. "1797 Olayı ve İzmir'in Yakılması." *Tarih İncelemeleri Dergisi* 2:117–61.

Veis, I. Nicos. 1948. "Το μεγάλο ρεμπελιό της Σμύρνης κατά νεώτατας πηγάς" [To megalo rebelio tis Smyrnis kata neotatas pigas] [The great rebellion of Smyrna according to newest sources]. *Μικρασιατικά Χρωνικά* [*Mikrasiatika Chronika*] [*Asia Minor Chronicles*] 4:411–22.

Yaycıoğlu, Ali. 2016. "Révolutions de Constantinople: France and the Ottoman World in the Age of Revolutions." In *French Mediterraneans: Transnational and Imperial Histories*, edited by Patricia Lorcin and Todd Shepard, 21–51. Lincoln: University of Nebraska Press.

# RELIGIOUS ROUTES TO RACIAL PROGRESS IN WEST AFRICA

Edward Blyden, Islam, and the Gold Coast Press

*Carina Ray*

The introduction of Islam into West Africa is typically associated with Arab and North African Muslim traders and scholars who plied the trans-Saharan trade routes that eventually linked North and West Africa into an expansive economic unit (Trimingham 1959, 1962; Levtzion 1994). This is certainly the case for the introduction of Islam into the northern reaches of modern-day Ghana by the fifteenth century (Silverman and Owusu-Ansah 1989, 326).[1] Farther south, however, the Tabon—formerly enslaved Afro-Brazilian Muslims who left Brazil and settled in a number of West African entrepots in the 1830s—are credited with first introducing Islam to Accra, an especially prominent port city on the Atlantic shore of what was then known as the Gold Coast (Quayson 2014, 47).[2] By the time the Tabon arrived in Accra, it had long been settled by the Ga people, who by the seventeenth century had already laid the city's first and most enduring blueprint in the form of the Ga Mashie and Osu townships, which were the oldest and most strategic nodes in the wider constellation of Ga littoral townships. But the Ga were not the sole makers of the town.

By the middle of the seventeenth century, the various European powers vying for control of the region's lucrative slave trade had built permanent footholds along the coast. Over the next century and a half, Osu became home to a prosperous Danish and Ga-Danish slave trading community based largely in and around Christiansborg Castle. Just as the Ga had strategically integrated the Danes into Osu, they would later integrate the Tabon into Ga Mashie during the nineteenth century. For a number of reasons, including a shared Portuguese pidgin that bridged the linguistic divide between the Tabon and their Ga hosts, as well as the lucrative and in-demand urban skill sets the Tabon introduced to Accra, they were easily and enthusiastically integrated by the Ga into the Otublohum *akutso*, or quarter, of the Ga Mashie, the ethnic heart of the six original Ga coastal settlements (Quayson 2014, 51–52). Thereafter, the Tabon were provided with additional tracts of arable land farther afield, ensuring that their presence was not limited to the spatial confines of the *akutsei* system.

What is important to emphasize here is that Islam was introduced into Accra at a time when its external origins by way of Brazil were arguably a prestige factor rather than an obstacle to its incorporation. That was no longer the case by the early twentieth century, by which time the British were firmly in control of the Gold Coast colony. In the decades after relocating their administrative capital from Cape Coast to Accra in 1877, the British colonial state usurped and co-opted Ga patrimony, most notably through land alienation and the introduction of indirect rule. The emergence of a rights of origin discourse among the Ga in response to the British colonial state's incursions helps explain why the Tabon, within about four generations, had adopted the religious practices of their Ga hosts (Quayson 2014, 60; see also Ray 2016, 507–9). As the Tabon shed their Islamic faith in order to more easily assimilate into Ga society, the continued presence of Islam along the coast was ensured by the increasing number of Muslim migrants from the north who were confined to *zongos* (quarters for "strangers") in different parts of colonial Accra. This point is noteworthy since the trajectory of Islam on the coast, and specifically in Accra, might have been quite different had the Tabon not been put under intense pressure to assimilate. Instead, Islam came to be associated pejoratively with northern migrants, and many of the colony's educated African elites, most of whom were Christians or Christian converts, regarded Islam as an inferior religion.

During the opening years of the twentieth century, Islam, however, found a powerful advocate in Edward Wilmot Blyden, the West Indian writer, scholar, and champion of Pan-Africanism, who settled in Liberia in the mid-nineteenth century and later lived in Sierra Leone and Lagos. In 1903, Blyden's writings triggered a debate over whether Islam offered an alternative and more appropriate path to racial progress for Gold Coasters than either Christianity or indigenous religions, the latter of which were dismissed as "pagan." This chapter traces the debate as it unfolded over a decade in two of the colony's leading African-owned newspapers, first in the *Gold Coast Leader* (1902–1929) and later in the *Gold Coast Nation* (1912–1920). These newspapers provided a natural home for such a debate, as the indigenous Gold Coast press had long been the primary venue in which the colony's politicized cosmopolitan writers debated contemporary matters of concern. During the opening decades of the twentieth century, as Audrey Gadzekpo has observed, "the chief advocates of social and political reform . . . could be found within the ranks of the politician/journalist" (2001, 74–75). Indeed, many of the men who formed part of the early nucleus of the nationalist movement in the Gold Coast, including Joseph Ephraim Casely Hayford, Samuel Richard Brew Attoh Ahuma, Frederick Victor Nanka-Bruce, Thomas Hutton-Mills, and James Hutton Brew, were closely associated with indigenous newspapers, either as founders, editors, or investors (74–75). They harnessed the power of the Gold Coast press to challenge colonial rule and to carve out alternative spheres of power and influence for themselves. Not all these papers shared the same political orientation. Indeed, the *Gold Coast Leader* and the *Gold Coast Nation* represented two different political trajectories: the former, one of increasing radicalization and anticolonialism; and the latter, one of increasing conservatism tied to the politics of indirect rule (Akurang-Parry 2006, 44; Jones-Quartey 1974, 19; Newell 2011, 84).

## Edward Blyden: An Unlikely Proponent of Islam in West Africa

Blyden is a towering figure in the intellectual history of Pan-Africanism. He was born to free Black parents in 1832, in what was then the Danish West Indian colony of St. Thomas. At the age of ten he moved to Venezuela, where he became fluent in Spanish. When his family returned to St. Thomas in 1845, Blyden became closely associated with the pastor of his Dutch Reformed Church, a white American named John Knox. Knox subsequently took Blyden to the United States in 1850 to enroll him in Rutgers Theological College, where he hoped to become ordained as a minister. Rutgers, along with two other theological colleges, refused to accept him because he was Black (Pawlikova-Vilhanova 2002, 120–21).[3] With few options open to him, Blyden traveled to Liberia in 1851 at the behest of Knox. These early experiences of racial discrimination in his pursuit of theological training troubled Blyden's thinking about Christianity as a plausible spiritual path for the "negro race," as he called it in his widely circulated book, *Christianity, Islam and the Negro Race*, first published in London by W. B. Whittingham in 1887.

Although there has been much speculation about Blyden's personal faith, there is no doubt that over the course of his life he came to regard Islam with special affection and sought to foster unity and cooperation between Muslim and Christian Africans. Blyden's commitment to the principle of religious coexistence was enacted, symbolically, at his funeral in Freetown in 1912, when Muslims carried his body to his final resting place, after which Christian burial rights were performed (Lynch 1967, 245–46). During his life, however, more was at stake for Blyden than just the question of religious tolerance. Indeed, the primary concern that came to dominate his work was the promotion of Islam as the most appropriate method for the spiritual and intellectual progress of the Black race, globally and in West Africa in particular.

Blyden spent his first several decades in Liberia engaged in journalism, government service, and teaching. A polyglot, he was already fluent in Greek, Latin, Spanish, and English when he traveled to Syria in 1866 to learn Arabic at the Syrian Protestant College (Lynch 1967, 47). Once fluent in Arabic, Blyden was able to participate in a program sponsored by the college that sent Arabic-language Bibles to Muslim communities in Liberia with the request that they return the favor by sending information about their communities to the college in Syria. It was this project that ushered in a phase of intense interaction between Blyden and Muslim communities in Liberia, and later in Sierra Leone. To facilitate this interaction, he established the Arabic Studies Program at Liberia College in 1867 (Lynch 1967, 48). He continued this work throughout the 1870s, with the result that he became deeply impressed by the high levels of education obtained by the region's Muslim populations, as well as by the apparent unifying effect of Islam on African populations. While he saw Islam as preferable to the region's traditional religions, or so-called "paganism," in his early years on the West African coast he still held on to the idea that Christianity was the ultimate spiritual destination of Africans and that Islam was but a stop on the way where "pagans" could be groomed to receive the true gospel. As the twentieth century opened, however, the Gold Coast press reported his unequivocal assertion that Islam was the faith "best adapted to the Negro race."[4]

In *Christianity, Islam and the Negro Race*, in published articles, in speeches delivered in West Africa and in England, and in the excerpts of his writing and speeches that appeared in the Gold Coast press, Blyden advanced several key arguments in favor of the adoption of Islam by West Africans. These arguments were grounded in a romanticized vision of Islam that was augmented by Blyden's trenchant critique of the uses and abuses of Christianity. Blyden's view that Islam had spread peacefully through trade and the conversion of African elites left no room for acknowledging that it also spread violently through jihad to establish the West African Muslim states of Futa Jalon and Futa Toro in the seventeenth and eighteenth centuries, and later the Fulani Empire under the leadership of Usman Dan Fodio in the early nineteenth century. Nor did Blyden acknowledge the possibility that Arab traders, scholars, and missionaries harbored pejorative ideas about Africans. Instead, he argued, whereas Europeans felt "repulsion" upon encountering Black Africans, Arabs felt sympathy and brotherhood (Blyden 1994, 23). "Christianity," he wrote, "came to the Negro as a slave, or at least as a subject race in a foreign land. Along with the Christian teaching, he and his children received lessons of their utter and permanent inferiority and subordination to their instructors." These circumstances, Blyden argued, meant that Christianity was hardwired to stymie the development of African people. "Owing to the physical, mental, and social pressure under which the Africans received these influences of Christianity, their development was necessarily partial and one-sided, cramped and abnormal," wrote Blyden. He also asserted that Christianity's stranglehold on African development had produced the tendency toward mimicry in Africans. "Their ideas and aspirations could be expressed only in conformity with the views and tastes of those who held rule over them. All avenues to intellectual improvement were closed against them, and they were doomed to perpetual ignorance" (14–15). Islam, in contrast, allowed the "African Personality" to flourish by drawing out the best aspects of African cultures, purging customs and traditions that were incompatible with the progress of the "Negro race," and promoting unity across ethnic divisions (67–68).

Unsurprisingly, given the importance of knowledge acquisition and production in Blyden's life, he championed Islam as a conduit of education. "Mohammadanism and learning to the Muslim Negro," wrote Blyden, "were coeval. No sooner was he converted than he was taught to read, and the importance of knowledge was impressed upon him" (1994, 15). In Blyden's view, this meant that Muslim converts could take on the fullness of their spiritual calling, while Christian converts were bound to be regarded as both racially and spiritually inferior. His view was soon confirmed when the various missionary churches enacted color bars within their ecclesial hierarchies. Blyden regarded this move as a death knell for Christianity in West Africa: whatever progress had been made by Christianity in converting West Africans had occurred during the early phase of its introduction, when the religion was largely in the hands of Africans. These individuals were often recaptives or "liberated" Africans such as Samuel Ajayi Crowther, who had been trained in Sierra Leone and subsequently fanned out across British West Africa. A further barrier to conversion was erected when the indigenization of the church gave way to Europeanization (Baum 2016, 83–85).

Blyden's view of this critical difference between Christianity and Islam was made clear in the first extract of his writings to appear in the *Gold Coast Leader* in early February 1903. "Islam makes room for all," declared Blyden, who then drew on the words of an interlocutor to preface his remarks about Christianity:

> Mr. Bryce in his Romanes lecture, a few months ago, confessed to the inability of Christianity on this subject compared with Islam. "Christianity," he said, "with its doctrine of brotherhood does not create the sentiment of equality which Islam does." This is not the fault of Christianity but of the earthen vessel in which the treasure is contained. An Imperial race is incompetent to maintain the simplicity of the Naza-

rene, and diffuse His teachings as he gave utterance to them. It is not the business of Imperialism to make men but to create subjects, not to save souls, but to rule bodies.[5]

The inferiority complex bequeathed by Christianity to its African converts had not only spiritual and intellectual implications but also a bodily dimension, which Blyden believed gave Islam an additional advantage.

Islam condemns idolatry and, by extension, discourages the depiction of God, Muhammad, and other prophets. As a result, Islam does not alienate potential converts, wherever they might be located in the world and whatever they may look like, by depicting the Prophet in phenotypically specific ways. By contrast, Christianity has a long tradition of iconography that over time came to represent Jesus/ God as white. By racializing God, Christian art gives whites what Blyden calls an "aesthetic advantage" over their Black counterparts with regard to conversion (1994, 17). Even when the depiction of Christ as white does not deter Blacks from converting, it nonetheless has a damaging impact on the psychology of the Black convert, argued Blyden, who presages Frantz Fanon in the following passage: "But to the Negro all these exquisite representations exhibited only the physical characteristics of a foreign race; and while they tended to quicken the tastes and refine the sensibilities of that race, they had only a depressing influence upon the Negro who felt that he had neither part nor lot, so far as his physical character was concerned, in those splendid representations" (Blyden 1994, 17).

While Christianity's racialized iconography had "impaired, if not destroyed, his [the Negro's] self-respect, and made him the weakling and creeper which he appears in Christian lands," Islam had no somatic deficit, argued Blyden: "The Mohammedan Negro, who is not familiar with such representations, sees God in the great men of his country" (1994, 17, 18). The physical dimension of Islam's advantage over Christianity had an additional layer: the Arab missionary in West Africa, said Blyden, is "often of the same complexion as his hearer and does not require any long habit to reconcile the eye to him," allowing for easier integration into host societies and greater success in spreading Islam (25). When Islam was eventually propagated by West Africans, the somatic gap was gone altogether. The trajectory for Christianity was reversed: with the increasing Europeanization of the missionary presence in West Africa, the somatic gap widened over time.

Blyden also extolled Islam's virtues as they related to the prohibition of liquor, a topic that was being vigorously debated during the early decades of the twentieth century across much of British West Africa (Dumett 1974; Olorunfemi 1984; van den Bersselaar 2007). He is quoted in the *Gold Coast Leader* contrasting favorable reports of the salubrious effect Islam had on the populations of northern Nigeria, signaled by their demand for a ban on liquor with negative reports that described the "drunken and slovenly habits of the chiefs" in the Gold Coast who had not come under Islamic influence.[6] Whatever good the Christian missionaries could do among native populations, according to Blyden, was undone by European traders who profited handsomely from the liquor trade. With such weak footing among West Africans, Blyden argued, Christianity inevitably would give way to Islam, and Islam would thus preserve West Africans' intellectual and physical strength, allowing them to avoid the physical and moral destruction faced by Native Americans, Pacific Islanders, and New Zealanders under Christianity.[7]

## Debating Islam and Christianity in the Gold Coast Press

Adaptations of and engagements with Blyden's arguments about Islam and Christianity soon began to appear in the Gold Coast press. Reflecting a broader political divide, writers associated with the more radical *Gold Coast Leader* saw in Islam a possible route to their own unique civilizational aspirations that circumvented the racial baggage and cultural imperialism of Christianity. Other writers, however, took to the more politically conservative pages of the *Gold Coast Nation* to caution against the idea that Islam was inherently superior to Christianity or more adaptable to African life, and rejected the claim that Africans could practice their Christian faith only as second-class citizens. What did unite these writers, however, was their shared assumptions about the inferiority of indigenous African religions, often derisively referred to as "paganism."

In October 1903 and again in May 1904, editorials in the *Leader* condemned the excessive litigation among Christianized Gold Coasters and pointed to the comparative lack of litigation among Muslims in the colony, leading the *Leader*'s editors to question "whether Christianity as it is being taught us, and the kind of civilization that is being forced down our throat is doing us as a race, good or harm."[8]

In early 1905, the *Leader* published a lengthy editorial under the title "Christianization or Denationalization," which pondered whether the shallowness of Christianity and its purported insalubrious effect on Africans in the colony were a result of "the religion or the way that the religion is taught."[9] Echoing Blyden's argument that Islam was easily adopted by Africans because it is a religion whose social and domestic practices are intelligible and easily compatible with their own, the *Leader*'s editors urged the missionary bodies in the colony to teach the Christian religion "divested of all its foreign elements." Instead of focusing on the "modes and customs belonging to other countries," they ought to focus on the gospel. If Christianization was tantamount to Europeanization, then what it amounted to in the end was denationalization of the African. Making matters worse was the fact that even when African converts had become denationalized, Christian missionaries looked down on them with scorn as mimics, while admiring Muslims for their authenticity of self.[10] Though the editorial was not advocating Islam over Christianity, it used the idea of cultural complementarity between Islam and its African converts to argue that if Christianity could not find a cultural common ground with Africans, it ought to dispense altogether with the "civilizing mission" in favor of Christ. Once the gospel had taken root, Africans would in due course shed cultural practices that were not compatible with their Christian faith.

Blyden had also argued that Islam had done the preparatory work of making West Africans amenable to education, uplift, progress, discipline, and authority— all qualities, he said, that colonial authorities had also observed in Muslims, causing them to praise Muslims over and above their "pagan" or quasi-Christian counterparts.[11] Echoes of Blyden's argument appeared in a series of articles about the implementation of direct taxation in West Africa. The authors of these articles employed a common refrain that direct taxation was bound to fail in areas that had not come under the influence of Islam and thus lacked the advanced state of civilization associated with Muslims. Therein, however, lay what would become the Gold Coast radical intelligentsia's major posthumous critique of Blyden: he had provided a template for the theory of indirect rule, which Lord Lugard had pioneered in northern Nigeria and subsequently exported to other British colonies. The intelligentsia were especially aggrieved with Blyden on this count, since they were the ones who would soon be displaced by the institutionalization of indirect rule.

Beginning in 1905, there was a lull in the public discussion of Islam in the colony's press, but that changed shortly before Blyden passed away in February 1912. At that time, a series of commentaries about the vexed "marriage question" in the Gold Coast revived interest in Blyden's ideas about Islam as a "natural" fit for Africans because of its acceptance of polygamy, which, according to its practitioners, allowed Africans to remain African. In a series of commentaries between late 1911 and early 1912, Sam Brew, a leading member of the Gold Coast intelligentsia, wrote in passionate defense of polygamy under native customary law.[12] He argued that polygamy preserved the morality of Africans, and that if granted the right to polygamous marriage within Christianity, Africans would not take advantage of the privilege. He pointed to Islam's protection of polygamy to show that it had not led to the moral degeneration of Muslims. The propagation of monogamous or ordinance marriages, conversely, was leading to all manner of moral decay in the colony because, in Brew's view, it encouraged men either to have affairs or to abandon their customary-law wives upon contracting a Christian marriage. Brew also argued that monogamous marriages were creating a surplus of single women who were driven into immorality, and encouraging women toward wifely insubordination by endowing them with greater rights than did customary law.

On February 24, 1912, the *Leader* announced Blyden's death. Appearing adjacent to his death notice was a column that argued that Islam was spreading in areas that had hitherto been inimical to it because it allowed polygamy. The Christian Church would cede more ground to Islam if it did not change course by Africanizing Christianity, in part by accepting polygamy. This sentiment was oft repeated in the pages of the *Leader*—in November of that year, regular columnist Quashie wrote that the prohibition of polygamy led to "Islam advancing by leaps and bounds [while] Christianity on the West Coast is vanishing." "Leave the people to adopt their own form of marriage," he said, "and then they will with devotion attend your Church."[13]

In 1913, the *Leader*'s rival, the more politically conservative *Gold Coast Nation*, made its own position on Islam clear. It published excerpts of an account it described as "controversial" by a former German missionary named Diedrich Westermann on "the Negro in Islam and in Christianity" that bore the ideological imprint of Blyden's thinking about Islam and Christianity in relation to Africans. Westermann condemned Christianity for "turning the Negro into a mere caricature of the European, while Islam makes him a self-respecting African" and allows him to join a global community, to enter "into a clearly defined relationship with Europeans," who treat him with respect due to his Islamic faith. In striking contrast, wrote Westermann, "The Europeanized negro never obtains among the whites that social equality to which Islam admits him readily."[14] In the next edition, the *Nation*'s editor politely but forcefully rejected the notion that Islam had any inherent advantage over Christianity as far as West Africans were concerned. What Islam did have, however, was a much longer history in West Africa, which made any comparison with Christianity disingenuous. It was premature, claimed the editor, to make comparisons between Christian missions and Islam. While the editor conceded that "the Crescent is superior by whole heavens to Wood and Stones"—a reference to what he later called "Paganism"—he went on to claim that in due course Christianity would find its footing on the West African coast when it no longer sought to replace African customs, modes of thought, and habits of life with European ones without qualification and necessary modifications.[15]

When Africans could embrace Christianity not as mimics but as equals, they would find in it the social equality made available by Islam. Thus, like the *Leader*, the *Nation* called for delinking the gospel from the racism of those who often preached it. But the *Nation* went a step further by declaring that "if Islam is the harbinger of fraternity, liberty, and equality to the native, much more so is the Christian Religion."[16] It was only a matter of time, the newspaper concluded, before Christianity reigned victorious over Islam. In this way, the *Nation*, unlike the *Leader*, did not express doubt about the fate of Christianity in relation to Islam.

In early 1914, news of a group of Gold Coast Christians who had converted to Islam in Warri (Nigeria) prompted the *Nation* to publish a fearmongering attack on Islam, which it described as a religion "fraught with base immorality" and "strong licentious passion."[17] Bypassing the familiar argument about whether conversion from "paganism" to Islam was favorable to no conversion at all, the paper reworked the terms of the debate to focus on the danger of Gold Coast Christians converting to Islam, arguing that the only inducement for such an act was "the desire to plunge into a polygamous state of life which has received the sanction of the Koran, and which Christianity prohibits."[18] Thus, while both newspapers regarded polygamy as a pull factor in favor of Islam, the *Nation*'s position was categorically different from that of the *Gold Coast Leader*, which regarded polygamy not as a source of moral debauchery but as a guard against it.

World War I brought an end to this decade-long debate about Islam and Christianity in the colony's African-owned newspapers. Instead, war-related events and their implications for the West African colonies dominated press coverage, with short human-interest stories about the region's Muslim communities appearing every now and again. After the war was over, debates about the racial and cultural appropriateness of Christianity for Africans emerged once again in the colony's newspapers, but rarely did they turn to Islam as an alternative. Indeed, the real battle that Christianity would have to fight in the Gold Coast was not against Islam but rather against itself.

## NOTES

1. According to historians such as Trimingham, Islam had no influence south of the Sudanic belt. To counter this claim, Silverman and Owusu-Ansah (1989) provide a comprehensive bibliographic account of the presence of Islam in the forest region of Ghana.

2. On the history of the Tabon, see Essien 2016; Amos and Ayesu 2002; and Schaumloeffel 2015.

3. The scholarly literature on Blyden is vast. The most recent study is Odamtten 2019.

4. "Dr. Blyden's Speech: Africa and the African," *Gold Coast Leader*, September 26, 1903.

5. "Extracts from Dr. Blyden's Paper on 'Islam in Western Soudan,'" *Gold Coast Leader*, February 7–14, 1903. Blyden's paper was first published in its entirety in the *Journal of the Royal African Society* 2, no. 5 (1902): 11–37.

6. "Extracts from Dr. Blyden's Paper."

7. "Extracts from Dr. Blyden's Paper."

8. "Editorial Notes," *Gold Coast Leader*, October 10, 1903.

9. "Christianization or Denationalization," *Gold Coast Leader*, February 4, 1905.

10. "Christianization or Denationalization."

11. "Extracts from Dr. Blyden's Paper."

12. Sam H. Brew, "The Marriage Question on the Gold Coast," *Gold Coast Leader*, December 16, 1911; December 30, 1911; January 13, 1912; January 20, 1912; January 27, 1912; February 3, 1912.

13. Quashie, "European Marriage and Its Effect on the Negro Race," *Gold Coast Leader*, November 16, 1912.

14. "Islam in Africa," *Gold Coast Nation*, February 20, 1913.

15. "Our Editor's Notes and Comments," *Gold Coast Nation*, February 27, 1913.

16. "Our Editor's Notes and Comments."

17. A Gold Coaster, "The Spread of Islamism in Warri," *Gold Coast Nation*, January 15, 1914.

18. A Gold Coaster, "Spread of Islamism in Warri."

## REFERENCES

Akurang-Parry, Kwabena O. 2006. "'Disrespect and Contempt for Our Natural Rulers': The African Intelligentsia and the Effects of British Indirect Rule on Indigenous Rulers in the Gold Coast c.1912–1920." *International Journal of Regional and Local Studies* 2 (1): 43–65.

Amos, Alcione M., and Ebenezer Ayesu. 2002. "'I Am Brazilian': History of the Tabon, Afro-Brazilians in Accra, Ghana." *Transactions of the Historical Society of Ghana* 6:35–58.

Baum, Robert M. 2016. "Historical Perspectives on West African Christianity." In *Routledge Companion to Christianity in Africa*, edited by Elias Kifon Bongmba, 83–85. New York: Routledge.

Blyden, Edward W. 1994. *Christianity, Islam and the Negro Race*. Baltimore: Black Classic Press.

Dumett, Raymond E. 1974. "The Social Impact of the European Liquor Trade on the Akan of Ghana (Gold Coast and Asante), 1875–1910." *Journal of Interdisciplinary History* 5 (1): 69–101.

Essien, Kwame. 2016. *Brazilian-African Diaspora in Ghana: The Tabom, Slavery, Dissonance of Memory, Identity, and Locating Home*. East Lansing: Michigan State University Press.

Gadzekpo, Audrey S. 2001. "Women's Engagement with Gold Coast Print Culture from 1857 to 1957." PhD diss., University of Birmingham.

Jones-Quartey, K. A. B. 1974. *A Summary History of the Ghana Press, 1822–1960*. Accra: Ghana Information Services Department.

Levtzion, Nehemia. 1994. *Islam in West Africa: Religion, Society and Politics to 1800*. London: Routledge.

Lynch, Hollis R. 1967. *Edward Wilmot Blyden: Pan-Negro Patriot, 1832–1912*. London: Oxford University Press.

Newell, Stephanie. 2011. "Writing Out Imperialism? A Note on Nationalism and Political Identity in the African-Owned Newspapers of Colonial Ghana." In *Exit: Endings and New Beginnings in Literature and Life*, edited by Stefan Helgesson, 81–94. Amsterdam: Rodopi.

Odamtten, Harry N. K. 2019. *Edward W. Blyden's Intellectual Transformations: Afro-publicanism, Pan-Africanism, Islam, and the Indigenous West African Church*. East Lansing: Michigan State University.

Olorunfemi, A. 1984. "The Liquor Traffic Dilemma in British West Africa: The Southern Nigerian Example, 1895–1918." *International Journal of African Historical Studies* 17 (2): 229–41.

Pawlikova-Vilhanova, Viera. 2002. "Christianity, Islam and the African World: Edward Wilmot Blyden (1832–1912) and Contemporary Missionary Thought." *Asian and African Studies* 11 (2): 117–28.

Quayson, Ato. 2014. *Oxford Street, Accra: City Life and the Itineraries of Transnationalism*. Durham, NC: Duke University Press.

Ray, Carina. 2016. "*Oxford Street, Accra:* Rethinking the Roots of Cosmopolitanism from an Africanist Historian's Perspective." *PMLA* 131 (2): 505–14.

Schaumloeffel, Marco A. 2015. "Afro-Brazilian Diaspora in West Africa: The Tabom in Ghana." In *Another Black Like Me: The Construction of Identities and Solidarity in the African Diaspora*, edited by Elaine Pereira Rocha and Nielson Rosa Bezerra, 185–99. Newcastle upon Tyne: Cambridge Scholars Publishing.

Silverman, Raymond A., and David Owusu-Ansah. 1989. "The Presence of Islam among the Akan of Ghana: A Bibliographic Essay." *History in Africa* 16:325–40.

Trimingham, John S. 1959. *Islam in West Africa*. Oxford: Oxford University Press.

——. 1962. *A History of Islam in West Africa*. Oxford: Oxford University Press.

Van den Bersselaar, Dmitri. 2007. *The King of Drinks: Schnapps Gin from Modernity to Tradition*. Leiden: Brill.

# THE LHASA UPRISINGS OF 1959 AND 2008

## Muslims in a Buddhist Land

*David G. Atwill*

Late in the evening of March 17, 1959, under the cover of darkness, a small group of trusted guards and advisers whisked the fourteenth Dalai Lama out the Norbulingka Summer Palace's front gate. Slipping unnoticed through the crowds that had gathered there to protect him, the Dalai Lama set out on what would be a harrowing two-week journey over some of the world's highest mountains to India. It was a momentous decision. After nearly eight years of attempting to rule Tibet as an autonomous region under the increasingly strict oversight of the People's Republic of China (PRC), the Dalai Lama had chosen to flee his homeland in exchange for a life in exile.

When word of his departure reached Tibetans, it sparked a massive insurrection that, while lasting only a few days, came precariously close to toppling the tenuous hold of the PRC over Tibet. It was a lesson that China's leadership did not soon forget. For Tibetans, the intervening decades have not diminished the memory of the failed uprising or the grief over the loss of their spiritual leader. From that year forward, every March, as Tibetans sought ways to mark the occasion, Chinese security forces would tighten access, restrict movement, and limit all religious activity across the Tibet Autonomous Region (TAR). As the forty-ninth anniversary of the 1959 uprising approached in 2008, China's preparations to host the Summer Olympic Games later that year unsettled an already delicate situation.

As one veteran China journalist wrote, "If there is one city in China where the authorities are truly worried about serious unrest that might spoil the Olympic games in Beijing in August, it is the Tibetan capital, Lhasa" (Miles 2008, 56).

China's concern over the threat of open dissent was palpable. Checkpoints were set up across Tibet, and the central government saturated Lhasa with police and paramilitary troops. Though many of the city's activities continued as normal—Tibetan Buddhists circled Lhasa's sacred pilgrimage sites and a steady stream of Chinese tourists milled around the central Barkor market—a sense of foreboding permeated the capital.

On March 14, 2008, riot police rushed to suppress and, as some reports say, opened fire on a small protest in the center of Lhasa. The reaction was immediate, overwhelming, and violent. For the next twenty-four hours, bands of Tibetans prowled the streets targeting Chinese businesses and residences, setting cars ablaze, and attacking any Chinese who crossed their path. By the time that Chinese troops regained control of the city in the early hours of March 16, several hundred Han Chinese and Tibetans—monks, civilians, and soldiers—had been killed (CTAIE 2010).

Within hours of the initial violence, global news media speculated as to the motivations behind the uprising. The front-page headline of the *New York Times* declared "Violence in Tibet as Monks Clash with the Police," and the article framed the chaotic scenes as representing "a major challenge to the ruling Communist Party as it prepares to play host to the Olympic Games in August" (Yardley 2008, 1). In the *People's Daily*, Jampa Phuntsog (Ch. Xiangba Pingcuo), chairman of the TAR, claimed that the riots, far from being caused by the Chinese government, had been "organized, premeditated and meticulously planned by the Dalai Lama and the 'Free Tibet' movement [Ch. *Zangdu*] at home and abroad" (*People's Daily* 2008). Even with differences of interpretation over the exact impetus of the clashes, most accounts, both inside and outside of China, related the sequence of events in surprisingly similar ways: tense protests followed by running skirmishes between Tibetans and Chinese forces. Yet, in the scores of articles written on the uprising in the weeks following the incident, only a handful mentioned Lhasa's Muslims. That omission is startling, given that Tibetans had attacked the Grand Mosque and set its main gate on fire, in addition to ransacking and looting Muslim restaurants and shops.

The repeated erasure of Muslims from the uprising is, on the one hand, the result of politicization of the Tibet issue, a tendency of those writing on Tibet to adopt a Chinese-or-Tibetan caricature that leaves little room for Tibet's vibrant social diversity. On the other hand, the subtle airbrushing of Muslims out of Tibet's past and present is part of a centuries-old tradition—a tendency by outsiders to regard Tibet as an idealized Buddhist land untouched by external influences. It comes as a surprise to many that the presence of Muslims in Tibetan society is neither remarkable nor objectionable to most Tibetans. Muslims have been a vibrant part of Lhasa society for nearly four centuries. Their presence was and is accepted and embraced by Tibetans.

The attack on the Grand Mosque in 2008 was not the first time that Tibetan rioters had targeted Muslims and sought to destroy one of their places of worship. As longtime residents of Lhasa would later recount, the storming of the Grand Mosque in 2008 brought to mind unpleasant parallels with the 1959 uprising, when the Grand Mosque and much of Lhasa's Muslim quarter were burned to the ground. What follows is an attempt to explain why, after centuries of embracing Muslims as their neighbors within Tibet's holiest city, Tibetans targeted them in 1959 and again in 2008, and why such attacks against Muslims are absent from most narratives of the two greatest insurrections against the Chinese rule of Tibet.

## Tibetan Muslims in Tibet's Buddhist Past

In the minds of Tibet's earliest foreign visitors, to be Tibetan was to be Buddhist. As a result, although many early accounts of Tibet confirmed the presence of Tibetan Muslims, most treated them as fundamentally un-Tibetan. For example, in his influential nineteenth-century memoir, French missionary Évariste Huc includes Tibetan Muslims as among "the permanent population of Lhasa," observing that they were "almost imperceptibly formed in the heart of Tibet." In spite of these discerning observations, he concludes, erroneously, that they were "a small community apart, having adopted neither the dress, nor the customs, nor the language, nor the religion of the natives" (Huc [1850] 1925, 2:247). Huc's description reflects a disturbing tendency of foreign narratives, up to the present, to affirm the presence of Muslims in Tibetan society but not to accept them as native Tibetans.

In fact, Muslims have been a prominent and demographically significant part of Tibetan society for four hundred years. Since the fifth Dalai Lama (1617–1682) granted land for Lhasa's first mosque on the outskirts of the city in the early seventeenth century, Muslims have served as Tibetan officials, have played a prominent role in Tibet's classical arts (Tib. *nangma*), and were renowned for their facility with the Tibetan language (Ramble 1993; Samuel 1976). By the early twentieth century, Muslims were a conspicuous element of Tibetan society. Lhasa alone had four mosques and two Muslim cemeteries, and mosques were present in every large central Tibetan city, including Shigatse, Gyantse, and Tsetang. Admired, accommodated, and welcomed, Tibetan Muslims were recognized as Tibetans in almost every realm of society.

Like many diasporic communities who trace their ancestry to foreign lands, Muslim communities in Tibet retained ties to their countries of origin: India and China. The Wapaling (Chinese) Khache (Tib. *wa pa gling kha che*) were primarily agriculturists who settled in the southeastern part of the city near the Lhasa River. The Barkor (South Asian) Khache (Tib. *bar skor khache*) were largely traders who lived in and around Lhasa's central Barkor market. In the intervening centuries, the Khache communities intermarried with each other and with Buddhists. Until 1959, the permanent Muslim population stood at about 10 to 15 percent of Lhasa's thirty thousand nonmonastic residents (Gaborieau and Muhammad 1973, 79; Kaul 1976, 103; Xue 1999, 70).

Muslims were integrated into every dimension of Tibetan daily life, and there is little evidence of anti-Muslim sentiment among the Buddhist community. In Tibetan Buddhist texts, Muslims are rarely referenced, and when they are, they tend to be glossed generically as "barbarian" outsiders (Tib. *kla klos* / Sanskrit: *mleccas*). John Newman, a specialist on Buddhism in Tibet, concedes that in some Buddhist tracts Islam is identified as the "perfect anti-religion which is the antithesis of Buddhism." He concludes, however, that such a view of Islam never translated into a broader "systematic attempt to demonize Muslims." Instead, Muslims tend to be characterized as "truthful, clean, honest and chaste" (Newman 1998, 331).

Similarly, Buddhists distinguish between Islam as an abstract set of beliefs that is opposed to Buddhism and Muslims as individuals. For example, adherents of the Dorje Shugden sect have accused the fourteenth Dalai Lama of being a "saffron robed Muslim" and thus a falsely recognized reincarnation (Chandler 2015, 84; Lopez 1999, 191). Even in this case, however, Islam is invoked to express the loss of Buddhist beliefs rather than to attack Muslims.

If Muslims have been a central part of Tibetan culture for centuries and if there are few examples of sustained anti-Muslim behavior, how are we to explain the attacks on Muslims during the uprisings of 1959 and 2008? Part of the answer lies in the manner in which China portrayed Tibet. China's narrative was shaped by an ethnoterritorial formula in which China is the sum of its Tibetan, Muslim (Hui), Mongolian, Manchu, and Chinese parts. In this narrative, Tibetan identity and Muslim identity are mutually exclusive.

Beginning with the Qing dynasty, established in 1644, Chinese officials have portrayed China as being composed of "five ethnicities" (Ch. *wuzu*): Tibetans, Muslim Hui, Manchu, Mongols, and Han Chinese. Invoking the five ethnicities served as a shorthand to signify "China." Among these five ethnic groups, the Hui category was particularly fraught. Unlike the other groups, Hui could signify a territory (Ch. *Huidi*), a race/ethnicity (Ch. *Huimin*), or a religion (Ch. *Huijiao*). With the founding of the PRC in 1949, this ambiguity deepened. At that time, the PRC carried out a state-sponsored ethnic classification project (Ch. *minzu shibie*) that identified fifty-six "nationalities" (Ch. *minzu*). Of these, ten *minzu* were Muslim. As the Chinese historian Jonathan Lipman points out, the

Chinese government's new classification system sought "to divorce its *minzu* paradigm from religion, divid[ing] its Muslim citizens into ten *minzu*, each supposedly distinguished by common territory, language, economy and psychological nature" (1997, xxii). This new classification system gave official status to ethnic groups who practiced Islam, especially in northwest China. However, the many Muslims, including those in China's heartland who had no territorial or linguistic markers other than their Muslim religious beliefs, remained Hui. For this reason, many Han Chinese suggested that the Hui were Han Chinese who practiced Islam. The renowned Hui scholar Bai Shouyi specified that those "who believe that Hui are Muslims and that Muslims are Hui are simply incorrect. . . . We must not say that all those who believe in the Islamic faith are all Hui, this is absolutely untrue" (1984, 8–9). Such academic assertions have done little to change popular perceptions.

The Chinese continue to use the term "Hui" to refer to any Muslim. The Chinese language does have terms for "Muslim" (Ch. *musilin*) and "Islam" (Ch. *yisilan jiao*), although most Chinese call Muslims "Hui people" (Ch. *Huimin*) and speak of Islam as the "Hui religion" (Ch. *Huijiao*). Following the adoption of an ethnic classification system in the 1950s, the label "Hui" came to be understood as signifying that one was culturally Chinese. In other words, "Hui" refers to a Chinese Muslim—not to one of the ethnically distinct Muslim *minzu* who lived in northwest China, such as the Uyghurs, Kazaks, Kirgiz, and Salars. This was not a trivial matter. In the PRC, one's ethnic classification is a central part of one's identity. It appears on one's identity card (Ch. *shengfenzhen*), residence permit (Ch. *hukou*), and, until recent decades, on one's permanent dossier (Ch. *dang'an*) (Wang 2005, 88). For Muslims in Tibet, this proved to be a delicate issue. Following a practice common among their Chinese Nationalist Party (KMT) predecessors, PRC officials referred to most Khache as Hui even though most identified themselves as ethnically Tibetan (Ch. *Zangzu*).

The history of labeling Muslims in Tibet as "Hui" has a more dubious pedigree. From the early twentieth century onward, the decision by the Chinese central government to identify the Khache as Hui was based on an effort to perpetuate the notion that just as Tibet has always been a part of China, so too the Muslims of Tibet have always been Chinese. This narrative was predicated on the portrayal and understanding of Khache as long-term Chinese residents of Tibet (of whom, in fact, there were very few). When the People's Liberation Army marched into Lhasa in October 1951, this linguistic sleight of hand was redeployed, once again confronting the Khache community with awkward choices about their political and religious allegiances as Tibetans, as Chinese, and as Khache (Atwill 2018, 53–58; Lin 2006, 73–75).

# Lost Citizens of the Himalayas

Between 1951 and early 1959, Lhasa quickly became a city of divided loyalties and ambiguous allegiances. This new era under PRC rule proved to be one of opportunity for the Barkor (South Asia) Khache, with their enduring ties to India, and the Wapaling (Chinese) Khache, with their shared linguistic bond with the Chinese. The Seventeen-Point Agreement, in which Tibet formally accepted Chinese rule, included numerous provisions allowing the Dalai Lama and his government to retain limited political control. Tibet retained its own currency, Tibetans could trade with the neighboring states of Nepal, Bhutan, and India, and Tibetans could travel abroad.

Under the new regime, both the Barkor and the Wapaling Khache thrived. The Barkor Khache quickly realized that the demand of the newly arrived Chinese for luxury goods imported from India far exceeded supply. Similarly, the Wapaling Khache realized that their facility in Chinese and Tibetan was indispensable to Chinese officials and soldiers, for whom many served as linguistic and cultural interpreters. While both Khache communities flourished, their situations set them on trajectories that would have distinctly divergent political consequences.

As the political situation deteriorated in the late 1950s, these separate consequences became increasingly apparent. For the Barkor Khache, earlier commercial opportunities dwindled while Chinese reliance on the language skills of the Wapaling Khache increased. The political implications for both communities were inescapable, as noted by Chinese government officials. As one early Hui cadre observed when posted to Lhasa, the Barkor Khache's exposure to "pro-British propaganda, [meant that they] were not terribly welcoming" (Xue 1999, 168). The Wapaling Khache were perceived as more responsive and open to the Chinese and thus "closer to the motherland" (168). By early 1959, Chinese officials in Lhasa were impatient with Tibet's perceived lack of political development and with the Tibetans' languid response to the push for them to embrace Chinese rule.

The March uprising began on March 19, 1959, days after the Dalai Lama's departure from Lhasa. The earliest violence was directed at several highly placed, pro-Chinese Tibetans who had openly collaborated with Chinese forces. The following day began differently. Tibetan rebels, fanning out across the city, targeted Chinese military outposts and government buildings. Bloody engagements between Tibetan and Chinese forces occurred near the Norbulingka Summer Palace and the Potala Palace northeast of Lhasa.

At the same time, although less well known, Tibetan groups attacked the Wapaling Khache community in southeastern Lhasa. These Tibetans did not hide their indignation over the Wapaling Khache's assistance to the Chinese during the previous decade, which they regarded as nothing less than collaboration.

They looted and burned the centuries-old Grand Mosque and several dozen homes. Tibetans were incensed that the Wapaling Khache failed to support their uprising and instead assisted "the Chinese soldiers as translators, oppressing and terrorizing the Tibetans" (Khétsun and Akester 2008, 150).

When the Chinese forces emerged victorious, political scores were settled—those seen as loyal were praised and those as disloyal were vilified. Sensitive to accusations that its suppression of Tibet was antireligious, the PRC in the first weeks and months adopted a strategy suggesting that it was the Tibetans, not the Chinese, who were antireligious. At the heart of this campaign was an effort to paint the Tibetan attacks against the Wapaling as religiously motivated. The *People's Daily* published a series of front-page articles underscoring the irony of the Tibetan rebels' insistence that they were protecting religion when the evidence showed that they attacked their Muslim neighbors. In one article, the headline, "Tibetan Rebels' 'Protect Religion Army,'" is juxtaposed to a photo of a Wapaling Khache standing forlornly in the remnants of his burned-out home (*People's Daily* 1959a, 2). The effectiveness of this strategy faded as the Wapaling themselves acknowledged that the rebels were primarily motivated by anti-Chinese rather than anti-Muslim feelings. In one article, Wapaling Khache Ma Mingliang went so far as to say that the Wapaling were attacked "only because they were opposed to the rebellion and refused to participate in the pro-uprising rallies" (*People's Daily* 1959b, 1). Such an admission is accentuated by the little-publicized fact that none of the other three, primarily Barkor Khache, mosques were targeted by the Tibetans during the uprising. Nor was this fact likely unnoticed by the Chinese officials.

By contrast, the Barkor Khache, who had remained openly aligned with pro-Tibetan elements, were detained, threatened, and accused of aiding and abetting the Tibetan rebels. Seeking an avenue of escape, like the tens of thousands of Tibetans who followed the Dalai Lama to India in the months after the uprising, the Barkor Khache declared themselves, by virtue of their ancestral ties to South Asia, "Kashmiri" and demanded to be allowed to return to India. After an eighteen-month standoff, and with added diplomatic pressure from India, the Chinese government acquiesced and allowed over one thousand Barkor Khache to immigrate to India. The disparate experiences of the Barkor and Wapaling Khache in the aftermath of the 1959 uprising challenge the suggestion that the rebels' actions against the Wapaling were motivated by religious considerations or that China's defense of the Wapaling was based on the government's concern for their religious freedom.

The exodus of the Barkor Khache from central Tibet altered the traditional balance of power among the Muslim communities. Their departure left the Wapaling Khache as the dominant Muslim community in central Tibet. As a result of the

Barkor Khache's departure and of antireligious political campaigns, particularly the Chinese Cultural Revolution (1966–1976), the Wapaling Khache stopped using the Grand Mosque, choosing to pray in Lhasa's other three mosques. The Wapaling Khache suffered to a degree that altered most Tibetans' attitudes toward them. In the late 1980s, one Lhasa resident commented that "in the beginning of the Sixties, their situation was almost worse than ours" (Bass 1990, 72).

As the Chinese Hui population of Lhasa grew, the Grand Mosque slowly came to be dominated by non-Tibetan Muslims who traveled to Lhasa from the interior provinces of China to work as merchants, as laborers, or, increasingly, as traders in the lucrative caterpillar fungus market (Ch. *chongcao*, Tib. *dbyar rtswa dgun 'bu*) (Fischer 2008). As a result, by the early 2000s, the Muslims who gathered and prayed at Lhasa's Grand Mosque were overwhelmingly Hui. Such a shift did not go unnoticed by Tibetans. In 2002, when the government authorized Hui Muslims to add a second story to the Grand Mosque that would dramatically alter the Lhasa skyline, many Tibetans protested the action. Tibetans argued that the renovations violated the centuries-old custom that the sacred Buddhist Jokhang Temple should be the highest building in Lhasa.

As Tibetan-Hui relations deteriorated, Tibetans and Chinese alike commonly suggested that the hostility emanated from an incompatibility between Buddhism and Islam. However, as Emily Yeh (2009, 77) has observed, the long history of an amicable relationship between Muslims and Buddhists in Tibet before 1951 "makes this an unsatisfying explanation." Her conclusion is consistent with the opinions of several imams and other Muslims who were interviewed in Lhasa in 2008. One Khache indicated that although tensions between Buddhists and Muslims had been on the rise, they had never "had anything to do with religion or involved the . . . officially recognized Muslims whose families have lived in Tibet for generations" (Consulate Chengdu 2008).

The fact that Tibetan-speaking Khache who were raised in Tibet did not identify with the Chinese-speaking newcomer Hui should come as no surprise. Similarly, it is hardly remarkable that Tibetans did not discriminate between Han and Hui Chinese in 2008. It was precisely this resentment toward Chinese, both Han and Hui, that erupted on March 14, 2008. Spontaneously instigated, and with little evidence of any organization, the violence caused the city to be awash in rumors, exaggerations, and half-truths. Storefront windows were smashed, goods were looted, and cars were overturned and set on fire. While conspicuous Chinese businesses and residences, such as the Bank of China, the Wenzhou Mall, and many police checkpoints, attracted the bulk of the Tibetan fury, so did the Grand Mosque.

The role of the Khache in the 1959 and 2008 uprisings reflects the often-unacknowledged place of Muslim communities in Tibet's past. Rather than being based on hostility to Muslims, the uprisings and attacks on the Grand Mosque were a consequence of hostility to the Chinese. That rioters did not disturb or target Lhasa's other three mosques in either 1959 or 2008 corroborates this hypothesis. It is only when we look for alternative motives for these attacks on the Grand Mosque that we can see how they align with the broader picture of the March uprisings. In the 1959 attack against the Wapaling Khache, one catches a rare glimpse of the internal tensions between Buddhists and Muslims who were accused of collaboration. Equally remarkable is the fact that the Wapaling Khache, who were severely maligned in 1959, found themselves in league with their Buddhist neighbors in opposition to Chinese rule in 2008.

This search for an answer as to why Tibetans attacked Lhasa's Grand Mosque in the 1959 and 2008 uprisings suggests that political alignments were more relevant than religious beliefs. It is my contention that the absence of references to Muslims in serious examinations of the uprisings in Tibet is a result of the misguided belief among Chinese and other non-Tibetan observers that Muslims were, and are, an alien element within Tibetan society. This understanding makes it possible for scholars to move beyond the perception of religious animosity as a driving force. In fact, the violence was less a result of underlying ethnic or religious antagonisms than a defense of Tibet's culture and way of life—a defense that includes preserving Tibet's deep and sustaining ties with its Muslim community.

## REFERENCES

Atwill, David G. 2018. *Islamic Shangri-La: Inter-Asian Relations and Lhasa's Muslim Communities, 1600 to 1960.* Oakland: University of California Press.

Bai Shouyi. 1984. "Guanyu Huizu shi gongzuo de jidian yijian." *Ningxia shehui kexue* 1:8–9.

Bass, Catriona. 1990. *Inside the Treasure House: A Time in Tibet.* London: Gollancz.

Chandler, Jeannine. 2015. "Invoking the Dharma Protector: Western Involvement in the Dorje Shugden Controversy." In *Buddhism beyond Borders: New Perspectives on Buddhism in the United States,* edited by Scott A. Mitchell and Natalie E. F. Quli, 75–91. New York: SUNY Press.

Consulate Chengdu. 2008. "Islam on the Tibetan Plateau—Two Local Perspectives." Wikileaks Cable: 08CHENGDU39_a, March 5, 2008. https://wikileaks.org/plusd/cables/08CHENGDU39_a.html.

CTAIE (Central Tibetan Administration-in-Exile). 2010. *2008 Uprising in Tibet: Chronology and Analysis.* Dharamsala: Narthang Press.

Fischer, Andrew M. 2008. "'Population Invasion' versus Urban Exclusion in the Tibetan Areas of Western China." *Population and Development Review* 34 (4): 599–629.

Gaborieau, Marc, and Ghulām Muhammad. 1973. *Récit d'un voyageur musulman au Tibet.* Paris: Klincksieck.

Huc, Evariste Régis. 1850. *Souvenirs d'un voyage dans la Tartarie, le Thibet, et la Chine pendant les années 1844, 1845 et 1846.* 2 vols. Paris: D'Adrien Le Clère et cie.

Kaul, Prem Nath. 1976. *Frontier Callings.* Delhi: Vikkas Publishing House.

Khétsun, Tubten, and Matthew Akester. 2008. *Memories of Life in Lhasa under Chinese Rule*. New York: Columbia University Press.

Lin, Hsiao-ting. 2006. *Tibet and Nationalist China's Frontier: Intrigues and Ethnopolitics, 1928–49*. Vancouver: University of British Columbia Press.

Lipman, Jonathan N. 1997. *Familiar Strangers: A History of Muslims in Northwest China*. Seattle: University of Washington Press.

Lopez, Donald S. 1999. *Prisoners of Shangri-La: Tibetan Buddhism and the West*. Chicago: University of Chicago Press.

Miles, James. 2008. "Monks on the March." *The Economist*, March 15, 2008, 56.

Newman, John. 1998. "Islam in the Kālacakra Tantra." *Journal of the International Association of Buddhist Studies* 21 (2): 311–72.

*People's Daily (Renmin Ribao)*. 1959a. "Xizang panfei de 'weijiao jun'—yiguan qinshou he pizhe jiasha de chailang" [Tibetan rebels 'protect religion army'—animals dressed in nice clothes; wolves wearing monk's robes]. May 5, 1959, 2.

——. 1959b. "Xizang renmin yongyuan zhongyu zuguo, Lasa liang wan ren kongqian da shiwei, Zai budalagong qian renmen fenfen kongsu panfei de taotian zuixing" [The Tibetan people are forever loyal to the homeland; an unprecedented twenty-thousand people hold rally in Lhasa in front of the Potala Palace; people one after the other denounce the rebels' monstrous crimes]. April 16, 1959, 1–2.

——. 2008. "Renhe pohuai xizang wending, zhizao fenlie de tumou dou zhuding yao shibai" [Any attempt to undermine Tibet's stability and create division is doomed to failure]. March 15, 2008, 4.

Ramble, Charles. 1993. "Whither, Indeed, the Tsampa Eaters." *Himāl* 6 (5): 21–25.

Samuel, Geoffrey. 1976 "Songs of Lhasa." *Ethnomusicology* 20 (3): 407–49.

Wang, Fei-Ling. 2005. *Organizing through Division and Exclusion: China's Hukou System*. Stanford, CA: Stanford University Press.

Xue Wenbo. 1999. *Xueling Chongze*. Vol 2. Lanzhou: Xindaxiao yingchang chubanshe.

Yardley, Jim. 2008. "Violence in Tibet as Monks Clash with the Police." *New York Times*, March 15, 2008, 1.

Yeh, Emily. 2009. "Living Together in Lhasa: Ethnic Relations, Coercive Amity and Subaltern Cosmopolitanism." In *The Other Global City*, edited by Shail Mayaram, 54–85. New York: Routledge.

# MUSLIMS AND POLITICS IN THE SOUTHERN PHILIPPINES

The 2017 War of Marawi

*Patricio N. Abinales*

On May 23, 2017, one thousand "militants" seized the Islamic city of Marawi in the southern Philippine island of Mindanao and held it until the Armed Forces of the Philippines (AFP) liberated the city on October 27. The so-called War of Marawi claimed the lives of 920 militants (including the group's leaders, the brothers Abdullah and Omar Maute), 165 soldiers, and 47 civilians. More than 100,000 families fled the city during the siege, and the AFP rescued 1,790 hostages (Amnesty International 2017). Scholars and journalists described the war as the work of the Maute brothers, who, inspired by the teachings of the Islamic State of Iraq and Syria (ISIS), wanted to establish an ISIS branch in the southern Philippines, with Marawi as its founding center. In this chapter, I examine the war from a different lens—that of the Muslim *datu* politicos who have been the most consistent presence in the political life of Mindanao's Muslims. For nearly five months in 2017, several of these politicians, known as Moros ("Moro" is a pejorative term used by the Spanish that was appropriated by separatist rebels in the 1970s), kept an armed coalition together.

The thousand-strong army led by the Maute brothers was, in fact, a confederacy of armed men and women related to the Maute family in several ways. The Mautes owned property in the area, and they managed a furniture shop, used car and construction businesses in a Butig municipality, south of Marawi, and a commodity trading business in Surabaya, Indonesia. The AFP claimed that the Jemmah Islamiya was using the Indonesian business as a transit point for sending its cadres to Mindanao.

The Mautes had a "private army" composed of uncles, cousins, and even aunts from both sides of the family. Some of the relatives belonged to the Moro National Liberation Front (MNLF) and other relatives had joined its rival, the Moro Islamic Liberation Front (MILF). They readily came to the aid of the brothers upon the request of the brothers' father, Cayamora Maute, himself a former MILF fighter. Units loyal to the MILF's late vice chairman of military affairs also joined out of respect for his second wife, who was a Maute cousin. When journalists asked about these connections, the MILF leadership acknowledged that its commanders in the area and the Mautes "have family ties either by blood or marriage," and that it was inevitable "that some of their fighters decided to help their relatives under military attack" (Zambrano 2016).

If the MILF fighters constituted the Left side of the Maute coalition, the Right side was represented by strongmen and their political clans who acted as feudal lords in their communities. These relatives readily sent their "troops" to Marawi. For example, the Midtimbangs, the bosses of a municipality adjoining that of the Mautes and known major arms traffickers, contributed some of their men to aid their Maute cousins. A former Marawi mayor, Fahad Salic, was arrested and charged with rebellion, on suspicions that he was aiding the Maute brothers—one of his wives was the sister of the matriarch, Farhana Maute (Saliring 2017). Like the Midtimbangs, Fahad and his brother Solitario (another ex-mayor of Marawi) were key players in the lucrative drug trade in the area (*Politiko* 2017).

Then there were the "ideologues"—that is, MILF fighters who were attracted to the Mautes' "idealism" and "bold and daring" actions. These young rebels were increasingly disappointed with their leaders' inability to forge and maintain a permanent peace agreement with the Philippine government (Fonbuena 2017). The MILF's older rival, the MNLF, soon discovered that its own cadres were involved in the fighting or were providing arms. On November 24, 2016, Malaysian authorities arrested Datu Mohammad Abdulijabbar Sema, son of the head of the largest MNLF faction and former mayor of Cotabato City (*Rappler* 2017). Sema was linked to the September 2016 bombing in Davao City, President Rodrigo Duterte's hometown, which the military claimed was the handiwork of the Mautes (Deogracias 2017).

ISIS ideology had only a minimal influence on this coalition of Islamic fundamentalists, drug lords, and insurgents. The Mautes and their followers were able to resist the Philippine army for four months because of the Moro politicos' money and guns. These officials participated in the politics of spoil and patronage, kept their constituents backward and poor, and engaged in the most sacrilegious of trades—selling arms and drugs and trafficking in humans. Although the MILF and ISIS militants were critical of these "traditional leaders," they could do little to oust them, owing to their long and deeply embedded histories in their communities. To understand how the Moro politicos came to dominate the pinnacles of power in Muslim Mindanao and why they were important players in the War of Marawi, it is necessary to review their origins and role in the formation of the Philippine nation-state and the reconfiguration of Mindanao as the country's largest land frontier.

## *"Datu and Mayor"*

Arab trader-missionaries from Hadramut in the Yemen brought Islam to Mindanao in the late fourteenth century (Wolters 1982, 5–9). To encourage mass conversion, they "adjusted" their proselytization efforts by incorporating indigenous beliefs such as ancestor worship and reverence for spirits into Islamic teachings. The Tausug, the largest ethnic group in the Sulu Archipelago, "bent some Moro orthodoxies (for example, the ban on the enslavement of fellow Moros) to local norms when it suited them" (Tagliacozzo 2013, 233). Local sultans and *datus* (the title given to these "men of prowess" in the Southeast Asian maritime region, which includes Mindanao and the Sulu Archipelago), in turn, adopted Islam for its spiritual value, as well as for the commercial opportunities associated with the religion. The missionaries became the mentors of these "men of prowess," teaching them how to navigate across Asia and how to deal with trading partners, military rivals, and, subsequently, Spanish colonizers.

Religious syncretism is a long-standing practice among Mindanao Muslims. The datu is *ima muwallam halipa* (priest) and "caliphal representative [over] the community . . . [who] ruled to establish the judgment of the Islamic religion" (Wolters 1982, 18–19). A powerful datu possesses "charismatic grace" (*baraka*), sexual and military prowess, and power (*daulat* or *dawla*) that allows his "words and commands" (*tita*) to reach "heaven, where they would be heard by the dead as well as the living" (Majul 1973, 16). He is "not much different from the Pope as the head of the Catholic Church, representing God on earth" (Laarhoven 1989, 41).

The Americans fared better than the Spanish did in subjugating the Muslims, mixing superior firepower and offering datus and sultans positions in the new colonial order (Hawkins 2013). They also promised their "Moro wards" that they would respect Islam and not persecute Moros on religious grounds (Jubair 1984, 62). As it turned out, Muslim leaders proved adept in colonial governance, acting as leaders and spokespersons of the community, on the one hand, and as administrative partners of the Americans, on the other. Thus, when Filipino leaders took over the colonial state in the second decade of US rule, Muslim elites readily adjusted to the new rules of the political game. They did so by adding new, modern designations (governor, congressman, mayor) to their older pedigrees (sultan, datu, and *ima muwallam halipa*), reinforcing their local power in the process (Saber 1967).

These hybrid titles carried over into the Philippine Republic Era. In their game of political patronage, the datu politicos used their multiple pedigrees to offer national leaders the solid "Moro vote" that would ensure their electoral victories. In exchange, national leaders gave them control over their territories and a share of state spoils. Datu politicos distributed small portions of state funds to their constituents, who showed their appreciation by voting for these politicians and offering their services when demanded (Abinales 2000, 206).

In the years immediately following World War II, the government kept only a small military and national police force on the island, and the relationship between datu politicos and "their people" was critical in keeping Mindanao stable (Abinales 2020, 200–201). One consequence of this rapprochement was the failure to implement state development projects in Muslim Mindanao; the funds allocated for them always ended up in the pockets of datu politicos. One of these projects was education, a critical tool in facilitating Muslim integration into a nation-state that they did not recognize and into a political system from which they had long been alienated. The creation of a network of primary and secondary schools might have corrected this "bias" by introducing Muslims to a "national history and culture" that included their stories. The schools also might have boosted the Philippine government's legitimacy by teaching young Muslims to read, write, and do arithmetic. The public school system established by the US army when it ruled Moro Mindanao laid a foundation for the "three R's." The new republic, however, did not continue what the army had started. In 1958–1959, "total public high school enrollment in the three provinces [was] only 7,060, representing 2.04 percent of the total school population." By contrast, 17.9 percent of Filipinos between the ages of thirteen and sixteen were enrolled in public secondary schools (Filipinas Foundation 1971, 102).

High illiteracy meant that Muslims learned very little about Philippine history and society, putting a virtual stop to their integration into the postwar body politic. When the state reneged on its civic responsibility, Muslims continued to rely on the only source of knowledge and authority that was accessible—datu politicos—who, in turn, reinforced their influence over their communities. A Muslim public intellectual's 1969 informal survey of people in his communities yielded one interesting response. When asked where they got their news, respondents pointed to their "*datu* and mayor." They gave the same answer when asked to whom they turn to mediate their differences or who gives them advice on economic matters: their "*datu* and mayor" (Glang 1969, 3).

# Diluting Radical Islam

While observers in Manila and elsewhere attribute Muslim Mindanao's insta-bility to the rebellions of the MNLF and the MILF, conflict was mainly due to endemic interclan revenge killings called *rido*. Feuding families engaged in fire-fights over petty disputes such as theft, insults, love affairs, jests, quarrels over land ownership, electoral rivalries, and defense of family honor. When a feud breaks out, everyone is expected to join and defend the clan's interest (Durante et al. 2014, 97–98).

In the 1970s, rido took a backseat to separatist politics. Muslim students who attended the University of the Philippines and al-Azhar University in Egypt were radicalized and formed the MNLF. To stop the Philippine government's geno-cidal campaign against Muslims, the MNLF vowed to separate Mindanao, the Sulu Archipelago, and Palawan Island from the national body politic. The MNLF received weapons from Libya and Malaysia and from the datu politicos whom President Ferdinand Marcos was trying to destroy (Ozerdem 2012, 393–41). A year after Marcos declared martial law, the MNLF launched its war.

The story of the MNLF revolt has been told by several scholars, and there is no need to retell it here (McKenna 1998; George 1980; Gutierrez 2000; Vitug and Gloria 2000). The one aspect of the war germane to this chapter is the fate of the datu politicos. In response to Marcos's campaign to disempower them, the datu politicos forged a military alliance with student radicals and formed the "right wing" of the "liberation" force. This united front did not last long: the regime successfully enticed datu politicos to abandon the radicals in exchange for con-tinuing control over their local bailiwicks (McKenna 1998, 161–63). After Mar-cos was overthrown, datu politicos were able to reclaim their power by switching sides and proclaiming their support for the new government of President Cora-zon Aquino. They consolidated their hold over local politics by taking advan-tage of the Aquino government's program to transfer some of the national agencies to the local level and by increasing local governments' share of the na-tional tax (Abinales and Amoroso 2017, 238–39). The apparatus put in place by Marcos to offer autonomy to the MNLF quickly fell apart. The Autonomous Re-gion for Muslim Mindanao (ARMM) became just another "bureaucratic layer providing little except position and privilege for self-interested Muslim politi-cians" (Lara 2014, 142).

The MNLF was largely a secular movement. Its leaders had been trained in secular state-run universities, and its chairman, Nur Misuari, promised to create a Bangsamoro *Republik*, whose "Declaration of Independence" would commit the MNLF "to the principle of establishing a democratic system of government which shall never allow or tolerate any form of exploitation and oppression of any human being by another or one nation by another nation" (MNLF 1974). Also, the MNLF was supported by republics, not caliphates: the Federation of Malaysia, the United Arab Republic's Gamal Abdel Nasser, and Libya's Muammar Gadhafi.

When MNLF cadres broke away from the organization and formed the MILF, they claimed that the "MNLF leadership [was] manipulated away [sic] from its Islamic basis, methodologies, and objectives and fast-evolving towards a Marxist-Maoist orientation" (Macasalong 2014, 7). They argued that the "ultimate aim of our Jihad is to make supreme the Word of Allah" (Liow 2006, 15). These MILF leaders had been mentored by the Egyptian Islamic reformers Hassan al-Banna and Sayyid Qutb while studying at al-Azhar University, and their commitment was subsequently reaffirmed when they joined the anti-Soviet *mujahidīn* resistance in Afghanistan. When the MILF publicly announced its presence, it had an army of fifteen thousand regulars and ten thousand auxiliaries, led by five hundred Afghan-trained commanders. Its organizational structure paralleled that of the Philippine government (Taya 2007, 63).

The MILF viewed the "traditional leaders" with suspicion. Its ideologue, Salah Jubair, described "traditional leaders" as possessing a "lackluster mentality [that] ultimately led to surrender [and] 'subservience'" (2007, 84–85). After the MILF entered into peace negotiations with the government, however, Jubair changed his tune. While conceding that these "warlord-politicians and vigilantes" used private armies "for highly suspect purposes, including the undermining of the peace process between the MILF and the government," he asserted that these datu politicos supported the peace talks because "in one way or the other . . . [they] stood for Moro rights and aspirations" (Jubair 1984, 144). By adopting the latter position, Jubair acknowledged the limits of the MILF's radicalism (Franco 2016, 170–89). He knew that the organization could not afford to go to war against the datu politicos. The MILF may have had an army of fifteen thousand, but its camps in Central Mindanao were surrounded by the forty-five private armies of its "traditional" rivals (Centre for Humanitarian Dialogue 2011, 24).

The government acknowledged that at "least eight out of every ten private armed groups the police are keeping a close watch on are in the two most volatile regions in Mindanao, the . . . ARMM and Central Mindanao" (Lacorte and Quiros 2016). These private armies were the albatross around the necks of both the MILF and the government. Rido immediately returned to the center of Muslim life. In a 2004 survey, 57 percent of the respondents listed family-involved conflicts as the most important, and between 44 percent and 47 percent reported that these ended in violence. When asked who can resolve these feuds, the respondents answered: their local officials. No one sought the MILF's help (Kamlian 2014, 40–41).

On January 25, 2015, forty-four members of the Philippine National Police's Special Action Force were killed in a clash with an MILF breakaway group, the Bangsamoro Islamic Freedom Fighters. The consequences of what was called the Mamasapano Massacre were immediately palpable: 16 percent of Filipinos nationwide had "much trust" in the Moros, 19 percent were undecided, and 61 percent showed little or no trust in the Moros (*GMA News Online* 2018). Once again, the search for peace in Muslim Mindanao unraveled.

## The "Real Economy" of Mindanao

The staying power of the datu politicos was closely linked to their involvement in Mindanao's illicit trade in pearls, jewelry, television sets, refrigerators, cars, trucks, motorbikes, and guns. In the 1980s, with the addition of heroin, methamphetamine, and Ecstasy, the illicit economy expanded considerably. The clans were flush with government cash when the 1991 Local Government Law mandated that 40 percent of taxes collected be returned to local governments. The combination of smuggled goods, drug money, and the "internal [tax] revenue allocations" made "the capture of local state power . . . more attractive for *datu* elites, [as these] enabled the clans to access the networks, links, and resources that could expand the capital and scope of their underground businesses and illegal operations" (Lara 2014, 165). A leaked cable from the US embassy in Manila warned of the rise of "narco-politics" in Muslim Mindanao. It characterized Lanao del Sur as a province where a "Lucky Seven Club" of mayors oversaw "various illegal activities which included, in addition to drug trafficking, gunrunning, kidnapping, car napping, armed robbery, and selling smuggled merchandise" (Cagoco-Guiam and Schoofs 2016, 113). Filipinos had known about these "narco-politicians" as early as 2012. Five years later, the Mautes declared their jihad.

The Marawi siege was not simply a revolt by Islamic fundamentalists in the name of ISIS. It was a product of a combination of Muslim separatist aspirations, religious zealotry, opioid racketeering, political rivalries, and clan feuds. The datu politicos—the historical glue of Moro society—provided the Maute brothers and their followers with additional firepower that enabled them to resist military attacks for over four months. After Marawi was "freed," Islamic radicalism never regained its footing, leaving these politicians as the sole political force operating in the city and the surrounding municipalities. This is the irony of Muslim politics in the southern Philippines. If the government tries to reduce the datu politicos' power to bring about lasting peace in Moro Mindanao, conflict will break out. If it tolerates these "traditional leaders," electoral rivalries quickly break into rido. If national leaders leave them alone, the datu politicos will expand their share of the profitable drug trade and offer a haven for Islamic fundamentalists. In the end, the national government will have to compromise with these datu politicos to ensure stability in the Mindanao war zone at the expense of perpetuating their never-ending "feudal" dominance.

## REFERENCES

Abinales, Patricio N. 2000. *Making Mindanao: Cotabato and Davao in the Formation of the Philippine Nation-State*. Quezon City: Ateneo de Manila University.

Abinales, Patricio N., and Donna J. Amoroso. 2017. *State and Society in the Philippines*. Lanham, MD: Rowman and Littlefield.

Amnesty International. 2017. *"The Battle of Marawi": Death and Destruction in the Philippines* London: Amnesty International.

Cagoco-Guiam, Rufa, and Steven Schoofs. 2016. "A Deadly Cocktail? Illicit Drugs, Politics and Violent Conflict in Lanao del Sur and Maguindanao." In *Out of the Shadows: Violent Conflict and the Real Economy of Mindanao*, edited by Francisco J. Lara Jr. and Steven Schoofs, 113–54. Quezon City: Ateneo de Manila University Press and International Alert.

Centre for Humanitarian Dialogue. 2011. *Armed Violence in Mindanao: Militia and Private Armies*. Geneva, Switzerland: Centre for Humanitarian Dialogue.

DayangLaylo, Carijane C. 2004. "Conflict Management in the Autonomous Region of Muslim Mindanao." Paper presented at the 4th Regional Conference of the World Association for Public Opinion Research, Asian Institute of Management, Makati, Metropolitan Manila, February 23–24, 2004.

Deogracias, Charmaine. 2017. "Duterte Bestows ISIS Status on Maute Group," *Vera Files,* May 29. https://verafiles.org/articles/duterte-bestows-isis-status-maute -group.

Durante, Ophelia L., Norma T. Gomez, Ester O. Sevilla, and Howard Manego. 2014. "Management of Clan Conflict and Rido among the Tausug, Maguindanao, Maranao, Sama, and Yakan Tribes." In *Rido: Clan Feuding and Conflict Management in Mindanao*, edited by Wilfredo Magno Torres, 90–117. Quezon City: Ateneo de Manila University Press.

Filipinas Foundation. 1971. *An Anatomy of Philippine Muslim Affairs: A Study in Depth of Muslim Affairs in the Philippines*. Makati, Rizal: Filipinas Foundation.

Fonbuena, Carmela. 2017. "MILF, Maute Group Battle for Legitimacy." *Rappler,* July 3, 2017. https://www.rappler.com/newsbreak/in-depth/174531-milf-maute-group -peace-process-marawi-crisis.

Franco, Joseph. 2016. "The Philippines: The Moro Islamic Liberation Front—a Pragmatic Power Structure?" In *Impunity: Countering Illicit Power in War and Transition*, edited by Michelle Hughes and Michael Miklaucic, 171–89. Washington, DC: Center for Complex Operations.

George, T. J. S. 1980. *Revolt in Mindanao: The Rise of Islam in Philippine Politics*. Kuala Lumpur: Oxford University Press.

Glang, Alunan. 1969. *Moro Secession or Integration?* Quezon City: R. P. Garcia.

GMA News Online. 2015. "The Mamasapano Report." March 13, 2015, 72–76. http:// www.gmanetwork.com/news/news/nation/451737/full-report-pnp-board-of -inquiry-report-on-mamasapano-encounter/story/.

Gutierrez, Eric U., ed. 2000. *Rebels, Warlords, and Ulama: A Reader on Muslim Separatism and the War in the Southern Philippines.* Quezon City: Institute for Popular Democracy.

Hawkins, Michael. 2013. *Making Moros: Imperial Historicism and American Military Rule in the Philippines' Muslim South.* DeKalb: Northern Illinois University Press and the Center for Southeast Asian Studies.

Jubair, Salah. 1984. *Bangsamoro: A Nation under Endless Tyranny.* Kuala Lumpur: IQ Marin Sendirian Berhad.

——. 2007. *The Long Road to Peace: Inside the GRP-MILF Peace Process.* Cotabato City: Institute of Bangsamoro Studies.

Kamlian, Jamail A. 2014. "Survey of Feuding Families and Clans in Selected Province in Mindanao." In *Rido: Clan Feuding and Conflict Management in Mindanao,* edited by Wilfredo Magno Torres, 30–43. Quezon City: Ateneo de Manila University Press.

Laarhoven, Ruurdje. 1989. *Triumph of Moro Diplomacy: The Maguindanao Sultanate in the 17th Century.* Quezon City: New Day Publishers.

Lacorte, Germelina, and Judy Quiros. 2016. "PNP: 80% of Private Armies Keep Hideouts in Mindanao." *Inquirer Net,* April 2, 2016.

Lara, Francisco J. 2014. *Insurgents, Clans, and States: Political Legitimacy and Resurgent Conflict in Muslim Mindanao, Philippines.* Quezon City: Ateneo de Manila University Press.

Liow, Joseph Chinyong. 2006. "Muslim Resistance in Southern Thailand and [the] Southern Philippines: Religion, Ideology, and Politics." East-West Center Washington, Policy Studies 24.

Macasalong, Marjanie Salic. 2014. "The Impact of Militancy on Liberation Movements: The Case of Mindanao." *Islamic and Civilisational Renewal* 5 (2): 225–38. https://icrjournal.org/index.php/icr/article/view/404.

Majul, Cesar Adib. 1973. *Moros in the Philippines.* Quezon City: University of the Philippines Press and the Asian Center.

McKenna, Thomas M. 1998. *Muslim Rulers and Rebels: Everyday Politics and Armed Separatism in the Southern Philippines.* Los Angeles: University of California Press.

MNLF (Moro National Liberation Front). 1990. "The Manifesto of the Moro National Liberation Front. April 28, 1974." *Muslim Separatism: The Moros of Southern Philippines and the Malays of Southern Thailand,* by W. K. Che Man, 189–90. Quezon City: Ateneo de Manila University Press.

Ozerdem, Alpaslan. 2012. "The Contribution of the Organisation of the Islamic Conference to the Peace Process in Mindanao." *Civil Wars Journal* 14 (3): 393–413.

*Politiko: The Bible of Philippine Politics.* 2017. "Duterte Drug Matrix: Salic Brothers Control All Drug Trade in Lanao del Sur; Sent Kill Orders against Rival Drug Lords." September 23, 2017. https://politics.com.ph/2017/09/23/duterte-drug-matrix-salic-brothers-control-drug-trade-lanao-del-sur-sent-kill-orders-rival-drug-lords-dealers.

*Rappler.* 2017. "Son of MNLF Leader detained in Malaysia," January 15, 2017. https://www.rappler.com/nation/158380-son-mnlf-leader-detained-malaysia/.

Saber, Mamitua. 1967. "The Transition from a Traditional to a Legal Authority System: A Philippine Case," PhD dissertation, University of Kansas.

Saliring, Alwen. 2017. "Former Marawi City Mayor Arrested for Rebellion." *Sunstar Philippines,* June 8, 2017. https://www.sunstar.com.ph/article/146440.

Tagliacozzo, Eric. 2013. *The Longest Journey: Southeast Asians and the Pilgrimage to Mecca.* New York: Oxford University Press.

Taya, Shamsuddin L. 2007. "The Political Strategies of the Moro Islamic Liberation Front for Self-Determination in the Philippines." *Intellectual Discourse* 15 (1): 59–84.

Vitug, Marites, and Glenda Gloria. 2000. *Under the Crescent Moon: Rebellion in Mindanao.* Quezon City: Ateneo Center for Social Policy and the Institute for Popular Democracy.

Wolters, O. W. 1982. *History, Culture and Region in Southeast Asian Perspectives.* Singapore: Institute of Southeast Asian Studies.

Zambrano, Chiara. 2016. "The Ties That Bind MILF and Maute Group." *ABS-CBN News*, March 3, 2016. https://news.abs-cbn.com/focus/03/03/16/the-ties-that-bind-milf-and-maute-group.

# Part 5

# WALLS, ARCHITECTURE, AND THE OTHER

In the opening chapter, Travis Zadeh reflects on walls as a spatial metaphor that separates "us" from "them" and civilization (the West) from barbarism (Islam), noting that walls are a common trope in the eschatological narratives of Judaism, Christianity, and Islam. The wall metaphor, he argues, is an ideological tool used to identify groups and to keep them separate from one another. The idea that Muslims must be contained behind a wall has a long history upon which the author muses by reflecting on Edward Said's *Orientalism* (1979) and HBO's *Game of Thrones* (2020). As the power of the West increased vis-à-vis the Muslim world, Westerners promoted a triumphalist narrative in which walls serve as a trope to associate Muslims with decline, stagnation, and superstition. Zadeh calls on scholars "to confront the ideational quality of spatial thinking, its immateriality, and its often fictitious, if factitive, nature."

In the second chapter, Angela Andersen argues that the modern Turkish state uses the visual rhetoric of architecture to convey a message about religious ideology and national identity. Since 1923, when Turkey achieved independence under Kamalist rule, the state has attempted to exercise control over all aspects of religion and society, including the Alevis, a religious minority that numbers between fifteen and twenty million people. The Turkish Republic views this minority with suspicion, and, over the past one hundred years, the state has refused to support Alevi *cemevi*s (houses of worship) at the same time that it underwrites the design, construction, and maintenance of Sunni mosques. The unstated goal of this policy, Andersen concludes, is to promote the primacy of Sunnism by marginalizing Alevi beliefs, practices, and ceremonial spaces. At present, the cemevi has become a symbol of resistance to the suppression of Alevism, to state-administered religious practices, and to the rhetoric of what Andersen calls "mosque culture."

Whereas the West uses the wall trope to associate Muslims with decline, stagnation, and superstition, the Turkish state uses architecture and the built environment to marginalize its Alevi minority.

# WALLS, WONDER, AND THE EDGES OF THE MUSLIM WORLD

*Travis Zadeh*

There is something that does love a wall. Our political horizons brim with them. So do our fantasies. For years, nativist crowds chanted "Build the wall" at rallies and demonstrations, while millions of viewers followed *Game of Thrones*, George R. R. Martin's medieval epic that has as one of its central plot lines a sprawling wall of stone and ice guarded by both men and magical spells, separating the living from the dead.

In a time marked by increasing identitarianism, it is not entirely surprising to encounter walls erected in our politics and entertainment. Not too long ago, politicians and pundits started to debate what the Middle Ages could teach us about the efficacy of walls, in response to a US president who asserted that fortifications along the southern border offered a tested defensive strategy taken from the medieval past (Gabriele 2019; Petri 2019). Where "the political suffuses the ordinary," one may well find a certain pessimism and cruelty beholding the storied proscenium of politics as theater and theater as politics (Berlant 2011, 230; Hsu 2019).

The medievalism of today's white supremacists takes its cues from the social nationalism of European fascists who also found the medieval to be a generative repertoire (Chan 2017; Gluckman 2017; Kim 2017; Schuessler 2019; cf. Utz 2017, 39–52). Like Hydra, the many-headed serpent, such medievalism takes numerous shapes. Neo-Nazis celebrate their militarism in the honor of Vikings and Crusaders, while the press, foreign policy analysts, and politicians regularly characterize jihadi militants, as well as ordinary Muslims, as motivated by a barbaric and medieval ideology—equated, in certain quarters, with monsters beyond the gates

(Pinfari 2019, 101–21). Many US legal authorities and ideologues who justified the use of torture at the beginning of the Global War on Terrorism premised their arguments on the grounds that medieval brutality was sadly necessary as Muslims only understood the language of violence (Holsinger 2007, 2016; Spiegel 2008; Sheehi 2011).

The forward progress implied in the historiography of the Middle Ages is designed to mark off the limits of civilization. It is in this context of boundary making that white supremacists and nativists wave their banners and pound their shields as self-appointed guardians of civilization, protecting the nation and the homeland against an onslaught of religious and racial others. Inversely, as a mechanism for defining the West, this particular temporal progression also lends conceptual ballast to the Muslim world as a coherent spatial category. The epoch-marking terms of enlightenment and modernity serve to affirm the supremacy of Western rationality, which has awoken from a stupor of medieval ignorance and superstition.

The medieval provides a specific teleology that leads through the Renaissance, the Age of Exploration, and the Enlightenment and culminates in modernity. The argument goes that as Muslims did not enjoy these stages of history, they remain, in some basic sense, in the throes of medieval darkness. The normalization of Islamophobia in political discourses across the world is merely one measure of a heightened attention to solidifying external boundaries. In the social imaginary of liberalism as an ideology of the secular and the democratic, Islam has played a shadowy archenemy, veiled in countless images of fanaticism, irrational traditionalism, and tyrannical oppression (Massad 2015; Devji and Kazmi 2019; cf. Al-Azmeh 1993, 11–12, 24–26).

These oppositional structures unfold not so much in geography but in the contours of the imagination. Like all ideological configurations, the boundaries of Western civilization are products of the mind and thus must be cultivated and asserted, generation after generation. This is true not only for the territorial or conceptual coherence of either the West or Europe but also for the very idea of civilization itself (Asad 2003, 172; Mazlish 2004). As with group formation in general, the common vocabulary, heritage, symbols, and ideology said to compose Western civilization must be continually restated and reaffirmed. This boundary work marks Muslims as quintessentially unintegrated and inadmissible (Zadeh 2021).

In the grand historical narratives that condition the possibilities of collective thought, the metonym that sets Islam against the West offers an evident and transparent postulate for self-definition. The juxtaposition generates an endless series of interrogations: Is Islam fundamentally hostile? Can Muslims be assimilated? Will they seek to implement Sharia law? Do they hate freedom? Can they have fun? Often posed as headlines, these queries animate our news, entertainment, and the language of domestic and foreign policy. It is a logic that resists any manner of synthesis. Here, as elsewhere, this definitional grammar conditions the contours of what can be thought or articulated. Importantly, such rhetoric need not have an actual relation to any particular group, body, practice, or belief to be politically powerful or motivating.

In addition to specific locations and ways of knowing, the conceptual borderlands drawn around the West are rooted in discrete visions of history. Our present is shaped not only by the material conditions of our past but also by the particular ways of invoking, imagining, and locating it. Theories to account for a great divergence, where Western powers emerged as hegemons of the world in political, economic, and technological terms, often proceed with triumphalist postures of exceptionalism mixed with thin stories of Oriental decline, stagnation, and superstition. Rather than interrogating the material and historically contingent factors that made the global conquest of capital possible, much time has been spent pondering the essential primitivism of the conquered and the unique genius of the triumphant (e.g., Huff 1993; Ferguson 2011).

In performative terms, it is here helpful to think of the notion of disqualification as a means of interrogating the "political forces, social cues, and moral virtues" that produce qualified knowledge, while also marginalizing other ways of knowing (Foucault 1980, 82–86; Gandhi 1998, 43; Stoler 2002a, 159–60; 2002b, 95). To recognize that knowledge systems are also evaluative invites a fuller engagement with the ethical implications and material conditions that govern the production and consumption of scholarly labor. In this current political landscape drenched in nativism, speaking out against Islamophobia is certainly a noble and necessary task.

Inversely, we would be naive not to acknowledge that a good measure of modern scholarship produced on Islam within the Western academy is motivated by a desire to combat Salafi radicalism and its own appropriations of Islamic history. Observing such motivations, stated or unstated, may help to historicize the values governing the language of academic and scientific objectivity (Daston and Galison 2007). Scholarship is always invested in specific evaluative systems. These values are not only historically conditioned; they are also constantly unfolding.

The often pithy narratives that condition how we come to view history as a "collective, singular subject" are intertwined with specific ethical and epistemic frameworks for understanding being, agency, and the possibilities of human flourishing. The secular frame of a disenchanted physical universe serves as one of the primary postulates for modern historical reasoning. The professional discipline of history has dispensed with any effort to read divine will in the annals of human strife. Such logic predicates both history and literature as consummately secular modes of viewing and fathoming the world (Asad 2003, 41–43). But the posture of disenchantment for both historical endeavors and social critique produces its own forms of estrangement that can make fathoming all the varieties of wonder and rarity that we encounter in the past and the present rather vexing.

# The Containment of Wonder

One response to this dilemma can be seen in efforts to "re-enchant, if not the world, at least the historical profession." This is precisely the terrain covered by Caroline Walker Bynum, who turns for inspiration to the medieval Latin history of wonder, not as a form of assimilation, conquest, or possession but rather as a "cognitive, perspectival, non-appropriative, and deeply respectful" mode for appreciating "the specificity of the world." In a compellingly crafted argument, Bynum concludes that this particular configuration of wonder, from its Latin roots in *admiratio*, should be the special concern of the historian. And yet, she is quick to recognize that history writing is always situated and perspectival and that such awareness may shatter "the possibility of writing any coherent account of the world" (Bynum 1997, 2, 24–25).

To be sure, the posture of detachment, of wondering at a distance, can easily turn attention away from the material means, social mechanisms, and contextual specificity by which knowledge is produced in the present. The illusion of scholarly neutrality and disinterest is designed to obtain authority through objective distance. These paratexts are no less strange and awe-inspiring, as they animate not only what we study and why, but how we go about doing so.

Early in the written record, wonder, as a form of perplexity and curiosity, came to represent a prime means for fathoming the world and our place in it. This theme is frequently traced back to Plato and his famed student Aristotle, who famously opens the *Metaphysica* with the argument that wonder arises out of a curiosity to uncover the puzzles of existence, leading from curiosity to contemplation and ultimately concluding with knowledge of truth. This idea, as Bynum and others have demonstrated, has a lasting influence in Latinate discourses on wonder as an affective disposition (Llewelyn 2001).

Yet similar statements can also be made about the epistemic and aesthetic influence of Aristotelian *thaumazein* in the formative development of Arabic philosophy. Amazement, perplexity, and wonder as the basis for obtaining wisdom animate a good deal of early Arabic writings on knowledge, nature, and being. Such wonder talk not only shapes classical Arabic and Persian letters but also runs throughout Islamic theodicy, philosophical optimism, natural history, and occult learning. There is a case to be made that as a means for conceptualizing the world, the language of wonders and rarities (ʿajāʾib-o-gharāʾib) functions as one of the primary aesthetic and cognitive methods for ordering the broad historical contours of Islamic thought, from the full array of sciences and arts to the very constitution of the cosmos.

Merely drawing attention to these areas of conceptual confluence is not to paper over the many points of divergence. Consider, for instance, the famed philosopher-physician Ibn Sīnā, who notably places a psychological emphasis on the mind's sensation of astonishment (taʿajjub) as aroused by the imitative quality of image-evoking statements. Further, Ibn Sīnā views imitation (muḥākāt) as a source of aesthetic pleasure. Such a line of argumentation locates wonder as a psychological response related to the faculty of representation (al-quwwa al-mutakhayyila), the cognitive faculty that is the site of phantasia in the Aristotelian tradition of the psyche or soul. For Ibn Sīnā, imitation possesses an element of amazement (taʿjīb) that truth or authenticity lacks—a sentiment drawn from his own reading of Aristotelian poetics and psychology (Zadeh 2010, 42–43; Harb 2020, 93–97). By contrast, Bynum suggests that medieval Christian theologians sought to separate admiratio from imitatio, often out of broader concerns regarding Christological devotion (Bynum 2001, 52–53). In comparative terms, the extent to which this tension between absorbing and admiring at a distance actually bears true for the history of wonder as a cognitive state, as an emotive response, and even as a prelude to pleasure or possession certainly deserves further attention.

On close inspection, it would appear, contrary to what Bynum suggests, that there is a good deal in medieval Latin discourses on wonderment and the mysteries of nature that is indeed concerned not only with cataloguing and explaining—and thereby exerting epistemic control over—but also with possessing and manipulating the full array of phenomena diffused throughout the cosmos (Eamon 1994, 38–90; Truitt 2015, 12–39). The storied adventures of Alexander the Great, who is known in Arabic Hermetic literature as a master of perfect nature (al-ṭibāʿ al-tāmm), provide a concise inventory for this variety of wonder as an articulation of imperial desire, if also an emotive impetus with therapeutic and practical ends. Cast as a natural philosopher, the world conqueror Alexander is a frequent guide in classical Arabic and Persian to ingenious devices and the wonders of creation, as he is in Greek and Latin. His famed teacher Aristotle dutifully records the special properties (khawāṣṣ) of sundry substances that Alexander uncovered on his conquests. The wonderous and strange properties hidden throughout existence were generally known in Latin as qualitates occultae; they were frequently catalogued, mined, extracted, tested, and consumed in compendiums of natural history and the secrets of creation that promote wonder very much as a prelude to possession. Wonders were not just far from home at the margins of existence; they could be encountered through all manner of quotidian fare, stretching through the cosmos from the gnat's wings to the daily motions of the planets.

It was Galen, after all, who turned to the wonders (*thaumata* in Greek, translated as *ʿajāʾib* in Arabic) of human anatomy in a paean to the perfect wisdom (*sophia/ḥikma*) of a divine creator, in true teleological fashion. It is this sensibility that leads the Persian natural philosopher al-Qazwīnī, following the theologian al-Ghazālī before him, to argue that wonder does not end by merely uncovering the cause behind a given phenomenon, as Aristotle would appear to have had it. Rather, beholding the innumerable wonders of creation is a basis for ethical discipline and spiritual pursuit. Such a contemplative practice leads to a greater appreciation of divine wisdom by seeking to continually see the world anew (Zadeh 2023).

Needless to say, writings on natural wonders circulated widely in countless languages—translated, repurposed, expanded, absorbed, and consumed. There is much in these elite, pre-industrial formations of philosophy, natural hierarchy, and imperial history that made them intelligible and interchangeable. Yet there is also a good deal of difference. Certainly, distinct theological and ideological commitments framed the various means of engaging this broader universe of ideas.

While strange creatures, often referred to as *gharāʾib*, populate Arabic and Persian collections of natural wonders, they generally abide in a world where evil has no ontological foundation in metaphysics, coded within a larger cosmology of Islamic theodicy of divine perfection and order. Yes, there are savages and all manner of beasts and barbarians. But this spectrum of difference represents a notable contrast to the various ideas of monstrosity that develop in Latin Christendom and then are transposed onto Africa, Asia, and the New World (Davies 2016, 13–17, 30–39). Thus, when confronting hybrid forms of animals and humans found throughout history, from Herodotus and Pliny to al-Qazwīnī and Mandeville and beyond, we should ask not only are they races, as they are frequently called today (Mittman 2015), but also are they truly monstrous, in the sense of uniformly representing baleful and unnatural deformity. It turns out that as categories, monsters and monstrosity are not nearly as universal or static as the modern scholarly usage that follows after them would suggest (Wengrow 2014, 108–12). Similarly, while there is much to be said about shared languages of bigotry, xenophobia, and climatic determinism, classical Islamic discourses, in all their variety, do not follow the same historical patterns or evaluative frameworks that give birth to the modern category of race (Gandhi 2022; cf. Anidjar 2015).

Yet, there remain numerous areas of conceptual overlap that put Arabic and Persian writings in conversation with a much broader array of ideas—wonderment

**FIGURE 12.1.** Voyages of Sir John Mandeville, in a collection composed circa 1410, known as *Livre des merveilles du monde*, Bibliothèque nationale de Paris, MS Français 2810, fol. 210a, featured in Bynum (1997, 25) as "Men carrying a western Marvel, the barnacle goose born from trees, meet wise men from the East bearing their comparable marvel, the vegetable lamb."

is merely one among many (Karnes 2015, 2022). Today to discuss the history of wonder as a prerequisite of philosophy without gesturing to developments beyond the confines of Latin Christendom is to risk a certain provincialism. To be sure, Bynum does evoke the wonders of the East, long part of a wider imagined geography. But as in the texts that contain them, Easterners, even when wise, are addressed largely as foils to the strange practices "back home" or as uncanny vehicles for wonders and themselves as objects of curiosity (figure 12.1). Even though they may well share an equivalent economy of marvels, the vocabulary of their wonderment and their intellectual capacity to deploy it, even when used for similar ends, are left ignored. Rather, Latin Christendom is used as the grounds for generalization, offered as the conceptual inspiration for the historian to re-enchant the profession through a wonderment that is both a mode and a method of historical inquiry. In less generous hands, such a narrow focus on Western Christians as agents of thought and emotion worthy of our exclusive attention and theoretical elaboration can lead to rather parsimonious treatments of intellectual and social history that occult from view contiguous and overlapping fields of concern. Such genealogies easily reinforce the false notion that ancient Greek learning was the unique prerogative of Europe or that Jews, Christians, and Muslims have occupied radically distinct ethical and intellectual worlds.

## Fantastic Entertainments

Even for those not so sanguine about the potential of wonder to apprehend without absorbing, there are numerous reasons to contemplate the power of wonderment as a cognitive sensibility and emotive disposition, in addition to its significance as an organizing area of inquiry (Hughes-Warrington 2019). The present-minded among us cannot miss how the strange, horrific, and grotesque shape popular culture and mass media. Yet, while etymologically related to the Greek *phantasia*, it would be a categorical solecism to view the conceptual labor of the fantastic today as neatly analogous to the classical conceptions of the imagination. Historically, the words *phantasma*, *takhyīl*, and *dimyon*, in Greek, Arabic, and Hebrew, respectively, are connected not only to a particular psychology of the soul, but also to a shared cosmology populated by demons, spirits, and angels, where microcosm and macrocosm are interconnected in the emanating power of a divine intellect spread throughout all existence, from the rays of the stars to the minerals spread throughout the earth.

Here the vocabulary of high-level Islamic metaphysics has a good deal to offer in the appeal to *al-umūr al-gharība*, strange, uncanny, weird, paranormal, extraordinary phenomena. It is a key category in Ibn Sīnā's natural philosophy, used as a basis to explain in scientific terms both magic and miracle; it also forms the theoretical backing to the category of the extraordinary sciences (*al-ʿulūm al-gharība*) frequently equated today, not unproblematically, with the "occult sciences" (Zadeh 2020, 614–24). In this repertoire of wonder and rarity, the value of the marvel to behold lies in its veridical ontological status, or the "there-ness" of any given phenomenon, as Bynum evocatively refers to it.

Contrast these discourses of the marvelous with the vertiginous subgenres of modern fantasy and science fiction filled with dragons, nymphs, and witches, along with aliens, mummies, mutants, and zombies. Supernatural wonders populate the fictive universes of our screens and printed pages. In the course of global industrialization and the vast circulation of memetic capital, these new forms of alternative worldmaking have found expression in countless languages and societies (e.g., Campbell 2018; Knickerbocker 2018). In many ways these wonderous worlds enchant for reasons that are quite distinct from earlier historical modes of fathoming existence. As an organizing principle, the modern variety of the fantastic is indelibly shaped by the values of fiction and the romantic notions of genius and the imagination that accompany its rise. The word "genius" notably provides a concise metric for measuring these historical changes, transforming from the Latin *genii*, or guardian spirits—themselves parallel to the *daimones* of Greek cosmology—into a secularized, even if re-enchanted, vision of individual ingenuity, creativity, and originality (Asad 2003, 50–52).

Book after book, film after film conjure up marvelous worlds as entertainment to be consumed in delight and diversion—in a series of alternative possibilities to the normal, quotidian, and predictable. In contrast to other models of wonder, the question of veridical status is generally not as important as the awe-inspiring spectacle of difference itself. Worldmaking has long been the coin of capital, for both imaginative endeavors and the extractive industries that condition modern consumption. Worlds of fantasy are served as salves to tedium, boredom, and isolation. Far from the seemingly intractable problems offered by the theater of everyday politics—environmental degradation, global pandemics, economic and racial inequalities, ongoing wars, gun violence, the rise of ethnonationalism—there is always a chance to escape it all through exotic travels across remote lands of time and space. Sublimated expressions of communal fears and desires, these otherworldly fascinations appear to speak back, as it were, to the disenchanting forces of a mechanized universe governed by the transparency of measured reason that has all but failed us.

We are now reminded with some frequency that the secular disenchantment of society is as much a myth as is the claim to modern rationality (Latour 1993; Partridge 2004–2005; Josephson-Storm 2017). Interest in the paranormal forms part of an increasing and renewed cultural value placed on such esoteric arts as astrology, New Age spirituality, and paganism (Kripal 2010, 2011). Although rejected in the dustbin of Enlightenment rationality, esotericism has important predecessors well before its rise in nineteenth-century transcendental thought (Hanegraaff 1996, 2012; Schmidt 2000; Saif 2019). A good deal of esoteric thinking in Latin Christendom came to derive its authority from a body of occult writing that circulated in the East, prominently in Greek, Hebrew, Arabic, and Persian.

The Orient has long been mined as a textual and ethnographic source of ancient wisdom and hidden knowledge. The stories of the *Arabian Nights*, in their gothic mazes and lairs, are important parties to the ongoing fascination with the imaginative powers to conjure and transform. The price of admission promises incantations, magical seal rings, flying carpets, and genies who can deliver harems of delight and horrific scenes of dismemberment in the wink of an eye. It is this sensibility of the Orient that pervades Wojciech Has's *Saragossa Manuscript* (1965), with its macabre scenes of enchantresses and erotic deceptions. The enticements and horrors of the East proceed along the push and pull of attraction and repulsion, as in the arabesque conceit that guides film noir—a viewer who is seduced into the action, only to be consumed and annihilated, both ethi-cally and corporally.

As a mode of entertainment, these modern enchantments respond to con-tinuing social demands for the spectacle of different worlds and ways of being. The uncanny landscapes summoned up are tantalizing, horrifying, racialized, and gendered all at once (Lavender 2014, 2017). They project reflections of self and other across imaginary geographies of difference, with all our present con-cerns of identity and politics thinly transformed into myth and metaphor. In a mesmerizing logic befitting Scheherazade, the markets of the imagination are moved by a collective desire for greater wonder and diversion. Today, the con-ceptual boundaries that guide these fascinations with the fantastic and paranor-mal are still usually set off at an oblique angle from the abiding authority of science, religion, history, and the general parameters of reality itself. Well be-fore our era of post-truth politics, the tension between the real and the unreal has offered a basis for both critique and consumption.

## Territory's End

Containment is an old strategy. Traces of the past remain in mammoth stone ramparts and impressive fortifications, as well as more modest boundary mark-ers and trenches that line the globe. Walls are not only built but also commem-orated. The memorialization of city ramparts and temple blocks stretches back to the earliest written records. Akkadian and Sumerian cuneiform tablets praise in epic form King Gilgamesh tending the city walls of Uruk (Damrosch 2007). Within the gates of the city, the walls of the temple mark the cosmic lines that generate sacred space. As with Hadrian's wall and the wall of China, these ar-chaeological remains reflect the very durable power of the wall as a symbol of territorial demarcation and epistemic control.

Yet beyond such generational, physical labor, walls also line the imagination as an ideological basis for fathoming human history. This can be seen in the di-viding lines that we impose neatly onto epochs and ages from antiquity through modernity to fathom history as discrete metonymic units of progress. Walls hold together so many of the myths we tell. The Freemasons were not the first to de-velop a Hermetic fascination with temples or ancient architects. Indeed, the story of Hermes, as the master mason and prophet of wisdom who teaches humanity the arts and sciences, travels widely beyond the Mediterranean and Mesopota-mia. The same holds true for Alexander the Great, the world conqueror whose feats have been celebrated in countless ages and tongues and whose name has long been associated with a particularly well-known barrier.

The episode of Alexander's wall to contain Gog and Magog crosses the East and the West in Arabic, Armenian, Ethiopic, Greek, Hebrew, Persian, Turkish, Syriac, and Urdu, not to mention the full array of languages written in Latin Christendom. Variously told, Alexander the conqueror, student of Aristotle, master of perfect nature, curious collector of wonders and rarities, journeys north to the edge of the inhabitable world on a godly mission. Sealing off the tribes of Gog and Magog behind a giant mountain barrier, Alexander succeeds in saving the world from savages set to devour humanity. Alexander's wall marks an outer boundary beyond which habitation and knowledge end.

The belief in an ancient, impenetrable barrier features in various forms of Christian, Jewish, and Muslim eschatology. Making their appearance in both the Bible and the Qur'an, Gog and Magog also surface in a sizable body of exegetical literature, parenetic prose, and geographical discourse. Protected by both guardians and talismans, the line against the others represents a shared idiom for conceptualizing space and territory, contained in cartographic terms quite literally at the edges of the world. As an ominous symbol, the scene, as with many others taken from prophetic and imperial history, came to feature as part of a standard repertoire in Islamic divinatory texts and images (Farhad and Bağci 2009, 25, 34, 152–53; see figure 12.2). Come the end of time, these savage tribes will break through the barrier, to spread across the world as hoards bent on destroying everything in sight. Like the language of wonder, or Ibn Sīnā's regimes of medicine and philosophy, the myth of the Alexandrian rampart spreads across diverse regions of the globe. Transported, adapted, assimilated, and retold, Alexander's adventures represent a shared horizon for conceiving the world and our place in it in cosmic terms (Zadeh 2011; Silverstein 2014; Akasoy 2016a, 2016b).

Conceptually, the barrier of Gog and Magog also exhibits many obvious parallels with the wall of Westeros in *Game of Thrones*, which protects the land of the Seven Kingdoms against the wildlings, armies of ravenous skeleton-zombies, and white walker overlords. Both walls guard humanity from apocalyptic destruction. Yet, for much of its history, Alexander's rampart was generally not valued as fantasy or fiction. The power of the wall and the numerous tales about it lies in its veridical "there-ness," as a physical edifice bottling up actual savages.

In the gap that separates Gog and Magog from the undead wights at the gates of Westeros is the space where fantasy, in its modern form, abides. The ancient myth of savages behind a wall can be torn down, ridiculed, and rejected as a primitive emblem of the ignorance and superstition that clouded the world before the totality of the globe and its two hemispheres became fully realized. And in the ceaseless configurations of "myth as ideology in narrative form" (Lincoln 1999), the story can also be recast along the enchanted landscapes of modern fantasy. The barriers against Gog and Magog and the creatures beyond the

**FIGURE 12.2.** Alexander (Iskandar) in conversation with the prophets Khiḍr and Elijah (Ilyās), while demons and men build a wall against Gog and Magog from a dispersed *Fāl-nāma* (Book of divination) for Shāh Ṭahmāsp (d. 1576). © The Trustees of the Chester Beatty Library, Dublin. Reprinted courtesy of Chester Beatty, CBL Per 395.2.

Seven Kingdoms of Westeros prove quite useful—if only as metonyms for measuring the conceptual distance between the disciplines that govern modern reason and the geographies and metaphysics that fashioned the world before the global spread of capital.

Such spatial thinking, it turns out, also reveals a good deal about how Islam as a discursive tradition functions territorially in the social imagination. Like the West, the modern conceit of the Muslim world offers a coherent and self-evident way of viewing the geopolitical present. The concept of a Muslim world that is neatly cordoned off has been remarkably productive. It is an immanently pliable idea employed by both detractors and advocates. Its territorial transparency has appealed to numerous reformists who have promoted Muslim unity as the basis for various pan-regional identities (Grewal 2013; Cemil 2017). For Islamophobes, by contrast, the coherence of its boundaries provides a conceptual framework to direct fear and hatred.

At a very basic level, the dilemma posed by such spatial binaries is amplified by the dialectic quality of language and the numerous forms of deixis—of I and you and here and there—that structure collective thought and action (Hanks 2011). Definitional logic of the in-crowd / out-crowd variety tends to govern both small and large-scale group formations (Sapolsky 2019). In order to critique the map, we must first confront the ideational quality of spatial thinking, its immateriality, and its often fictitious, if factive, nature. To do so is to witness the complexities of being located in space and of being named in language. It is to recognize that while the meaning of the barrier at the edge of the map may shift over time, its power to captivate, contain, and condition is no less real.

## REFERENCES

Akasoy, Anna. 2016a. "Geography, History and Prophecy: Mechanisms of Integration in the Islamic Alexander Legend." In *Locating Religions: Contact, Diversity and Translocality*, edited by Nikolas Jaspert and Reinhold Glei, 16–36. Leiden: Brill.
——. 2016b. "Iskandar the Prophet: Religious Themes in Islamic Versions of the Alexander Legend." In *Globalization of Knowledge in the Mediterranean World of Post-Antiquity, 700–1500*, edited by Sonja Brentjes and Jürgen Renn, 167–204. New York: Routledge.
Al-Azmeh, Aziz. 1993. *Islams and Modernities*. London: Verso.
Anidjar, Gil. 2015. "The History of Race, the Race of History." *Jewish Quarterly Review* 105 (4): 515–21.
Asad, Talal. 2003. *Formations of the Secular: Christianity, Islam, Modernity*. Stanford, CA: Stanford University Press.
Berlant, Lauren. 2011. *Cruel Optimism*. Durham, NC: Duke University Press.
Bynum, Caroline Walker. 1997. "Wonder." *American Historical Review* 102 (1): 1–26.
——. 2001. *Metamorphosis and Identity*. New York: Zone Books.
Campbell, Ian. 2018. *Arabic Science Fiction*. Cham, Switzerland: Palgrave MacMillan.
Cemil, Aydin. 2017. *The Idea of the Muslim World*. Cambridge, MA: Harvard University Press.

Chan, J. Clara. 2017. "Medievalists, Recoiling from White Supremacy, Try to Diversify the Field." *Chronicle of Higher Education* 63 (42): A3.

Damrosch, David. 2007. *The Buried Book: The Loss and Rediscovery of the Great Epic of Gilgamesh*. New York: Henry Holt.

Daston, Lorraine, and Peter Galison. 2007. *Objectivity*. New York: Zone Books.

Davies, Surekha. 2016. *Renaissance Ethnography and the Invention of the Human: New Worlds, Maps, and Monsters*. Cambridge: Cambridge University Press.

Devji, Faisal, and Zaheer Kazmi, eds. 2019. *Islam after Liberalism*. Oxford: Oxford University Press.

Eamon, William. 1994. *Science and the Secrets of Nature: Books of Secrets in Medieval and Early Modern Culture*. Princeton, NJ: Princeton University Press.

Farhad, Massumeh, and Serpil Bağci. 2009. *Falnama: The Book of Omens*. Washington, DC: Smithsonian Institution.

Ferguson, Niall. 2011. *Civilization: The West and the Rest*. New York: Penguin Press.

Foucault, Michel. 1980. *Power/Knowledge: Selected Interviews and Other Writings, 1972–1977*. Edited by Colin Gordon. Hertfordshire: Harvester Press.

Gabriele, Matthew. 2019. "Trump Says Medieval Walls Worked. They Didn't." *Washington Post*, January 10, 2019.

Gandhi, Leela. 1998. *Postcolonial Theory: A Critical Introduction*. Edinburgh: Edinburgh University Press.

Gandhi, Supriya. 2022. "Locating Race in Mughal India." *Renaissance Quarterly* 75 (4): 1180–220.

Gluckman, Nell. 2017. "A Debate about White Supremacy and Medieval Studies Exposes Deep Rifts in the Field." *Chronicle of Higher Education* 64 (4): 43.

Grewal, Zareena. 2013. *Islam Is a Foreign Country: American Muslims and the Global Crisis of Authority*. New York: New York University Press.

Hanegraaff, Wouter. 1996. *New Age Religion and Western Culture: Esotericism in the Mirror of Secular Thought*. Leiden: E. J. Brill.

——. 2012. *Esotericism and the Academy: Rejected Knowledge in Western Culture*. Cambridge: Cambridge University Press.

Hanks, William. 2011. "Deixis and Indexicality." In *Foundations of Pragmatics*, edited by Wolfram Bublitz and Neal R. Norrick, 315–46. Berlin: De Gruyter.

Harb, Lara. 2020. *Arabic Poetics Aesthetic Experience in Classical Arabic Literature*. Cambridge: Cambridge University Press.

Holsinger, Bruce. 2007. *Neomedievalism, Neoconservatism, and the War on Terror*. Chicago: Prickly Paradigm.

——. 2016. "Neomedievalism and International Relations." In *The Cambridge Companion to Medievalism*, edited by Louise D'Arcens, 165–79. Cambridge: Cambridge University Press.

Hsu, Hua. 2019. "Affect Theory and the New Age of Anxiety." *New Yorker*, March 25, 2019, 61–65.

Huff, Toby. 1993. *The Rise of Early Modern Science: Islam, China, and the West*. Cambridge: Cambridge University Press.

Hughes-Warrington, Marnie. 2019. *History as Wonder: Beginning with Historiography*. New York: Routledge.

Josephson-Storm, Jason. 2017. *The Myth of Disenchantment: Magic, Modernity, and the Birth of the Human Sciences*. Chicago: University of Chicago Press.

Karnes, Michelle. 2015. "Marvels in the Medieval Imagination." *Speculum* 90 (2): 327–65.

——. 2022. *Medieval Marvels and Fictions in the Latin West and Islamic World*. Chicago: University of Chicago Press.

Kim, Dorothy. 2017. "Teaching Medieval Studies in a Time of White Supremacy." In the Middle, August 28, 2017. https://www.inthemedievalmiddle.com/2017/08/teaching-medieval-studies-in-time-of.html.

Knickerbocker, Dale, ed. 2018. *Lingua Cosmica: Science Fiction from around the World.* Urbana: University of Illinois Press.

Kripal, Jeffrey. 2010. *Authors of the Impossible: The Paranormal and the Sacred.* Chicago: University of Chicago Press.

——. 2011. *Mutants and Mystics: Science Fiction, Superhero Comics, and the Paranormal.* Chicago: University of Chicago Press.

Latour, Bruno. 1993. *We Have Never Been Modern.* Translated by Catherine Porter. Cambridge, MA: Harvard University Press.

Lavender, Isiah, III, ed. 2014. *Black and Brown Planets: The Politics of Race in Science Fiction.* Jackson: University Press of Mississippi.

——, ed. 2017. *Dis-orienting Planets: Racial Representations of Asia in Science Fiction.* Jackson: University Press of Mississippi.

Lincoln, Bruce. 1999. *Theorizing Myth: Narrative, Ideology, and Scholarship.* Chicago: University of Chicago Press.

Llewelyn, John. 2001. "On the Saying That Philosophy Begins in Thaumazein." *Afterall: A Journal of Art, Context and Enquiry* 4:48–57.

Massad, Joseph. 2015. *Islam in Liberalism.* Chicago: University of Chicago Press.

Mazlish, Bruce. 2004. *Civilization and Its Contents.* Stanford, CA: Stanford University Press.

Mittman, Asa Simon. 2015. "Are the 'Monstrous Races' Races?" *postmedieval* 6 (1): 36–51.

Partridge, Christopher. 2004–2005. *The Re-enchantment of the West: Alternative Spiritualities, Sacralization, Popular Culture, and Occulture.* 2 vols. London: T and T Clark International.

Petri, Alexandra. 2019. "Medieval Things Still Work Fine!" *Washington Post,* January 12, 2019.

Pinfari, Marco. 2019. *Terrorists as Monsters: The Unmanageable Other from the French Revolution to the Islamic State.* New York: Oxford University Press.

Saif, Liana. 2019. "What Is Islamic Esotericism?" *Correspondences* 7 (1): 1–59.

Sapolsky, Robert. 2019. "This Is Your Brain on Nationalism: The Biology of Us and Them." *Foreign Affairs* 98, no. 2 (March/April): 42–47.

Schmidt, Leigh Eric. 2000. *Hearing Things: Religion, Illusion, and the American Enlightenment.* Cambridge, MA: Harvard University Press.

Schuessler, Jennifer. 2019. "Symbols of Past Used by Right Upset Scholars." *New York Times,* May 5, 2019, A1.

Sheehi, Stephen. 2011. *Islamophobia: The Ideological Campaign against Muslims.* Atlanta: Clarity Press.

Silverstein, Adam. 2014. "Enclosed beyond Alexander's Barrier: On the Comparative Study of 'Abbāsid Culture." *Journal of the American Oriental Society* 134 (2): 287–306.

Spiegel, Gabrielle. 2008. "Getting Medieval: History and the Torture Memos." *Perspectives on History: The Newsmagazine of the American Historical Association,* September 1, 2008, 3–6.

Stoler, Ann Laura. 2002a. *Carnal Knowledge and Imperial Power: Race and the Intimate in Colonial Rule.* Berkeley: University of California Press.

——. 2002b. "Colonial Archives and the Arts of Governance." *Archival Science* 2:87–109.

Truitt, Elly. 2015. *Medieval Robots: Mechanism, Magic, Nature, and Art*. Philadelphia: University of Pennsylvania Press.

Utz, Richard. 2017. *Medievalism: A Manifesto*. Kalamazoo, MI: ARC Humanities Press.

Wengrow, David. 2014. *The Origins of Monsters: Image and Cognition in the First Age of Mechanical Reproduction*. Princeton, NJ: Princeton University Press.

Zadeh, Travis. 2010. "The Wiles of Creation: Philosophy, Fiction, and the ʿAjāʾib Tradition." *Journal of Middle Eastern Literatures* 13 (1): 21–48.

——. 2011. *Mapping Frontiers across Medieval Islam: Geography, Translation, and the ʿAbbāsid Empire*. London: I.B. Tauris.

——. 2020. "Cutting Ariadne's Thread, or How to Think Otherwise in the Maze." In *Islamicate Occult Sciences in Theory and Practice*, edited by Liana Saif et al., 607–50. Leiden: Brill.

——. 2021. "Unruly Subjects." *Verge: Studies in Global Asias* 7 (1): 98–111.

——. 2023. *Wonders and Rarities: The Marvelous Book That Traveled the World and Mapped the Cosmos*. Cambridge, MA: Harvard University Press.

# ALEVI *CEMEVIS* AND "MOSQUE CULTURE" IN TURKEY

*Angela Andersen*

Muslim minorities in Turkey, such as the hereditary Turkish and Kurdish spiritual lineages (*ocaks*) grouped under the umbrella of Alevism, are part of the public, media, and academic discourses on religion and society. The Alevi population, unofficially estimated (owing to a lack of census data) at between 15 and 20 million people, forms a significant portion of the total Turkish population, projected at 84.3 million people in 2020 (United Nations Population Division 2019). However, Alevi concerns regarding religious education, the recognition of historical oppression, and the safety of their homes and community members are not always acknowledged by the state. Furthermore, Turkish policy continues to restrict the right of Alevis to construct, license, and operate their places of worship, often referred to as *cemevis*—that is, the houses (*evis*) for Alevi congregational ceremony (*cem*). That cemevis do not manifest a specific architectural type or design tradition leads to misunderstandings of their historical role. In this chapter, I will briefly examine the Turkish Republic's (1923–) restrictive policy on cemevis and the impact of this policy on Alevi architecture. By contrast, the state's administration, financial support, and construction of mosques for the Sunni Muslim majority result in a strategic statement about sanctioned Islamic identities in Turkey and a visual rhetoric in which building design supports the government's underlying religious ideology.

A petition submitted to the Turkish Grand National Assembly (Türkiye Büyük Millet Meclisi) in 2012 unsuccessfully challenged the state's refusal to acknowledge the role of cemevis in Alevi praxis (Andersen 2015b, 372–78). A different cemevi case was brought to the Turkish Supreme Court of Appeals (Türkiye

Cumhuriyet Yargıtay Başkanlığı), also in 2012. The court ruled that a cemevi is not a "place of worship" (*ibadethane*), because such a designation is "not possible" for Islamic religious buildings other than mosques (*Hürriyet* 2012). In the twenty-first century, cemevis have been propelled from their place in Alevi local traditions into a public and legal role as markers of resistance. They stand as an architectural indicator of the variety of traditional practices in Turkey. The laws and policies of the Turkish Republic have been interpreted in such a way as to disregard and impede other Islamic and non-Islamic religious sites, while at the same time offering increasingly visible official support for mosques.

On April 26, 2016, the European Court of Human Rights (ECHR) ruled on a Turkish cemevi case. The decision noted that the Turkish Republic had violated Alevi freedom of religion under Article 9: Freedom of Thought, Conscience and Religion, and Article 14: Protection from Discrimination, as they appear in the *European Convention on Human Rights* document (ECHR 2015; ECHR Press Unit 2022). The ECHR issued this statement on the ruling:

> The absence of a clear legal framework governing unrecognised religious minorities such as the Alevi faith caused . . . legal, organisational and financial problems. The ability to build places of worship was uncertain and was subject to the good will of the central or local authorities; the communities in question could not officially receive donations from members or State subsidies; and, since they lacked legal personality, these communities did not have access to the courts in their own right but only through foundations, associations or groups of followers. (ECHR Registrar 2016)

In 2018, the Turkish Supreme Court of Appeals ruled on another cemevi-related case, this time considering the cemevi to be a place of worship. This made it possible to rule that the government is responsible for the electrical expenses of cemevis (*Sendika* 2018). At that time, the governing Justice and Development Party (Adalet ve Kalkınma or AK Partisi) was campaigning for the spring 2019 municipal elections, so the nod to cemevi concerns was interpreted by analysts as a solicitation of the Alevi vote (Erdemir 2018). Indeed, the Supreme Court's language and ruling had limited resonance, as Alevi centers, including the city of Diyarbakir's Pir Sultan Abdal cemevi, had their electricity cut in the following months when the power authority failed to receive payments from the state (*Independent Turkçe* 2019).

The ECHR's Turkish cemevi ruling and cemevi cases in the Turkish legal system represent the systemic issues faced by those who attempt to build, license, operate, and assemble within sites of Alevi worship. During my interactions with Alevi communities in several regions of central Anatolia between 2008 and 2015, interviewees repeatedly spoke of ongoing challenges at the regional and state levels. Several used the phrase "mosque culture" (*cami kültürü*) as a way of referring to systemic conditions for minorities in a majority society. "Mosque culture" refers to the government and its associated hegemonic structures, past and present, as well as its overt and bureaucratically initiated efforts to obstruct, deny, and oppress Alevis and their practices. Without criticizing Sunnism (the majority Islamic identification among Turkish Muslims), the term also contrasts a certain quotidian appearance and communal ethos expressed by Alevi places of worship with the imperial legacy and formal design language of mosques, which Alevis do not typically visit for prayer and congregation.

Architecture, one of the most publicly accessible and visually immediate modes of communicating dominant religious affiliations in Turkish society, conveys messages that form the basis for a visual rhetoric of state-fostered religious power in the twentieth and twenty-first centuries. This architectural rhetoric of places of worship and ceremony draws directly on the Ottoman past (1299–1923), Islamic traditions, and contemporary political voices and appears in official discussions of religious architecture in Turkey. Architecture communicates authoritative messages about identity and Islam, and architectural siting, scale, materials, and historical references are used to promote Turkish political ideologies. For Alevis, who have been forced to advocate for cemevis as their traditional places of worship while the state focuses on the administration and ongoing construction of mosques, the notion of a "mosque culture" is conveyed and vividly reinforced through such architectural messaging.

## The Cemevi

There is no consensus on precisely when Alevis and their ancestors began holding cem ceremonies, although specific sites may have been selected for use as cemevis as early as the thirteenth century (Kaygusuz 1983, 29). Temporary congregational settings for the cem were frequently adapted from other local building types, including rooms in homes. However, the architectural record does not contain many examples of houses used for the cem or dedicated ceremonial halls built by Alevi communities that can be dated before the twentieth century (Akın 1985; Andersen 2015a). No set building type or decorative approach is prescribed by Alevi teachings and liturgical practices (Andersen 2020). The space must be safe, accommodate the ceremony, and receive approval from the community. By serving the requirements of ceremonial participants, cem architecture aligns with Alevi teachings regarding community and with the rural economy and its accompanying architectural needs. The imperative to remain inconspicuous in the face of oppression is likely to have supported the tradition of holding cems in the home.

The quotidian nature of cemevis shifted in the late twentieth century, when Alevi associations (*derneks*) began to construct multipurpose centers to provide services to Alevi people migrating to Turkish cities. The meaning of the cemevi has been further modified in the first two decades of the twenty-first century, when the cemevi became a symbol not only of Alevi spiritual traditions and teachings but also of the Alevi political struggle to achieve full rights in the Turkish Republic. This change in meaning takes place in a state that is increasingly reviving the powerful design language of the Ottoman Empire's Sunni mosques as part of a commanding and visually manifest architectural rhetoric. "Mosque culture" is signified in form and substance in a way that is easily replicated in architectural design, with a reciprocal relationship between cultural and religious behaviors, on the one hand, and infrastructural decision making, on the other. For centuries, Alevi teachings have supported the adaptability of cemevi sites, in part because of the general prioritization of community over a visible language of architectural symbolism. As a result, Alevi communities today are in the challenging position of wanting to serve their people and advocate for their rights, without being able to showcase dedicated ceremonial halls as verification of their history on the Anatolian religious landscape. Architects who are working to design new iterations of Alevi centers and cem spaces also struggle to communicate ideas and ideals without the shorthand of an established, recognizable history of monumental architecture (Andersen 2022).

The complicated history of Alevis and their ancestors in the Ottoman Empire (Ocak 1997) has contributed to long-standing misconceptions regarding Alevi communities. Alevis, who often supported the ruling dynasty of the neighboring Safavid Empire (ca. 1501–1736) (Karolewski 2008), were accused of religious heterodoxy by the Ottoman authorities and conservative segments of the Sunni population. Following the creation of the Turkish state in 1923, Alevis continued to encounter restrictions on their religious and political practices; many Alevis aligned themselves with leftist movements in the 1970s and 1980s, in an atmosphere of increasing tensions. At present, many Alevis regard the Turkish bureaucracy, legal system, and licensing authorities as forces that restrict their rights (Andersen 2019). As of the writing of this chapter, syncretic and marginalized practitioners such as the Alevis are not granted the rights that are assigned on the basis of religious status, whether they seek acknowledgment as a distinct group or as non-state-mandated Muslims.

Distinctions between Alevi and Sunni practice are visible in the architectural record, particularly as it relates to social organization and comportment. Many Alevis traditionally met on a seasonal basis for cem ceremonies, but contemporary

Alevi centers provide weekly cem assemblies and a variety of important services, from funerals to child care and education. Sunnis aspire to perform regular daily prayers in mosques as a tenet of their faith. Many mosques constructed between the eleventh century and the present also provide social services.

The Turkish Ministry of Religious Affairs (Diyanet İşleri Başkanlığı), established in 1924, acts in accordance with the principles and directives of the state. Originally intended to exercise oversight over Muslim religious education and its administration within the republic, the ministry has been granted a broader purview through constitutional changes passed by the Grand National Assembly in the intervening decades. By 1998, the ministry was in charge of staffing and administering all mosques in Turkey, and it continues to oversee the promotion of Sunni Islamic education, as well as the training and appointment of imams, aspects of mosque construction, and the coordination of the Meccan pilgrimage. Proper Muslim behavior is suggested and promoted under the category of "morality" (*ahlak*), and ministry statements are referenced by other government ministries. A budget derived from taxes, which Alevis protest as it includes their taxes as well, is used to pay the utilities and the wages of religious staff for mosques.

The Directorate General of Foundations (Vakıflar Genel Müdürlüğü) oversees Christian churches, hospitals, and similar properties. Alevis and their sites are not regulated by this authority or by the Diyanet Ministry. As a result of their exclusion from the constitutional definition of a "place of worship," cemevis are typically called "cultural centers" (*kültür merkezleri*) so as not to contravene restrictions. Alevi associations are formed by Alevi citizens who want to build, license, and operate cemevis. Constitutional debates about the role of the cemevi reflect tensions between Alevis and the state, as well as Alevi resistance to outside definitions of their religious identity (Pinar 2013). Specifically, Alevis may insist that they are not Muslims, in order to escape the official argument that they should congregate in mosques. This matter of status is highlighted by a 2014 proposal to provide funding for cemevis on the condition that they accept the designation of "prayer room" (*ibadet yeri*) and acknowledge the mosque as the rightful place of Islamic worship. This sticky concession, which would have left the place of the cemevi unaltered, has been described by one analyst as a "suggested political formula" (Özkan 2018, 90). Like many other such strategic efforts, this one has not been accepted by Alevis.

In tables prepared for its *Strategic Report* for 2012–2016, the Ministry of Religious Affairs counted 18,757,740 worshippers in attendance for Friday congregational prayers in Turkish mosques and an average of 1,420,662 people in attendance for the five daily prayers (Diyanet İşleri Başkanlığı 2012, 58). The report did not explain the system used to collect this information, nor did the subsequent *Strategic Report* released for 2017–2021 provide similar data sets, instead announcing plans to increase services and attendance numbers for mosque-goers (Diyanet İşleri Başkanlığı 2016). According to statistics for 2018, the ministry operates 88,021 mosques (Diyanet İşleri Başkanlığı Strateji Geliştirme Başkanlığı 2018), including congregational mosques (*camis*) and smaller prayer buildings (*mescits*), historic monuments, and newly constructed sites. Private patrons, including towns and associations, can sponsor and construct mosques, but they too are administered by the ministry. Anecdotal evidence suggests that some mosques are frequently used while others are all but empty; demographics and need are sometimes overridden by political expediency and messaging when sites are selected for the erection of new mosques. For example, Alevi communities are regularly identified for mosque construction, in spite of the fact that most residents will not use the new building beyond making a visit to welcome the imam (Andersen 2015b).

In January 2007, the General Directorate of Security (Emniyet Genel Müdürlüğü) released its ledgers of registered architecture, which included 900 Alevi sites, 321 churches of various Christian denominations, and 36 synagogues (Gürel and Konuralp 2007). In 2013, Hüseyin Aygün, a deputy in the Grand National Assembly, requested a count of Turkish cemevis based on data from the Ministry of the Interior (İçişleri Bakanlığı). At that time, 937 cemevis and five projects slated for construction were listed (AleviNet 2013; INTERNETHABER 2013). These counts do not include sites that have not been designated or registered as Alevi "cultural centers" and cemevis, including private homes and pilgrimage sites. More recent and detailed statistics are not yet available.

## Mosques in Turkey, the Ministry of Religious Affairs, and the Academic Record

The regional mosques of the pre-Ottoman principalities, Byzantine churches that were converted into mosques, and the large Ottoman imperial mosques present some of the most compelling examples of engineering and craft in the global history of architecture. These places of prayer and complexes offering social services provide a remarkable heritage for Islamic architecture in Turkey, although the response to Islamic monuments, their status, and their symbolism has fluctuated as the result of shifting power dynamics. The properties of some Sufi religious orders were confiscated and reallocated or demolished during the late Ottoman period to limit the authority of those living within their walls (Andersen 2018; Barnes 1986).

During its formative years, Turkey strove to distance itself from symbols of the failed empire and attempted to eradicate the role of Islam in the state's governance and cultural affairs by closing tombs, religious schools, and mosques. The nascent Turkish state regarded control over architecture as one of its most important communication tools, an idea it put into practice by leaving Istanbul and its Ottoman monuments to create a new capital in Ankara with freshly designed Republican buildings. Within decades, Sunni Islam reemerged as part of the political landscape, and, beginning in 1960, a series of military coups purportedly sought to quell the reintroduction of Islamic ideology into state leadership. The Kocatepe Mosque in Ankara, a prominent Sunni mosque begun in 1967, is frequently cited as a prime example of the return to the Ottoman architectural idiom. But Kocatepe was built on top of the razed foundations of a newly begun modernist, concrete mosque, selected from competition entries in 1963. The initial design presented a new language for modern Turkish Muslim sensibilities (As 2006; Bozdoğan and Akcan 2012, 171–202) but was rejected in favor of the familiar: a large, central dome over a prominent entrance, flanked by slender minarets.

The Diyanet Vakfı (Religious Foundation) operates as the charitable arm of the Diyanet Ministry. Together, they have coordinated mosque restoration and construction projects in Turkey and in several cities around the world. Many of these efforts are directed at communities with long-standing Muslim populations. For example, the Tokyo Camii and its adjoining Turkish Cultural Center, opened in 2000, replaced the mosque built for the Kazan Turks, who migrated to Japan from Russia following the October Revolution. The neo-Ottoman mosque type built in Tokyo is visually striking and clearly associated with Turkey, and, like Diyanet mosques constructed in other countries, it is an effective representation of both Islam and the republic (Rizvi 2015). In Turkey, architectural specifications for Ottoman revival mosques, including floorplans, have been made available by the Diyanet (As 2006, 59; Batuman 2016, 331). The relationship of these mosques to the state is explicit. According to its website, the "Diyanet Center of America receives its major support from [the] Presidency of Religious Affairs (Diyanet), an institution of the Turkish Government" (Diyanet Center of America 2019). Their imams are also appointed by the Diyanet, as in Turkey.

As a charitable foundation, the Diyanet Vakfı has had access to construction financing that is not generated by taxes. Donations to the Mosque Construction Assistance Campaign (Cami İnşaatı Yardım Kampanyası) are collected via text messaging or through the provision of bank codes. The donation portal is a prominent part of the Diyanet Vakfı's website (Diyanet Vakfı 2019). The generosity and good intentions of donors who wish to support Sunni mosques and community services are not under scrutiny here, nor should the needs of those communities be conflated with the publicity strategies of the state and its ministries. What should be scrutinized is the fact that Alevis and other minority Muslim and non-Muslim communities in Turkey do not have the same infrastructural support for creating and licensing places of worship. Different policies, political motivations, and financing strategies as well as a centralized approach to mosque design directly impact the appearance of mosques while indirectly impacting the appearance of cemevis and Alevi centers, both inside and outside of Turkey.

Diyanet Ministry statements describe both the architectural and the functional capacities of the mosque. Followers of the ministry's Islamic teachings are instructed to "seek the ways of placing the mosques at the center of the city and [their] lives, and turn them into cradles of civilization again." They are to "consider once again how important the mosques are" (Diyanet İşleri Başkanlığı 2017). The contents of Friday sermons (*hutbes*) delivered in congregational mosques across the country are prepared and distributed by the Diyanet Ministry through a centralized committee (Korkut and Eslen-Ziya 2018, 39). The Diyanet has institutionalized Turkish Islamic praxis on behalf of the state as if it were singular in its Sunni manifestation. The visual and architectural culture of the mosque falls under state purview, allowing for strategic oversight of the country's new mosque projects and heritage mosques, inclusive of maintenance, restoration, and preservation.

This architectural centralization has clear parallels with the Ottoman *has* system under which the court architect and his workshop controlled imperial commissions and exercised oversight over architecture across the empire. Centralization suited the court's rhetorical and infrastructural needs, and it was reluctant to give up this control: a proposal to revise the *has* system was rejected during a period of widespread reforms in the nineteenth century (Cerasi 1988). At the same time, Alevis were making community pilgrimages to tombs in Anatolia (*ziyarets*), and some visited the lodges (*tekkes*) of Sufi orders such as the Bektashis, with whom a number of Turkish Alevi lineages share teachings and exemplars (Birge 1937). However, the regional, user-built architecture that forms the basis of Alevi communities is not now, nor was it previously, regulated by a central religious or state authority.

Alevi cemevis and pilgrimage sites remain little-studied subjects (Akın 1995; Andersen 2015a). The rich historiography of other religious architectures in Turkey and its surrounding states and studies on Alevism from sociological, political science, and religious studies perspectives (Dressler 2013) highlight the absence of Alevi architectural issues from the literature. In his review of publications on Rum Seljuk (1077–1328) and Ottoman Turkish Islamic architecture, published between the 1940s and the early 1970s, Howard Crane notes the Turkish "chauvinism" that marks much of that literature. Authors attribute pan-Turkish design character and "uniqueness" (Aslanapa 1971, 29) to buildings that represent a vast range of linguistic, temporal, and geographical contexts (Crane 1972, 310). Similarly, Sibel Bozdoğan argues that mid-twentieth-century Ottoman-Turkish architectural historiography promotes the idea of "latent Turkishness" in the service of revealing the "'latent modernity' of Ottoman forms and building practices" (2007, 202) in the face of Western criticisms. While authors did challenge this "Turkish" typology (Kuban 1965) and have subsequently developed the analysis of other Islamic architectural forms for congregational worship, such as Sufi *tekkes* (Tanman 1992, 2005), the idea that mosques are central to a uniquely Turkish-Muslim architectural heritage pervades scholarship produced in some of Turkey's renowned mid-twentieth-century architecture schools. In the new republic, constitutional language made all citizens "Turks" in an effort to remove from the discourse the divisive conflicts between Turks, Greeks, Armenians, Arabs, Kurds, and others. Yet, the design contributions of all these religio-linguistic groups are part of the Anatolian architectural landscape. The scholarly record of architectural history may perpetuate political rhetoric, but currents of architectural design may perpetuate an imagined history of monolithic Islamic practice.

Ongoing opposition to official acknowledgment of Alevi places of worship, unrealized preelection promises to Alevi constituents, official language and legislation restricting Turkish places of worship, and the historically lax punishment for crimes committed against Alevis and Alevi architecture combine to create oppressive circumstances for Alevis. The very absence of a historical Alevi architectural footprint across the Turkish landscape may be attributed in part to this list of Republican-era factors and in part to restrictive precedents from earlier periods. In recent years, buildings within which Alevis live and worship have been subjected to anonymous vandalism. On May 3, 2018, the walls of an Alevi cemevi in Bursa were spray painted with graffiti, described by the press as "insults" (*Hürriyet Daily News* 2018). A photograph published in the daily *Hürriyet* establishes that the slur coursing down the cemevi staircase is an accusation that the cemevi president was a member of the PKK or Kurdistan Workers' Party, regarded as a terrorist organization by the Turkish authorities (*Hürriyet Daily News* 2018). In fact, the cemevi and its president are not implicated in PKK activities. Rather, the ethnocentric accusation of terrorism serves as a shorthand for the belief that Kurds and Alevis, and even more so Zaza and Kurmanci-speaking Kurdish Alevis, are outsiders who resist a prescribed Turkish or Sunni identity.

"Mosque culture" signals the power imbalance and marginalization of Alevis and their beliefs, practices, and ceremonial spaces. The term, used by Alevis during interviews in several parts of Turkey, alludes to the Sunni mandate of the Diyanet Ministry and to the leaders who grant the ministry increasing powers. The language of architecture is a powerful indicator of socioreligious trends in the Turkish Republic, where the mosque is currently a proxy for religiously motivated state authority. The rhetoric of mosque architecture eloquently conveys the intended primacy of Sunnism through great domed spaces that reference a long history: mosque patronage and administration have become ideological tools of the Turkish state, as they were during the Ottoman Empire. The state, in turn, through the rhetorical statements of the courts, the Diyanet Ministry, and its representatives, has accorded the mosque moral authority and a status above that of other places of worship. This shaping force in Turkish architecture has been called "Islamism" (Batuman 2018) to distinguish it from the oversight of Islamic doctrine itself. The AK Party, which rose to power in 2002, has continued the mid-twentieth-century project to solidify and perpetuate recognizable, authoritative Ottoman-revival mosque forms. Bureaucratic processes succeed in reducing knowledge of Islamic religious architecture's diverse heritage to a single form, and marginalize other ways of thought, belief, action, and their architectural manifestations.

The legal construction of Alevis as a religious minority brings numerous heterogeneous groups together into a "corporate body" that is vulnerable to state determinations of identity (Hurd 2014, 417). Alevi advocacy for the right to identify themselves with either religious or cultural criteria, and as either Muslims who do not congregate in mosques or as non-Muslims, is closely tied to their petition for the right to a place of worship that is distinct from the mosque and any other congregational setting. Even as the cemevi remains a largely quotidian structure in service to its community, it has become an emblem of resistance to the oppression of Alevism, to state-administered religious practices, and to the rhetoric of the mosque.

## REFERENCES

Akın, Günkut. 1985. *Doğu Ve Güneydoğu Anadolu'daki Tarihsel Ev Tiplerinde Anlam.* PhD diss., Istanbul Teknik Üniversitesi.
——. 1995. "The Muezzin Mahfili and Pool of the Selimiye Mosque in Edirne." *Muqarnas* 12:63–83. *AleviNet.* 2013. "Türkiye'de hangi ilde kaç cemevi var?" March 15, 2013. https://alevinet.com/2013/03/15/turkiyede-hangi-ilde-kac-cemevi-var/ (site discontinued).
Andersen, Angela. 2015a. *Cemevleri: An Examination of the Historical Roots and Contemporary Meanings of Alevi Architecture and Iconography.* PhD diss., Ohio State University.
——. 2015b. "Muslims Viewed as 'Non-Muslims': The Alevi Precincts of Anatolia." In *Sacred Precincts: Non-Muslim Sites in Islamic Societies,* edited by Mohammad Gharipour, 57–75. Leiden: Brill.
——. 2018. "The Transfer of Turkish Bektashi *Tekkes* to Alevi *Cemevleri.*" In *15th International Congress of Turkish Art, Naples, Università di Napoli "L'Orientale" 16–18 September 2015,* edited by Michele Bernardini, Alessandro Taddei, and Michael Douglas Sheridan, 109–21. Ankara: Ministry of Culture and Tourism, Republic of Turkey.
——. 2019. "One House of Worship with Many Roofs: The Attempted Imposition of Architecture to Mediate Mainstream Sunni, Alevi and Gülenist Islam in Turkey." *International Journal of Islamic Architecture* 8 (2): 283–305.

———. 2020. "'He Who Is the Wondrous Green Dome Is 'Ali': The Relationship between Narratives of the Prophet Muhammad's Ascension and the Communal Religious Architecture of the Alevis." In *Saintly Spheres and Islamic Landscapes*, edited by Daphna Ephrat, Sara Ethel Wolper, and Paulo G. Pinto, 301–34. Leiden: Brill.

———. 2022. "The Anecdotal Archive: Building Design, Oral History, and the Notion of an Alevi Place of Worship." *International Journal of Islamic Architecture* 11 (1): 25–43.

As, Imdat. 2006. "The Digital Mosque: A New Paradigm in Mosque Design." *Journal of Architectural Education* 60:55–59.

Aslanapa, Oktay. 1971. *Turkish Art and Architecture*. New York: Praeger.

Barnes, John Robert. 1986. *An Introduction to Religious Foundations in the Ottoman Empire*. Leiden: Brill.

Batuman, Bülent. 2016. "Architectural Mimicry and the Politics of Mosque Building: Negotiating Islam and Nation in Turkey." *Journal of Architecture* 21 (3): 321–47.

———. 2018. *New Islamist Architecture and Urbanism: Negotiating Nation and Islam through Built Environment in Turkey*. New York: Routledge.

Birge, John Kingsley. 1937. *The Bektashi Order of Dervishes*. Hartford, CT: Hartford Seminary Press.

Bozdoğan, Sibel. 2007. "Reading Ottoman Architecture through Modernist Lenses: Nationalist Historiography and the 'New Architecture' in the Early Republic." *Muqarnas* 24:199–221.

Bozdoğan, Sibel, and Esra Akcan. 2012. *Turkey: Modern Architectures in History*. London: Reaktion.

Cerasi, Maurice. 1988. "Late-Ottoman Architects and Master Builders." *Muqarnas* 5:87–102.

Crane, Howard. 1972. "Recent Literature on the History of Turkish Architecture." *Journal of the Society of Architectural Historians* 31 (4): 309–15.

Diyanet Center of America. n.d. "Who We Are." Accessed April 15, 2019. https://diyanetamerica.org/about-us/what-is-dca (site discontinued).

Diyanet İşleri Başkanlığı. 2012. *Stratejik Plan 2012–2016*. Ankara: Diyanet İşleri Başkanlığı.

———. 2016. *Stratejik Plan 2017–2021*. Ankara: Diyanet İşleri Başkanlığı.

———. 2017. "The Mosque, the City and the Civilization." October 12, 2017. https://www.diyanet.gov.tr/en-US/Content/PrintDetail/10396.

———. n.d. Homepage. Accessed May 10, 2019. https://www.diyanet.gov.tr.

Diyanet İşleri Başkanlığı Strateji Geliştirme Başkanlığı. 2018. *Cami Sayısı*; and *İstatistiki bölge birimleri sınıflamasına göre cami sayısı*. December 31, 2018. https://stratejigelistirme.diyanet.gov.tr/sayfa/57/istatistikler.

Diyanet Vakfı. 2019. "Online Bağış." Accessed May 2, 2019. https://bagis.tdv.org/Pages/DonationDetail.aspx?dsc=5001&dc=5000#/0 (site discontinued).

Dressler, Markus. 2013. *Writing Religion: The Making of Turkish Alevi Islam*. Oxford: Oxford University Press.

ECHR (European Court of Human Rights). 2015. "Guide to Article 9: Freedom of Thought, Conscience and Religion of the European Convention on Human Rights," p. 46. http://www.echr.coe.int/Documents/Guide_Art_9_ENG.pdf.

———. Press Unit. 2022. "Press Country Profile: Turkey." Updated July 2022. https://www.echr.coe.int/Documents/CP_Turkey_ENG.pdf.

———. Registrar of the Court. 2016. "Press Release: The Refusal to Provide a Public Service to the Applicants, Followers of the Alevi Faith, Entailed a Breach of Their Right to Freedom of Religion." April 26, 2016. Grand Chamber judgment in the case of İzzettin Doğan and Others v. Turkey (application no. 62649/10).

Erdemir, Aykan. 2018. "AKP Eyes Alevi Voters—Again and to No Avail." Foundation for Defense of Democracies, November 30, 2018. https://www.fdd.org/analysis /2018/11/30/akp-eyes-alevi-voters-again-and-to-no-avail/.

Gürel, Soner, and Okan Konuralp. 2007. "İbadethane zenginiyiz." *Hürriyet*, January 11, 2007. http://www.hurriyet.com.tr/gundem/ibadethane-zenginiyiz-5756356.

Hurd, Elizabeth Shakman. 2014. "Alevis under Law: The Politics of Religious Freedom in Turkey." *Journal of Law and Religion* 29 (3): 416–35.

*Hürriyet Daily News*. 2018. "Unidentified Assailant Graffitis Bursa Cemevi with Insults, Swearing." May 4, 2018. http://www.hurriyetdailynews.com/unidentified-assailant -graffitis-bursa-cemevi-with-insults-swearing-131336.

*Hürriyet (Gündem)*. 2012. "Yargıtay: Cemevi ibadethane değil." July 26, 2012. http:// www.hurriyet.com.tr/gundem/21068846.asp.

*Independent Türkçe*. 2019. "Diyarbakır Cemevi'nin elektriğinin kesilmesi Meclis'e taşındı." April 25, 2019. https://www.independentturkish.com/node/25211/haber /diyarbak%C4%B1r-cemevi%E2%80%99nin-elektri%C4%9Finin-kesilmesi -meclise-ta%C5%9F%C4%B1nd%C4%B1.

INTERNETHABER. 2013. "Türkiye'de hangi ilde kaç cemevi var?" March 15, 2013. https://www.internethaber.com/turkiyede-hangi-ilde-kac-cemevi-var-513052h .htm.

Karolewski, Janina. 2008. "What Is Heterodox about Alevism? The Development of Anti Alevi Discrimination and Resentment." *Die Welt des Islams* 48:434–56.

Kaygusuz, İsmail. 1983. *Onar Dede Mezarlığı ve Adı Bilinmeyen Bir Türk Kolonizatörü Şeyh Hasan Oner*. Istanbul: Arkeoloji ve Sanat Yayınları.

Korkut, Umut, and Hande Eslen-Ziya. 2018. *Politics and Gender Identity in Turkey: Centralised Islam for Socio-Economic Control*. London: Routledge.

Kuban, Doğan. 1965. *Anadolu-Türk Mimarisinin Kaynak ve Sorunları (The Source and Problems of the Anatolian-Turkish Architecture)*. Istanbul: İTÜ Mimarlık Fakültesi.

Ocak, Ahmet Yaşar. 1997. "Un apercu general sur l'hétérodoxie musulmane en Turquie: Réflexions sur les origines et les caractéristiques du Kızılbachisme (Alévisme) dans la perspective de l'historie." In *Syncretistic Religious Communities in the Near East*, edited by Krisztina Kehl-Bodrogi, Barbara Kellner-Heinkele, and Anka Otter-Beaujean, 195–204. Leiden: Brill.

Özkan, Nazlı. 2018. "Infrastructures of Urban Religious Management: Who Should Pay for the Utilities of Cemevis in Turkey?" *Middle East—Topics & Arguments* 10:86–94. https://doi.org/10.17192/meta.2018.10.7588.

Pinar, Candas. 2013. "Religion-State Relations in Turkey since the AKP: A Changing Landscape? Evidence from Parliamentary Debates on the Alevi Matter." *Journal of Muslim Minority Affairs* 33 (4): 507–20.

Rizvi, Kishwar. 2015. *The Transnational Mosque: Architecture and Historical Memory in the Contemporary Middle East*. Chapel Hill: University of North Carolina Press.

*Sendika*. 2018. "Yargıtay: Cemevleri ibadethanedir, elektrik faturalarını devlet karşılamalı." November 27, 2018. http://sendika63.org/2018/11/yargitay-cemevleri -ibadethanedir-elektrik-faturalarini-devlet-karsilamali-519756/.

Tanman, Baha M. 1992. "Settings for the Veneration of Saints." In *The Dervish Lodge: Architecture, Art, and Sufism in Ottoman Turkey*, edited by R. Lifchez, translated by M. E. Quigley-Pinar, 130–71. Berkeley: University of California Press.

——. 2005. "Ottoman Architecture and the Sufi Orders: Dervish Lodges." In *Sufism and Sufis in Ottoman Society*, edited by Ahmet Yaşar Ocak, 317–86, with plates. Ankara: Türk Tarih Kurumu.

United Nations Population Division, Department of Economic and Social Affairs, Population Division. 2019. *World Population Prospects 2019: Highlights*. New York: United Nations Population Division, Department of Economic and Social Affairs, Population Division. ST/ESA/SER.A/423.

# Part 6

# REPRESENTING MUSLIMS

Poetry, Film, and News Media

In the first of three chapters in this part, Nerina Rustomji explores English views about the other—in this instance, Islam—by examining Muslim heroines in nineteenth-century poetry. Lord Byron (d. 1824) famously popularized the idea of the houri, a figure whom he portrays as pure, beautiful, and desirable. By creating a repertoire of Muslim heroines, Byron transformed the houri from an Orientalist trope into a universal ideal, suggesting that the grace, beauty, and sensuality of Muslim heroines might serve as a model for English women. Byron's positive representation of "ideal" Muslim women subsequently made its way to the United States, where American poets used the model of the houri to construct their own ideas about feminine purity and sensuality.

In the second chapter, Anindita Banerjee analyzes an inaugural cinematic collaboration between Soviet and Indian filmmakers in 1957. The product of this collaboration was a film that tells the story of a fifteenth-century Russian merchant named Nikitin, who, in 1468, traveled from Greek Orthodox Moscow to Muslim India. Dubbed "the Russian Columbus," Nikitin crossed the Volga River, the Caspian Sea, and the Arabian Sea before "discovering" India. He landed on the southwestern coast of the subcontinent, where he spent four years engaging in trade, albeit with little success. After visiting Muslim royalty on the Deccan Plateau, Nikitin set out on his return journey to Russia but died near the port of Kaffa before reaching home, leaving a short but detailed travelogue (*The Journey beyond the Three Seas*) written in colloquial middle Russian with a healthy smattering of Arabic, Farsi, and Turkish. Four hundred years later, the travelogue manuscript was translated into English by Count Wielhorski, a secretary of the Russian legation at the court of St. James, and published in 1868 by the Hakluyt society of London. From a close reading of the translation, Banerjee establishes that Wielhorski redacted and/or modified the original text in an effort to hide Nikitin's powerful attraction to Islam. Similarly, the 1957 Russo-Indian film does not include any images of the Muslims encountered by the Russian merchant in the Bahmanid Deccan or any manifestations of the Deccan's multiethnic and multilingual society. The film reduces Nikitin to a pious and devout Greek-Orthodox Christian. These editorial choices, Banerjee argues, were motivated by a desire to align the Russian past with Indo-European civilization, that is to say, by "a particular set of desires regarding religious identity and political ideology." The movie, she concludes, reflects transimperial and transcultural tensions that shaped contesting social identities across three continents.

In the third chapter, Annika Marlen Hinze analyzes the representation of Muslims in news media in the United States and Germany, two of the largest democracies in the West. Her main sources are the *New York Times* and the *Süddeutsche Zeitung*, whose coverage of Muslim societies—on subjects that include immigrants and refugees, the Israel-Palestine conflict, and the Middle East— "frames" public opinion about Islam and Muslims among educated elites in these two countries. For comparative purposes, Hinze includes two conservative media in her sample, *Fox News* and *Bild*. These four media outlets, which reach millions of people daily, not only play an instrumental role in shaping public opinion on issues relating to Islam and Muslims but also contribute to the polarization of politics and social relations in Germany and the United States. By "fabricating" news, the media steer public opinion toward one or another extreme, with little middle ground, thereby exacerbating our current ideological predicament.

The representation of Muslims in poetry, film, and the media is a fluid and dynamic process that responds to changing power relations, political ideologies, and ideas about identity.

# 14

# VISUAL DEPICTIONS OF MUSLIM HEROINES

## Byron's *Beauties* and American Houris

*Nerina Rustomji*

This chapter explores the notion of what constitutes a Muslim heroine in nineteenth-century English literature. By focusing on the poems of Lord Byron (1788–1824) and the compendiums of his excerpted poems, I question the idea of a Muslim society and ask if, in fact, one must be Muslim to be considered a Muslim heroine. The conceptual exploration is valuable since English writers in the nineteenth century often made assertions about religious and civilizational differences between Islam and Christianity in essays, poems, and Oriental tales. Byron's poems suggest another possibility: Christian ladies of England and the United States emulated Turkish, Muslim heroines. Indeed, Byron played an important role in popularizing Muslim heroines by invoking houris, or the pure, female companions of Islam. By suggesting that the poems have different levels of significance, I highlight the manner in which labels endure and shape identities. While English writers articulated the difference between English or American societies and Turkish or Muslim ones, they were also inspired by the aesthetics of Muslim societies. Unlike William Cantwell Smith (1991, 18), who developed a model of external and internal perspectives of identifying faiths, English writers in the nineteenth century used religious and civilizational identifications to assert and subvert ideas of difference to create feminine Christian identities that depended on Muslim concepts of feminine purity.

# Houris

Both the Qur'an and hadith highlight purity as a value for men and women. The Qur'an presents a model of purity in the form of the houris, or the pure, female companions of paradise. In the Qur'an, houris are an ambiguous reward. They are named four times (Q. 44:54, 52:20, 56:22, 55:72) and alluded to in verses that discuss "restraining in their glances" (Q. 27:48, 38:52, 55:56), "companions of an equal age" (Q. 38:52, 56:35–37, 78:33), and companions of purity "whom no man or jinn before them has touched" (Q. 55:56, 55:74). While their purity is often signified by metaphors about pearls, it is also invoked by the term *abkār*, or virginal (Q. 56:35–37). Building on these references, Qur'an commentators puzzled over the characteristics of the houri and suggested that she was a feminine being whose wide eyes had an intense contrast between the sclerotic coat (the white of the eye) and the pupil with the result that her eyes resembled those of a cow or gazelle. In hadith, the houri is a female figure who embodies the landscape of paradise since she is composed of opulent materials such as musk and amber. She appears as a feminine companion awaiting her designated male believer. In later eschatological literature, meeting the houri in paradise is often a central point of the drama: the presumed male believer sees the many rewards that he has earned over a lifetime of righteousness (Rustomji 2009, 96).

Qur'an commentators and theologians were not the only scholars interested in the houri and her meaning. Theologians in Latin Christendom were fascinated by the material dimension of descriptions of Islamic paradise. In particular, they focused on the idea that men could enjoy sex in Muslim paradise. For example, Prester John's ideal kingdom reinforced the idea that the Islamic heaven has virgins (Heng 2012, 260). In the sixteenth century, Johannes Andreas Maurus (1487–1515 CE) calls these virgins "hourin" and "hora" in his anti-Islamic polemic, *Confusión o confutación de la secta Mahomética* (1652, 158). In the mid-seventeenth century, the French traveler Nicolas Du Loir (1654, 178) mentions the word "houri" in his letter about women in the Ottoman Empire. While Du Loir uses the term "houri" in his section on Turkish women, English writers also began to employ the term as a way to describe English women. In the eighteenth century, the term "houri" was used to identify English women who were "handsomer than one of the houris" (Walpole 1745, 11–13). By the nineteenth century, one finds references to houris in English novels, poems, travel accounts, and monthly magazines.

While interest in houris may have begun as a theological concern about sex in paradise, nineteenth-century English writers understood the houri through gender relations. English writers who invoked the houri often asserted that Islam oppresses Muslim women and that a female companion could be sensual and pure at the same time. English writers did not find these two assertions as contradictory. Most importantly, these two assertions highlight the usefulness of the houri for English writers, as it provides evidence that Islam is inferior because it allows for sex in paradise; at the same time, however, the houri provides a possible model for how females may represent a sublime sensuality.

If the houri became commonplace as a term and idea in English literature, then Lord Byron transformed the houri from an Orientalist trope to a universal ideal for all women. English writers may have understood the houri as a beautiful feminine being of Islamic paradise, but Byron's expansion of the idea challenged how nineteenth-century writers understood what constituted a Muslim society. What did it mean for English and American ladies to be called houris? How did the images of these heroines acknowledge religious difference? At the same time that Byron's language reinforced Muslim difference, the characters he provided erased that very difference. That is to say, he simultaneously reinforced and undermined visions of the Orient. By creating a repertoire of Christian and Muslim heroines, he subverted the idea of the distinctiveness of Muslim society. Instead, he suggested that English and American ladies could be as strong and sensual as Muslim heroines.

# Byron and the Houri

George Gordon, the sixth Lord Byron, traveled to Greece, the Balkans, Spain, and Anatolia in 1809 and 1810. In his poems, he presents the image of the fearful Turk who dominates and enslaves pure women. In some of his poems, he depicts women as pure beauties who are enslaved by Turks. Byron refers to these women as houris in *Childe Harold* (1812), *Bride of Abydos* (1814), *The Siege of Corinth* (1816), *Giaour* (1813), and *Don Juan* (1819).

In *Childe Harold*, the poet compares houris with Spanish women:

> Match me, those houris, whom ye scarce allow
> To taste the gale lest Love should ride the wind
> With Spain's dark-glancing daughters—deign to know
> There your wise Prophet's paradise we find,
> His black-eyed maids in Heaven, angelically kind
> (Byron 1890, canto I, stanza lix).

In a cluster of poems that make up the "Turkish Tales," Byron uses houris to depict an Oriental setting. In the *Bride of Abydos*, he refers to the houri while invoking music: "But soft as harp that Houri string / His long entrancing note!" (Byron 1814a, canto II). The musical metaphor extends to Giaffer's daughter Zulieka. When she enters a room, Giaffer exclaims: "But hark!—I hear Zulieka's voice, / Like Houris' hymn it meets mine ear" (canto I, stanza v, lines 146–47). In the same poem, Byron invokes the houri in connection with comforting love: "Oh! who so dear with him could dwell? / What houri soothe his half so well?" (canto II, stanza vii, lines 112–13). In *The Siege of Corinth*, the houri promises men eternal love: "Secure in paradise to be / By Houris loved immortally" (Byron 1835, stanza vii).

In other poems, the houri represents an ideal of beauty. In the *Giaour*, Leila's dark eyes recall the image of the houri (Byron 1814b, lines 480–86), and other houris await "at the Prophet's gate" (lines 1045–47), where heaven is described as the "dark heaven of Houris' eyes" (lines 738–44).

In *Don Juan*, Byron understands houris as sexual reward for men in paradise (1858, canto viii, stanza cxi). Yet, these houris also experience desire and prefer young men, not old warriors:

> And what they pleased to do with the young khan
> > In heaven, I know not, not pretend to guess;
> But doubtless they prefer a fine young Man
> > To tough old Heroes, and can do no less.
> And that's the cause, no doubt, why, if we scan
> > A Field of Battle's ghastly Wilderness,
> For one rough, weather-beaten, Veteran body,
> > You'll find ten thousand handsome Coxcombs bloody. . . .
>
> Your Houris also have a natural pleasure
> > In lopping-off your lately married men,
> Before the Bridal Hours have danced their measure,
> > And the sad, second moon grows dim again,
> Or dull repentence hath had dreary leisure
> > To wish him back a bachelor now and then:
> And thus your Houri (it may be) disputes
> > Of these brief blossoms the immediate fruits.
> (Byron 1858, canto viii, stanza cxiii)

The houri inspires the khan to rush into battle.

> Thus the young Khan, with Houris in his sight,
> > Thought not upon the charms of four young brides,
> But bravely rush'd on his first heavenly night;
> > In short, howe'ver *our* better faith derides,
> These black-eyed Virgins make the Moslems fight,
> > As though there were one heaven, and none besides—

Whereas, if all be true we hear of Heaven
And Hell, there must at least be six or seven.
(canto viii, stanza cxiv)

In these poems, Byron develops the image of Islam as sexually motivating men to engage in battle while oppressing and enslaving pure women.

# Byron's *Beauties*

The compilation of Byron's poems—*The Gallery of Byron Beauties: Ideal Pictures of the Principal Female Characters in Lord Byron's Poems*, sometimes titled *Les Dames de Byron*—presents readers with positive depictions of Byron's heroines, unlike the poems that highlight their oppression (Byron 1867).

The compilation was first published in London in 1836, and several volumes were republished in New York with some variations in the engravings. Each poem is matched with an engraving of the heroine and significant passages from the poem, allowing the reader to appreciate the beauty of the heroine in both visual and textual form. Here, I draw on images from a volume published by Appleton in New York in 1867.

In the compilation, both Leila of the *Giaour* and Zulieka of the *Bride of Abydos* are referred to as houris. While the accompanying selection from the poem does not mention the houri, the passages recall the strengths of the heroines. Leila gazes into the distance (figure 14.1). Her pearl diadem, jewels, and costume signify her worldliness and her luxurious surroundings. Zulieka projects youthful beauty with her sweet expression (figure 14.2). While these two figures depict a gentle stillness, in Byron's other poems females engage in more actions. The heroine called Light of the Heavens in *Childe Harold* tends to her infant child, while Gulnare has a fearful look and displays fierce determination.

In the engravings of *Childe Harold* and of the minor poems, Muslim and Christian heroines look alike: Marion, Inez, and Generva all have a similar gaze, accompanied by a defining prop, such as cascading curls or a fan—although Generva, exceptionally, is depicted with a crucifix. In these images, the heroine represents universal purity, which allows for a restrained sensuality adorned by luxury goods. They suggest that Byron's beauties are pure and cosmopolitan and can enjoy an expanding world of consumer products in England and the United States. Byron's Muslim heroines become heroines for all time.

The engravings of Byron's beauties play a significant role in the development of the houri as a descriptor for American females and the highlighting of Muslim

**FIGURE 14.1.** Leila. From *Gallery of Byron Beauties*, 1867, B8225B99 F7 1867, Rare Book & Manuscript Library, Columbia University in the City of New York.

**FIGURE 14.2.**   Zulieka. From *Gallery of Byron Beauties*, 1867, B825B99 F7, Rare Book & Manuscript Library, Columbia University in the City of New York.

heroines in Byron's poems. By focusing on feminine grace and beauty, rather than religious markers or narrative context, the images highlight Muslim heroines as a universal aspiration for American ladies. The American reading public was able to access his message about feminine beauty in the *Gallery of Byron Beauties* and also in monthly magazines in which houris symbolized feminine virtue.

## American Houris

Byron transformed the idea of the houri by depicting her as a pure, beautiful, and desired heroine. He introduced houris to American literature through the model of universal purity. In fact, in love poems about American ladies, their beauty is likened to that of the houri (Hines 1840, 16). Thus, the appearance of the American houri points to the transformation of the Muslim female companions of paradise from religious figures in an eschatological drama to protagonists in a gendered drama in which males try to oppress beautiful females. The houri, then, became one way in which a distinctly Muslim idea became a universal ideal. For example, in a poem titled "Star of Love," published in the American magazine *Ladies' Companion*, the poet, identified only as R.H., depicts the female role model as follows:

> Beauty and soul in wreath divine,
> Are twined around thy forehead's shrine,
> While sweetest thoughts and sunny smiles,
> Gleam out 'midst love's ambrosial wiles,
> Like twin stars on the crest of night,
> Thin eyes are flashing lustrous light,
> And on they lips of crimson hue,
> Thy breath dissolves in balmy dew,
> Just as the night's tears on the rose,
> Melt when the gates of morn unclose.
> Houri of Fancy's fairest dream,
> So sweetly does thine image beam,
> As if some angel with his wing,
> Had waked thy young heart's slumbering,
> From visions clothed in glory's light,
> In realms of Paradise all bright,
> That doubly strong thy claims should prove,
> Young beauty to—the Star of Love!
> (R.H. 1840, 31)

The Romantic imagery of feminine beauty draws on Byronic language, and the reference to the "Houri of Fancy's fairest dream" shows how the Muslim feminine figure is appropriated without religious significance for an American audience.

Byron not only developed Orientalist images but also developed the framework for undermining them. Like houris, English or American women expressed their pure Christian selves while aspiring to luxury and adornment. The image of the houri may have arisen from Islamic religious traditions, but her representation allowed English and American ladies to aspire to a higher status. In doing so, the American ladies borrowed from the Muslim image of the houri to craft their own visions of feminine purity and sensuality.

## REFERENCES

Cantwell Smith, William. 1991. *The Meaning and End of Religion*. Minneapolis, MN: First Fortress Press.

Du Loir, Nicolas. 1654. *Les Voyages du Sieur du Loir*. Paris: Chez Gervais Closvzier.

Heng, Geraldine. 2012. "Sex, Lies, and Paradise: The Assassins, Prester John, and the Fabulation of Civilizational Identities." *Differences* 23 (1): 1–31.

Hines, David Theo. 1840. *The Life, Adventures and Opinions of David Theo Hines, of South Carolina: Master of Arts, and, Sometimes, Doctor of Medicine*. New York: Bradley and Clark.

Lord Byron. 1814a. *The Bride of Abydos: A Turkish Tale*. London: John Murray. HathiTrust Digital Library.

——. 1814b. *The Giaour: A Fragment of a Turkish Tale*. London: John Murray. HathiTrust Digital Library.

——. 1835. *Siege of Corinth*. Paris: B. Cormon and Black. HathiTrust Digital Library.

——. 1858. *Don Juan*. Boston: Phillips, Sampson. HathiTrust Digital Library.

——. 1867. *The Gallery of Byron Beauties: Ideal Pictures of the Principal Female Characters in Lord Byron's Poems; From the Original Paintings by Eminent Artists*. New York: D. Appleton.

——. 1890. *Childe Harold's Pilgrimage*. New York: Lovell Brothers. HathiTrust Digital Library.

Maurus, Johannes Andreas. 1652. *The Confusion of Muhamed's sect or a confutation of the Turkish Alcoran. Being a discovery of many secret policies and practices in that religion, not till now revealed. Written originally in Spanish, by Johannes Andreas Maurus, who was one of their bishops and afterwards turned Christian*. Translated by Joshua Notstock. London: H. Blunden. Early English Books Online.

Rustomji, Nerina. 2021. *The Beauty of the Houri: Heavenly Virgins, Feminine Ideals*. New York: Oxford University Press, 2021.

Walpole, Horace. 1745. *The Yale Edition of Horace Walpole's Correspondence, Letter to Sir Horace Mann, February 28, 1745*. New Haven, CT: Yale University Press. Online edition.

# A RUSSIAN COLUMBUS

## From Victorian England to Bombay Cinema

*Anindita Banerjee*

The first collaboration between the Soviet and Indian film industries took place in 1957. The year marked the tenth anniversary of India's independence from British rule, the fortieth anniversary of the October Revolution, and the launch of Sputnik. The year 1957 was also the apex of the political and economic liberalization called the "Thaw," instituted by Nikita Khrushchev after thirty years of Stalinist austerity, which manifested itself in the realms of consumer culture and public taste as a newfound hunger for the colorful and the exotic. This was the economy of desire to which the largest state studio, Mosfilm, responded by coproducing, with Naya Sansar Studio of Bombay, a three-hour technicolor extravaganza called *Khozhdenie za tri moria* (subtitled in English as *The Journey beyond Three Seas*). While nodding to contemporaneous cultural trends in each of the two countries involved in the production, the film also presents itself as an archival project. It purports to reconstruct the legendary journey of a fifteenth-century merchant whom the medievalist Ia S. Lur'e had famously christened the "Russian Columbus" (Lur'e and Semenov 1986, 32).

Afanasy (Athanasius) Nikitin, born and raised in the small town of Tver' north of Moscow, arrived in the Indian subcontinent approximately three decades before Vasco da Gama famously discovered the Cape Route to the Indian subcontinent in 1498 and opened up the region to European trade.[1] Like the expeditions of Christopher Columbus, his itinerary was determined more by chance than by deliberation. Nikitin's original intention of stopping at the trading posts in the southern Volga and returning home was foiled by numerous robberies and swindles, which compelled him to continue southward beyond the

Caspian Sea. Unable to turn a profit in northern Iran, he made the fateful decision to sail *Dorya indostanskaia*—the stretch of the Arabian Sea known as the
Hindustan Passage to Persian and central Asian traders—that his fellow merchants advised Nikitin to cross if he wanted to tap the rich markets located on
its other shore. After landing on the southwestern coast of the Indian subcontinent, the merchant from Tver' spent almost four years in the kingdom of the
Bahmani sultans on the Deccan plateau with little commercial success but a good
deal to say. This sojourn is the principal subject of the short but minutely detailed account that survived the traveler's untimely demise on his way back home.

    *Khozhdenie za tri moria*, as the fifteenth-century travelogue came to be called,
has no obvious precursor either in the Western canon or in the Russian literary
tradition. Its medium of narration, moreover, is a remarkably heterogeneous amal-
gam of languages. Permeating the merchant's colloquial middle Russian is a phonetically transcribed mixture of Arabic, Farsi, and Turkic invocations to Allah
and His prophet. This macaronic tongue, probably acquired during his long journey across Iran and the Arabian Sea, provides Nikitin with vital access to the Muslim elite on the Indian subcontinent, the "boyars and big men" (*KTM*, 20) of the
Bahmanid sultanate to whom he presents himself as "Yusuf Khorasani" (21).[2]
The non-Russian interpolations, which increase in frequency and intensity as the
account progresses, metamorphose into a lengthy, emotional passage consisting
entirely of Islamic topoi at the conclusion of the narrative (30).

    The cinematic rendition of this extraordinary text represents the iconic for-
malization of a phenomenon that has only recently begun to attract scholarly
attention: the Soviet Union as an early field for the globalization of the Indian film
industry. As Sudha Rajagopalan (2008, 5) notes in her seminal study, the popularity of Bombay blockbusters among Russian-speaking audiences—especially
those in the central Asian republics who identified with Indian cinema's many
engagements with a shared Perso-Islamic heritage—began with the runaway success of Khwaja Ahmed Abbas's 1951 hit *Awara* (*The Vagabond*, translated into
Russian as *Brodiaga*, starring Raj Kapoor and Nargis Dutt). It is not coincidental
that *Khozhdenie* was codirected by Abbas and featured Nargis as the female lead;
Raj Kapoor's father, the pioneering actor and producer Prithviraj Kapoor, appeared in an instrumental role. The film served as India's official entry in the
Cannes Film Festival the following year and inaugurated a rich tradition of collaboration between Soviet and Indian studios over the next two decades.

    A striking correlation between the production of Nikitin's original account
and the conditions of its adaptation on the big screen explains why the fifteenth-
century text, rather than a contemporary narrative, may have provided the ideal
platform for the first Indo-Soviet cinematic venture. Just as the original travelogue inscribed a zone of contact with the Indian subcontinent unmediated by the

Western gaze, the Russian encounter with popular Indian cinema circumvented the influence of the US and European film industries. With lavish sets, lush colors, and musical interludes, *Khozhdenie* manifests a remarkable convergence between the softer aesthetic of Khrushchev's Thaw and the conventions of Bollywood, which, as the film historian M. Madhava Prasad (1998, 109) put it, "managed to combine fragments of utopian ideology and enactments of the pleasures of commodity culture." The choice of the fifteenth-century *Khozhdenie* also provides a unique lens for examining how the Soviet and Indian film industries' newfound aesthetic synergy was fueled by a particular set of desires regarding religious identity and political ideology. If films, as Lalitha Gopalan asserts, are the most powerful mode of "communicating our utopian imaginings of collective social life" (2002, 29), what did Nikitin's journey, first from Orthodox Muscovy to the Islamic Bahmanid kingdom and then from text to screen across the vast span of almost half a millennium, contribute to the utopian longings of both Russian and Indian cinema in the postwar twentieth century? This chapter addresses the question by looking backward an additional century and traveling to a third space, London in the Victorian era, to the first introduction of Nikitin's travelogue to a global audience via translation into the English language. By situating the Indo-Soviet *Khozhdenie* in the *longue durée* of literary translation and cinematic adaptation, I seek to examine the transimperial and transcultural tensions that contributed to the transformation of the fifteenth-century text into a powerful field of contesting social identities across three continents.

Ironically, it was the indeterminacy of the traveler's voice that opened his text to a stunning diversity of modern co-optations. Both the Islamic polyphony of his linguistic medium and the contingent nature of his arrival in the Indian subcontinent, catalyzed by encounters with Muslim fellow traders rather than any mandate from the church or state in his homeland, complicate the task of identifying Nikitin within any monolithic imagined community of the modern world. In order to understand how the film harmonizes the mobile bodies and languages of the fifteenth-century text with the utopian ideals of nation, history, and culture on the twentieth-century screen, we must first map the Indo-Soviet adaptation of *Khozhdenie* onto the Victorian English portrayal of the Russian Columbus.

Almost a century before the Mosfilm–Naya Sansar collaboration, the English language transformed the merchant from an obscure eccentric, whose manuscript had languished in his homeland for more than three hundred years, into a crucial metonym for defining Russia's unique place in global geopolitics. *The Journey beyond Three Seas* appeared for the first time in a non-Russian language in 1858 in a volume published by the Hakluyt Society of London, a venerable Victorian institution named after the sixteenth-century explorer Sir Richard Hakluyt. Supplemented by the subtitle *The Travels of Athanasius Nikitin to India*, it was included in a volume titled *India in the Fifteenth Century*. The translation from Russian to English was credited to "Count Wielhorski, secretary of the Russian legation at the court of St James" (*JTS*, iv).[3] Like the 1957 film, the English *Journey* introduced Nikitin to an international audience in a highly charged political atmosphere: on the eve of the Crimean War and immediately following the infamous Sepoy Mutiny, an uprising of Muslim soldiers in the service of the British East India Company.

Wielhorski's text is the only account in the volume framed by an extended introduction by the translator himself. Even before the reader encounters the fifteenth-century merchant, this introduction imposes two kinds of order on what the translator calls "the striking peculiarities of Nikitin's narrative" (*JTS*, xix). First, it attributes a deliberate intentionality to the merchant's unusual trajectory. Wielhorski begins with a citation from Nikolai Karamzin, the celebrated author of the first monumental history of the Russian empire in 1820: "Hitherto, geographers have ignored the fact that the honor of one of the oldest voyages to India, undertaken and described by a European, belongs to the age and country of Ivan III" (*JTS*, xix). The implications of invoking this particular passage from Karamzin's history extend well beyond an acknowledgment of the document's importance for reconstructing the past. By retrospectively appending a higher purpose to Nikitin's voyage, Wielhorski, via Karamzin, positions his journey squarely within the greater European projects of discovering the Orient and asserting imperial power.

The strategy of simultaneously nationalizing and globalizing the fifteenth-century merchant finds a much more elaborate counterpart in Wielhorski's second mode of resolving the intrinsic "peculiarities" of Nikitin's account: creating a selective order of linguistic access to the heteroglossic text. The translator explains his choice of rendering "the frequent recurrence of Oriental words and sentences, spelt in Russian letters and embodied in the original text" (*JTS*, xix) as follows: "Of these words and sentences," he warns, "some have been translated, while others have been necessarily left without explanation" (*JTS*, xx). One explanation of this "necessity" is offered in a footnote to one of the untranslated passages: "Even when the meaning can be guessed at, it has sometimes, as in the present instance, been thought undesirable to supply it in English" (*JTS*, 18). What was so "undesirable" in Nikitin's document that the translator refused to convey it to the English-speaking world?

As the account progresses, these "undesirable" passages appear to share one common element: Islam. Significantly, Wielhorski does not hesitate to communicate facts concerning Islamic societies and cultures, such as descriptions of trading routes and wry observations on local communities; what is omitted is the speaking subject's personal communion with the faith. The first example of

filtering occurs in the wake of a censorious description of the Hindu community. Recalling the hospitality extended to itinerant traders by the wives and
daughters of local merchants, Nikitin invokes what seems to be the Christian
God: "*O God, true God, merciful God, gracious God*" (*JTS*, 10). In the original,
however, the italicized sentence appears as a transliteration, "Bismillah e rahman ur rahim" (*KTM*, 20), a readily identifiable call to "Allah the Compassion-
ate and Merciful." As I have examined elsewhere, the exclamation was a common
response to cultural shock and moral outrage in contemporaneous Islamic travel
narratives (Banerjee 2003, 74).

As formulaic utterances such as the Bismillah give way to introspective reflections in which the merchant ponders his spiritual state, the translation likewise begins to change. Nikitin confesses, for example, "I am between two faiths.
*But I pray to the only God that he may preserve me from destruction. God is* one,
king of glory and creator of heaven and earth" (*JTS*, 13). While the italicized
words in Wielhorski's translation suggest that the narrator is still holding on to
his Christian faith, the translation diverges significantly from the source. The
"*only God*" to whom he prays does not appear as "Bog," the Russian word for
the Christian God, in the original; instead, it is "Ollo," a phonetic variation of
Allah. A more literal rendition of the original passage would thus yield: "I am
between two faiths. But I pray to Allah, the only God" (*KTM*, 24).

This typographic strategy of italicized Christianization, however, soon gives
way to a new style of managing the "irregularities" of Nikitin's text. Wielhorski's
version of another confession of faith reads, "I prayed to God Almighty who
made heaven and earth; and no other god of any other name did I invoke: Bog
Ollo, Bog kerim, Bog garym" (*JTS*, 15). Just as scorn toward Hindu women
spurred the merchant's first call to Allah, this prayer is an attempt to purge himself of a brief contact with the same community's polytheistic ritual objects, "stat-
uaries of beasts as naked as their worshipers" that have nothing in common with
the shrines of "Jerusalem or Mecca" (*JTS*, 24–25). As antipathy toward Hindu
spiritual and social life pushes Nikitin closer to the monotheistic worldview of
the Bahmanid Muslim elite, Wielhorski refuses to translate Islamic invocations
altogether. Thus, when a governor challenges the traveler for not being a true
Muslim, the merchant responds in the following terms: "Do not lead me, O Lord,
from the path of truth, but direct my steps to wander in righteousness. For in my
trouble I did no good for thy sake, O Lord, and have spent the whole of my days in
evil. Ollo pervodyger, Ollo tykarym, Ollo karim, Ollo ragymello, Akhalim du-
limo. I have already passed the fourth great day [of Easter] in the Mussulman
country, and have not renounced Christianity. But what may come hereafter, God
alone knows" (*JTS*, 18). While this utterance implies that the merchant is repent-
ing his observance of Ramadan rather than Easter, the phrase "But what may

come hereafter, God alone knows" acquires a very different meaning in light of the untranslated passages in Arabic and Persian that immediately precede it.

The extended closure of the narrative, composed sometime before the traveler's death near the port of Kaffa on the return journey and left untranslated in its entirety by Wielhorski, constitutes the final and most extensive example of the deafening silence that surrounds Nikitin's interlocutions with Islam in the English translation. Apart from a bland statement tucked into the introduction— "Nikitin terminates his narrative by a long sentence in corrupt Turkish, expressive of his gratitude to heaven for his preservation and safe return to his native country" (*JTS*, xxi)—the English translation remains conspicuously speechless for a very long moment at the end. As I have previously argued, the closing passage of the original consists of a series of commonplaces frequently used by Muslim travelers to conclude the narratives of their adventures (Banerjee 2003, 76–77). It is significant, therefore, that Wielhorski chose not to convey this ultimate testimony to his English-speaking audience.

The trajectory of selective translation, which begins by re-Christianizing the Islamic components of *Khozhdenie* and culminates in the complete aphasia of the narrator, performs a kind of linguistic containment under the guise of communication. By flattening out the "peculiarities" of the speaking subject, Wielhorski's English version of the *Journey* erases the rich contact zones of spirituality and culture that define the fifteenth-century travelogue. Instead, it establishes an important set of parameters for reclaiming the merchant both as an exemplary representative of the modern Russian empire and as an exception among European explorers who subsequently documented their own journeys to the Indian subcontinent. While the translation accords the merchant, and by extension Russia, a unique mode of access to the fabled "land of Ind" (*JTS*, xi)—long enshrined in the European imagination through documents as varied as the mysterious letter of Prester John, Marco Polo's *Travels*, and John Mandeville's majestic *Itinerarium*—the fact that the reader has no access to his inimitable linguistic heterogeneity protects both the corpus of his narrative and its embodied narrator's identity against the Islamic component of the East.

The same impulse of de-Islamicization marks the transcription of Nikitin's adventures onto the big screen a century later. In a remarkable departure from the merchant's actual fate, the Indo-Soviet *Khozhdenie* frames his journey as a flashback bracketed between two identical landscapes that cannot be identified with anything other than Orthodox Christian Russia. The film opens with a close-up of the blond-haired, blue-eyed protagonist wearing an oversize cross at the neck of his open shirt. He gradually wakes up as the camera pulls back to reveal a panoramic vista of the Volga River, with an onion-domed wooden church on the horizon and a Gregorian chant in Old Church Slavonic playing softly in the background. As the merchant begins to recognize his surroundings, he repeats the words of the background chant, at first hesitantly and then with increasing joy. Finally, he kneels and kisses the ground before him while fervently making the Orthodox sign of the cross.

The carefully designed continuum between the merchant's body, the surrounding landscape, and the language that returns to his lips is conspicuously devoid of any traces of Islam or the Orient. As the audience learns from the flashback immediately following the opening scene, it was from this very riverbank and with the blessings of this very church that Nikitin had departed several years earlier. His motive, as explained to his grieving mother and the perplexed village priest, was not to turn a profit but "to satisfy my burning desire to see India."

Desire lends a powerful affective dimension to the intentionality that Wielhorski's translation imposed on the merchant's contingent trajectory. Whereas the translator invoked Karamzin to align Nikitin's journey with contemporaneous European quests of discovering the fabled land of India, the film accomplishes the same effect with light, color, and sound. As dawn slowly dispels the darkness of the long passage over the Arabian Sea, Nikitin leans against the ship's mast, whispering, "India, my dream, my love! How long have I waited to meet you!" The camera then turns to reveal the feminized object of his passion: a panoramic beach, adorned by ancient Hindu temples and full of men and women chanting the Sanskrit *Gayatri mantra* to the rising sun. This establishing shot is striking in its obvious parallels with the inaugural scene of the merchant's return to the bosom of Orthodox Christian Russia. The very first image of India thus obscures all traces of both the Muslim population and the Islamic architecture of the Bahmanid sultanate that likely greeted the merchant in the fifteenth century. Classical Sanskrit on the soundtrack likewise occludes the mixture of languages that he must have encountered on shore and that would later find its way into his writing.

Whereas the English translator struggled to contain the Islamic eruptions in Nikitin's text, the film manages to produce a monolithic, monolingual vision of both his origin and his destination. In fact, the Indo-Soviet *Khozhdenie* goes one step further than Wielhorski by replacing the multiethnic and multifaith community of the Bahmanid Deccan with an unabashedly Orientalist imagination of India. Just like its Russian counterpart in the opening scene, the object of the merchant's desire appears on the screen as a timeless repository of mystical Hinduism, replete with temples, sacred cows, and even a noble elephant.

Such confluences of utopian longings, however, are not a product of the film's twentieth-century context alone. Their roots reach back to a complex politics of world culture that took shape between the late eighteenth and late nineteenth centuries and informed both Karamzin's historiographical project and the Hakluyt Society's mission. During this period, the ancient Sanskrit language acquired a powerful new signification as a naturalized index of origins and identities. As Raymond Schwab put it, the "discovery" of Sanskrit in the late eighteenth century by European colonial officials was akin to stumbling upon "the America of languages" (1984, 176)—a new repository of the past that was quickly co-opted to construct a hierarchized network of human culture through the distribution and interaction of languages. The first humanistic field to take on the mantle of the natural sciences and attempt to describe this new world system was comparative philology. Drawing freely from the idiom of biology to construct an elaborate structure of equivalence and difference, the emerging academic discipline divided languages into families, while dialects and idiolects served as genera and species.

Sanskrit occupied a peculiar place in this system, as demonstrated by Max Muller's famous pronouncement: "Thanks to the discovery of the ancient language of India, and thanks to the discovery of the close kinship between this language and the idioms of the principal races of Europe, a complete revolution has taken place in the method of studying the history of the world" (quoted in Krishnaswamy 2005, 8). Valorized as the apex of the linguistic and cultural perfection of a world lost to the mists of time, the classical, by now "dead" language of the Indian subcontinent paradoxically became the principal frame for defining Europe's global primacy in the historical present. By the mid-nineteenth century, as Revathi Krishnaswamy (2005, 9–12) has documented, the typological links between Sanskrit and the principal languages of western Europe had become inextricably attached to concepts of racial and cultural superiority in Germany, England, and France.

The impact of comparative philology most germane to this study was the internal division it created within the very concept of the Orient. As Maurice Olender (1992) elegantly demonstrated, the systematic contrast between Indo-European and Semitic language families resulted in the construction of a grand supranational tribal prehistory whose implicit protagonist was white Christian Europe. Although the tremendous enthusiasm over Sanskrit cast colonial India in a somewhat positive light, it was only by erasing the long presence and rich history of Islam on the subcontinent that Indian culture could be aligned with Western imaginations of the self. This concept of two Orients, differentiated by language, race, and religion, is likewise essential for understanding the little-examined but crucial role of India in the construction of modern Russian identity. By laying a special claim to the discovery of India untainted by Islam, Wielhorski's translation not only aligned Russia's past with the Indo-European civilizational continuum but also counteracted its orientalization under Western eyes. The portrayal of Hinduism as the cultural counterpart of Nikitin's

Orthodox Christian faith was the logical next step for rescuing Russia, as the historian Martin Malia put it, from being "cast out into Asia's outer darkness" (1999, 147).

As the Russian empire entered the Great Game with Britain to gain control of the Eurasian heartland in the late nineteenth century, the Indian subcontinent emerged as a significant point of reference for its geopolitical and cultural identity. India represented a pure Orient: its classical Hindu past seemed disconnected from Russia's long history of contact and conflict with Islam, starting with the twelfth-century Mongol occupation of Kievan Rus' and culminating in the Soviet occupation of central Asia after the October Revolution. By staging a grand encounter between Hinduism and Orthodox Christianity at the critical intersection between decolonization and de-Stalinization, the Indo-Soviet adaptation of Nikitin's journey suppresses several centuries of imperial violence and cultural contamination through which Islam embedded itself in the cultures of both nation-states. It is from this revisionist perspective of de-Islamicization that the film also performs a literal enactment of Khrushchev's slogan "friendship of the peoples," a soft-power project that aligned modern Russia's revolutionary trajectory with the emerging emancipatory narratives of newly decolonized nations. The inherent contradictions of such a goal are again resolved by Bombay cinema's conventions of desire. Nikitin's relationship with his screen environment is mediated through two intimate relationships with the Hindu community conspicuously absent from the fifteenth-century original—relationships that, in turn, correspond with the spiritual and secular, historical and contemporary axes of his journey. Instead of commercial and religious communion with influential Muslims of the Bahmanid sultanate, which in the fifteenth century proved highly advantageous to the narrator, the cinematic merchant gains access to Indian society and culture through characters who are unabashedly Hindu. Setting the tone and determining the trajectory of his journey are two distinct love plots: the first of romantic love with a woman named Champa and the second of fraternal love with a man called Sakharam. Both Hindu characters bear "speaking names," or *nomens omens*, more typical of classical theater: while "Champa" means a fragrant flower, Sakharam is both literally and figuratively a fellow traveler.

In a radical repudiation of the original text, a family of Hindu pilgrims provides Nikitin with his first point of entry into local society and customs. At a seaside temple, the merchant forges a deep kinship with this family by reviving the daughter, Champa, from a poisonous snakebite. No linguistic or religious barrier prevents the newcomer from identifying himself, anachronistically, as a "Russian" or from adopting the very customs that the fifteenth-century narrator had found so abhorrent. Dressed in a *dhoti* and sporting a resplendent caste mark on his forehead, he overcomes the Hindu taboo of sharing food with people of other castes and religions—a point noted with disdain and accompanied by indignant invocations to Allah in the original *Khozhdenie*—when Champa serves him food from the same vessel as her father. The hospitality extended to visitors by Hindu women that had inspired the first linguistic turn to Islam in the fifteenth-century text turns to joyous acceptance on the screen as she flouts the rules of gender sequestration and entertains the foreigner without any chaperones. The film's introduction of a love interest that was absent in the original text performs a significant symbolic function. It invents a powerful counternarrative to the merchant's uneven attempts at passing as a Muslim in order to gain the favor of Bahmanid elites. Rather than having to prove his Khorasani credentials to a bevy of administrators and fellow traders, Nikitin's cinematic avatar receives immediate recognition and respect from the same religious community that alienated his fifteenth-century original.

The tantalizing prospects of miscegenation that arise from this alliance are kept at bay by another stock convention of Bombay cinema: the dream sequence in which protagonists act out their most transgressive desires. Champa, dressed in a kitschy peasant maiden's costume and gliding across the snowy plains of Russia, replicates Nikitin's gesture of dressing as a Hindu Brahmin in her family home. The visual harmony produced by this reciprocal act is shattered, however, when she sorrowfully informs him that her religion prohibits union with those of other faiths. Even though Champa's platonic relationship with Nikitin—like medieval Russia's identification with classical Sanskrit—seems preordained by their mutual antipathy to Islam, the blond-haired, blue-eyed embodiment of Orthodox Christianity is ultimately spared both spiritual and ethnoracial contamination from any kind of Orient.

In popular Indian cinema, the dream sequence usually foreshadows resolution rather than capitulation. By inverting its narrative function, the scene imposes a very specific set of limits on the potentialities of Indo-Soviet intercultural communion. The sudden wall that springs up between the lovers exposes an inviolable hierarchy between the masculine figure of the savior superpower and the feminine, newly decolonized object of salvation. Whereas the Great Game provided the impulse to de-Islamicize Nikitin's translation into Victorian English, the subplot of thwarted romance attests to the persistent imperial unconscious underlying the utopian imagination of Khrushchev's "friendship of the peoples."

A very different friendship with a Hindu man sublimates the threat of Nikitin's romantic desire and realigns his quest with a more salubrious narrative of the Indo-Soviet alliance. Following the separation from Champa, the merchant is adopted by Sakharam, a wandering minstrel and universal do-gooder, who promises to show him "the real India." The brotherly love between the two men shifts the index of the merchant's identification from spirituality to the secular parameters of class, a much less treacherous terrain with a powerful message of social justice. Upon learning that Sakharam is a "penniless wanderer," Nikitin—contradicting both his self-identification as a merchant and his relentless aspiration to join the Khorasani circle of "boyars and big men" in the original text—warmly declares that he is a fellow proletarian, the "destitute son of a landless ploughman."

It is through the secular index of class, surprisingly, that the film achieves the ultimate separation of the traveler from the Islamic elements of his narrative. As observed by a number of commentators, including me, the nexus between economic success and social prestige was the most powerful motivator for the fifteenth-century merchant to ally himself with the language, religion, and culture of the Khorasanis, the mobile community of traders and statesmen who connected the commercial circuits of west-central Asia with the Muslim principalities of the Indian subcontinent (Lenhoff and Martin 1989, 328; Banerjee 2003, 72–73). The "real India" that Sakharam shows Nikitin capitalizes on this asymmetry of class and religion to highlight the vast gaps in wealth and power between the Hindu majority and the primarily Muslim commercial and political elite. Through the eyes of Sakharam, played by Balraj Sahni, the traveler takes on the mantle of a progressive tourist in the third world. Nikitin's shock at the squalid poverty of the Hindu masses translates into outrage directed toward wily Muslim traders and the despotic "boyars" who prey on the common man. Among his many encounters with villainous Muslim figures—who, unlike the Hindus on the seashore, are framed against the famous Bahmani architecture of southwestern India—only the governor Mahmud Ghawan appears to possess any depth of character.

Nikitin's exchange with Mahmud Ghawan, played by Prithviraj Kapoor, constitutes the climax of the cinematic journey beyond three seas. Stunned by the opulence of the governor's palace, the merchant nevertheless preserves his personal integrity while petitioning the powerful man on behalf of the Hindu peasants. Impressed by the "strength of the Russian's soul," Ghawan accedes to hearing the visitor's testimony. It is in the context of this confrontation that the merchant becomes a true proselytizer, though not in the religious sense of the word. With his fiery advocacy of a more equitable social order, he manages to transform the stereotypical figure of the oppressive Oriental despot into a somewhat enlightened one. Promising to acquaint himself with his subjects' plight, the governor performs a small gesture that is faithful to the fifteenth-century context of Nikitin's journey. He hands the trader written permission to conduct commercial activities on his territory.

The merchant thus departs the Indian subcontinent not as a conflicted pseudo-Khorasani convert but rather with his territorial, racial, and religious identity intact and unmarked. An additional modern role as an agent of revolutionary change supplements this nostalgia of restoration from the Islamic Orient. What he leaves behind in the real world is the perpetual possibility of religious intolerance. Genocidal violence between Hindus and Muslims, which constituted the dark underbelly of decolonization ten years before the making of the film, continues to haunt political and social life on the subcontinent to this day. Paradoxically, the spectralization of Islam that connects the English translation and screen adaptation of the Russian Columbus's journey does not just undermine the idea of India as a secular nation-state. It also exposes the fault lines of the "friendship of the peoples."

## NOTES

1. The dates of Nikitin's journey are estimated as either 1466–1472 or 1468–1474 (Lur'e and Semenov 1986, 34; "Russkii chuzhezemets").

2. Lur'e and Semenov reproduce two versions of *Khozhdenie za tri moria Afanasiia Nikitina*: one from the L'vov (Ermolinsky) Chronicle, 5–17, and the other from the Troitsky-Sergiev redaction, 18–31. Subsequent references to the Russian source correspond with the second, fuller version. All citations from the Russian source appear in parentheses in the body of the text as *KTM*. All translations are mine.

3. The Troitsky-Sergiev redaction provided the source material for Count Wielhorski's English translation, published by the Hakluyt Society of London in 1858. References to the English text appear in parentheses in the body of the text as *JTS*.

## REFERENCES

Banerjee, Anindita. 2003. "By Caravan and Campfire: Khorasani Narratives about Hindustan and Afanasii Nikitin's Journey beyond Three Seas." *Die Welt der Slaven* 48:69–80.

Gopalan, Lalitha. 2002. *Cinema of Interruptions: Action Genres in Contemporary Indian Cinema*. London: British Film Institute.

"Journey beyond Three Seas by Athanasius Nikitin, The." 1858. Trans. Count M. Wielhorski. In *India in the Fifteenth Century*, ed. R. H. Major, 1–32. London: Hakluyt Society.

Krishnaswamy, Revathi. 2005. "History in Language, Language in History." *Clio* 34 (1): 7–16.

Lenhoff, Gail, and Janet Martin. 1989. "The Commercial and Cultural Context of Afanasii Nikitin's Journey beyond Three Seas." *Jahrbucher fur Geschichte Osteuropeas* 37 (3): 321–44.

Lur'e, Ia. S., and L. S. Semenov, eds. 1986. *Khozhdenie za tri moria Afanasiia Nikitina*. Leningrad: Rossiskaia Akademiia Nauk.

Malia, Martin. 1999. *Russia under Western Eyes*. Oxford: Oxford University Press.

Olender, Maurice. 1992. *The Language of Paradise: Race, Religion, and Philology in the Nineteenth Century*. Cambridge, MA: Harvard University Press.

Prasad, Madhava M. 1998. *Ideology of the Hindi Film: A Historical Construction*. New Delhi: Oxford University Press.

Rajagopalan, Sudha. 2008. *Indian Films in Soviet Cinemas: The Culture of Movie-Going after Stalin*. Bloomington: Indiana University Press.

Schwab, Raymond. 1984. *The Oriental Renaissance: Europe's Rediscovery of India and the East, 1680–1880*. New York: Columbia University Press.

# MEDIA COVERAGE OF ISLAM IN CONTEMPORARY GERMANY AND THE UNITED STATES

*Annika Marlen Hinze*

**The media is the most powerful entity on earth. They have the power to make the innocent guilty and to make the guilty innocent, and that's power.**

—Malcolm X

In 1981, Edward Said predicted that, as the world grows smaller through sophisticated means of travel and communication, cultural identity would become more important and mistrust regarding "the other" would grow. He noted that the "production and diffusion of knowledge" would "play an absolutely crucial role" (Said 1981, 153) in the realm of intercultural relationships. Unless knowledge is produced and diffused in the name of community and mutual understanding, Said predicted, the relationship between the Muslim world and the West would be bleak.

In *Covering Islam: How the Media and the Experts Determine How We See the World*, Said addresses the Iranian Hostage Crisis and subsequent Western media coverage thereof. The book analyzes how print media and the television screen brought the crisis to Western, specifically US, audiences. In this chapter, I revisit the coverage of Islam in the public sphere in the second decade of the twenty-first century, with a focus on the United States and Germany. By analyzing the coverage of topics relevant to Islam, such as immigrants and refugees from predominantly Muslim countries, the Israel-Palestine conflict, and international policies toward predominantly Muslim countries in the Middle East and North Africa, I seek to expose media coverage as an "invisible screen" that affects policy and public opinion in Germany and the United States, two of the Western world's richest and most powerful nations. I also seek to understand how popular media sources may function differently in the United States and Germany, especially in an age of increasing criticism of what certain policymakers refer to as the "mainstream media." To this end, I present a content analysis of media headlines in popular mainstream news sources in both countries over the past three years, from January 2017 through December 2019. My analysis focuses on the two newspapers with the highest circulation in each country: the *New York Times* (*NYT*) in the United States and the *Süddeutsche Zeitung* (*SZ*) in Germany. Both newspapers have largely Center Left audiences, with the *NYT*'s audience leaning slightly more to the left of the US political spectrum than the *SZ*'s audience on the German political spectrum (Pew 2014, 2017). To account for increasing political polarization in both countries, I supplemented the analysis by adding two populist news outlets with a more conservative audience: *Fox News* in the United States and *Bild*, a print and online tabloid, in Germany. These additional news sources add some nuance to this analysis and allow me to paint a more detailed picture of Islam-related media coverage in both countries.

## Islam and the West

The relationship between the West and the Muslim world in the twentieth and twenty-first centuries has been marked by distance, occasional fascination, and war. The reification of "Islam" and "the West" has not helped matters. Over the past thirty years, tensions have increased significantly: the 1979 Iranian Revolution; the 1980 hostage crisis in Tehran; the hijackings of several airplanes; the ongoing conflict between Israel and Palestine; and the terrorist attacks of the past two decades, culminating in the September 11, 2001, attacks in New York, Washington, and Pennsylvania, the March 11, 2004, attacks in Madrid, and the July 7, 2005, attacks in London. In the aftermath of 9/11, the United States and its allies waged wars in both Iraq and Afghanistan and are now embroiled in the (proxy) war in Syria. Tensions with Iran have continued to increase since the Trump administration announced that it would pull out of the Iran Nuclear Deal in 2018. In Europe, the number of working-class Muslim immigrants has increased dramatically, as has the level of xenophobia, and nativist, anti-Muslim immigration discourse has established itself solidly on the Far Right. In the United States, Muslims have been targeted by racists and xenophobes as well, but in contrast to Europe, "denunciations of Muslims and their beliefs have been couched in terms of security" (*The Economist* 2011, 23).

Since 2015, tensions between Islam and the West have escalated. The Syrian refugee crisis has displaced approximately 5.6 million people (UNHCR 2018), the vast majority of whom reside in refugee camps in Turkey, Lebanon, Jordan, Iraq, and Egypt. In addition, hundreds of thousands of Syrians have fled to Europe, most to Germany and Sweden (Connor 2018). The influx of predominantly Muslim refugees from Syria to the European Union was followed by a right-wing populist backlash in many European countries, several of which already had a tense and often racially charged relationship with their mostly Muslim immigrant communities. In Germany, in particular, the right-wing populist party Alternative für Deutschland (AfD) gained in popularity. In the 2017 parliamentary elections, the AfD won 11.5 percent of the popular vote, on the basis of its anti-immigration, Euro-skeptic platform, and it became the third-strongest party in the German parliament, the Bundestag. Since 2017, it has become even stronger, especially in the five German *Länder* (states) of former East Germany.

Similarly, in the United States, where the Muslim population is smaller than in Europe (about 1 percent of the US population is Muslim, compared with 5 percent in Europe, and 6 percent in Germany, according to Sahgal and Mohamed 2019), tensions have grown. Since the election of President Donald Trump in 2016, the United States has reduced immigration from Muslim countries, mostly through a "Muslim ban" that blocks entry to the United States for citizens from several Muslim-majority countries. In addition to restrictions on immigration, in general, and from Muslim-majority countries in particular, the Trump administration has engaged in an unpredictable foreign policy, which, according to Hassan (2017, 187), is characterized by "Orientalism, Islamophobia, and the securitization of Islam . . . more than any other strategic rationale." Trump has been famously outspoken about Islam. When he announced the first version of his "Muslim ban" in 2017, he declared during a speech in Youngstown, Ohio, that "the hateful ideology of radical Islam must not be allowed to reside or spread within our own communities" (quoted in Shane, Rosenberg, and Lipton 2017).

Despite the influence of right-wing populism inside the US government and in the German parliamentary opposition, both countries are deeply divided on Islam, although Americans are more open to Muslims than are Germans: a 2019 Pew survey reports that 89 percent of Americans are willing to accept Muslims as neighbors, and 79 percent are willing to accept them as family members. According to the same survey, 77 percent of Germans are willing to accept Muslims as neighbors, and 55 percent as family members (Sahgal and Mohamed 2019). The survey indicates that a higher level of education correlates with an increased level of acceptance of Muslims in both countries: 86 percent of Americans who hold a college degree are willing to accept a Muslim into their family, compared with 75 percent without a college degree. In Germany, 67 percent of individuals with a college degree are willing to accept a Muslim into their family, while the figure falls to 52 percent among those without a college degree (Sahgal and Mohamed 2019).

# The Media

The media play a special role in shaping public opinion and the policy discourse about Islam in Germany and the United States. Although the media do respond to public opinion, the public generally invests little time in following political issues (Baum and Potter 2008), perhaps because paying attention to politics generates only marginal utility (Downs 1957). The media provide a platform for elites to insert their views on crucial political and social issues into the public discourse and to influence public opinion (Zaller 1992). But elites sometimes change their views in response to public opinion (Page and Shapiro 1983). For this reason, the effects of media framing, public opinion, and elite discourse are multidirectional, spilling over into and crucially influencing one another: elite discourse influences the public and the media, but public opinion can sway media coverage and elite behavior. The public's main mechanism of influence is its choices in media consumption and the electoral accountability of elites.

Elites can strongly influence public opinion based on their prominence and their ability to "frame" the media (Baum and Potter 2008). "Framing" is a term that emphasizes certain aspects of an event or issue, which are woven together into a story that supports a specific interpretation and evaluation of the event or issue and proposes a solution for it (Entman 2004). According to Entman, the administration in charge has the greatest ability to frame an issue. The president of the United States and the chancellor of Germany are the most trusted sources of information for the media. Owing to their position of leadership, their views are most heavily cited in the media, giving them the ability to wield the greatest influence on public debate (media scholars refer to this as the bully pulpit). A "story" that supports a certain frame generates emotions and terminology that are incorporated into the public debate and give a certain segment of the political spectrum the upper hand in the "framing war."

In the United States, the news organizations hierarchy is headed by the *NYT*, whose coverage is used as a cue by other media. News organizations rely on specific norms when selecting their sources and the frames that they use to describe news events. This general process is referred to as indexing (Bennett 2016; Zaller 1992). These norms are widely shared among news organizations and outlets, which tend to make similar decisions in the selection of their sources. In democracies, news outlets base their indexing decisions on guesses made by journalists about the likely balance of power among political elites. Therefore, elites that exercise power in the political process tend to dominate media coverage (Bennett 2016). According to Bennett (1990), the democratic ideal of an independent press is rarely achieved, and true freedom of press is limited, in part because media tend to index levels of dissent among political elites. If political decision makers disagree on an issue, the media will present multiple frames that reflect those diverging opinions. If there is agreement among elites, however (as during major national crises, e.g., the Cold War), the media will accept elite consensus at face value and not pursue alternative perspectives. In my view, Bennett underestimates the overall influence of both the media and public opinion (e.g., Page and Shapiro 1983; Baum and Potter 2008). In the aftermath of 9/11, however, indexing is an important factor to consider in connection with national and international crises and anti-Muslim sentiment. With increasing partisan polarization, we can expect indexing to become incrementally weaker, especially on topics such as Islam.

Public opinion on certain issues is typically strengthened by "focusing events" that allow new issues to move onto the policy agenda (Baumgartner and Jones 1993; Kingdon 1995). Entman (2004) argues that 9/11 was a "focusing event" that unified and streamlined public opinion in ways that only the Cold War had done previously. More than twenty years later, after two major wars, 9/11 may have lost its immediate force, but it remains a powerful symbol for policymakers and mainstream media, especially because of its association with Islam.

According to Edward Said (1981), the West has invented its own Islam. In response to century-old political tensions, he argues, the West portrays Islam as extremist and a threat to Western civilization: "Muslims and Arabs are essentially covered, discussed, apprehended, either as oil suppliers or as potential terrorists" (26). This negative frame suggests that the West must protect itself against any threat to its security posed by Islam. He adds that the Western framing of Islam is rooted in political motivations rather than sociological or anthropological fact, and it therefore tells us very little about Islam. Rather, the West projects itself onto its description of Islam:

> All in all, present coverage of Islam and non-Western societies in effect canonizes certain notions, texts, and authorities. The idea that Islam is medieval and dangerous, for example, has acquired a place in both culture and in the polity that is very well defined: authorities can be cited for it readily, references can be made to it, arguments about particular instances of Islam can be adduced from it—by anyone, not just by experts or by journalists. And in turn such an idea furnishes a kind of *a priori* touchstone to be taken account of by anyone wishing to discuss or say anything about Islam. From being something out there, Islam—or rather, the material invariably associated with it—is turned into an orthodoxy of *this* society. It enters the cultural canon, and this makes the task of changing it very difficult indeed. (149)

On both sides of the Atlantic, popular discourse portrays Islam as "medieval and dangerous" (Said 1981). According to Elizabeth Poole (2002), the media create their own version of Islam. In the United States, policymakers often conflate Islam with threats to national security and terrorism. Kalkan, Layman, and Uslaner (2009) find that 9/11 has had no significant impact on American attitudes toward Muslims. Unlike other religious groups, American Muslims are perceived more as a cultural minority than as a religious or racial minority. This finding has two implications: (1) Muslims are not regarded as part of an immigrant minority group, as Hispanics are, and (2) they are not treated as part of the American mainstream.

In Germany, Muslims are associated with blue-collar immigrants who threaten to "take over" German democratic society. Muslims represent both the largest immigrant minority and a cultural out-group. German political discourse, on the left and the right, tends to portray Muslims as a cultural minority whose cultural values are a threat to German (or European) values.

Similarly, in Britain, as Rusi and Cinnirella observe, negative media portrayal of Muslims has the effect of enhancing "the distinctiveness and self-esteem principles" of the dominant population group (i.e., white, nonimmigrants), "since the in-group is delineated *evaluatively* from the out-group in the clearest manner" (2010, 304). Thus, out-grouping serves not only to reject the "other" but also to affirm the in-group. Such self-affirmations are produced, reproduced, and communicated by the media, which thus participate in the process of identity negotiation.

Media frames are important factors that shape public discourse and influence policy implementation. In both the United States and Germany, the media frame Muslims as the "other," albeit for different reasons. But do the media frame Muslims in exclusively negative terms? By framing Muslims in a more balanced manner, the media would be fulfilling their democratic function of impartiality and telling both sides of the story. A more balanced portrayal of Muslims in key media sources with high circulation/viewership would suggest that elites in both countries are not unified in their negative framing of Muslims and that the discourse on the "Muslim issue" has changed since Said wrote *Covering Islam* in 1981.

# Methodology

At a time of increasingly extreme political polarization on both sides of the Atlantic, media framing and the power of the bully pulpit have changed. In their quest for readership, media sources increasingly cater to a polarized public. The analysis of the media by academics has been influenced by this polarization.

For my analysis of US media discourse on Islam, I use two popular news sources: one "traditional" newspaper and one news outlet that caters to conservative-populist views. For Germany, I analyze the two most highly circulated newspapers: *Bild*, a conservative-populist tabloid that sold 1.47 million papers in the third quarter of 2019 (Statista 2019b), and *SZ*, which has a more left-leaning readership. During the last quarter of 2019, *SZ* had a circulation of 327,000, second only to *Bild* (Statista 2019a).

For the US sample, I selected *Fox News*, a conservative-populist news outlet, with 2.4 million primetime viewers and 1.4 million total-day viewers in the third quarter of 2019, according to a Nielsen report (Johnson 2019). The *NYT*, the country's leading "traditional" newspaper, had a circulation of 484,000 in January 2019 (Statista 2019b), ranking it third in circulation behind the *Wall Street Journal* and *USA Today*.

I chose to perform a content analysis of news headlines in an effort to provide a general overview of coverage regarding Islam. The time frame was January 1, 2017, through December 31, 2019. In the United States, this period covers roughly the first three years of the Trump presidency, as well as the signing, partial implementation, and litigation of the three "Muslim travel bans." In Germany, this period includes the nine months leading up to the September 2017 parliamentary elections, which made the AfD the third-largest party in Parliament and the strongest opposition party. The three-year time frame also includes a period of intense political debate among German policymakers who addressed the aftermath of the Syrian refugee crisis.

I collected samples through a LexisNexis search for the word "Islam" in article headlines for each of the four news sources, between January 1, 2017, and December 31, 2019. I used all headlines listed in the LexisNexis search engine for this time period. However, if the same article was published in two or more sources a few hours apart, I included only one in the sample to avoid repetition. The search yielded 12 headlines containing the word "Islam" from *Fox News*, 70 headlines from the *NYT*, 108 headlines from the *SZ*, and 26 headlines from *Bild*.

I recorded the publication date of each article and assigned an evaluative category to each headline: "positive," "neutral," or "negative."

## Analysis

Table 16.1 summarizes the results of my content analysis of news headlines from all four news sources. The two traditional news outlets had many more articles on Islam than the two populist ones. The *NYT* coverage of Islam was almost seven times greater than that of *Fox*, and *SZ*'s coverage of Islam was approxi-

**TABLE 16.1**  Headline framing of Islam from all four news sources

| HEADLINE FRAMING OF ISLAM | FOX NEWS | NEW YORK TIMES | BILD | SÜDDEUTSCHE ZEITUNG |
|---|---|---|---|---|
| Positive | 1 | 7 | 0 | 8 |
| Neutral | 3 | 51 | 8 | 87 |
| Negative | 8 | 12 | 17 | 13 |
| Total | 12 | 70 | 26 | 108 |

mately four times greater than that of *Bild*. The coverage of Islam in the German sources was slightly higher than that in the US sources: 134 Islam-related headlines versus 92 Islam-related headlines.

In both countries, the tone and framing of headlines on Islam in conservative-populist news sources were more negative than those in the traditional sources. The sample of headlines also indicates considerably less overall coverage of Islam in conservative-populist media.

The traditional news sources, the *NYT* and *SZ*, published more articles on Islam than the conservative sources, but of the "non-neutral" headlines, a majority were negative, a sign that skepticism toward Islam is not exclusive to conservative circles. As Khan argues, Islamophobia is not exclusive to the political Right, and it manifests itself in a more subtle form on the Left, often "under the guise of inclusion" (2017, 51). For example, headlines about Islam coded as "negative" in the *NYT* refer to Islam as "radical," "violent," or "dangerous," usually in connection with the oppression of women or in the context of national security threats.

The neutral and positive coverage of Islam in the two traditional newspapers, the *NYT* and *SZ*, differed significantly. Positive coverage of Islam in the *NYT* often addressed its diversity, humanist elements, inclusiveness, and tolerance of other religions. In *SZ*, by contrast, positive headlines were formulated with a note of surprise, such as "A peaceful Islam is possible" or "Women's rights in Islam." The tone of the article headlines suggests that the basic assumption is that Islam is *not* peaceful and does *not* recognize women's rights.

The conservative-populist media and the traditional newspapers appear to address two different Islams. The traditional newspapers tend to cover Islam from a variety of angles, with an overall neutral tone, while the conservative-populist sources frame Islam as a violent and hateful religion that poses a serious threat to national security and the democratic order. This finding supports the observation that indexing and the general media landscape are increasingly affected by political polarization and that alternative, populist media sources are increasingly catering to audiences different from those of traditional media sources. The populist media audience tends to have lower levels of education, endorses more restrictive views on immigration, and manifests greater xenophobia. The finding also supports previous observations that the media create their own Islam (Said 1981; Poole 2002).

In Western democracies, traditional media are under attack not only from populist policymakers who challenge their truth-value but also from within their own ranks. As policy landscapes become increasingly polarized, so too does media coverage. Topics such as Islam are particularly vulnerable to polarization.

*Fox News* and *Bild*, both leaders within their respective domestic media fields, have an obligation to provide accurate and balanced yet critical journalistic coverage of sensitive issues. However, their coverage of Islam, as documented in this chapter, caters strongly to the more-negative-than-average opinions of their audiences. Arguably, they are more interested in selling images of Islam that are consistent with their readers' views than in upholding journalistic values of truth, fairness, impartiality, and humanity.

But traditional left-leaning news sources also manifest skepticism of Islam (Khan 2017). Almost forty years after the publication of Edward Said's *Covering Islam*, Islam remains a contentious topic in two of the world's most powerful Western democracies. Traditional and left-leaning news media tend to cover Islam from a Western-centric and often demonizing perspective, allowing little space for open, intellectual inquiry. This rather negative coverage may indicate that media sources across the board are not living up to the democratic standards of impartiality on the topic of Islam.

My findings here require important caveats: my analysis offers only a small glimpse into a large and complex topic that merits further inquiry. News headlines are not always indicative of the full content of a news article. The purpose of a news headline is to capture the attention of readers, while the content of the article often offers a more nuanced treatment of the subject. A content analysis of the full articles, therefore, may identify a more sophisticated treatment of Islam and may yield different conclusions. Further research is warranted.

### REFERENCES

Baum, Matthew A., and Philip B. K. Potter. 2008. "The Relationships between Mass Media, Public Opinion, and Foreign Policy: Toward a Theoretical Synthesis." *Annual Review of Politics* 11:39–65.

Baumgartner, Frank R., and Bryan D. Jones. 1993. *Agendas and Instability in American Politics*. Chicago: University of Chicago Press.

Bennett, W. Lance. 1990. "Toward a Theory of Press-State Relations in the United States." *Journal of Communication* 40 (2): 103–25.

——. 2016. "Indexing Theory." In *The International Encyclopedia of Political Communication*, edited by D. Mazzoleni. https://doi.org/10.1002/9781118541555.wbiepc 180.

Connor, Phillip. 2018. "Most Displaced Syrians Are in the Middle East, and about a Million Are in Europe." Pew Research Center, January 29, 2018. https://www.pew research.org/fact-tank/2018/01/29/where-displaced-syrians-have-resettled/.

Downs, Anthony. 1957. *An Economic Theory of Democracy*. New York: Harper.

*Economist, The*. 2011. "Can Careless Talk Cost Lives? The Growth of Islamophobia." July 30, 2011.

Entman, Robert M. 2004. *Projections of Power: Framing News, Public Opinion, and U.S. Foreign Policy*. Chicago: University of Chicago Press.

Hassan, Oz. 2017. "Trump, Islamophobia and US-Middle East Relations." *Critical Studies on Security* 5 (2): 187–91.

Johnson, Ted. 2019. "Fox News Tops Cable Networks in Third Quarter." *Deadline*, October 1, 2019. https://deadline.com/2019/10/fox-news-cable-news-network-ratings -1202749534/.

Kalkan, Kerem Ozan, Geoffrey C. Layman, and Eric M. Uslaner. 2009. "'Band of Others?' Attitudes toward Muslims in Contemporary American Society." *Journal of Politics* 72 (3): 1–16.

Khan, Saeed A. 2017. "Fallacies of Foundational Principles: Rawls's Political Liberalism and Islamophobia." *ReOrient* 3 (1): 50–64.

King, Jawara D. 2010. *The Awakening of Global Consciousness: A Guide to Self-Realization and Spirituality*. Bloomington, IN: AuthorHouse.

Kingdon, John W. 1995. *Agendas, Alternatives, and Public Policies*. Boston: Addison-Wesley Educational Publishers.

Page, Benjamin I., and Robert Y. Shapiro. 1983. "Effects of Public Opinion on Policy." *American Political Science Review* 77 (1): 175–90.

Pew Research Center. 2014. "American Trends Panel (wave 1)." Survey conducted March 19–April 29, 2014. https://www.journalism.org/2014/10/21/political-polari zation-media-habits/.

——. 2017. "In Western Europe, Public Attitudes toward News Media More Divided by Populist Views Than Left-Right Ideology." Survey of eight western European countries conducted October 30–December 20, 2017. https://www.pewresearch .org/global/fact-sheet/news-media-and-political-attitudes-in-germany/.

Poole, Elisabeth. 2002. *Reporting Islam: Media Representations of British Muslims*. London: I.B. Tauris.

Rusi, Jaspal, and Marco Cinnirella. 2010. "Media Representations of British Muslims and Hybridized Threats to Identity." *Contemporary Islam* 4 (3): 289–310.

Sahgal, Neha, and Besheer Mohamed. 2019. "In the U.S. and Western Europe, People Say They Accept Muslims, but Opinions Are Divided on Islam." Pew Research Center, October 8, 2019. https://www.pewresearch.org/fact-tank/2019/10/08/in -the-u-s-and-western-europe-people-say-they-accept-muslims-but-opinions -are-divided-on-islam/.

Said, Edward. 1981. *Covering Islam: How the Media and the Experts Determine How We See the Rest of the World*. New York: Random House.

Shane, Scott, Matthew Rosenberg, and Eric Lipton. 2017. "Trump Pushes Dark View of Islam to Center of U.S. Policy-Making." *New York Times*, February 1, 2017. https://www.nytimes.com/2017/02/01/us/politics/donald-trump-islam.html.

Statista. 2019a. "Auflagenstärkste Zeitungen in Deutschland nach verkaufter Auflage im 3. Quartal 2019." https://de.statista.com/statistik/daten/studie/73448/umfrage /auflage-der-ueberregionalen-tageszeitungen/.

Statista. 2019b. "Leading Daily Newspapers in the United States in September 2017 and January 2019, by Circulation." https://www.statista.com/statistics/184682/us-daily -newspapers-by-circulation/.

UNHCR (United Nations High Commissioner for Refugees). 2020. "Situation Syria Regional Refugee Response." Data. https://data2.unhcr.org/en/situations/syria#_ga =2.221086296.1502741189.1578850611-87893757.1578850611.

Zaller, John R. 1992. *The Nature and Origins of Mass Opinion.* Cambridge: Cambridge University Press.

# Part 7
# MUSIC, ART, AND THE NATION

In the first chapter, Rachel Fell McDermott tells the story of two friends and musicians: Nazrul Islam, a lyricist, and Abbasuddin Ahmed, a singer. Both men worked for His Master's Voice (HMV), the record label of the Gramophone Company. In the middle of 1931, the two men approached their boss at HMV and submitted a proposal to record Muslim devotional music. Initially, the proposal was rejected as too risky, but six months later the record company agreed to take on the project. Between 1932 and 1941, HMV recorded 189 Islamic songs. Through an act of cultural translation, the two friends and musicians created a new musical genre known as Islāmī Gīti, a Bengalized musical tradition about God, Islam, Muhammad, and Islamic religious celebrations. This new musical genre was modeled on a tradition of songs composed for Hindu deities. In the lyrics, Nazrul used the term *svāmī* for Allah and *dharma* for *dīn*. This bold musical innovation was extremely popular among Muslims in East and West Bengal. In 1942, however, Nazrul developed dementia and stopped writing (he died in 1976). Subsequent generations of musicians ignored the Islāmī Gīti genre, no doubt owing to the risks associated with composing Bengali Islamic songs. McDermott situates this story in the context of the end of British colonialism, political unrest in South Asia, and the struggle over the two Bengals in the third decade of the twentieth century.

In the second chapter, Amr Kamal examines the Qatari decision to build a world-class art museum that quickly came to rival the Met, the British Museum, and the Louvre. In 2010 the Qataris invited several distinguished intellectuals, including Eric Hobsbawm, a renowned historian of imperialism, to visit the country in order to reflect on the museum and to situate it in the context of the country's art holdings. Their resulting reflections were published as a collection of essays in 2011. By writing about relics produced over a period of 1400 years across three continents, these intellectuals connected severed pasts to the present. In doing so, Kamal argues, they displaced history, wittingly or unwittingly, by legitimizing Qatar's claim to be the guardian of Islam's imperial past. In fact, Kamal concludes, the Qatari interest in art is directly related to contested issues—nationalism, faith, and memory—that are, literally, part of the fabric of the museum.

# MUSLIM DEVOTIONAL SINGING IN TWO BENGALS

## A Bold Experiment

*Rachel Fell McDermott*

In mid-1931 in Calcutta, a Muslim singer persuaded his lyricist and song composer friend to join him in a bold move: they would approach the "rehearsal in charge" of His Master's Voice (HMV), the record label of the Gramophone Company, for which they both worked, and propose that they record a disc of Islamic devotional songs. In those days, a record had only two songs, one on each side, each lasting no more than three minutes. The two friends had been working together at HMV for two years, composing and singing songs in Bengali on patriotism, love, nature, and Hindu devotionalism; thus, the singer thought, branching out into Islamic songs did not seem an onerous request.[1] However, their boss, Bhagavati Babu, denounced the idea. Published poetry on Islamic themes was one thing, but songs set to music was another.[2] Six months later the singer tried again. This time Bhagavati Babu acquiesced and said that the two friends could produce one record as an experiment. The composer, Kazi Nazrul Islam (1899–1976), wrote the songs in the HMV rehearsal room and then taught them to his friend, the singer Abbasuddin Ahmed (1901–1959). Abbasuddin sang and played the harmonium, and a staff tabla player joined them for the production. In February 1932, the record was ready.

The two songs were released during Īd, the conclusion of the monthlong Ramadan fast, and were an instant hit. Even those Muslims who previously had avoided listening to songs took an interest in the Nazrul-Abbasuddin productions. The songs were short, two to four stanzas each, on God, His unity, the Prophet, the call to prayer, fasting, the Hajj, charity, Īd, animal sacrifice, the tragedy of Moharram at Karbala, the Prophet's birthday and death day, and the revelation of the Qur'an.

Some of them were calls for a renewal of Islamic heroism and bravery. All of them were couched in a devotional musical mode parallel to the then extremely popular devotional songs addressed to Hindu deities. Abbasuddin was hopeful that the creation of this genre would mollify the many orthodox Muslims who found Nazrul's earlier overtures to the Hindu tradition offensive and labeled him a *kāpher* (heretic) or even a *saytān* (satan) (Ahmed 2014, 66; Khan 1960, 150).[3]

The experiment proved extremely popular, and Bhagavati Babu was enthusiastic to continue it, so Abbasuddin recruited several Muslim singers of note to join him. For one such singer, the opportunity was poignantly fortunate. Muhammad Kasem (1888–1959) had become a famous exponent of Hindu songs to Kālī under the Hindu pseudonym K. Mallik; when he learned that he could sing Islamic songs he reverted to using his birth name. Over the next ten years, he recorded twenty-nine of Nazrul's compositions. A third young man with a sweet voice, Abdul Latif (d. 1940), also sang. He recorded seventeen songs from 1935 to 1940.

In all, Nazrul composed about 189 Islamic songs (Islāmī Gīti) that were recorded between 1932 and 1941, when illness prevented him from composing any more.[4] Twenty-seven singers or singing groups performed, mainly for HVM and Twin Records. Abbasuddin sang the most—sixty-two of the total. Established Hindu singers, some of them women, took Muslim stage names to facilitate the selling of the songs, and Nazrul wrote songs in the voice of Muslim women: Amina, Muhammad's mother; Fatema, Muhammad's daughter; and the women of Medina.[5] Fifteen of the twenty-seven singers sang just one record of two songs each.

Nazrul rose to prominence in Bengal as an anti-British poet in the 1920s and 1930s, earning the soubriquet the "Rebel Poet." His scathingly critical poetry, championing of the poor and downcast, sympathy for the nascent Communist Party, and twelve volumes of novels, short stories, dramas, and romantic and devotional poetry are all celebrated in India, where Nazrul is remembered as a liberal, all-encompassing, even secular man. In his most prominent photos he stands with his arms crossed in a gesture of defiance, a youth facing down the injustices of life. In the years after 2011, when I began my research on Nazrul in India, I often heard the devotional songs that he composed to Hindu deities like Kālī and Kṛṣṇa, but I never heard his Islamic songs. Imagine my surprise when I began to visit Bangladesh—where Nazrul lived between 1972 and 1976, during which time he was designated as the national poet of the new country—and found people downplaying Nazrul the rebel poet in favor of Nazrul the poet of Muslim regeneration who composed Islamic songs. In Bangladesh the photograph most often seen is of the slightly older, more thoughtful Nazrul of the late 1930s, wearing a Muslim cap. The monthlong Ramadan fast cannot conclude without Nazrul's "O mon Ramjāner ai"—his most famous song and the one recorded on the first album in 1932—being played on the radio. The devotional songs are integral to people's spiritual lives.

To approach the Islāmī Gīti in a scholarly fashion therefore demands a cross-border approach. In February–March 2019, after preparing my own translations, I went to Dhaka, Bangladesh, and read almost the entire corpus of songs with Nashid Kamal, granddaughter of Abbasuddin and herself a professional singer. In June and July 2019, I went to Kolkata, India, and read the songs again with Pratima Dutt, my Indian scholar-mentor. The three of us—Nashid, Pratima, and I—were astonished by two aspects of the songs and their history: the instability of the genre in terms of its recognition and popularity, and the "unorthodox" contents of some of the lyrics. What happens when the Muslim tradition, which views icons and music with suspicion, borrows a non-Islamic musical genre? In what follows I introduce the songs and then discuss the surprising aftereffects of Nazrul's newly created genre, from the 1930s to the present.

# "Wandering from Country to Country I Sing Songs of Your Name / Oh Khoda, This Is Your Order, Your Farman"

Let us start where Nazrul's audiences started—with the first record. One of the two songs on that disc is the most popular of his 189 Islamic songs. It celebrates Īd, the festival that concludes the month of fasting, or Ramadan (in Bengali, Ramjān), when Muslims come together in peace and solidarity:

> O mind, at the end of this Ramadan fast
>     comes the Īd of happiness.
> Give yourself away today;
>     listen to the heavenly demand.
> Your gold and ornaments, your palatial buildings,
>     keep them all in God's name.
> Give alms to dead Muslims
>     to break their sleep.
> Pray the prayers of Īd, my mind,
>     in this gathering place
> where all Muslim heroes
>     became martyrs.
> For today, forget friend, forget enemy;
>     join hands.

With your love make the whole world
   faithful followers of Islam.
The poor, the wretched, orphans
    those who, ever-abstinent,
    keep the fast throughout their lives—
give them something to help them.
Into your heart's dish
    pour the sweet dessert of God's oneness,
    an invitation for Hazrat that I suspect he will accept.
The bricks and stones thrown at you throughout your life,
gather them up and build with them
    a mosque of love.[6]

In this chapter, I can mention only a few of Nazrul's songs while providing an overview of his favorite topics. Repeated themes include "wake-up" songs directed at Indian Muslims; pride in a putative unified Muslim community, where "Allah is my Lord," Muhammad my Prophet, the Qur'an my battle drum, and all Muslims of the world my brothers; the mercy of the Prophet, or Hazrat, who ferries his followers across the flooded desert; and the chest-beating grief of all nature at the death of the Prophet, or the slaughter at Karbala.[7] Sometimes Nazrul petitions, chides, teases, or plays with God in a manner reminiscent of *bhakti* poetry, which was popular in Bengal in his time. In the following song, recorded in 1939 but unknown today, the poet needles the Prophet. Amina is the Prophet's mother, and "Kamaliyala" means the "shawl-wearing one":

Just as the Arab desert called you,
Oh my dear Prophet Al Arabi,
   if I also call you in that way—won't you come?
Just as the Tigris and Euphrates Rivers cry,
calling ceaselessly,
hey, my desert-wandering prophecy-bearing one,
   if I also weep that way—won't you come?
Just as Medina and Mount Hera
remained awake in hope of you,
hey Hazrat mine, Oh my beloved,
   if I also remain awake, like them—won't you come?
    Just as the oppressed cried
    at the home of the Kaba
Oh Darling of Amina, Oh my Kamaliyala,
If I also desire you like that—won't you come?[8]

Nazrul composed some songs for women singers—for example, songs in which the female voice is the narrator: Fatima singing about her sacrifice of Hasan and Hossein; Khadija representing all women when she says that she is a "proud Muslim woman"; or women trapped in purdah who cannot see the Prophet and who cry out to him. Seven women recorded twenty-five Nazrul songs in 1936–1937 and 1940–1941.[9] Only four of these are widely known today. "Everyone sings this one," said Nashid Kamal of the following song, recorded by Sakina Begum, about a woman peddling the five pillars of Islam.

> I am a woman peddling prayer, fasting, the Hajj, and alms-giving;
> calling out the Prophet's profession of faith, I wander on the road day
>     and night.
>
> Oh my Prophet's sweethearts,
>     come running, Muslim women!
> Come if you want to trade the merchandise of religion,
> if you want freedom.
> My birth was a thousand years ago in Arab lands;
> the entire world has given me a place
>     out of love.
>
> My call of prayer sounds
> in the hearts of all true believers;
> I am the imaginary daughter of the Prophet, and Allah is my Lord.[10]

I conclude this brief potpourri of Islāmī Gīti with two famous songs in the first-person singular, as if from Nazrul's own lips. The first reflects the fact that Nazrul never left British India and traveled no farther west than Karachi. Certainly, he never visited Medina.

> Are you going to the tomb in Medina?
> Deliver my greetings to the grave of the Nabi-ji.
>     On the pilgrimage road of the Hajjis
>     I am standing since morning, weeping.
> If only someone would take my *salam*s.
> I am crippled; how will I leap across the Arabian Sea?
> That is why day and night I stay by the road that goes to that tomb.
>
>     I say, oh waves of the ocean,
>     No one took my *salam*s;
> You carry my *salam*s to a hot desert wind,
>     oh, to the door of that tomb.[11]

The final song, the second most famous in the genre, was used to justify Nazrul's burial on the Dhaka University campus, next to a mosque. The song was composed near the end of Nazrul's active creative life, in July 1940, and sung by Muhammad Kasem.

> Bury me next to the mosque, brother,
> so even from the grave I can hear the muezzin's call.
>
> People will pass my grave on their way to prayer.
> This slave will hear the sound of their holy feet,
> this sinner escape the punishment of the grave.
>
> So many pious people, devotees of Khoda and followers of the Nabi-ji,
> read the beautiful Qur'an in this mosque;
> I listen; let my heart be soothed.
>
> So many dervishes and fakirs, brother,
> invisible in the courtyard of this mosque
> deep in the night
> recite Allah's praises.
> I want to weep with them
>    and repeat Allah's name.[12]

## Penury, Mental Death, the Politics of Partition, and the Temptations of Music

As a genre, these lyrics bring a Bengali sensibility and intimacy to Islamic themes. But two interpretive puzzles demand attention. First, why is this popular genre so unstable in Bangladesh? More than a full half of the corpus is unrecognized by Nazrul singers, and only a select percentage of the total lives in public performance. The Nazrul Institute, founded on the site of the house where Nazrul lived in Dhaka between 1972 and 1976 (the last four years of his life), is trying to retrieve the old records and issue remastered renditions, but the process is slow. Except for a few Bengali composers who, following Nazrul's lead, tried to write Islāmī Gīti but did so poorly,[13] the genre is not living—no one is releasing new songs.[14] It is as if a musical genre that dared to be born in the 1930s took on life and imparted inspiration but did not reproduce itself, remaining a treasured aural and oral period piece. Why? And what about India, where Nazrul is not the national poet?

There are three chief reasons for the shifting sands, so to speak, on which this genre attempts to stand. The first is the ephemera of sheets of paper, of notebooks, in the hands of a man from whom speed was required and who lived in penury. Nazrul had two children to support, as well as a wife and a mother-in-law, and he was always in debt—especially after his wife fell ill in 1939. In 1932 and 1933, the first two years of his collaboration with Abbasuddin, the lyrics came from songs he had already published in literary journals.[15] Increasingly, however, he wrote songs on the spot, often while sitting in the recording companies' studios, drinking tea and eating pan. He would finish a song, teach it to whichever singer was on hand, and then record it. Mohammad Kasem remembers Nazrul composing an Islamic song for him on a train; he wrote it on a piece of paper and handed it to him (Haq 2000, 20). By 1936, only one of the thirty-six songs released by the Gramophone Company had been published in a printed compilation of Nazrul's work; the rest were recovered after 1970 by listening to the recordings and transcribing the words. Some of Nazrul's songbooks and royalty contracts specifying the song titles to appear on particular records were recovered from the 1950s onward. After Nazrul experienced mental death in 1942, his wife Pramila allowed the songs to be rerecorded and published in order to earn a small income, but in many cases the royalties had been forfeited years earlier, when Nazrul sold his rights for paltry sums to support his family. The corpus is unstable because there was no institutional base from which to preserve his artistry. This is in stark contrast to his older contemporary, Rabindranath Tagore (1861–1941), whose wealth, elite status, and familial and institutional support base ensured that everything he wrote or said was preserved.

Another reason for the uneven fate of the Islamic songs is political turmoil. Nazrul went silent in 1942. His family and friends tried unsuccessfully to find a cure for him, but this was wartime Calcutta, his family had no income, and many of Nazrul's friends deserted him. Then came 1947 and the Partition of Bengal. The upheaval experienced by the Muslim community split families and, in our case, singing traditions. In India, the 1950s and 1960s witnessed several literary ventures on behalf of Nazrul, with the publication of previously unpublished material. This did not occur with the Islamic songs, however, because the most important singer, Abbasuddin, had moved to Dhaka, where he set up a singing school and trained students. By contrast, Abdul Latif and Muhammad Kasem stayed in West Bengal, the former dying young in 1940, and the latter ceasing to perform in the same year. These three were the top performers of the Islāmī Gīti genre. The recorded songs of fourteen of the fifteen additional singers, each of whom recorded two songs, were unknown to and unrecognized by Nashid Kamal. Thus, the genre moved east because the Muslim community and Abbasuddin moved to East Pakistan while Nazrul sat in mental vacuity in West Bengal.

Indeed, the popularity of the Islāmī Gīti in West Bengal today bears marks of the Partition and, more importantly, of current Indian politics and Hindu-Muslim tensions. Numerous West Bengali Muslims have assured me that they too love the Islamic songs; in June 2019, however, two prominent West Bengali singer/teachers of Nazrul—Kalyani Kazi and Ramanuj Dasgupta—insisted that "there is no study of the Islamic songs here" (*ekhāne Islāmī-gītir carcā nei*) and that "no one does any work on that topic here" (*ekhāne ei niye keu kāj karche nā*).[16] In part this must be because, as stated above, none of the prominent singers of the genre made it a point to teach or sing it in West Bengal, save—much later—new singers like Kamal Dasgupta (1912–1974) in the 1960s, before moving with his Muslim wife to Bangladesh, and Manabendranath Mukhopadhyay (1931–1992) also in the 1960s, whose singing style was later criticized for the "liberties" he took with Nazrul's musical notations.[17] Today, West Bengali Muslims hear the Islāmī Gīti on discs recorded in Bangladesh, as sung by Bangladeshis who perform concerts in Kolkata, or on the internet. The All-India head of Hindustan Records, S. L. Saha, told me that reproducing Nazrul's Islamic songs in India is something he does periodically (e.g., at Īd), but that if someone else were to come to him with a proposal of recording new Bengali Islamic songs, he would not do it. "Definitely not," he commented. "It is too dangerous politically."[18] With the new and unprecedented tilt toward the anti-Muslim Hindu Nationalist Bharatiya Janata Party in the state, coupled with the clear and unpopular favoring of Muslims by the BJP's rival, Mamata Banerjee, the current chief minister of the state, the patronage of Muslims or Muslim art forms is greeted by the Hindu upper classes with skepticism.

A third factor for the shifting nature of the Islāmī Gīti genre may be the uncomfortable place of music in Islam (see Ahmed 2017, 424–30; Baig 2011; and Shiloah 1976, 161–80). This is what caused HMV's Bhagavati Babu such pause in 1931, and it is also the reason why, today, many of Nazrul's Islamic songs are rendered in Bangladesh, on YouTube, as they would have been in the 1930s, without showing live singers. Music in a devotional setting may be permissible as long as it does not rouse sensual feelings.

In Bangladesh, then, Partition and the creation of a Muslim-majority cultural environment, as well as institutional and state patronage channeled toward the national poet, have allowed Islamic songs to flourish and dominate the field of Nazrul's compositions, even if not all the songs are known. By contrast, it is not a surprise that in Hindu-majority India, where Nazrul is respected but not the national poet, his Islamic songs are overshadowed by other genres, other sides of his richly complex artistic output.

# Vernacularization or Affront? The Open Secret That No One Seems to Hear

There is a second puzzle here—namely, the openly "Hindu" valence of many of Nazrul's Islamic songs. The genre astounded me when I read it. When I mentioned my surprise to my reading partner in Bangladesh, Nashid Kamal, she too began to notice the Hindu elements, although in her entire singing career (she is now in her mid-sixties) she had never noted or marked such influences.

To give a few examples of many, Nazrul refers to God as "Prabhu," a term for "Lord" that derives from the Hindu part of the overall Bengali cultural context. Nashid commented that songs in which "Prabhu" is mentioned are very popular among Muslims, and that Nazrul had rendered the use of Prabhu acceptable, but only when singing his songs. Prabhu is unique to Nazrul, she said. Even Nazrul's choice of *svāmī* for Allah, while shocking and unprecedented, does not detract from the poet's overall popularity. His use of *dharma* instead of *dīn* for "religion" is also a liberal choice. Further, he asks God to appear to him, to give him his sight (sometimes *darśan* but more often the Persian *didār*). Still more daring is Nazrul's use of the Hindu Vaiṣṇava term *viraha*, or pining love in separation, to characterize the way God feels for the Prophet. In the Hindu context, *viraha* is what the human devotee feels, not what God feels for His devotee.

There are many other Hindu, or Hindu-connoting, images in Nazrul's 189 songs. These images include a focus on the Prophet's pink feet and ruby lips; petulant complaints to God for striking the poet with blows; requests to God for initiation (*dikṣa*), strength (*śakti*), and devotion (*bhakti*); repeated references to the world as a place of *samsāra*, *māyā*, and *moha* (illusion and the cyclic process of birth and death); a *bhakti*-esque denunciation of animal sacrifice during the sacrificial Īd; a preference for "*japa*" instead of "*dhikr*" when describing the repetition of God's name; and poems portraying Muhammad as a Hindu avatar who descends to earth to take upon himself sin and suffering.[19] Many, but not all, of these songs are unknown, and several were written near the end of Nazrul's productive life, in 1940 and 1941.

To date I have not been able to find a Muslim in Bangladesh or India who finds this language offensive, off-putting, or even visible. Nashid introduced me to several prominent Bangladeshi Nazrul singers, none of whom had noticed such elements—certainly not as deriving from the Hindu tradition—in the songs they routinely sing. I think there are four reasons for this: first, the singing tradition emphasizes the teaching of performance, not the understanding of content; second, Muslims in Bangladesh do not listen to Nazrul's (or anyone else's) Hindu devotional lyrics, where the parallels might become evident; third, Nazrul is so revered that "if he writes it, it must be all right"; and, fourth, in pre-Partition Bengal, Nazrul inherited a hybrid religious culture. Mustafa Zaman Abbasi told me that Nazrul came from a syncretic background, as do all Bengali Muslims, and that this accounts for the characteristics of the songs that I noted.[20] Mohit Ul Alam (2019) argues that the success of Nazrul's "vernacularization" of the Islamic tradition is demonstrated in the total fit of the songs in the context of Bengali society. But might Nazrul's creativity be considered part of a pan–South Asian Muslim expression of intimacy toward the figure of the Prophet, who in Sindhi and Urdu poetry, for example, is an intercessor, lamp, and pilot, for whom poets express *viraha* (Asani 1995)? The parallels are intriguing, but even if Nazrul had been familiar with such poetry and tried to imitate it, he still would have had to engineer the fit in Bengali. He was apparently so successful at this that a very orthodox Bengali Muslim gentleman said that he could not imagine these poems upsetting even members of the ultraconservative Jamaat-e-Islami. And yet, one wonders about songs with the off-putting language, the five poems never recorded, and the ones no one sings. That this gift of Muslim songs, while too precious to lose, also creates its own barriers is supported by the fact that no, or very few, composers are creating Islamic devotional music in Bengali. Everyone sings Nazrul. His status provides the excuse for exception making.

It seems, then, that what Abbasuddin planned for his friend Nazrul Islam in 1931—writing Islamic songs will rehabilitate you in the eyes of the mullahs—may actually have worked, more or less. Bengali Hindus have been singing love songs to their deities since the twelfth century, but because of the dubious status of music in Islamic contexts, such songs came very late to Bengali Muslims. What our two Bengali friends initiated, then, was an exercise in "translation," where the product was a new creation, a thoroughly Bengalized *bhakti* genre on Allah, the Prophet, festivals, Karbala, and the message of Islam that succeeded in charming Bengali Muslim audiences. The Hindu-tinted language in some of the songs seems neither to upset Muslims nor to interest Hindus, who, at least in India, are largely unaware of the Islāmī Gīti. The fate of that genre has turned, shifted, and altered course—like the rivers on Bengal delta—through the poet's illness and silence, the bifurcation in 1947 of the Bengal in which he lived and the creation of the new state of Bangladesh in 1971, the dislocation or relocation of people and artistic traditions, and the democratizing, border-vanishing abilities of the gramophone, the radio, the CD, and now the internet. Following the course of 189 small songs, watching where they rush in torrents and where they stagnate in eddies, allows one a new perspective on the ongoing relationship between the two halves of Bengal, as well as domestic conversations and debates within each. These two Bengals were Nazrul's world, where, as he wrote, "wandering from country to country I sing songs of [God's] name."[21]

## NOTES

1. Nazrul, the lyricist, joined the company in 1928, Abbasuddin, the singer, in 1930.

2. Nazrul wrote many poems on Islamic themes from 1922 to 1930, but none were set to music or sung.

3. In this chapter I use Bengali transliteration and spelling conventions—for example, Īd instead of ʿĪd, and Kābā instead of Kaʿba.

4. Nazrul probably wrote more than 189 songs: at least nine were never recorded, some were composed extemporaneously during his teenage years when he was a member of a *leṭo* singing group, and some straddle the line between philosophical and Islamic. It is difficult to determine the exact number of Nazrul's Islamic songs, and my estimate is conservative. I have seen totals ranging up to 282 (Haq 2000, 80).

5. For instance, Ashcaryamayi took the name Sakina Begum, Dhiren Das took the name Gani Miya, Girin Cakrabarti became Golam Haydar, and Usharani sang as Rabeya Khatun.

6. "O man Ramjāner ai" (Islam 1932, poem 7), sung by Abbasuddin for HMV N4111 (February 1932).

7. "Āllāh āmār Prabhu" (Islam 1932, poem 11), sung by Abbasuddin for HMV N7109 (May 1933). "Tauhideri bān ḍekeche" (Islam 1952, poem 11), sung by Abbasuddin for Twin FT 12355 (April 1938). Although the trope of flooded plains is appropriate for alluvial Bengal, it is less understandable for Arabia; in the Arabian context, the trope is understood as a reference to the mercy of God or the Prophet, the tears of Karbala, tears over personal sins, or weeping at the Prophet's demise. "Hāy hāy uṭhiche mātam" (Islam 2009, poem 81), sung by Abdul Latif for Twin FT 4400 (June 1936). This song is moderately well known.

8. "Tomāy yeman kare ḍekechilo" (Islam 1952, poem 43), sung by A. Sirajur Rahman for Twin Records FT 13006 (October 1939).

9. In 1936–1937, four women recorded twenty-one Islāmī Gīti: Roshan Ara Begum sang six songs, three of which were on women's themes; Sakina Begum sang seven songs, two of which were on women's themes; Rabeya Khatun sang six songs, three of which were on women's themes; and Lutphaunnissa sang two songs, neither of which was on women's themes. In 1940, Anantabala sang one song, in 1941 Nilam Khatun two, and in 1944 Duli Bibi one.

10. "Nāmāj rojā hajva jākāter pasāriṇī āmi" (Islam 2009, poem 50), sung by Sakina Begum for HMV N7487 (February 1936). The last three words read "*Āllāh āmār swāmī.*"

11. "Kābār jiyārate tumi ke yāo Madināy" (Islam 1952: poem 31), sung by A. Sirajur Rahman for Twin Records FT 12769 (April 1939).

12. "Masjideri pāśe āmār kabar dio bhāi" (Islam 2009, poem 43), sung by M. Kasem for HMV 17476 (July 1940).

13. For a sampling of such songs by Golam Mustafa (1897–1964), Azizur Rahman (1917–1978), Kazi Golam Akbar (1921–1988), and Said Siddiki (n.d.), see *Ābbāsuddiner Gān* (1961) 2014.

14. I distinguish between Islamic songs and the songs of the Bauls. The latter, which employ Muslim and Hindu themes, have a distinctive mystical, often intentionally obfuscating, vocabulary.

15. Nazrul published his early songs in literary journals such as *Bulbul, Jayatī, Kārtik, Mohammadi,* and *Muezzin.*

16. Kalyani Kazi and Ramanuj Dasgupta, interview by the author, June 18 and 19, 2019.

17. Music is controversial in relation to Nazrul. If one is going to have music, it must be "authentic"—that is, tunes and musical arrangements that go back to Nazrul and reflect his intentions. Dhaka's Nazrul Institute is committed to establishing the precise intonations of the early recordings, when Nazrul's presence would have guaranteed

authenticity; and it condemns any departure from those patterns. In West Bengal, Nazrul's singing tradition was promoted inter alia by Manabendranath Mukhopadhyay, who in the mid-1960s rerecorded many of Nazrul's most famous songs with more complex instrumental music and new tunes. Although these renditions were popular, the Dhaka Institute in Bangladesh pillories Manabendranath because of his nontraditional interpretations. A few years ago, Sujit Mustafa, a prominent Bangladeshi singer, applied to the Bangladesh government for funding to allow him and a team of musicians to add tunes to the 1,700 or so untuned Nazrul songs (these include all songs, not just those in the Islamic category), so that people would be able to sing them. The government rejected his proposal. A man who made it his career to write out, in staff notation, all the tunes that Nazrul had composed for the recorded songs threatened a fast unto death if Sujit were allowed to undertake the project. Sujit Mustafa, interview by the author, March 8, 2019.

18. S. L. Saha, interview by the author, June 27, 2019.

19. "Āllājī go āmi bujhi nā" (Islam 2009, poem 31), sung by Abbasuddin for Twin Records FT13217 (March 1940); "Iyā Āllā, tumi rakṣā karo" (Islam 2009, poem 44), sung by Golām Hāydār and Party for Twin Records FT 13261 (April 1940). See "Īdjjohār cānd hāse ei" (Islam 1933: poem 77), sung by Mohammad Kasem for HMV N7101 (May 1933); "Īdujjohār takbīr śon Īdgāhe" (Islam 1952, poem 22), sung by K. Mallik and Manikmala for HMV N17046 (February 1938); "Hāte hāt diye āge col" (Islam 2006, poem 350), sung by Abbasuddin for Twin Records FT 13545 (March 1941); and "Natun cānder takbir śon" (Islam 2006, poem 572), sung by Dhiren Das and Roshan Ara Begum for HMV N7478 (January 1936). Not one of these songs is known today. The following song—"The Protector of Orphans, becoming an orphan, / came on this earth. / Without the pain of orphaned humanity, / he would not have understood," from "Khodār habib halen nājel" (Islam 1933, poem 84)—was never even recorded.

20. Mustafa Zaman Abbasi, interview by the author, March 4, 2019.

21. "Deśe deśe geye beḍāi" (Islam 2009, poem 90), sung by Muhammad Kasem for HMV N17008 (December 1937). All song translations in this chapter are my own.

## REFERENCES

*Ābbāsuddiner Gān.* (1961) 2014. Compiled by Mustafa Zaman Abbasi. 5th ed. Dhaka: Muktodesh Prakashan.

Ahmed, Abbasuddin. 2014. *My Life in Melodies*. Translated by Nashid Kamal. Dhaka: Adorn Books.

Ahmed, Shahab. 2017. *What Is Islam? The Importance of Being Islamic*. Princeton, NJ: Princeton University Press.

Alam, Mohit Ul. 2019. "Nazrul's Way of Vernacularizing Islam." In *Kazi Nazrul Islam: Poetry, Politics, Passion*, edited by Niaz Zaman, 130–54. Dhaka: Writers.ink.

Asani, Ali. 1995. "In Praise of Muḥammad: Sindhi and Urdu Poems." In *Religions of India in Practice*, edited by Donald S. Lopez, 159–86. Princeton, NJ: Princeton University Press, 1995.

Baig, Khalid. 2011. *Slippery Stone: An Inquiry into Islam's Stance on Music*. Garden Grove, CA: Openmind Press.

Haq, Asadul. 2000. *Islāmī Aitihye Najrul-Saṅgīt*. Dhaka: Nazrul Institute.

Islam, Kazi Nazrul. 1932. *Zulfikār*. Reprinted in *Najrul-Racanābalī*. Edited by Rafiqul Islam. Vol. 4 of 12, 287–308. Dhaka: Bangla Academy, 2007.

——. 1933. *Gulbāgicā*. Reprinted in *Najrul-Racanābalī*. Edited by Rafiqul Islam. Vol. 5 of 12, 219–79. Dhaka: Bangla Academy, 2007.

——. 1952. *Zulfikār*. 2nd ed. Reprinted in *Najrul-Racanābalī*. Edited by Rafiqul Islam. Vol. 7 of 12, 89–110. Dhaka: Bangla Academy, 2008.

——. 2006. *Najrul Sangīt Sangraha*. Edited by Rashidun Nabi. Dhaka: Nazrul Institute.
——. 2009. "Agranthita Gān" [Uncollected songs]. In *Nazrul-Racanābalī*. Edited by Rafiqul Islam. Vol. 10 of 12, 189–343. Dhaka: Bangla Academy.
Khan, Azharuddin. 1960. *Bānglā Sāhitye Najrul*. 4th ed. Calcutta: D. M. Library.
Shiloah, A. 1976. "The Dimension of Sound: Islamic Music—Philosophy, Theory, and Practice." In *The World of Islam*, edited by Bernard Lewis, 161–80. London: Thames & Hudson.

# REFLECTIONS ON ART AND NATION BUILDING

## The Museum of Islamic Art in Doha, Qatar

*Amr Kamal*

**Invented traditions is taken to mean a set of practices . . . which automatically implies continuity with . . . a suitable historic past.**

—Eric Hobsbawm, *The Invention of Tradition*

Reflecting on a portrait of the emperor Shah Jahan in the Museum of Islamic Art (MIA) in Doha, the historian Eric Hobsbawm writes:

> On 10 January 1401 (by the Western calendar) an event occurred at which I would dearly like [*sic*] to have been present. It was the first meeting between the Mongol world conqueror, Timur of Samarkand (Tamerlane), and the greatest social and historical mind of the medieval world, Ibn Khaldun, who had reluctantly interrupted his studies to return to be an adviser to governments. I can see the old scholar—he was almost seventy—being lowered by ropes from the walls of Damascus, which Timur was then besieging. . . . Timur needed information about North Africa, on which Ibn Khaldun was the leading expert. He received the required memorandum, but Ibn Khaldun was sufficiently worried to produce an equivalent memorandum on the Eastern conqueror for the Sultan of Morocco. (2011, 85)

Hobsbawm's visit to Doha bears many resemblances to Ibn Khaldun's experience in Damascus. Like Ibn Khaldun, the English historian was summoned by a royal figure for his scholarly expertise: Hobsbawm's invitation came from Qatar's Museums Authority, an organization chaired by the emir of Qatar's daughter, Sheikha al-Mayassa bint Hamad bin Khalifa al-Thani. Hobsbawm, who was in his nineties, traveled to Doha to write on the MIA. Most likely, the sight of a museum designed to resemble a fortress brought to Hobsbawm's mind Ibn Khaldun's meeting with Tamerlane before the walls of Damascus.

Beyond this architectural similarity, Hobsbawm's reverie about Ibn Khaldun exposes other similarities between these two experiences: both historians occupied a precarious position by participating in a narrative that confirms the power of a ruler. Ibn Khaldun's reputation as a renowned Arab scholar served to legitimize the sovereignty of the new king in the Muslim world. Although Ibn Khaldun shared his knowledge with Tamerlane, he was also expected to communicate his impressions to the Mongol emperor's foe, the sultan of Morocco. In Damascus, the scholar was both an outsider and an insider, both guest and hostage, both friend and enemy.

Like Ibn Khaldun, Hobsbawm was both an insider and an outsider in his host country. In Doha, the author of *The Invention of Traditions* (1983) witnessed firsthand certain aspects of nation building that he had studied throughout his career. Perhaps, this was not a coincidence. Hobsbawm was born in colonial Egypt in 1917, and his research focused on the rise of European nationalism and imperial hegemony during the nineteenth century. The scholar's personal connection to the Middle East and his writings on European history contributed to the promotion of the museum on a global scale. Hobsbawm's presence established an authoritative continuity between his writings on the history of empire and Qatar's rise as guardian of the Muslim imperial past.

Hobsbawm's memorandum is part of an edited volume, *Reflections on Islamic Art* (2011; hereafter *RIA*), which brings together impressions of the MIA by twenty-seven authors. In addition to Hobsbawm, this group includes the cultural critic Slavoj Žižek and several world-recognized intellectuals, mainly of Middle Eastern and South Asian origins. The articles, edited by the British Egyptian writer Ahdaf Soueif and prefaced with a statement by Sheikha al-Mayassa, are designed as an ekphrastic exercise: the authors are invited to wander through the museum in search of an object to describe (Soueif 2011b). Like Ibn Khaldun, Hobsbawm and the other guest writers were invited to the museum to witness a historical moment in which Qatar asserted itself as a regional economic and cultural leader.

In this chapter, I seek to untangle the connection between the museum and its representation in *RIA* as a multidimensional memory project shaped by culture experts (scholars, writers, and intellectuals) and rulers. In *Of Hospitality*, Jacques Derrida draws attention to the etymological link between the French word *hôte*, which signifies both "host" and "guest," and the Latin *hostis*, or enemy. For Derrida, the role of the guest—and by extension that of the immigrant—is both ominous and performative: the guest, as a hostage in the host's house, witnesses, questions, and reinforces the patriarchal order (Derrida and Dufourmantelle 2000, 5). As guest-experts wandering through the museum, the authors who contribute essays to *RIA* mirror the ambiguous status of many communities in Qatar. They are both insiders and outsiders who witness, question, and participate in fabricating the country's global image and its cultural memory. As Michael Rothberg posits, "Memory emerges from unexpected, multidirectional encounters—encounters between diverse pasts and a conflictual present . . . between different agents or catalysts of memory." Memory, he adds, develops as a *"noeud de mémoire,"* a "knot" or a nodule, shaped and reshaped by a web of "rhizomatic" connections extended amid diverse elements (Rothberg 2010, 7). Ann Rigney draws our attention to the instability inherent in the construction of memory, as several narratives and representations "converge" to create a social framework of reference (2005, 16). Expanding on this idea, Astrid Erll argues that memory undergoes a process of "mediation," "pre-mediation," and "remediation." By "mediation," Erll refers to the representation of memory in mass media (i.e., literature and visual culture). "Pre-mediation" signifies "that existent media, which circulate in a given society, provide '*schemata*' [models] for the representation of new experience." "Remediation" means that "an event which has turned into a site of memory . . . seems to refer not so much to what one might cautiously call the 'actual event' but instead to a canon of existent medial constructions, to the narratives, images and myths circulating in a memory culture" (Erll 2009, 111).[1] As commemorative acts, the museum and its remediation in *RIA* mobilize a repertoire of preexisting cartographies and historical narratives belonging to regional and global culture memory.

## Spatial Schemata of Urban Modernity

The states of the Arab Gulf, including the United Arab Emirates (UAE) and Qatar, are currently engaged in a dynamic competition for the creation of state-of-the-art museums and monuments designed by world-renowned architects.[2] In addition to the MIA, Qatar is funding several art/memory projects, such as the National Museum of Qatar, the Mathaf; Arab Museum of Modern Art; and the Echo Memory Project at the city center of Doha (Exell 2016a, 264). Similarly, the UAE has built the Louvre Abu Dhabi, the Guggenheim Abu Dhabi, and the Museum of Modernity (Elsheshtawy 2009; Kazerouni 2017; Exell 2016b). Museums are emblematic spaces, components of what I call *spatial schemata of urban modernity*. By *spatial schemata*, I refer to the configurations and elements of an urban plan, which acquire a symbolic significance in cultural memory, and whose meaning is shaped not only by the urban history of these spaces but also by their various manifestations worldwide and by their "remediation"—that is, their recurrent representation in art, literature, and media.

Museums, universal exhibitions, department stores, opera houses, and (in a later epoch) skyscrapers are the building blocks of these spatial schemata, which crystallized in global collective memory as embodiments of a western European modernity, change, and economic prosperity. As cities apply these schemata to their own environments, they project an imaginary continuum with a "progressive" narrative typically associated with the Enlightenment. However, once integrated in a different setting, these symbolic spaces fashion new meanings particular to their new locations, beyond the original context of European social and intellectual history.

The museum's official website sheds light on the resignification processes of these urban schemata. According to the website, "MIA represents Islamic art from three continents over 1,400 years. MIA . . . is transforming the State of Qatar into a cultural capital of the Middle East."[3] This statement echoes the motive behind the establishment of museums and world fairs at the height of French and British imperialism, projects that were designed to foreground France and Britain as leading modern powers by carefully curating and displaying artifacts from different parts of the globe. The layout and design of French and British museums created a teleological narrative that highlighted the role played by both nations as keepers of world history and direct heirs of the Egyptian, Hellenic, and Roman empires (Bennett 1995, 76; Mitchell 1991, 6–13). Similarly, by building MIA, Qatar presents itself as the guardian of a diverse Islamic imperial heritage that extends from Spain to China.

The design and location of the museum provide insight into the tensions within the new national image that Qatar seeks to establish. Located on a small island off the shore of Doha, the museum mirrors the liminal geography of its host country, whose territory borders the eastern shore of the Arabian Peninsula, facing Iran, Pakistan, and India. The design combines geometrical Islamic and postmodern aesthetics: a five-story building composed of a stack of cubes whose exterior limestone walls reflect the interplay of light. I. M. Pei, the museum's architect, specifies that the main aesthetic feature of his design was "the architecture of defense and fortifications." After studying Islam and traveling across the Middle East, Pei took his inspiration from Ibn Ṭūlūn's mosque in Cairo and a fortress in Tunisia (Ouroussoff 2008). Although the design is influenced by two Arab monuments, it is also informed by European perceptions of the Middle East. Pei explains, "Doha in many ways is virginal. . . . There is no real context there, no real life unless you go into the souk. I had to create my own context. It was very selfish" (Ouroussoff 2008). Pei's statement strikes an Orientalist chord: the gendered geography of Qatar is devoid of meaning except for the iconic spaces significant for Western imagination, namely the Orientalist spatial schemata: the desert dunes and the bazaar. Any aspect of the local heritage that does not fit the European model of culture registers as empty space. This impression of the city's urban landscape prompted the architect to ask the emir of Qatar to build an island off the shore of Doha as the location for the new museum. In the end, Pei constructed his own cultural utopia/heterotopia, a fortress floating on water, connected to the mainland by a passageway lined with palm trees, facing Qatar's modern skyline.[4]

Ahdaf Soueif's introduction to *RIA* sets the tone for the representation of Qatar as guardian of the Arab heritage. Soueif imagines the Filipino taxi driver who takes her to the museum but has never set foot in it as the embodiment of the last Arab king of al-Andalus, Abu Abdallah Muhammad XII, who ended nearly eight hundred years of Arab presence in the Iberian Peninsula (711–1492) by surrendering to Ferdinand and Isabella (Soueif 2011a, 11). The nostalgia for the idyllic multicultural, multiethnic legacy of al-Andalus and its luxurious green and serene landscapes surfaces frequently in Arabic literature and media and in contemporary Spanish national narratives (e.g., Calderwood 2014; Ashour 2003). The museum's landscape reinforces this geopolitical imaginary: on the shoreline, a large park functions as a transitional space between the city and the museum, connected to the mainland by a bridge. This spatial configuration evokes the Strait of Gibraltar crossed by Ṭāriq ibn Ziyād, the Muslim commander who led the conquest of Iberia, and whose name is eponymous with the rock overlooking the path to Europe.[5]

## Some Similarities between the Urban Histories of Qatar and France

Museums and other urban development projects in the contemporary Arab Gulf are often viewed through an Orientalist lens as disingenuous performances of modernity. Urbanists and culture critics express their ambivalence toward Qatar's urban changes. Doha's landscape, with its (un)familiar urban schemata, is often perceived as an inorganic top-down urban plan that threatens to dissolve the country's traditional social fabric.[6] This development project, however, is better assessed in the context of global urban history and contemporary politics, not as an anomaly fueled by oil wealth. For instance, the creation of the Louvre Abu Dhabi triggered public outcry in France over the sale of the national heritage to wealthy sheikhs (Cachin, Clair, and Recht 2006; Kazerouni 2017). Ironically, this Orientalist image exposes many common aspects between the history of France and that of the Arab Gulf. The emblematic monuments of Parisian modernity were the product of a long-term top-down urban project that gained momentum during the Second Empire (1852–1870) under the leadership of Baron Haussmann. He humorously nicknamed himself the "Pacha" to allude to his authoritarian decisions (Benjamin 1999, 127–28). The French lavish plan was motivated by social and political anxieties, in particular regarding the control and visibility of the working class in public spaces. At present, Haussmann's Paris is celebrated as an integral part of the French cultural heritage; its violent history of displacing the working classes and erasing urban memory has receded into the background (Clark 1999, 40–60; Harvey 2003; Papayanis 2004).

Anxieties about urban migrants and workers are central to contemporary French and Qatari politics. The majority of the migrant population in France, concentrated in the economically disadvantaged suburbs of Paris, remains the object of racial and sexual clichés that mark them as outsiders (Mack 2017; Wallach Scott 2007). Similarly, Doha's "Haussmannized" urban plan is fraught with social tensions between the state and its migrant labor population, who outnumber native Qataris and who are the victims of racial prejudices (Gardner and Watts 2012). Currently, native Qataris account for only 12 percent of its population, while 16 percent of the labor force comes from the Arab world, and 60 percent from South Asia (Exell 2016a, 261; Kennedy, Hargreaves, and Al Khater 2016, 74). The native Qatari population comprises several religious, social, and ethnic groups, including Sunni and Shi'a, Bedouin (nomad), and Hadar (urban). Each Qatari community has its particular historical experience that informs its contemporary social status. Some groups are descendants of manumitted slaves, while others are members of tribes that settled temporarily on the Persian coast and later returned to Qatar (Hammadi 2018, 1–5; Montigny 1996; Zahlan 1997).

It is particularly the consciousness of the demographic and social changes triggered by the oil economy that propelled the funding of memory projects. As Karen Exell observes, immediately after Qatar's independence in 1971, the state transformed the ruling palace, which had belonged to the emir Sheikh Abdullah bin Jassim al-Thani, into its first national museum. The museum included tableaux from contemporary Qatari society, about which the British travel writer Jonathan Raban commented that the museum visitors and the exhibited mannequins strikingly mirror each other in their dress and appearance (Exell 2016a, 263). This meticulous staging of everyday life in Qatar echoes the state-sponsored universal exhibitions of nineteenth-century France, which sought to frame the "world as [a] picture" and, by extension, to establish its own distinctive homogenous national image (Colla 2007, 1–9; Mitchell 1991, v–xiii). As Exell posits, "The [first national] museum setting situated the living culture in a past time frame and homogenized it through the presentation of 'typical and authentic' artifacts that synthesized local culture as heritage" (2016a, 263).

# Territorialization through Art:
# Nationalism, Faith, and Memory

The urban plan of Doha is also rooted in a specific regional politics. In shaping its national and global image, Qatar attempts to create a continuum between a pan-Arab identity and a pan-Islamic heritage that extends beyond the Arab world in a manner that speaks to its contemporary social demographics and its geographical location between the Arab world and South Asia.

As Tony Bennett argues, the representation of a modern state requires both the endowment of territory with a history and, simultaneously, the circumscription of history within a defined territory. This historical narrative "is the result of an active process of organization through which other histories—other possible frameworks for organizing events into sequences and interpreting their significance—are either eliminated or annexed to and inscribed within the unfolding unity of the nation's development" (Bennett 1995, 141). However, fitting past political frameworks organized around faith into a defined secular national narrative poses several challenges. According to Bennett:

> Benedict Anderson . . . contrasts the spatio-temporal matrices of the modern nation-state with those of dynastic realms or religious communities [which precede or overlap with the establishment of the modern state] (Anderson 1983, 31).[7] For the unifying traditions which characterize the latter, Anderson argues, are neither bound to a particular territory nor especially historical to the degree that they evoke a world of eternal permanences. The unity of a nation, by contrast, is always conceived as more limited in scope, the unity of a people who share the same space and time, the occupants of a territory which has been historicized and the subjects of a history which has been territorialized. (1995, 141)

Islamic history, with its transcendental temporality, spans a plethora of dynasties (each with its own frame of reference, context, and languages), which complicates the process of its integration into a streamlined national narrative. A focus on Islamic art circumvents these complications by creating a representation of Islamic civilization unified by material culture. According to Anderson, sacred language constitutes a transcendental system that binds together the members of a religious community (1991, 12–24). Art, with its secular aura and its universal claim over human experience, provides an alternative secular imaginary to express communal ties. To construct the history of Islamic civilization, the MIA curates the artworks of people who practiced Islam or lived under Muslim rule. Using objects of the everyday to represent Muslim empires allows the museum to anchor Islamic history in a globally recognized, secular timeline—what Anderson calls the "'homogenous empty time'... measured by clock and calendar" (1991, 24).[8] In this manner, Islamic art bridges the differences among Muslim dynasties and constructs a unified map of Islamic heritage, easily attached to a national—in contrast to a religious—narrative.

# Between a Museum and a Royal Gallery

The MIA activates social functions that are associated with the royal gallery, a forerunner of the modern museum. In his survey of the birth of the museum, Bennett highlights that the public function of the modern museum has shifted from a direct representation of the sovereign to public cultural reform. The museum visitor undergoes a didactic cultural experience that places the middle-class European man at the center of an evolutionary narrative suggested by the museum's curatorial practices (Bennett 1995, 23–24). Before the emergence of the museum, Bennett explains, royal galleries communicated a different political message, emphasizing the wealth and power of the sovereign. As Carol Duncan and Alan Wallach argue:

> The princely gallery spoke for and about the prince. The visitor was meant to be impressed by the prince's virtue, taste and wealth. The gallery's iconographic programme and the splendour of the collection worked to validate the prince and his rule. In the museum, the wealth of the collection is still a display of national wealth and is still meant to impress. But now the state, as an abstract entity, replaces the king as host. This change redefines the visitor. He is no longer the subordinate of a prince or lord. Now he is addressed as a citizen and therefore a shareholder in the state. (cited in Bennett 1995, 38)

Qatar Museums, a government entity chaired by a member of the royal family, oversees the MIA and the creation of similar cultural memory projects.[9] As a hybrid space, both modern museum and royal gallery, the MIA reinforces the image of the sovereign while advocating a didactic nationalist mission. In contrast to Qatar's national agenda implemented by the ministry of culture, Qatar Museums, with its global outreach, aims to distinguish Qatar from its neighbors, Saudi Arabia and the UAE in particular (Kazerouni 2017, 136, 56). This role reflects the shift in Qatar's political objectives after the first Gulf War (1990–1991). While Gulf tribes and royal families still proudly trace their roots to early Muslim communities in the Arabian Peninsula, the contemporary national policies of Qatar and the UAE attempt to transcend the limits of this traditional regional and spiritual identity by situating themselves within a global culture (Anscombe 1997; Kazerouni 2017, 136–56).

On the global level, as Alexandre Kazerouni suggests, the joint European-Gulf sponsorship of Islamic art (as in MIA) gives both European and Arab governments a role in shaping a narrative about Islam that aligns with their respective cultural and regional policies. On the one hand, this cultural collaboration conveys a positive image of Europe's attitude toward its Muslim community by emphasizing the former's role as a protector of Islamic heritage (Kazerouni 2017, 190–92). On the other hand, the museum collection, which includes artifacts from three continents, mirrors the diverse origins of Qatar's contemporary migrant populations and residents who, even after maintaining residency in the country for years, have to satisfy a set of complicated conditions to acquire Qatari citizenship (Hammadi 2018, 10; Babar 2014). In addition, the United Nations has frequently decried Qatar's *kafāla* (sponsorship) employment system, which facilitates the exploitation of migrant workers by placing them under the complete control of their employers (Gardner et al. 2013).[10] A unified representation of Islamic art, as part of a larger world heritage, allows guest workers to establish a common frame of reference with Qatari citizens; by extension, the residents of Qatar and the international community may perceive their host country as guardian of a common global past, rather than as a temporary workplace (Kennedy, Hargreaves, and Al Khater 2016, 87). As Bennett puts it, "That we walk through a museum, walk past the art, recapitulates in our act the motion of art history itself, its restlessness, its forward motion, its power to link" (1995, 45). As visitors to the museum walk through its galleries, they become part of a shared imagined map, marked by several cultural and historical encounters represented by artworks and charted by the linear progressive narrative suggested by the museum's organization.

## From Museum to Cabinet of Curiosity: Becoming a Belt Buckle

Whereas the museum constructs a linear historical narrative, *RIA* mobilizes a third spatial practice related to another precursor of the modern museum: the cabinet of curiosity. In contrast to the museum, organized around a linear timeline in which each piece fits within a specific moment of history, the classification principle of the cabinet of curiosity revolves around the fetishistic quality of the object on display or its potential to evoke wonder (Bennett 1995, 40, 213). Like the Qatari residents who visit the museum, the guest writers become part of the MIA imaginary map. By inviting the authors to stroll through the museum and write about any two objects of their choice, the editor of the volume shifts attention from the diachronic to the synchronic representation of history. As *flâneurs*, or wanderers in the museum, the writers establish random connections with the artifacts they encounter, regardless of their epoch and context. They break the historical and geographical barriers between these objects by creating a rhizomatic (random, nonlinear) itinerary guided by the power of objects to beckon the subject.

In thinking of this experience, I am reminded of an essay by the Palestinian writer and translator Anton Shammas, "The Nightmare of the Translator," included in *RIA*. Contemplating a belt buckle dating from fourteenth-century Granada, Shammas posits: "For a buckle, I thought, to be worthy of the name, it needs to establish a connection of sorts between two ends; that is its mission, its purpose. . . . But now the buckle is bereft of its belt, distant Granada bereft of its sultan. . . . The words in relief . . . assert . . . 'Glory to our lord the Sultan.' At first, I wanted to mistake the 'glory' of the first word . . . for . . . 'return,' as the 'z' and 'd' in Arabic calligraphy look beguilingly alike, and I wanted to think that the words were actually saying: 'Return to our lord The Sultan!'" (2011, 181–82). The title of Shammas's essay humorously alludes to Walter Benjamin's text "The Task of the Translator" and to himself as a translator. As Shammas suggests, in their quest for an object to describe, the guest authors resemble the beltless buckle that has lost its function as a connector between two ends. The verb *to translate*, which signifies to interpret and "to move from one place to another," is key to understanding Shammas's allegory.[11] By writing on relics from different places and times, the guest writers become the buckle that connects severed pasts to the present. They *translate* history in the double sense of that word: they interpret and displace history. Perhaps, in doing so, they symbolically return Granada to a *new* sultan. Crucially, the world-renowned authors are both subjects and objects. As they weave their narratives around the objects of their choice, their names and biographies become part of the collection.

By operating as a cabinet of curiosity, the edited volume restores the collection to a moment before the birth of the modern European museum and its classificatory practices, which frequently reduce artifacts to ethnographic objects. As the authors reframe the collection through narrative, they re-create the artifacts' long-lost aura by suggesting other ways to view the museum content. For instance, describing a dish from the tenth century, Slavoj Žižek writes:

> Item number PO.24 . . . a . . . circular dish from Nishapur or Samarkand . . . decorated with a (Farsi) proverb . . . "Foolish is the person who misses his chance and afterwards reproaches fate." Such dishes were meant to solicit an appropriate conversation among the learned eaters during and after the meal. . . . This is the integration of the dish

> as art into its environs . . . in clear contrast to the standard European practice of isolating the object of art into the sacred space of its exposition, exempting it from daily practices. . . . Let us then step down from the archeological and art-historical heights into today's ordinary life. Let us imagine a group of poor immigrant workers resting on the grass south of the central market on Friday, eating a modest meal . . . on our dish. . . . One of them says: "But what if this applies to us? What if it is not our fate to live here as outcasts? What if, instead of bemoaning our fate, we should seize the chance and change this fate?" (2011, 69–73)

By removing the dish from the "sacred space of its exposition," Žižek produces a multilayered analysis of its meaning as an object of the everyday and explores its implication within contemporary Qatari politics. The cultural critic restores the dish to an earlier moment in time when its aura vacillated between art and commodification. As Kaja Silverman puts it, "Aura . . . is the glow with which objects shine in the first stage of commodity fetishism, a glow created through exhibition value" (2015, 24). Žižek reactivates the dish's dual function as tableware and conversational piece. He initiates a symbolic dinner chatter, inviting the reader to reflect on the proverb by comparing European and Islamic philosophical views on form and function, high art and the quotidian, fate and freedom of choice. He argues that "Western Christians often mistake *Islam*, a specific surrender to God, with *istislam*, a general surrender" (Žižek 2011, 71).[12] For Žižek, the proverb on the dish discredits this faulty identification, pointing instead toward the presence of choice. He asks, "Does Islam effectively contain [a] radical-emancipatory dimension?" (73). Unlike Christianity and Judaism, he claims, Islam rejects the concept of a society organized around a patriarchal deity. In doing so, it creates a domain where politics and religion are not mutually exclusive. This particular aspect of Islam, paradoxically, opens the possibility for social change and, at the same time, renders it amenable to co-optation by the state (73). By criticizing the institutionalization of Islam, Žižek subversively exposes the irony of his participation in a state-sponsored project on Islamic art that attempts to annex Islamic history to a national narrative.

Interestingly, the language of the proverb—Farsi, not Arabic—brings to mind other obstacles to the fulfillment of the Qatari project. In addition to language, these include the difference between the cultural memories of Shi'is and Sunnis and between the social organization of these two groups. The figure of the imam (the spiritual leader) as a descendant of the prophetic line among Shi'is is a key doctrinal difference that influences the way both religious groups institutionalize Islam and fuels the competition over regional leadership (Pinault 2010, 46). Like the unifying narrative constructed by the MIA, Žižek's essay elides these tensions.

Instead, the writer directs the reader's attention toward the question of migration.[13] He imagines the dish in the hands of migrant workers, outside the walls of the museum: precisely, at the marketplace, the same site that the MIA's architect dismissed as a source of inspiration and sought to keep at bay. There, at the marketplace, Žižek muses, workers discuss the emancipatory possibility suggested by the proverb.

Drifting through the museum in search of an artwork, the guest authors legitimize Qatar's claim to be guardian of Islamic heritage by associating their own names with its cultural project. Through their tales, Qatar establishes roots in a multicultural global past, paved by diverse Muslim "religious communities" and "dynastic realms" (Anderson 1990, 12). Qatar situates itself on a transnational map that ambiguously recognizes its contemporary guest residents and simultaneously erases them. Walter Benjamin posits, "Each epoch dreams the one to follow" (1999, 4).[14] Or perhaps every epoch dreams the ones that precede it by realigning the present, in Hobsbawm's words, with "a suitable past": a phantasmagoric beginning shaped by the interplay between authors and authority, experts, artifacts, and rulers (2012, 1).

## NOTES

I thank Olga Greco, Nancy Linthicum, Anne-Marie McManus, Christopher Meade, Patrick Tonks, and the participants of the 2019 Rifkind Seminar at the City College of New York for their valuable feedback on this chapter.

1. Erll's understanding of remediation draws on the scholarship of Jay David Bolter and Richard Grusin on mass media. See Bolter and Grusin 1999; Grusin 2004.

2. Consider similar political strategies in Egypt, the renaming of the Museum of Arab Arts in Cairo as the Museum of Islamic Arts in 1952 at the cusp of political independence, and the later reopening and promotion of the museum in 2010. See Leturq 2015.

3. "About Us," Museum of Islamic Art, accessed July 5, 2020, http://mia.org.qa/en/about.

4. For a critique of contemporary Orientalist visions of Qatar's cultural landscape, see Exell and Rico 2013.

5. Gibraltar is from the Arabic "Jabal Ṭāriq"—that is, "the mountain of Ṭāriq."

6. See Elsheshtawy 2009; Kazerouni 2017; see also *The Economist* 2010, 2012.

7. My addition in brackets.

8. In the extract cited at the beginning of this chapter, Hobsbawm uses the Western calendar to refer to the date of Ibn Khaldun's encounter with the emperor, thereby inscribing the event in a global historical framework.

9. See *The Economist* 2012; Scott 2014.

10. See "Universal Periodic Review" of Qatar in 2010, 2014, and 2019, United Nations Human Rights Council, accessed July 22, 2020, https://www.ohchr.org/EN/HRBodies/UPR/Pages/QAindex.aspx; see also UN High Commissioner for Refugees (UNHCR), *UNHCR Submission on Qatar: 33rd UPR Session*, May 2019, https://www.refworld.org/docid/5ccad3d07.html.

11. *OED* Online, s.v. "translate, v." https://www-oed-com (accessed July 26, 2020).

12. Žižek is referring to the etymological link between the words *islām* and *istislām*.

13. For a brief summary of contemporary polemics between Sunnis and Shi'is, see Pinault 2010; Armstrong 2002.

14. Benjamin is referring to a quote by the French historian Jules Michelet.

## REFERENCES

Anderson, Benedict. 1983. *Imagined Communities: Reflections on the Origins and Spread of Nationalism*. Rev. ed. 1991. London: Verso.

Anscombe, Frederick F. 1997. *The Ottoman Gulf: The Creation of Kuwait, Saudi Arabia, and Qatar, 1870–1914*. New York: Columbia University Press.

Armstrong, Karen. 2002. *Islam: A Short History*. New York: Modern Library.

Ashour, Radwa. 2003. *Granada*. Translated by William Granara. Syracuse, NY: Syracuse University Press.

Babar, Zahra R. 2014. "The Cost of Belonging: Citizenship Construction in the State of Qatar." *Middle East Journal* 68 (3): 403–20.

Benjamin, Walter. 1999. *The Arcades Project*. Translated by Howard Eiland and Kevin Mclaughlin. Cambridge, MA: Belknap Press.

Bennett, Tony. 1995. *The Birth of the Museum: History, Theory, Politics*. New York: Routledge.

Bolter, Jay David, and Richard Grusin. 1999. *Remediation: Understanding New Media*. Cambridge, MA: MIT Press.

Cachin, Françoise, Jean Clair, and Roland Recht. 2006. "Les musées ne sont pas à vendre." *Le Monde*, December 12, 2006.

Calderwood, Eric. 2014. "The Invention of al-Andalus: Discovering the Past and Creating the Present in Granada's Islamic Tourism Sites." *Journal of North African Studies* 19 (1): 27–55.

Clark, T. J. 1999. *The Painting of Modern Life: Paris in the Art of Manet and His Followers*. Rev. ed. Princeton, NJ: Princeton University Press. First published in 1984.

Colla, Elliott. 2007. *Conflicted Antiquities: Egyptology, Egyptomania, Egyptian Modernity*. Durham, NC: Duke University Press.

Derrida, Jacques, and Anne Dufourmantelle. 2000. *Of Hospitality*. Translated by Rachel Bowlby. Stanford, CA: Stanford University Press.

*Economist, The*. 2010. "He'll Do It His Way; Qatar and Its Emir." May 29, 2010.

——. 2012. "Qatar's Culture Queen; Art and the Middle East." March 31, 2012.

Elsheshtawy, Yasser. 2009. *Dubai: Behind an Urban Spectacle*. London: Routledge.

Erll, Astrid. 2009. "Remembering across Time, Space, and Cultures: Premediation, Remediation and the 'Indian Mutiny.'" In *Mediation, Remediation, and the Dynamics of Cultural Memory*, edited by Astrid Erll and Ann Rigney, 109–38. Berlin: De Gruyter.

Exell, Karen. 2016a. "Desiring the Past and Reimagining the Present: Contemporary Collecting in Qatar." *Museum and Society* 14 (2): 259–74.

——. 2016b. *Modernity and the Museum in the Arabian Peninsula*. London: Routledge.

Exell, Karen, and Trinidad Rico. 2013. "'There Is No Heritage in Qatar': Orientalism, Colonialism and Other Problematic Histories." *World Archaeology* 45 (4): 670–85.

Gardner, Andrew, Silvia Pessoa, Abdoulaye Diop, Kaltham Al-Ghanim, Kien Le Trung, and Laura Harkness. 2013. "A Portrait of Low-Income Migrants in Contemporary Qatar." *Journal of Arabian Studies* 3 (1): 1–17.

Grusin, Richard. 2004. "Premediation." *Criticism* 46 (1): 17–39.

Hammadi, Mariam I. Al-. 2018. "Presentation of Qatari Identity at National Museum of Qatar: Between Imagination and Reality." *Journal of Conservation and Museum Studies* 16 (1): 1–10.

Harvey, David. 2003. *Paris: Capital of Modernity*. New York: Routledge.

Hobsbawm, Eric. 2011. "Reflections on a Mughal Portrait." In *Reflections on Islamic Art*, edited by Ahdaf Soueif, 84–89. Doha: Bloomsbury Qatar Foundation Publishing.

——. 2012. "Introduction: Inventing Traditions." In *The Invention of Tradition*, edited by Eric Hobsbawm and Terence Ranger, 1–11. Cambridge: Cambridge University Press. First published in 1983.

Kazerouni, Alexandre. 2017. *Le miroir des cheikhs: Musée et politique dans les principautés du golfe persique*. Paris: Presses Universitaires de France.

Kennedy, Thalia, Jo Hargreaves, and Aisha Al Khater. 2016. "A Study of Visitor Behaviour at the Museum of Islamic Art, Doha." In *Museums in Arabia: Transnational Practices and Regional Processes*, edited by Karen Exell and Sarina Wakefield, 70–91. New York: Routledge.

Leturq, Jean-Gabriel. 2015. "The Museum of Arab Art in Cairo (1869–2014): A Disoriented Heritage?" In *After Orientalism: Critical Perspectives on Western Agency and Eastern Re-appropriations*, 145–65. Leiden: Brill. 145–65.

Mack, Mehammed Amadeus. 2017. *Sexagone: Muslims, France, and the Sexualization of National Culture*. New York: Fordham University Press.

Mitchell, Timothy. 1991. *Colonising Egypt*. Berkeley: University of California Press.

Montigny, Anie. 1996. "Les Arabes de l'autre rive." *Cahier d'études sur la Méditerranée orientale et le monde turco-iranien* 22:51–82.

Ouroussoff, Nicolai. 2008. "In Qatar, an Art Museum of an Imposing Simplicity." *New York Times*, November 23, 2008.

Papayanis, Nicholas. 2004. *Planning Paris before Haussmann*. Baltimore: Johns Hopkins University Press.

Pinault, David. 2010. "Sunni Shia Sectarianism and Competition for the Leadership of Global Islam." *Tikkun* 25 (1): 45–75. *Gale in Context: Biography*.

Rigney, Ann. 2005. "Plenitude, Scarcity and the Circulation of Cultural Memory." *Journal of European Studies* 35 (1): 11–28.

Rothberg, Michael. 2010. "Introduction: Between Memory and Memory: From Lieux de Mémoire to Noeuds de Mémoire." *Yale French Studies* 118/119:3–12.

Scott, Victoria. 2014. "Qatar Museums Authority Announces Re-branding amid Layoff Uncertainty." *Doha News*, May 11, 2014. https://dohanews.co/qatar-museums-authority-announces-re-branding-amid-job-loss-uncertainty/.

Shammas, Anton. 2011. "The Nightmare of the Translator." In *Reflections on Islamic Art*, edited by Ahdaf Soueif, 180–91. Doha: Bloomsbury Qatar Foundation Publishing.

Silverman, Kaja. 2015. *The Miracle of Analogy, or the History of Photography*. Part 1. Stanford, CA: Stanford University Press.

Soueif, Ahdaf. 2011a. "Introduction." In *Reflections on Islamic Art*, edited by Ahdaf Soueif, 10–17. Doha: Bloomsbury Qatar Foundation Publishing.

——, ed. 2011b. *Reflections on Islamic Art*. Doha: Qatar Museum Authority.

Wallach Scott, Joan. 2007. *The Politics of the Veil*. Princeton, NJ: Princeton University Press.

Zahlan, Rosemarie Said. 1979. *The Creation of Qatar*. London: Croom Helm.

Žižek, Slavoj. 2011. "Choosing Our Fate." In *Reflections on Islamic Art*, edited by Ahdaf Soueif, 68–75. Doha: Bloomsbury Qatar Foundation Publishing.

## Part 8

# TRANSLATION, MODERNIZATION, AND CULTURE

The Abbasid caliph al-Ma'mun (d. 833) reportedly had a dream in which he engaged Aristotle in conversation about "the good." It was because of this dream that the caliph created the Bayt al-Ḥikma, an institute for the translation of texts by Aristotle, Plato, Archimedes, Euclid, Galen, and others into Arabic. Some of the translators were Muslims; others were Christians.

Eight hundred years later, Ottoman sultans eager to learn more about European civilization and to formalize contact with the West sponsored the translation of writings in French, English, and other languages into Turkish. These Ottoman translation efforts are the subject of the chapter by Mehmet Darakcioglu. The first translators were multilingual Greek Orthodox Christians. In the aftermath of the 1821 Greek Revolution, however, Christian translators were replaced by Muslims who were more "trustworthy." The Translation Bureau made it possible for the Ottomans to incorporate foreign ideas (initially from Europe, but later from the United States and Japan) and to adapt them to the needs of Ottoman nationalism and loyalty to the empire. The Translation Bureau created a cadre of sophisticated bureaucrats whose ideas paved the way for the political and cultural modernization of Ottoman society. For one hundred years, it served as a launch pad for high-ranking Ottoman diplomats and occupied a central place in Ottoman administrative and political life, a primus inter pares among important government agencies.

In the second chapter, Mary Youssef argues that the hyphen in the term "Arab-American" signals a political and cultural power imbalance between Arabs and Americans, an asymmetry that is a product of American neocolonialism, racism, and the political and cultural subordination of Arabs. In place of a hyphenated approach to identity, Youssef proposes the adoption of a relational approach to the two elements separated by the hyphen. This relational approach, which encourages hybridity and dialogue, is reflected in the "new arrival" novels of Arab writers who have immigrated to the United States. In her analysis of two such novels, Youssef draws attention to "border crossings," that is to say, to the connection between premigration experiences in the Arab homeland and postmigration life and culture in the diaspora. In their homelands and in the diaspora, Youssef argues, Arabs confront "authoritarianism, essentialism, parochialism, dominance and political subordination." These "new arrival" novels are sites of resistance to these forces.

# 19

# OTTOMAN MODERNIZATION AND THE TRANSLATION BUREAU

*Mehmet Darakcioglu*

The Translation Bureau of the Sublime Porte (Bâb-ı Âli Tercüme Odası) received much attention as the channel for new ideas from Europe in the Ottoman Empire during the period that culminated with the proclamation of an Ottoman constitution in 1876.[1] Nearly all members of the Young Ottomans, a group of bureaucrats and literati, served in this office at some point in their careers (Mardin 2000, 11). The renowned Nâmık Kemâl, called "the poet of the fatherland" by subsequent generations, learned French and became receptive to European ideas while working in this office. In his plays, novels, poems, histories, and essays, he popularized the idea of an Ottoman homeland and freedom (Mardin 2000, 283–84). Another translator was Agâh Efendi, who in 1860 launched *Tercüman-ı Ahvâl* (The Interpreter of Conditions), the first private weekly published by a Muslim Turk in the Ottoman Empire (Çakır 2011; Lewis 1968, 147). Prominent political leaders who rose to the highest echelons within Ottoman civil officialdom, like the grand viziers Âli and Fuad Pashas, also worked at the Translation Bureau.

Historians of the Ottoman Empire frequently refer to the Translation Bureau in conjunction with the biographies of important figures who emerged from its ranks. To date, however, there has been no comprehensive study of the bureau that analyzes its contribution to the modernization process in the nineteenth century.[2] In this chapter, I will attempt to answer two questions: What was the Translation Bureau, and why was it important for Ottoman modernization?

Between 1669 and 1821, the Greek Orthodox Christian Phanariots monopolized the position of imperial court translator (*divân-ı hümayûn tercümanı*). The

Greek Revolution of 1821, or "the Rebellion," as the Ottomans called it, which started in the Danubian Principalities and spread to the Peloponnese, had significant consequences for the Phanariots of Istanbul, who occupied a privileged position within the Ottoman bureaucracy (Uzunçarşılı 1988, 72–73).[3] Sultan Mahmud II (r. 1808–1839) ordered the firing of imperial court translator Constantine Mourouzi, whose integrity and loyalty purportedly had been compromised. Mourouzi's translations were no longer considered to be reliable, and he was executed in the turbulent days of the revolution (Findley 1972, 400). As a result, the Phanariots lost their position as intermediaries between Europe and the Ottoman government. In the long term, this administrative shift led to the emergence of a learned Muslim bureaucratic elite who were proficient in European languages and played an important role in the political and intellectual life of the Ottoman Empire. The imperial court translator was an important official who connected the Sublime Porte with European governments. His work involved translating the diplomatic correspondence of European powers. Eight assistants, called language boys, aided the imperial court translator in his work. In addition to the translation of foreign papers, this official also served as an interpreter for European envoys during audiences with high-ranking Ottoman officials, including the grand vizier, and his office was usually the first stop for European diplomats when they visited the Sublime Porte.[4]

Following the removal of Mourouzi and confronted with the pressing need to translate the accumulating foreign correspondence, the Ottoman administration experimented with the organizational structure of the Translator's Office (Tercüman Odası), as it was called at the time. The transition, however, was hampered by the scarcity of Muslim officials with proficiency in European languages who were able and willing to serve. Initially, Yahya Efendi, an instructor from the Imperial Engineering School (Mühendihâne-i Hümayûn), and his son, Ruheddin Efendi, were appointed to translate these papers. When it was determined that Yahya Efendi's language skills were not sufficient for the task, Stavraki Aristachi, another Greek Orthodox, was appointed as the deputy translator (*tercüman vekili*). Although Stavraki was considered impartial, the Sublime Porte must have been ambivalent about his loyalties, and Yahya Efendi was asked to monitor his translations.[5] This arrangement did not last long. Stavraki was dismissed in 1822 after serving less than a year (Findley 1972, 400).

Notwithstanding the shortcomings of his language skills, Yahya Efendi was charged with training Muslim Ottoman officials in European languages. After Stavraki's dismissal, Yahya Efendi was appointed as the imperial court translator, and the burden of language instruction fell to Zenop Manas, an Armenian staff member of the Imperial Engineering School.[6]

According to British diplomatic records, in 1822 Muslim officials were studying foreign languages in a "Collegiate Establishment" at the Sublime Porte and translating articles related to the Ottoman Empire from European newspapers (Findley 1972, 401). An Ottoman document dated 1824 mentions a Language Office (Lisan Odası) along with the Translator's Office and provides details about institutional arrangements for language instruction at the Sublime Porte.[7] Zenop was the chief instructor in the Language Office, and a certain Abdurrahman was hired as a conversation instructor for these clerks-in-training.[8] According to this document, employees of the Translation Bureau, who were chosen from among talented clerks at the Imperial Chancery, were assigned to make neat copies of the translations, translated some light paperwork, kept records of newspapers, and conversed among themselves in French during their free time in the office. When one of these clerks was appointed to another administrative position, a clerk from the Language Office would replace him. Thus, the Language Office served as a training ground for the Translator's Office.[9]

Despite Sultan Mahmud II's eagerness to train Muslim officials in European languages, mainly in French, the Language Office did not produce the desired results.[10] Frustrated with the lack of progress of clerks who studied under Zenop, the Ottoman administration closed the office circa 1828. This decision was influenced by other factors, such as Zenop's banishment from Istanbul along with Catholic Armenians and the availability of French instruction in the newly reorganized Imperial Medical School (Tıbhâne-i Âmire).[11]

In 1824, following the death of Yahya Efendi, İshak Efendi, an instructor from the Engineering School, became the imperial court translator (İhsanoğlu 1989, 17). It was during his tenure that the institutional structure of the Translation Bureau began to take shape. His son-in-law, Halil Esrar Efendi, was appointed as the assistant translator, and his son, Sami Efendi, was employed as a translator. In addition to this core staff, other translators worked in the Translation Bureau when their help was needed.[12] In 1830, the Ottoman administration decided to reassign İshak Efendi to the Engineering School and promoted Halil Esrar Efendi in his place. James E. De Kay, an American who visited the Ottoman Empire between 1831 and 1832, provides a rare and detailed account of Halil Esrar Efendi and his office:

> The present incumbent is a native Turk, a son-in-law of the principal of the College of Engineers. He received us with great affability, and while smoking the customary pipe, he entered readily into general conversation. Near the corner of the divan where he sat, and within reach, was a small japan [sic] tray containing a few narrow strips of paper, a couple

of reed pens, an inkstand sand-box, and his official seal. With these simple implements, unaided by clerks, and independent of an organized bureau, he daily transacts all the complicated business connected with his department. He seemed to be well acquainted with the situation, political condition, character, and manners of our country; at least rather better informed than we are on the subject of Turkey. . . . During our interview several persons entered on business, which was transacted in a low tone of voice approaching a whisper, and this we learned was the established official etiquette. Several dragomen of the foreign powers also dropped in, apparently to lounge away their time and relieve the ennui of their situation. They have a room in this building allotted for their use and are expected to be within call in case their services are required. They are each provided with a pair of yellow shoes, which they slip on over their boots, when they visit the dragomen of the Porte, or are summoned by him. (1833, 282–83)

In 1833, around the time of the Egyptian Crisis, the increasing load of translation work led to an expansion of the Translation Bureau. It was during this expansion that future grand viziers Âli and Saffet Efendis joined its ranks (Findley 1972, 403). More translators were hired in the next two years, and by 1835 there were eight officials working under the imperial court translator. The appointment of Mehmed Tecelli Efendi as imperial court translator in 1835 signals the beginnings of the refinement of ranks in the bureau. The chief subordinate of the imperial court translator, previously referred to as an assistant (*yamak*), was now called the primary translator (*mütercim-i evvel*). Shortly after the beginning of Mehmed Tecelli's tenure (Darakcioglu 2010, 92–96), the Translation Bureau became a subdivision of the Ottoman Foreign Ministry, established in 1836 (Findley 1972, 407–8). He was also the last imperial court translator before the Tanzimât (Reorganization) reforms, which resumed in 1839, when the entire Ottoman administrative system was overhauled (Darakcioglu 2010, 95–96).

By 1841, the Translation Bureau had two groups of employees besides the imperial court translator and the primary translator: five officials, or translators, of the first class and five officials of the second class. In addition, there were seventeen supernumeraries and an instructor, and the total size of the office was thirty. Around this time, the English lexicographer James Redhouse, whose Turkish-English dictionary is still in use in Turkey, joined the bureau (Findley 1972, 404). As the Ottoman state became increasingly bureaucratized, the Translation Bureau continued to grow in size, and by 1851 it employed sixty-six officials.[13] In the mid-1850s, the Crimean War created increased paperwork for the Ottoman bureaucracy that required administrative adjustments in offices like the Translation Bureau. In 1855, an examining clerk (*mümeyyiz*) was appointed to the Translation Bureau to check the translations of correspondence with the embassies of allied powers in Istanbul.[14] In 1856, the imperial court translator Mehmed Kabûli Efendi proposed an extensive set of regulations for language training at the Translation Bureau.[15]

The institutional development of the Translation Bureau paralleled the development and expansion of the Ottoman bureaucracy in the second half of the nineteenth century. In 1883, the Translation Bureau reached its institutionally most sophisticated form. By this time, the Translation Bureau had first-, second-, and third-class employees with well-defined ranks and functions. The bureau was divided into three subdivisions.[16] During the reorganization of the Ottoman Foreign Ministry in 1914, however, its staff size was reduced, and it was renamed the Translation Directorate (Findley 1980, 317). In 1920, two years before the collapse of the Ottoman Empire, it recovered its earlier name, the Translation Bureau of the Sublime Porte.[17]

What made the Translation Bureau such a pivotal institution for Ottoman modernization? The Ottoman administration created the Translation Bureau following the Greek Revolution of 1821, when the Phanariots fell out of favor, so that official translation work could be performed by trustworthy Muslim officials. But the establishment of an institution like the Translation Bureau was inevitable as the Ottoman state became more bureaucratized and as its diplomatic needs became more sophisticated. Major international problems like the Egyptian Crisis (1831–1833), during which the survival of the empire was at stake, and the Crimean War (1853–1856), after which the empire was admitted to the Concert of Europe, required an institutional infrastructure and educated cadre of statesmen who could navigate the choppy waters of European diplomacy.[18] The Translation Bureau emerged as a prominent office that provided the Sublime Porte with trained diplomats and handled the communications of the imperial government.

Proficiency in French provided avenues for upward mobility to higher levels in the Ottoman bureaucracy for statesmen like Âli Pasha in an era when the survival of the empire depended as much on the strength of its diplomatic corps as on the strength of its military (Lewis 1968, 118). About Âli Pasha, whose father was a shopkeeper at Istanbul's Spice Bazaar,[19] Bernard Lewis writes, "For the shopkeeper's son, as for the others, French was the talisman that made the clerk a translator, the translator an interpreter, the interpreter a diplomat, and the diplomat a statesman" (Lewis 1968, 118). The language skills of Ottoman officials who were trained in the Translation Office were deployed not only in diplomacy but also in other important areas. In 1839, Saffet Mehmed Esad Pasha, who joined the bureau at the same time as Âli Pasha, was put in charge of the publication of the French version of the official Ottoman gazette, *Takvîm-i Vekâyi* (Özcan 2008). Although the Sublime Porte initially struggled to institutionalize language instruction and official translation work, within a decade of the removal of the Phanariots in 1821, the Ottoman administration had established the nucleus of a successful office and a key component of its foreign ministry.

The Translation Bureau, which served as a launch pad for high-ranking statesmen, also created a cadre of learned bureaucrats whose ideas paved the way for larger political changes in the Ottoman Empire. Proficiency in French and exposure to the ways of Europe opened the gates of a new world of ideas for figures like Nâmık Kemâl, who was exposed to the works of European thinkers such as Rousseau, Voltaire, Robespierre, Turgot, and others. In Paris, Kemâl took private lessons from the French jurist Emile Acollas, and he was heavily influenced by the idea of the separation of powers (Mardin 2000, 333–34). According to Serif Mardin, it is likely that Nâmık Kemâl learned about the idea of national cohesion from his French tutor, Mehmed Mansur Efendi, a Christian Macedonian convert to Islam. An amateur historian and "relentless enemy" of Greek revolutionary activities, Mehmed Mansur was a defender of the cultural achievements of Islam. He was the first Ottoman to publish a newspaper, which he titled *Vatan* (The Fatherland) (Mardin 2000, 211). In addition to proficiency in French, which made it possible for employees of this office to explore European thought, the Translation Bureau provided an atmosphere in which some of these ideas were transmitted in the form of master-disciple or collegial relationships.

Knowledge of European languages and the West was a recipe for success for aspiring Ottoman clerks in an era when the survival of the empire was highly dependent on diplomacy. In the first quarter of the nineteenth century, however, the avenues for acquiring these skills were limited. Besides the Imperial Engineering Schools for the navy and the army, established in the last decade of the eighteenth century, and the Imperial Medical School, which was opened in 1827, there were not many opportunities for specialized training in general, and for the study of European languages in particular (Lewis 1968, 83–84). Under Yahya Efendi and Zenop Manas, the language instruction was less than ideal, but following the removal of the Phanariots, the Translation Bureau provided Ottoman officials with an opportunity to study foreign languages at a time when language skills were a high priority for the Sublime Porte. Although we know little about the language instruction in the early years of the Translation Bureau, we do know that the employees of this office read and translated European newspapers as a part of their training. The language skills acquired by these officials at the Translation Bureau provided them with an opportunity to follow the affairs of Europe.

While some of these aspiring clerks, such as Âli and Fuad Pashas, went on to hold high offices in the grand vizierate or foreign ministry, Young Ottomans such as Nâmık Kemâl transformed the political landscape of the empire with their ideas and publications. The contributions of the Translation Bureau to the professional development and intellectual formation of an educated bureaucratic elite and influential literati played a pivotal role in the transformation and modernization of the Ottoman Empire in the nineteenth century.

## NOTES

1. "Sublime Porte" is the French equivalent of Bâb-ı Âli (literally "The Exalted Gate"). It refers to the complex that contained the administrative offices of the grand vizier and his household. Europeans and Ottomans used this term to refer to the Ottoman central government. See Findley 1980, 5. I use "Sublime Porte" to signify the Ottoman central government and its administration.

2. On connections between the Young Ottomans and the Translation Bureau, see Mardin 2000, 11. Scholarship on the institutional structure of the Translation Bureau is limited. Lewis discusses foreign languages and the Translation Bureau in his account of late Ottoman history (1968, 87–89). On the establishment of the Translation Bureau, see Findley 1972, 400–404; 1980, 132–35. On the education of officials in the Translation Bureau in the mid-1850s, see Akyıldız 1993, 72–78. On the Ottoman Foreign Ministry and the Translation Bureau, see Karaarslan 1999. On the institutional history of the Translation Bureau, see Balcı 2013, which is an expanded version of his dissertation, "Osmanlı Devleti'nde Tercümanlık ve Bab-ı Âli Tercüme Odası" (Ankara Üniversitesi, 2006). In both the book and the dissertation, Balcı cites all available archival documents on the Translation Bureau, albeit without placing this material in a coherent framework or advancing an argument. On the Translation Bureau between 1821 and 1883, see Darakcioglu 2010.

3. The Phanariots were a group of affluent Greek families from the Phanar (Fener) district of Istanbul who held important offices in the Ottoman government in the eighteenth and nineteenth centuries, such as imperial court translator and the voivodeships of Moldavia and Wallachia (Decei 1945, 547–50).

4. Orhonlu 1979; Türkiye Cumhuriyeti Cumhurbaşkanlığı Devlet Arşivleri Başkanlığı Osmanlı Arşivi (BOA) Istanbul, Turkey, Kamil Kepeci (KK.d) Teşrifat Defteri no. 676, Mükerrer 2, p. 178.

5. BOA, Hatt-ı Hümayun (HAT) 48823.

6. BOA, HAT 16749. On the Zenop and Manas families, see Çark 1953, 135–43.

7. BOA, Mühimme Defterleri (MD) no. 241, p. 392.

8. BOA, Cevdet Maarif (C.MF) 3760.

9. BOA, MD no. 241, p. 392.

10. BOA, HAT 16749.

11. BOA, HAT 24621; Beydilli 1995, 8.

12. BOA, HAT 21304.

13. BOA, Maliyeden Müdevver Defterler (MAD.d) no. 9210, p. 217.

14. BOA, İrade Dahiliye (I.DH) 20079.

15. BOA, İrade Hariciye (I.HR) 6900.

16. BOA, Hariciye Tercüme Odası Evrakı (HR.TO) 477/31.

17. BOA, Dosya Usûlü İrade Tasnifi (I.DUİT) 57/63.

18. On the Ottoman-Egyptian War of 1831–33, see Shaw and Shaw 1977, 32–44. On the Crimean War, see Aksan 2013, 476.

19. İnal 1964, 4.

## REFERENCES

Aksan, Virginia. 2013. *Ottoman Wars, 1700–1870: An Empire Besieged*. New York: Routledge.

Akyıldız, Ali. 1993. *Osmanlı Merkez Teşkilâtında Reform*. Istanbul: Eren Yayıncılık.

Balcı, Sezai. 2013. *Babıâli Tercüme Odası*. Istanbul: Libra Kitapçılık ve Yayıncılık.

Beydilli, Kemal. 1995. *Recognition of the Armenian Community and the Church in the Reign of Sultan Mahmud II (1830)*. Cambridge, MA: Harvard University, Department of Near Eastern Languages and Civilizations.

Çakır, Hamza. 2011. "Tercümân-ı Ahvâl." In *Türkiye Diyanet Vakfı İslam Ansiklopedisi*, 40: 495–97. Istanbul: TDV İslâm Araştırmaları Merkezi.

Çark, Y. G. 1953. *Türk Devleti Hizmetinde Ermeniler, 1453–1953*. Istanbul: Yeni Matbaa.

Darakcioglu, Mehmet. 2010. "Rebuilding the Tower of Babel: Language Divide, Employment of Translators, and the Translation Bureau in the Ottoman Empire." PhD diss., Princeton University.

Decei, Aurel. 1945. "Fenerliler." In *İslâm Ansiklopedisi*, 4:547–50. Istanbul: Milli Eğitim Basımevi.

[De Kay, James E.] 1833. *Sketches of Turkey in 1831 and 1832 by an American*. New York: J. & J. Harper.

Findley, Carter V. 1972. "The Foundation of the Ottoman Foreign Ministry: The Beginnings of Bureaucratic Reform under Selim III and Mahmud II." *International Journal of Middle East Studies* 3 (4): 388–416.

——. 1980. *Bureaucratic Reform in the Ottoman Empire: The Sublime Porte, 1789–922*. Princeton, NJ: Princeton University Press.

İhsanoğlu, Ekmeleddin. 1989. *Başhoca İshak Efendi, Türkiye'de Modern Bilimin Öncüsü*. Ankara: Kültür Bakanlığı Yayınları.

İnal, İbnülemin Mahmud Kemal. 1964. *Osmanlı Devrinde Son Sadrıazamlar*. Istanbul: Milli Eğitim Basımevi.

Karaarslan, Uğurhan. 1999. "Osmanlı Dış Politikasında Değişim ve Babıali Tercüme Odası." Master's thesis, Marmara Üniversitesi.

Lewis, Bernard. 1968. *The Emergence of Modern Turkey*. London: Oxford University Press.

Mardin, Serif. 2000. *The Genesis of Young Ottoman Thought: A Study in the Modernization of Turkish Political Ideas*. Syracuse, NY: Syracuse University Press.

Orhonlu, Cengiz. 1979. "Tercüman." In *İslâm Ansiklopedisi*, 12:175–81. Istanbul: Milli Eğitim Basımevi.

Özcan, Azmi. 2008. "Saffet Mehmed Esad Paşa." In *Türkiye Diyanet Vakfı İslam Ansiklopedisi*, 35:467–69. Istanbul: TDV İslâm Araştırmaları Merkezi.

Shaw, Stanford J., and Ezel Kural Shaw. 1977. *History of the Ottoman Empire and Modern Turkey*. Vol. 2, *Reform, Revolution, and Republic: The Rise of Modern Turkey, 1808–1975*. Cambridge: Cambridge University Press.

Uzunçarşılı, İsmail H. 1988. *Osmanlı Devletinin Merkez ve Bahriye Teşkilâtı*. Ankara: Türk Tarih Kurumu Basımevi.

# 20

# READING CULTURAL TRANSLATION IN TWO "NEW ARRIVAL" ARAB AMERICAN NOVELS

*Mary Youssef*

Arab American writers have long been telling stories about immigration, displacement, and belonging, as well as sharing experiences relating to community formation and where home may be; yet, for most of the twentieth century, their writings have been underrecognized by mainstream publishers and literary readership in the United States. In recent years, and especially toward the end of the twentieth century, the novels—the literary genre upon which this chapter focuses—of a younger generation of Arab American writers have come into the spotlight in the United States, marking a shift in the production of Arab American literature and its reception.

This cultural recognition is reflected, first, in the nomination of Arab American writings for prestigious literary prizes and honors, such as the PEN American Center Award for Fiction, the American Book Award, the American National Series Award, and the Pulitzer Award. It is also reflected in the dedication of a special issue to Arab American literature and its status in the journal *MELUS, The Society for the Multi-Ethnic Literature of the United States*. These awards, and the integration of Arab American literature into multiethnic literature in the United States, acknowledge the contribution of Arab American creative voices to American racial, religious, and cultural diversity and to narratives about the immigrant experience. The awards conferred inter alia upon Naomi Shihab Nye (b. 1952), Diana Abu-Jaber (b. 1960), Mohja Kahf (b. 1967), and Suheir Hammad (b. 1973), and their acquisition of a wide readership, signal appreciation for their nuanced articulations of American experiences and identities and their contributions to the redefinition of the American literary canon.

During the early period of the Mahjar, or Arab Diaspora in the United States, Arab immigrants produced an influential body of literature—largely in Arabic—that serves as the foundation for modern writings of Arab and Arab American authors alike. Although Arabophone immigrant literature continues to be produced in the United States, the growing appreciation for Arab American literature has been accompanied by a surge in popular interest in Arabic literature in translation, especially contemporary fiction produced in Arab countries. The award of the Nobel Prize in Literature to Egyptian novelist Naguib Mahfouz in 1988 was followed by a substantial increase in the number of English translations of Arabic literary works, especially novels. Ironically, that watershed in the history of modern Arabic literature and the global appreciation of its translated works was surpassed by a spike in interest after the events of 9/11 (Khalifa and Elgindy 2014, 50–53).[1] This recent attention is a double-edged sword: on the one hand, it reflects popular curiosity about Arab culture as part of the larger reservoir of human experience; on the other, it reflects Arabophobic prejudice that has targeted Arabs in the United States ever since. Sinan Antoon (b. 1967), the Iraqi-born US immigrant, award-winning novelist, academic, and translator, calls the latter type of attention a "forensic interest" that reduces Arabic literature and culture to sources of information for deciphering the discursive mystification of Arabs and Muslims (Qualey, quoted in Khalifa and Elgindy 2014, 53).

That confounding interest has prompted contextually sensitive inquiries and approaches to translation studies and practices in the Arab world, which, in turn, have begun to be acknowledged in the American cultural landscape. For example, the Libyan-born, US-based poet, critic, and translator Khaled Mattawa (b. 1964) was awarded the PEN America Center Award for Poetry Translation for his English translation of Adonis's poetry, and the Egyptian-born US-based literary critic and translator Samah Selim (b. 1966) was awarded the University of Arkansas Translation Award for her translation of the Lebanese writer Jurji Zaydan's historical novel *Tree of Pearls, Queen of Egypt*.

These shifts in the assessment and appreciation of Arab and Arab American literature and its translational relationship have occurred at a moment of cultural, political, and military power imbalance between the formerly colonized Arab countries, the original homelands of Arab Americans, and the United States, their adopted homeland.[2] This historical context entwines both Arabs (immigrants or those dwelling in the Arab homeland) and Arab Americans (US born or with Arab ancestry) into a joint fate of "political racism" in American social and political discourses, where they are vilified as a single racialized global group alien to the purportedly homogeneous American national structure and identity. These discursive antagonisms have been used to justify US interventions in the Arab world: after World War II and the waning of modern European colonialism, the United States emerged as the world's new superpower and is reenacting the colonial practice of divide and conquer to maintain political and economic domination in the Arab world. Over the past fifty years, Arabs and Arab Americans have suffered from the predicament of *othering* as a consequence of the US neoimperialist role in Arab-Israeli wars (1967 and 1973), the Lebanese Civil War (1975–1990), the Gulf War (1990–1991), the invasion of Afghanistan (2001), 9/11 (2001), the invasion of Iraq (2003), and the subsequent war on terror (2003) (Fadda-Conrey 2015, 1–2). Following the Arab Spring in 2011, a new wave of US-led military interventions in Libya, Syria, and Yemen has exacerbated the already asymmetrical global power relations and forced thousands of Arabs into homelessness and migration, factors that play a significant role in the current Middle East refugee crisis.

These political entanglements have stimulated pernicious discourses and practices that target Arabs and Arab Americans while generating among both groups a sense of political and cultural interdependence and entwined political fates, historical and contemporary. These entanglements have also inspired an awakening among Arabs and Arab Americans of their collective consciousness, their shared heritage, and the need to counter racial and political subordination as a group rather than as individuals. These political complications support the understanding that just as Arabs are in constant flux and on the move across borders and continents—despite bans, walls, and border control laws—so too their culture and identity are fluid and changing. As Paul Gilroy writes, "Culture can never be immobilized in the way that [the] . . . pursuit of absolute identity demands. To seek to fix culture is a problem because, if we arrest its unruly motion, we ossify it" (2005, 434). In the context of current historical transformations, Arab and Arab American writers, scholars, and translators have sought to make sense of two phenomena: first, the "unruly" openness, fluidity, and mobility of the translation process—not only in the performative act of translating a text from its source language into the target language but also in the sense of translating meanings and experiences across the spatial and metaphorical borders of nationalisms, linguistic affiliations, and fields of knowledge and specialization; and, second, the creative negotiation and pursuit by migrants of what Homi Bhabha calls "hybrid sites" located in the midst of power asymmetries that perpetuate the subordination of Arabness to Americanness (1994, 25).

I argue that Arab cultural translation efforts are decentered, multivalent, and heteroglossic sites of resistance to all forms of authoritarianism, essentialism, parochialism, dominance, and political subordination, both in Arab homelands and in the US diaspora. In their multivalence, these efforts manifest themselves on several overlapping cultural planes—the academic, the activist, and the literary—which are responsive to current historical conditions and the ensuing discursive subordination of Arabness to Americanness, without regard for their dialogic connections.

On the academic level, in 2015, *The Translator* published a timely special issue on translation in and of the Arab world. The coeditors, Richard Jacquemond and Samah Selim, stated that their goal was to examine new ways in which translation reorients the field away from the former focus on "textual questions of language and ethics" and toward the contentious historical forces and political economy of asymmetrical power relations that shape the theory and practice of Arabic translation into Western languages (Jacquemond and Selim 2015, 122). In an equally timely publication, the 2018 special issue of *Alif: Journal of Comparative Poetics*, on translation and the production of knowledge(s), Mona Baker asserts the vital role of translation in the transfer of knowledge, not in a disinterested manner, as formerly believed, but to impact the "production, renegotiation, and reification of knowledge" (Baker 2018, 9). Similarly, a special issue of *MELUS* (2006) devoted to Arab American literature, coedited by Salah Hassan and Marcy Jane Knopf-Newman, while designed to respond to the "pressure to educate students and the general public and also to intervene in the dominant discourses on Arabs in the US," expresses concern about "a disabling disconnect between the political determination of Arabs in the US, their cultural production, and the academic study of Arab Americans" (Hassan and Knopf-Newman 2006, 3). The coeditors call for "an unrelenting critique of the racialization of Arabs in the US and at the same time a thoughtful scrutiny of the political and cultural self-representation of Arabs" (5). Hassan and Knopf-Newman argue that the hyphen in hyphenated identities such as "Arab-American" reinforces the binary in, and power asymmetry between, its two sides rather than their hybridity and dynamism. On this point, they agree with Ella Shohat, who argues that it is necessary to abandon "segmenting and differentiating among various American ethnic identities" and to adopt "a relational approach to multicultural studies that does not segregate historical periods and geographical regions into neatly fenced off areas of expertise, and which does not speak of communities in isolation, but 'in relation'" (Shohat, quoted in Hassan and Knopf-Newman 2006, 6). This relational approach is modeled in a cross-ethnic study by Therí A. Pickens, *New Body Politics: Narrating Arab and Black Identity in the Contemporary United States* (2014), in which she makes insightful connections between mundane corporeal experiences in Black and Arab American narratives and the authorial deployment of such experiences in response to marginalizing social and political discourses in the United States.

The relational approach echoes Edward Said's cautionary admonition to postcolonial scholars to avoid lapsing into "parochial dominations and fussy defensiveness" when making claims to exclusive insider experience and knowledge in the name of "fragmentation and specialization" (Said 1985, 107). Under current historical contingencies, I argue, Said's call is relevant and urgent not only in the nascent field of cross-ethnic literary explorations but also in the cross-examination of Arab and Arab American literary production and criticism and their "unruly" cultural exchanges and translations.

On the activist plane, nuanced cultural translation efforts have recognized and solidified cross-border, literal and metaphorical, Arab and Arab American cultural dialogic interactions as a strategy for countering the discursive subordination of Arabness to Americanness. By "border crossing," I refer to the recent spatial and cultural movement cum translation cum border crossing of Arabs—their political consciousness, linguistic affiliations, social experiences, and knowledge(s)—from the Arab homelands to the United States and Arab America. Their unique position as new immigrants "at the metropolitan site," as Bhabha phrases it, facilitates distinct translational and interstitial reconfigurations of Arabness, Arab culture, and the Arab homelands in the Arab diasporic consciousness (Bhabha 1994, 213). These configurations contribute to redefining "Arab" in the phrase "Arab American."

A word about the changing demographic of Arab immigrants in the United States: before the 1960s, Arab immigrants to the United States were predominantly Christians from Lebanon and Syria; by contrast, the Arab immigrants who arrived in subsequent years were more diverse with respect to religion, ethnicity, politics, and educational background (Al Maleh 2009, 11; Majaj 2008). These new immigrants included Arab writers and intellectuals who were fleeing from political unrest and who came to the United States to write with freedom unattainable in their homelands. Sometimes, their creative writing is in Arabic, as with Sinan Antoon and Miral al-Tahawy; other times it is in English, as with Laila Lalami and Rabih Alameddine. As a group, they write about exile, displacement, gender, belonging, and social and political injustices. According to Layla Al Maleh, the diaspora has attracted both Anglophone and Arabic-speaking Arab writers: "Diasporic space, despite its inevitably concomitant pain, appeals because it grants the Arab intellectual, regardless of the linguistic tools at his disposal, an open forum for raising his voice in protest or clarification. Today, most literary, political, and cultural activity is taking place beyond Arab borders" (Al Maleh 2009, 14).

In 1993, Elie Chalala, a Lebanese-born, US-based social scientist, founded and became the editor of *Al Jadid: A Review & Record of Arab Culture and Arts*. Initially, the magazine appeared monthly in Arabic and English; since 1997, it has been published as a quarterly in English (a change facilitated by the robust translation of its Arabic content). *Al Jadid* exemplifies decentered, border-crossing cultural translation efforts that connect Arabic speakers with the Arab diasporic community in the United States and vice versa. Chalala has identified an American obsession with Middle Eastern politics and seeks to shift that focus to Arab cultural production. Such a shift is, in its own right, a political act that contributes to resisting the essentialization of Arabs in the United States (Gabriel 2001). Similarly, the Arab American Book Award, established in 2006 by the Arab American National Museum, recognizes new literary production across different genres as well as scholarship that examines the histories and present conditions of Arabs and their descendants in the United States. The expansion of the award categories to include adult fiction, nonfiction, children and young adult fiction and nonfiction, and poetry reflects the increase in border-crossing and translational efforts, linguistic and cultural, between the Arab world and the United States.

That expanding recognition is evident in literary awards for novels that bring premigration lives and experiences in the Arab homeland to the fore of the American, postmigration cultural landscape. In 2015, Laila Lalami received the Arab American Book Award in the category of adult fiction for her novel *The Moor's Account*. In the same year, Rabih Alameddine received this award for his novel *An Unnecessary Woman*, and again in 2017 for *The Angel of History*. In 2014, Sinan Antoon received the first Arab American Book Award in the category of adult fiction for self-translating his Arabic novel on Iraq, *The Corpse Washer*; the award signaled the critical value of translations from Arabic to English in the Arab American cultural context and, by extension, appreciation for the translational and border-crossing efforts of Arab authors, not only between Arabic and English but also between Arab and Arab American literary production. That pioneering critical acknowledgment aligns with the decision by two literary critics, Munir Akash and Khaled Mattawa, to include translations of writings by Mahmood Darwish and Tawfiq al-Hakim, neither of whom immigrated to the United States, in their coedited anthology, *Post-Gibran: Anthology of New Arab American Writing* (2000). This decision was based in part on the understanding that, since its inception, Arab American literature has been influenced by its roots in the Arabic literary tradition, as asserted by Arab American poet Elmaz Abinader (Hassan and Knopf-Newman 2006, 9).

I read Lalami's *The Moor's Account* (2014) and Alameddine's *The Angel of History* (2016) as examples of cultural translation and border crossing, on the literary plane, that contribute to the dialogic interaction between Arabness and Americanness. Both novels describe and foreground premigration lives and experiences in the Arab homelands in what I interpret as a political undertaking that, on one level, emphasizes the impact of experiences in the Arab homeland on postmigration life and culture and, on another, portrays border crossing and cultural translation as a process that began in Arab homes, before departure to the United States. In both novels, the Arab home and its culture, otherwise perceived as peripheral to the (neo)colonial center, is at the heart of the ongoing cultural exchange between Arabness and Americanness.

The main characters, Mustafa al-Zamori in *The Moor's Account* and Ya'qub in *The Angel of History*, give lengthy accounts of their homes in the Arab world. Unlike "canonical" American diasporic literature, these novels exemplify Bharati Mukherjee's "Literature of New Arrival" (Mukherjee 2011, 683). Both novelists write unapologetically about their "bond to the land" of their birth and family, about separation anxiety, and about the lack of exultation upon arrival in America (681). Grounded in his Arab hometown of Azemmur in the Maghreb, al-Zamori fondly invokes the memory of his mother, who cooked meals for her children and told them captivating stories, and of his father, a learned and locally respected notary and scholar of Islamic jurisprudence. For Ya'qub, home is the whorehouse in Cairo where he, his mother, and his "aunties" were welcomed and given shelter by the house leader, Badeea, a maternal figure whose lap, kitchen table, and bosom are all sites for his identity formation and sense of belonging. Ya'qub's recollection of Badeea's teaching of Egyptian lyrics, the Qur'an, and classical Arabic poetry disrupts the common association of home and knowledge with patriarchy.

*The Moor's Account*, set in the sixteenth century, and *The Angel of History*, set at the beginning of the twenty-first, embed neoimperial power dynamics in their complex border-crossing representations. These "New Arrival" novels do not limit the process of cultural translation and border crossing to the postmigration site. Rather, they call attention to the Arab world as the premigration site where the process of culture translation and border crossing begins with the (neo)colonial encounter. The premigration lives of Mustafa and Ya'qub are filled with loss, forced relocations, and cultural exchange within violent (neo)colonial contexts, destabilizing attempts to insulate the (neo)imperial peripheral site, people, and culture from their metropolitan counterparts, and vice versa. In the end, Mustafa and Ya'qub transfer their pre- and postcolonial experiences in the Arab homeland(s) to the postmigration setting. On the day Mustafa is born, his father and pregnant mother are forced to cross the river on a raft in search of a safer home and life, still in their homeland; however, two imperial soldiers sever Mustafa's father's arm because he was defending locals. Thus, Mustafa is born into the world as a harbinger of change, loss, and imminent border crossing. Fulfilling his ominous trajectory, Mustafa refuses to become a scholar like his father, despite his training in Sharia. Instead, he becomes a merchant who is lured into the lucrative slave trade. Things fall apart, and Mustafa must sell himself as a slave to support his mother and his siblings.

Conceived out of wedlock in Beirut at the family house of his wealthy Christian father, Ya'qub, while still in the womb of his poor Muslim, Yemeni mother, is banished from his father's house. Mother and child travel from Lebanon to Yemen, where his mother is driven out of her hometown and forced to cross unnamed borders and deserts, all within the Arab world, until they find support and protection in a whorehouse in Cairo. Here Ya'qub discovers his sexuality and love for the "blond god" who shatters his and his mother's dream of deliverance from exile. This premigration trajectory signals that being Arab born and living in the Arab homeland does not necessarily protect Arabs from the experience of exile due to imagined and lived racial, religious, and national distinctions. Ya'qub says, "I'm the congenital immigrant. . . . I left parts of me everywhere. I was born homeless, countryless, raceless, didn't belong to either my father's family or my mother's, no one could claim me, or wanted me" (Alameddine 2016, 15).

These premigration depictions of home in the Arab world point to the indelible connection of Mustafa and Ya'qub to the land and its people as well as their memories of identity formation. At the same time, they indicate that the winds of change, set in motion by the (neo)colonial enterprise, have been blowing through their homelands, sending the characters on journeys of rooting and uprooting, anguish, and border crossing. Mustafa leaves the Maghreb on a slave ship bound for Spain and then La Florida (a former Spanish territory that includes present-day Florida in the United States). In his postmigration life he witnesses the mass enslavement of Black Africans like himself, coerced baptism, and rape, as well as the robbing and massacre of the Native American population in La Florida. Similarly, summoned by his Christian father to Beirut, Ya'qub experiences compulsory baptism and education in a French Catholic boarding school, both attempts by his father to lift him above his mother's perceived inferior racial and religious affiliation. At school, Ya'qub's humanity, like that of his mother, is violated by rape and coercion.

While still in the homeland, Mustafa and Ya'qub acquire knowledge and experience of empire and learn about Arabic poetry and the Qur'an. In addition, Mustafa is taught the principles of Islamic law, whereas Ya'qub discovers Eastern Christian mysticism and the fourteen saintly helpers of the Lebanese church tradition. Their premigration lives and homes are unapologetically translated (i.e., transferred with them) to the metropolitan site. They are multilingual and have the ability to translate from the languages of empire, like Spanish and English, into the languages of the marginalized communities to which they belong, like Arabic and Native American, and vice versa. Relying on their knowledge of both Arab tradition and empire, Mustafa and Ya'qub form new affinities and solidarities—Mustafa with other African slaves in Europe and with Native Americans in La Florida, and Ya'qub with the homosexual community in San Francisco. These postmigration solidarities among the similarly marginalized empower Mustafa to survive the fate suffered by his companions on the imperial expedition and help Ya'qub survive the AIDS epidemic that claimed the lives of his companions. Whether in the sixteenth century or the twenty-first, these two premigration and postmigration stories remind readers that the metropolitan site has been suffering from "postcolonial melancholia" owing to its loss of what it is supposed to be, a glorious empire, as Paul Gilroy characterizes it—with the British imperial example (Gilroy 2005, 434–38). Now, the foreign-born, new arrivals from the (former) colonial margins, like Mustafa and Ya'qub, the "semi-strangers who, disarmingly, knew . . . [the metropolitan] culture intimately as a result of their colonial education" like spirits, or perhaps mystical Eastern Christian saints, or even angels, haunt the history of the metropolis by retelling it from their hybrid sites of resistance, translating (i.e., transposing) the migration narrative beginning—spatially and temporally—to the Arab homeland and translating the Arab homeland to that narrative present, lest these homes be forgotten and pass into oblivion.

## NOTES

1. Expanding on S. J. Altoma's identification of three phases in the translation of modern Arabic literature, Abdel Wahab Khalifa and Ahmed Elgindy demonstrate that the translation of Arabic literary works into English, particularly fiction, unfolded in four stages. The "Initial Phase" stretched from 1908 (the publication date of the first English translation of a work of fiction, a 1902 novella by Shukri Khuri) to 1967. This was followed by an "Expanding Phase" (1968 to 1988), which witnessed an increase in Arabic literature courses for scholars and aspiring specialists. The year 1988—in which Naguib Mahfouz was awarded the Nobel Prize for Literature—marks the beginning of the "Post-Nobel Phase," during which the translation of Arabic fiction reached "a turning point." Finally, during the fourth or "Post-9/11 Phase," interest in Arabic literature has risen to new and unprecedented levels. See Khalifa and Elgindy 2014, 53.

2. The Arab and Arab American population in the United States is one of the fastest-growing immigrant groups. According to the Arab American Institute (AAI) website, at least 1.9 million Americans are of Arab descent (the AAI Foundation subsequently increased this estimate to 3.7 million). The AAI website states that the statistical source for the estimate is the U.S. Census Bureau, American Community Survey 1-Year Estimate (2017) and AAI's research and surveys. See demographics page on AAI website: https://www.aaiusa.org/demographics.

## REFERENCES

Alameddine, Rabih. 2016. *The Angel of History*. New York: Grove Press.
Al Maleh, Layla. 2009. "Anglophone Arab Literature: An Overview." In *Arab Voices in the Diaspora: Critical Perspectives on Anglophone Arab Literature*, edited by Layla Al Maleh, 1–63. Amsterdam: Rodopi.
Baker, Mona. 2018. "Translation and the Production of Knowledge(s)." *Alif: Journal of Comparative Poetics* 38:8–10.
Bhabha, Homi. 1994. *The Location of Culture*. New York: Routledge.
Fadda-Conrey, Carol. 2015. *Contemporary Arab-American Literature: Transnational Reconfigurations of Citizenship and Belonging*. New York: New York University Press.

Gabriel, Judith. 2001. "Emergence of a Genre: Reviewing Arab American Writers." *Al Jadid* 7 (34). https://www.aljadid.com/content/emergence-genre-reviewing-arab-american-writers.

Gilroy, Paul. 2005. "Multiculture, Double Consciousness and the 'War on Terror.'" *Patterns of Prejudice* 39 (4): 31–43.

Hassan, Salah D., and Marcy Knopf-Newman. 2006. "Introduction." *Multi-Ethnic Literature of the United States* 31 (4): 3–13.

Jacquemond, Richard, and Samah Selim. 2015. "Introduction to Translating in the Arab World." *The Translator* 21 (2): 121–31.

Khalifa, Abdel Wahab, and Ahmed Elgindy. 2014. "The Reality of Arabic Fiction Translation into English: A Sociological Approach." *International Journal of Society, Culture, and Language* 2 (2): 51–56.

Majaj, Lisa Suhair. 2008. "Arab-American Literature: Origins and Developments." *American Studies Journal, Arab-American Literature and Culture* 52. http://www.asjournal.org/52-2008/arab-american-literature-origins-and-developments/.

Mukherjee, Bharati. 2011. "Immigrant Writing: Changing the Contours of a National Literature." *American Literary History* 23 (3): 680–96.

Said, Edward. 1985. "Orientalism Reconsidered." *Critical Inquiry* 1:89–107.

# Part 9

# REMEMBERING—
# AND FORGETTING—
# THE DEAD

In the first chapter, Fabio López Lázaro (like Mary Youssef in part 8) engages in an exercise of border crossing by comparing the tombstone inscriptions of Muslim and Christian rulers in the Western Mediterranean between the tenth and the fifteenth centuries CE. These inscriptions, he argues, are "transliminal" pronouncements that display a striking pattern. Whereas inscriptions on the tombs of Muslim rulers are formulated in terms of people and personalities (e.g., "the excellent sultan, the honor of Islam, a handsome man among men" or "defender of the faithful"), those on the tombs of Christian rulers are formulated in terms of territory (e.g., "King in Castile," "King of France," or "King of Sicily, Duke of Apulia and Prince of Capua"). Muslim and Christian elites paid close attention to each other's tombstone proclamations and made calculated decisions about how best to project power across faith lines that were fluid and changing. Tombstones, López Lázaro concludes, are signs of accommodation, collaboration, and competition between and among Muslims and Christians, a dynamic process that involved not only *convivencia* but also *disvivencia*.

In the second chapter, Nancy Um reflects on the destruction of heritage sites during the current civil war (2014–present) in Yemen. Her focus is on the tomb of Abu al-Hasan al-Shadhili, the thirteenth-century Sufi mystic and patron saint of Mocha, who is often associated—albeit mistakenly—with the introduction of coffee to Arabia. According to one report, Abu al-Hasan discovered the power of caffeine while visiting Ethiopia, where he noticed that berry-eating birds were unusually chipper. Following his death in Mocha in 1424, al-Shadhili was buried in a tomb located inland from the coast. In 1590–1591, the Ottoman governor of Yemen ordered the renovation and enlargement of the tomb. Shortly thereafter, the governor ordered the construction of what would come to be known as the Great Mosque of al-Shadhili, adjacent to the saint's tomb. It was only at this time (that is to say, in the sixteenth century)—that Mocha became a major producer of coffee and that al-Shadhili became the patron saint of the beverage. Circa 2017, Salafi members of the coalition forces that reclaimed Mocha from the Huthis targeted al-Shadhili's tomb—in their eyes, a symbol of detested saint veneration—and reduced it to a pile of rubble. According to a Sufi maxim, human consciousness is woven of forgetfulness. How will al-Shadhili be remembered five hundred years from now? Or will he perhaps be forgotten?

# TRANSLIMINAL COMPARISONS IN THE TOMBSTONE INSCRIPTIONS OF MUSLIM AND CHRISTIAN RULERS IN THE MAGHRIB AND IBERIA

*Fabio López Lázaro*

**You desire the goods of the world, but God desires [for you] the Hereafter.**

—Qur'an 8:67

Aristotle may have been wrong: we are not *political* animals by nature but *comparing* animals, for arguably comparison constituted the polis and sustained it (*Politics*, book 3, chapters 1–3, 9). Discounting ethnic or geographical unity, Aristotle emphasized how citizens hold each other to the common goal of their particular "constitution." This unresolved part of his argument—spawning the many meanings of "political" and "policing"—might be paraphrased as "neighbors policing each other against unacceptable divergence from the perceived common good" (a troubling argument not least because it suggests that Antonio Gramsci's theory about conformism was right). Evolutionary psychologists call this uniquely hominin capacity for self-reflective comparison with others "theory of mind"—that is, the ability to discern multiple levels of difference in astonishing synchronic and diachronic ways. As Oxford University's Robin Dunbar explains, "The capacity to understand another individual's mind state," especially his or her intentions, is something children do not possess at birth but acquire slowly beginning at age four or five; most adults never achieve proficiency beyond "fifth order intentionality," as in the phrase "I think that you believe that I suppose that we understand that Jane wants . . ." (2014, 439–40).

Historical comparison is inextricably intertwined with cognition of difference, either diachronically, when historians deploy comparison as a heuristic, or synchronically, when differentiation was a hermeneutic intent of persons in the past (I use the past tense intentionally to highlight temporal difference). Three preliminary observations must be made to clarify how the epitaphs inscribed on the tombstones of western Mediterranean rulers are considered in this chapter as "transliminal" pronouncements—cross-boundary theory-of-mind instantiations of their creators' reciprocal limits of comparison (if the pun is allowed).

Generally, Christian rulers before circa 1300 CE shared with Muslim rulers a sense that the highest *nomos* binding them to their subjects, in theory, was divine law, not physical nature (*phusis*). However, in addition to sharing this ancient monotheistic conviction with Jews—the specific source for much dispute between Jews and Christians because they shared scripture (Cohen 1994, 26–29)—Christian and Muslim rulers were exposed to nonscriptural theories concerning starkly divergent "environmental determinisms." These floating theories privileged *phusis* as a differentiating category, making for natural groupings among humans, such as climactic origin, horoscopic predetermination, and somatic aspect (Futo Kennedy and Jones-Lewis 2016, 1–2). Such environmental and legal rationalizations for sameness and difference, which have been studied by several generations of scholars as part of "othering," are beginning to be superseded by the study of ethnicity, identification, and membership "regimes" (Caplan and Torpey 2011; Aktürk 2012; Bosma, Kessler, and Lucassen 2013; About, Brown, and Lonergan 2013; Hyde 2018)—a salutary theoretical refocusing on documenting events and not just representations. Arjun Appadurai's notion of "scapes" (e.g., ethnoscapes, financescapes, ideoscapes) hones this new appreciation for agency in the hegemonic construction of difference (Appadurai 1990, 296), moving us beyond the pitfalls of "methodological nationalism" (Wimmer and Schiller, 2003) and complementarily revealing phenomena previously obscured, such as "national indifference" (Zahra 2010). The inscriptions on rulers' tombstones, I argue, proclaimed membership regimes that ultimately diverged on what should be *scaped*: people, in Muslim epitaphs, and lands, in Christian ones.

Comparison, however, is an embattled heuristic. Many historians avoid it, despite its commercial popularity among general readers, or probably because of it—airport bookstores abound in convincing yet imprecise books like Fons Trompenaars and Charles Hampden-Turner's best-selling *Riding the Waves of Culture: Understanding Diversity in Global Business*. Critics decry that comparison distorts; cautious comparatists acknowledge that it often "smuggl[es] preconceived and uncritical concepts" into inappropriate contexts (Lawrence 2017, 5); staunch advocates retort against "myopic microanalysis" (Hentschel 2014, 1). Regardless, certain historical questions cannot be answered unless we resist the recent trends *against* comparison (Steinmetz 2014; Levine 2014), especially when attempting to determine how persons in the past thought comparatively about each other. This requires not only comparing their comparisons (when they were reciprocal)—their theory-of-mind politics of comparing—but also (I would emphasize, drawing on Michael Werner and Bénédicte Zimmermann's *histoire croisée* or crossed histories approach [2006]) thinking hermeneutically about the crossed lines between their comparisons and our own, of ourselves and of them.

What is offered here, then, is a heuristically comparative but diachronically reflexive questioning of how Islamic and Christian political rhetoric operated as theory-of-mind reciprocal differentiation. The evidence of elite tombstone inscriptions suggests a degree of intentional distancing in how epitaph references to higher things evolved dialectically—Muslim rulers holding to a monotheistic emphasis on religion transcending earthly identity, and Christian ones dabbling increasingly in the environmental determinism of territorializing political identity (in neither case need one see a "lack" of the other development but rather an ever-evolving and re-volving spectrum of choices). This approach contributes to the growing scholarship on cemeteries as sites of not only transnational entanglement and interaction (e.g., Standaert 2008; Herren 2014) but also "transjurisdictional" disentanglement. Put differently, the particular context analyzed witnessed the fragmentation of an Abrahamic *nomos convivencia* through territorializing *disvivencia* (a dialectical interpolity differentiation between Christian and Muslim rulers).[1]

The hypothesis proposed is that *disvivencia* is a useful object of historical study that raises precise comparative questions about how rulers kept an eye on each other's activities and proclamations, not just within religiously defined parameters—sultans on each other within the *umma*, for Muslim legitimacy, and kings within Christendom for Christian—but also across the *umma*-Christendom divide. In both instances rulers to some degree made what I call "transliminal" comparisons.[2] The evidence of Andalusī (Granadan), Maghribī (Sa'dian), and Castilian tombstones illustrates one key discursive issue: rulers' self-ascriptive titles. Adopting a tripartite typology recently formulated by Samuel Moyn and Andrew Sartori for studying "global intellectual history" (sorting out their "global" qualities) allows greater precision in our reconstruction of comparisons by persons in the past; and it has the added benefit of dovetailing with the *histoire croisée* approach. In this application of the Moyn-Sartori typology, comparisons or analogies imposed by the historian between contexts that were not in fact connected constitute "meta-analytical" instances—for example, contexts in which rulers did not explicitly compare themselves or even know of each other's existence. By contrast, comparisons or connections made between contexts in which rulers were indeed in contact but did not explicitly engage in thinking about each other comparatively constitute "substantive" instances. Finally, those occasions in which they did explicitly express themselves dialectically, as in treaty negotiations, constitute "subjective" instances (Moyn and Sartori 2013, 3–20). Importantly, these varying crossed histories can have diachronically subjective dimensions, as in those cases when Muslim and Christian rulers or their councillors either perpetuated or broke with pre-monotheism political antecedents, such as Roman emperors, Persian shahs, or Egyptian pharaohs (a choice that posed more problems for Muslim rulers than for Christian ones, as we shall see).

# The Tombstones of Muslim Rulers

Muslim thinkers' suspicion of state authority well into the modern age (down to the present) evinced deep knowledge of the way absolute power corrupts absolutely. By "absolute power," I do not mean the modern stereotype of unrestrained power but rather the original medieval Latin meaning of "sovereignty," here in the world of *phusis*, that is free from a higher standard of judgment of religiously derived *nomos*.[3]

Certainly the increasing prominence of ulama after the 1100s as political arbiters to whom commoners could appeal for juristic pronouncements against tyrannical rulers (Bulliet 2004, 61–68) must have deepened rulers' anxieties about secular authority—for lack of a better term. The imperative to stay within the parameters of religious legitimacy reinforced the normalization circa 1000 of a new juridical logic for "just war" thinking that inverted the earlier caliphal standard of judgment based on a unique legitimacy tied to a dichotomy between *dār al-islām* and *dār al-ḥarb*. As Fred Donner explains, "Muslim rulers did not consult the jurists to discover whether they were legitimate and therefore entitled to wage *jihad*, but rather by waging *jihad* they offered evidence of the legitimacy of their claim to rule" (1991, 51).

The more fragmented the *umma* was de facto, the more the actions of rulers were exposed to the scrutiny of ulama who catered to rulers' political rivals seeking de jure justifications in orthodoxy. Despite a proliferation of references to pre-Islamic kings in courtly literature, it became increasingly dangerous in official rhetoric to promote parallels with Egyptian, Persian, or Roman rulers. The Persian polemicist 'Abd al-Jabbār (d. 1025) was certainly not the only state official to accuse early Christians of selling out true Christianity to the Romans in exchange for worldly power (Stern 1968, 133–36). And pharaonic precedent became the ideological and religious epitome of illegitimate rule and worldliness, a key way of undermining opponents by implying their *jāhilī* or pre-Islamic politics (Broadbridge 2008, 33–35, 49–50, 113, 139–45). As these critiques were refined, between the Fatimid and Ottoman periods, absolute authority stemming merely from secular power, like that of Persian shahs or Egyptian pharaohs, increasingly became ideological anathema. Smart rulers realized that too much diachronically transliminal similarity with shahs and pharaohs was political suicide.

Erosion of the legitimacy of rulers, like the conformism of commoners, might thus involve criticism of burial practices suspected as corrupt or too similar to pre-Islamic practices (Renaerts 1986, 9–20, 48–73; Granqvist 1965, 54; Aldeeb Abu-Sahlieh 2002, 103; Ho 2006, 84). Certainly, early Muslim rulers preferred simple tombs, which, not surprisingly, frequently affirmed God's *mulk* or sovereignty, citing Qur'an 67:1. Almost two centuries passed before epitaphs became the norm on Muslim tombs, still against the better judgment of pietists who argued that "inscribing tombstones" constituted "a blameworthy innovation that violated the customs of Medina": Muḥammad's grave, after all, was a simple niche in his wife's mud-brick bedroom and possessed no epitaph (Halevi 2007, 15). The oldest biography of Muḥammad recorded him forecasting that "a nation . . . which makes the graves of its prophets into places of worship" falls into idolatry—and also recorded his widow confirming that that was precisely what took place: "When the apostle of God died many Arabs relapsed into idolatry: Judaism and Christianity rose again, and Hypocrisy became common" (Ibn Isḥāq 1964, 177; translation modified).

The proliferation of polities in a fragmented *umma* heightened juristic concerns about official burials. Circa 1100 CE Ibn Rushd the Grandfather (d. 1126 CE) recalled that the founder of the Mālikī school—in a conflation of the powerful with thieves that would have pleased Saint Augustine—"abhorred the 'inscribed flagstone' because the practice was one of the innovations (*bidʻa* [*sic*]) by which powerful magnates (*ahl al-ṭawl*) seek glory and fame" (Halevi 2007, 237). However, both Umayyads and Abbasids built mausoleums, and the former's dynastic descendants in al-Andalus brought the questionable habit westward (Peral Bejarano 1995, 7–10), undoubtedly exacerbating sociopolitical tension, for even the wealthiest Muslims continued to prefer tombs so simple that modern archaeologists cannot easily differentiate them from commoners' graves (Martínez García, Mellado Sáez, and del Mar Muñoz Martín 1995, 107; Galve Izquierdo 1995, 127). Archaeological evidence establishes that tombstone epitaphs nevertheless became common as highly visible tools of socioeconomic competition by the fourteenth century (Kervran 1996, 69–71; Vatin and Yerasimos 1996, 39; Moazz 1996, 80; Marcus 1996, 103; Renaerts 1986, 76). For this reason many ulama remained suspicious of cemeteries (Masulović-Marsol 1996, 121–34), and not merely in extreme cases such as the anthropomorphic Muslim gravestones of early Ottoman Bulgaria (Mikov 1996, 189–98). Al-Wansharīsī (d. 1508), for instance, "did not recommend" epitaphs but was willing to allow scripturally relevant ones, though Qur'anic quotations had to be installed in a manner that made it impossible to trample on them (Halevi 2007, 40–41). What, then, did the tombstones of Muslim rulers tell Andalusī and Maghribī passersby?

The design of Granada's Alhambra tombs seems to have conformed to wide-spread practices, but little remains of them (Amador de los Ríos 1896, 1906, 1910; Torres Balbás 1926, 1936, 1957; Martínez Núñez 2011). Muslim tombs were regularly appropriated for construction purposes not just during Muslim rule but especially after Christian conquest (López López et al. 1995, 138). Happily, a copy of the epitaphs on the tombstones of the Nasrid sultans of Granada survives in a little-known book titled *The Luminous Light of the Full Moon (al-Lamḥa al-badrīya)*, written circa 1360 by a well-known Granadan native, chief minister to several sultans, and prolific author, Ibn al-Khaṭīb (1313–1375). The epitaphs of the Nasrid rulers that he transcribed belonged to the graves of Muḥammad I (d. 1275), Muḥammad III (d. 1314), Naṣr (d. 1322), Ismāʿīl I (d. 1325), Muḥammad IV (d. 1333), and Yūsuf I (d. 1354). Three of these tombstones, "alabaster stones vertically driven into the ground with golden lettering on a blue background," were discovered in 1574 near Charles V's palace, located inside the grounds of the Alhambra, and corresponded to the graves of the first Muḥammad, Ismāʿīl and Yūsuf; the other three stones were apparently lost (Torres Balbás 1936, 186–88; Casciaro 1998, lxxiii–lxxv).

None of the princely epitaphs contained any references to Granada as a territorial entity. Each was composed of two inscriptions, one prose and the other a poem. That of Muḥammad I read: "This is the tomb of the excellent sultan, the honor of Islam, a handsome man among men, glorious by day and night, the deliverer of the common people, the shower of mercy, the North Pole of religion," and so on, without any reference to a specific territorial jurisdiction. The poetic epitaph spoke to Muḥammad's orthodoxy in religion, bravery in battle, generosity in government, and sanctity in behavior: "These were the signs of his noble actions, more manifest and more evident than fire on a star [*min nār ʿalā ʿalam*]" (Ibn al-Khaṭīb 1978, 49). Muḥammad III's epitaph contained encomia relating how he "opened the doors for his subjects to enter prosperity and safety" and "remained steadfast in the war against unbelievers." Specific titles appeared alongside, such as "Emir of the Muslims" and "Defender of the Faithful" (*ẓāhir al-muʾminīn*), but there was no mention of the specific territory he defended or the city in which he was buried (68). As far as we can tell, the early panegyric style was followed by the rest of the dynasty (76–77, 87–89, 96–98, 110–12). From these nonterritorial and nonethnicized titles one might not even know that the Nasrids reigned in Granada or ruled what was one of western Europe's most densely populated regions.

Of course, Muslim contemporaries divided their world into territories, ethnicities, and other useful categories. The terms *quṭr* (region or zone), *waṭan* (homeland, nation; Sp. *patria*), and *bilād* (country or homeland in the Spanish sense of

*patria chica*) all appeared regularly in Ibn al-Khaṭīb's writing, as did Castile, Aragon, Tlemcen, Tunis, and Marrakech (though, revealingly, unlike the former two
politonyms, the latter three originated in city names). Nothing in the terminology
of these Arabic epitaphs, however, corresponded to either contemporary geographical jurisdictions or pre-Islamic Roman provincial politonyms (Baetica, Lu-
sitania, Hispania, Tarraconensis, Carthaginensis, Mauretania, Tingitana), and
certainly nothing like the Latin *regnum* or kingdom appeared in them. On occasion, rhetorical comparisons to rivals brought home the dangers of kingship *tout
court*. One important tomb in Marrakech, that of the sixteenth-century Saʿdian
founding hero, Abū ʿAbdallāh Muḥammad al-Shaykh (r. 1555–1557), mentioned
how he conquered Fez "at the time of the Maghribī kingship [*mulk*]" of the Marinid dynasty (*MPSM*, 1:33). This territorialization intentionally reduced the
Saʿdian's Marinid rivals to mere kingship, emphasizing geographical and political
instead of religious or moral qualities.[4] Arabic chroniclers likewise deployed such
terms judiciously: in one piece of Almohad propaganda, the Almoravids' attachment to power over "our land" (*bilādunā*) and "our state" (*dawlatunā*) rhetorically
delegitimized them (al-Baydhaq 1928, 69). And when the pro-Marinid Ibn Abī
Zarʿ described the 1285 meeting near Jerez between the Marinid ambassador ʿAbd
al-Ḥaqq and the defeated Castilian ruler Sancho IV (who was suing for peace that
autumn), both ambassador and historian made sure that any Christian leader—
and future readers of the Arabic text—would understand that ʿAbd al-Ḥaqq's
Muslim lord, Yaʿqūb Abū Yūsuf, was "a commander of the faithful" and not merely
a "king" like Castilian rulers: after the Christian emissaries demeaned the Muslim
ruler by greeting him as "Oh victorious king," Abū Yūsuf instructed his ambassador to "go and tell this miserable wretch that it is the emir of the faithful who
speaks to him," which Sancho submissively (or diplomatically) did when he met
the emir in person on October 21 (Ibn Abī Zarʿ 1999, 466–74). Concrete examples
of exchanges such as these are telling evidence of the import of subjectively transliminal comparisons (adapting the Moyn-Sartori typology).

Muslim political protocol thus considered the typically territorialized titles
of Christian rulers as demotions when compared with nonterritorial Muslim
ones, a mode of thinking that allowed for derision of a more precise nature.
This probably explains why Ibn al-Khaṭīb called Fernando III (Firnānda ibn
Alfūnsh) and his son Alfonso X (Alfūnsh) kings "in Castile [*fī Qashtāla*]" and
not kings "of Castile" (Ibn al-Khaṭīb 1978, 45), putting them *in* their place, if
the pun is allowed, even more condescendingly than Ibn Abī Zarʿ. With a subjectively transliminal Christian-Muslim alternation between Arabic "in" and
Castilian/Latin "of," the wise Muslim politician may have been shrewdly reject-
ing what by the 1200s had become the normal practice of Christian kings, who

called themselves rulers *of* places (as discussed below). The Christian practice, in Ibn al-Khaṭīb's view, must have sounded ridiculously self-defeating within a broader, shared Abrahamic understanding of God's sovereign and universal *mulk* or kingship (a fact that savvy bilingual contemporaries would have picked up on).[5]

The epitaphs on Saʿdian tombs in Marrakech are consistent with the Granadan practice, as are epitaphs on other North African dynastic tombs into the nineteenth century. Over forty inscriptions survive from the 128 Saʿdian tombs still extant (plus several lapidary inscriptions), not counting dozens of now illegible or originally blank tombstones marking graves of *sharīf*s or descendants of the prophet Muhammad. Like Queen Isabel's tomb, which we shall analyze shortly, that of the dynasty's most powerful ruler, al-Manṣūr, was made of Italian marble. Not all the tombs were royal, but a courtly association can be presumed, including an émigré Granadan nobleman, a few ministers and courtiers, and many of the sultans' wives. Despite possible pre-Islamic Persian design influence (Bagherzadeh 1996, 172), the inscriptions in the Saʿdian mausoleum paralleled Nasrid discourse, describing the successes, merits, and eternal glory of rulers while eschewing territorial references, with one vague exception.[6] Glories might include reestablishing the "caliphate," as in the case of the Saʿdian conqueror of Fez mentioned above (*MPSM*, 1:32). Al-Manṣūr's (r. 1578–1603) inscription played on his nickname, "The Golden [*al-dhahabī*]," by praising God for "chasing away our sadness [*adhhaba ʿannā al-ḥuzn*]." Whatever hyperbole was deployed by epitaph authors, territorial specificity was avoided: "This is the tomb of he whose deeds are glorified, Aḥmad of the victorious standard [*manṣūr al-liwāʾi*] . . ." The epitaph of his son Zaydān (r. 1603–1627/28), "the triumphant hero" of the tombstone's poetic eulogy, had no clear geopolitical affiliation either, though, significantly, it did quote Qurʾan 2:255 on the general topic of kingly authority and power: "His throne [viz. God's] extends over the heavens and the earth [*al-samawāt waʾl-arḍ*] and He feels no fatigue in guarding them; He is the Most High, the Most Powerful" (*MPSM*, 1:11–13).

The contrast could not have been more striking: Zaydān, glorious in his military and political struggle for Islam, bound by the difficulties of worldly authority, versus God, effortless in His power and boundless in His presence. If Saʿdian monarchs were expected to reach out to protect Islam against infidels (e.g., *MSPM*, 1:24), it was nevertheless also true that their reach, unlike God's transcendent power over all things physical, should remain without territorial invocation: only God could rule the two worlds of earth and the afterlife. A ruler's lot was to guard *nomos*, not to possess *phusis* (*arḍ*).

# The Tombstones of Christian Rulers

Unlike the tombs of medieval Muslim rulers, those of Christian rulers were suffused with ever more carefully territorialized jurisdictional ascriptions, expressed with reference to ethnonyms constructed either prepositionally or adjectivally ("King of the Franks" or "French king") or—the later trend—with jurisdictional politonyms ("king of" or "in France"). The shift became discursively hegemonic within Christendom in the twelfth century, most famously as part of Abbot Suger's (ca. 1081–1151) program for sacral monarchy. Gothic architecture enshrined the difference between individual mortal kings and an intentionally less mortal kingdom. This was why Suger preferred to call Louis the Fat "King of France" instead of the previously more common "King of the Franks" (Suger 1979, 258, 268, 280), a tendency mirrored in chronicles (a separate question would be why Muslim epitaphs did not match the bias of Arabic chroniclers toward dynastic and ethnic/tribal ascriptions). Europe's churches and cemeteries became so full of epitaphs with interlocking territorialized jurisdictional titles, like Suger's description of Roger as "King of Sicily, Duke of Apulia and Prince of Capua" (Suger 1979, 258, 268, 280), that the quite different discursive practice of the Granadan and Marrakech epitaphs may surprise the reader today—as it undoubtedly surprised discerning bilingual travelers back then. Space precludes analyzing how this Christian territorializing practice consciously evoked Roman imperial practice or Carolingian elaborations, but one initial observation suggests itself.

Without essentializing Islamic notions of territory, jurisdiction, or authority, it may be argued that principles inspired by Islamic legal reasoning, especially after circa 1000 CE, increasingly encouraged Muslim elites to prioritize legitimating their polities as religiously bounded *communities* instead of religiously bounded *land*. This new practice broke with both pre-Islamic assumptions and contemporary Christian political trends (we will return briefly to diplomatic evidence that helps us understand the latter). This Muslim prioritization had long-lasting political consequences, liberating Muslim rulers from the discursive nightmare faced by Christian rulers who sought to reconcile principles of secular authority grounded in Roman law with religious ones grounded in God's biblical *nomos*. Significantly, for our purposes, the twelfth-century intellectual crisis caused by merging Bible and canon law with the *Corpus Iuris Civilis* (a title invented then and not under Justinian) was compounded by the "legal revolution" that created "a unified theory of *ius*" as opposed to "law" in Christendom (Tolan 2015, 67, 71); and both of these developments coincided with the territorialization of jurisdiction in fisc and administration (Bisson 1989,

147; Goemans 2006)—in my view causally. Not surprisingly, chronicles, royal seals, and epitaphs also began to assign territorial titles to kings much more systematically. These legal reform projects posed challenges in the Iberian kingdoms in subsequent centuries because they encouraged litigious *disvivencia* hardliners to decry the personal jurisdiction of their subject neighbors who lived according to the Law of Moses or the Law of Muhammad within putatively merged Romano-canonically territorialized jurisdictions. Even without that added complication, however, Christian ruling elites were obsessed with reconciling the model of Rome's territorial polity with the papacy's spiritual polity. The perennial struggles of Muslim rulers with the ulama, despite the eclipsing of effective, unitarian caliphal power, thus never matched the aporia faced by Christian thinkers who attempted to syncretize Rome with the Bible.

How did territorialization play out in Christian-ruled Iberia? Iconographic and heraldic identifiers mattered more than territoriality in the early medieval tombs of Asturian-Leonese royalty. Those of Ordoño I (d. 866) and Urraca (d. 956) identified the deceased simply as "king," "queen," or "prince" (*rex, regina, princeps*) without politonymic or ethnonymic specificity. The first piece of unambiguously territorial Iberian epigraphic evidence is the twelfth-century inscription added by Fernando II (r. 1157–1188) to the tomb of his father, Sancho el Mayor (r. 1004–1035), in Leon: "Here lies Sancho King of the Pyrenees Mountains and of Toulouse, in all things a Catholic man and defender of the Church . . ." (Arco 1954, 47–48, 56, 60–63). The shift from ethnonyms to politonyms is also attested in royal seals: from Alfonso VI's eleventh-century "most victorious king in Toledo and in Spain and Gaul [*victoriosissimus rex in Toleto et in Hispania et Gallaecia*]" to Alfonso VIII's twelfth-century "King of Toledo and Castile [*Rex Toleti et Castell[a]e*]." Thereafter the Leonese tombs were filled with references to "Kings of Leon" and "Counts of Castile," and—in the case of one Fernando who aimed to surpass Sancho el Mayor's imperialist ambitions—"King of all Spain, son of Sancho King of the Pyrenees Mountains and Toulouse [*rex totius Hispaniae filius Sanctii Regis Pirenaeorum et Tolosae*]." So common did this territorializing practice become that Alfonso VI extended the courtesy to a Muslim ruler in the twelfth century (a backhanded compliment given contemporary Muslim preferences) by describing his wife Isabel, née Zaida, as "the daughter of Ibn ʿAbbād, king of Seville [*filia Benabet regis Siviliae*]," the famous monarch and poet al-Muʿtamid, who died in Almoravid-imposed exile in North Africa (Arco 1954, 56–57, 185ff.).

At the level of royal neighborliness, from England to Castile, tombstone evidence confirms that by the 1250s Christian territorialization of sovereign titles was a transliminally policed elite norm. The tomb of Queen Eleanor at Westminster, daughter of Fernando III of Castile and wife of King Edward I of England, is a testament to the integrated nature of the Christian political transformation by the time she died in 1290: "Here lies Eleanor, once queen of England [*Icy gist Alianor, jadis reyne de Angleterre*]" (Blore 1826, 5). And on the extreme southern frontier of Christendom, Alfonso X, the famous "king of the three faiths" and Eleanor's contemporary, told the story, in *Cantiga* number 292, of how he had the bodies of his parents, Saint Fernando III and Beatrice of Swabia, transferred to Seville's cathedral (architecturally a mosque until the 1401 Gothic refurbishment). The four epitaphs on his father's tomb, one each in Latin, Castilian, Arabic, and Hebrew, transformed territorial accumulation into his father's glory: "King of Castile, Toledo, Leon, Galicia, Seville, Cordoba, Murcia, Jaen; he who conquered all of Spain" (the Hebrew and Arabic versions omitted the last phrase [Arco 1954, 107, 230–31]).

Analogous lists of kingdoms on the tombstones of Christian rulers would be repeated down through the centuries. The tombs of the Catholic monarchs in Granada, sculpted in Carrara marble by the Italian Domenico Alessandro Fancelli between 1514 and 1517, exemplify the Renaissance practice of aggrandizing rulers as human synecdoches for territories. Isabel was as conscious as Muslim rulers were of the tension between earthly power and metaphysical sanctity, requesting in her will that her grave be made "low" with "no large structure at all except for a flat stone on the ground carrying the graven inscription." The queen desired a modest epitaph because no soul could be sure of "justification" before God, least of all "those of us who must give account [to Him] of how we ruled great Kingdoms and States." But the second article in her will (after the pro forma doxology) carried the predictable territorial formula: "I, Doña Isabel, Queen of Castile, Leon, Aragon, Sicily, Granada, Toledo, Valencia, Galicia, Mallorca, Seville, Sardinia, Cordoba, Corsica, Murcia and Jaen" (Ballesteros Gaibrois 1964, 236–37). The sepulcher built by Fernando for both of them before his death, completed by Charles V in 1521, ignores Isabel's plea for simplicity, rising so high that visitors could barely make out the supine alabaster statues of the monarchs on the top (Gallego Burín 1961, 320–35). But the inscription ensured that "Aragon" and "Castile" would be understood as synonymous with a territorialized orthodoxy that had crushed both internal heresy and external enemies, an example of explicitly subjective *disvivencia* transliminality. It reads: "Fernando of Aragon and Isabel of Castile, man and wife conjoined [*unanimes*], known as the Catholics, destroyers of the Muhammadan sect and extinguishers of heretical depravity, are buried in this marble tomb." The chapel entrance inscription told visitors that it was built "by the most catholic [monarchs] don Fernando and doña Isabel, king and queen of the Spains, Naples,

Sicily, and Jerusalem, who conquered the kingdom of Granada and reduced it to our faith" (Gallego Burín 1961, 326, 329).

What does the striking difference in territorialization emphasized in this brief analysis suggest about rulers' *convivencia* coexistence or *disvivencia* demarcations on a reciprocally monitored political plane? Clearly, the importance of reciprocal comparisons was something rulers understood (well before R. Bin Wong and Kenneth Pomeranz began praising it as an analytical corrective). Contemporaries like Castile's Alfonso X and Granada's Muḥammad I (in *histoire croisée* fairness, I should not say "Granada's") intended to convey different meanings when they chose descriptions extolling territorial jurisdiction—in the Christian case: Castile, Toledo, Seville, and so on; and in the Muslim, nonterritorial and admittedly hyperbolic but remarkably modern PR-sounding characterizations: "excellent sultan, the honor of Islam, a handsome man among men, glorious by day and night, the deliverer of the common people, the shower of mercy, the North Pole of religion" (Ibn al-Khaṭīb 1978, 49).

These comparisons—using tense precisely—*are* not meta-analytical in the Moyn-Sartori sense (i.e., made by a historian after the fact) but rather *were* substantive (happening within very real contacts) and, in many cases, even subjective, most notably in diplomacy. In Iberia and North Africa, epitaphs inscribed on royal tombstones were themselves rhetorically inscribed, as is well known, within a much larger context of enduring and deep-seated, if disjointed, *convivencia* within and across Christian and Muslim jurisdictional and territorial boundaries. The movement of people—the mercenary, diplomat, or migrant but also the "renegade, convert, adventurer, and opportunist merchant," as the young Robert Burns once observed wryly—shaped images of multiple Others in an "intertwined Christian-Muslim society at the military-aristocratic-commercial level" (1972, 342, 353). All this was more than just contact: it was, particularly in elite interactions, well-documented transliminal gazing at each other's quotidian, courtly habitus, including, undoubtedly to some degree, burials and visits to tombs. Alfonso X and Muḥammad I, for instance, knew each other "professionally," as erstwhile allies (against both Christian and Muslim enemies in Europe and Africa), as lord and vassal (Muḥammad had helped Fernando III, Alfonso's father, as his sworn vassal, to conquer the Muslim kingdom of Seville), and as bitter enemies (Muḥammad promoted a Castilian civil war led by Alfonso's brothers and allied aristocrats). Over the centuries, other rulers, both Christian and Muslim, repeated what Muḥammad did in 1254 by sending "a ceremonial guard of Moorish knights to attend his lord's funeral" in Castile (Mackay 1977, 64).

At least until the 1300s (and to a lesser degree thereafter), a not inconsiderable number of diplomats, aristocrats, knights, and exiled princes (and their families and servants) visited or lived in royal and aristocratic courts run according to the customs and laws of a different religion. The eleventh-century border-crossing careers of Castile's king, Alfonso VI (who spent time living in Muslim Toledo before conquering it in 1085), and the Cid (whose career as a knight focused on serving the Muslim sultan of Zaragoza) functioned as transliminally disturbing tropes about the significance of stepping into thresholds of difference. Muḥammad and Alfonso knew such cases well: Alfonso's rebellious brothers Enrique and Fadrique served the sultan of Tunis in the 1260s along with an important group of Spanish, British, and French knights. In the next decade an even more significant group of top Castilian aristocrats under Alfonso's other brother Felipe moved to Granada and swore feudal homage in writing to Muḥammad, an ironic reversal of the sultan's previous subjection to Alfonso's father (Sánchez de Valladolid 1953, 7–8, 29–47). Muslim princes and military contingents also served Christian rulers and sought help from them against their rivals, as did the "son of the last Almohad caliph of Morocco," 'Uthmān, when "he fled to the court of King James" of Aragon in the mid-1200s (Burns 1972, 353).

The more than occasionally ironic juxtapositions of such sustained intimacy may surprise novice students when they read, for instance, that "the founder of the [Christian] Order of Santiago, Fernando II of León (1157–88)," allied himself "with the [Muslim] Almohads in order to prevent the town of Badajoz falling to the [Christian] Portuguese" (Mackay 1977, 33); these students may also be surprised if they visit the Castilian mausoleum in the monastery of Las Huelgas, Burgos, and see the phrase "Praise be to God" written in Arabic on the textiles wrapped around the bodies of two of Alfonso X's sons. Berenguela, the mother of the sainted king Fernando III, great hero of Reconquista ideology, was buried in green brocade bearing numerous Arabic inscriptions, and other royal bodies were surrounded with equally Islamic messages: "Happiness and power," "Permanence is God's," "To You belong highest honor and completeness," and, of course, the perennial "There is no God but God." Islamic references suffused the Las Huelgas royal burials.[7] Importantly, they were literally interwoven with heraldic castles and lions shouting out, not Christological conviction but an insistent territorial version of identity unselfconsciously transliminal, intended to inspire in those gazing upon them in the past (less successfully to us today) an unambiguous Christian *nomos* made *phusis*.

However, amongst all the surviving glimpses into how past persons gazed transliminally at each other—the "Maurophilia" and "Maurophobia" of Christian elites, significant "sartorial mimesis" on the part of both Muslim and Christian elites, the complex attitudes of intellectuals toward the other faith (Fuchs 2009;

Feliciano 2005, 110; López Lázaro 2013)—diplomacy may afford us the clearest corroborating evidence for our hypothesis concerning tombstones. (I say "persons" because I agree with Sanjay Subrahmanyam that cross-cultural contact happens not between cultures or people as a whole but between individuals and small groups [2012, 212]). Diplomacy, after all, is theory-of-mind incarnate. The back-and-forth trilingual work of treaty negotiators, mediators, and scribes required effective familiarity with Arabic, Latin, or various Romance languages as well as each other's *dīwān* and chancellery practices, though documents provide few details. Sufficient evidence survives, however, to indicate intense gazing across the table and careful checking of Arabic and Romance translations.[8] Naturally, the more diplomacy was sustained, as in interactions between western Mediterranean rulers, the greater the familiarity bred by the unfolding of such reciprocal gazing—but also, on many occasions, the greater the contempt (Mas Latrie 1964, 1:291).

Practitioners inevitably realized that there were stylistic inconsistencies between rulers' titles in the various language versions of treaties and tombstone epitaphs, even if exactly literal translations were not the diplomatic norm before the nineteenth century (Mas Latrie 1964, 1:270–71). It is not too much to picture Muḥammad I of Granada pondering the substantive contrast—and, I would argue, transliminally insisting on maintaining his side of it—between the religiously and philosophically eloquent titles of tombstone epitaphs of Muslim rulers and the much more terse identification of him, in the Castilian version of his 1272 seditious alliance with Alfonso X's rebellious brothers, as "Abū ʿAbd Allāh Muḥammad ibn Yūsuf ibn Naṣr, King of Granada and Emir of the Muslims" (Sánchez de Valladolid 1953, 32). The noticeable absence of territorial ascriptions for Muslim rulers in Arabic treaties with non-Muslim polities suggests that nonterritorial tombstone descriptions and treaty texts were transliminally declarative de-territorializations, not just nonterritorializations conforming to tradition.[9] Likewise, that translators into Latin and Romance languages are known to have added "more precise [i.e., geographical] designations," substituting, for instance, "king of Tunis" and "kingdom of Tunis" for the original Arabic phrases "our lord" and "our country" (Mas Latrie 1964, 1:293), only reinforces our appreciation that such reciprocal theory-of-mind practices were geared toward multiple receptions by different "political neighbors."

Perhaps the most remarkable example of the depth of rulers' transliminal sensitivities is the tortuous efforts by Aḥmad al-Manṣūr after triumphing at the famous 1578 battle of Makhāzin (Alcazarquivir). In a personal letter to Philip II on November 2, in which al-Manṣūr faced the difficult task of informing Philip of the death of his nephew, the young King Sebastian of Portugal, the new sultan took pains to let Philip know Sebastian's body had been retrieved from the battlefield and treated with all possible (Christian-like) respect. But the sultan's transliminal consciousness also led him to pay the Christian monarch the ultimate Muslim compliment, which was to completely de-territorialize Philip's royal titles in his epistolary address, proffering instead encomiums like "king of the *millet* of the Messiah [*malik al-milla al-masīḥ*]." Not doing so, in the sultan's perspective—like not treating Sebastian's corpse properly—would have been tantamount to kicking the Christian king while he was down. Equally, we should pause to weigh the theological-political import of al-Manṣūr's choice of words as he explained to Philip that his actions fulfilled "a code of mutual conduct" among "kings" that applied even across a war-torn Islamic-Christian divide (Cabanelas Rodríguez 1958, 29–34); for the word al-Manṣūr chose for this code, *madhhab*, was the hegemonic term for designating the four Sunni law schools.

The point I am making is not about redressing a balance between European Orientalist stereotypes of Muslim rulers' grandiose, artificially elaborate titles and Muslim anti-Occidentalist smugness at Christian rulers' simple-minded laundry lists of property. We need not restate the valid, if modernocentric, argument that sultans eventually had to face the challenge of reconciling "traditional religio-political obligations with the alien European concepts of territorial sovereignty and neutrality" (Bennison 2002, 108). The goal instead is to add serious analysis of the degree of transliminal consciousness in rulers' scaping of peoples or lands to Patrick Geary's trenchant idea that all identity monikers and titles are "situationally" constructed (1983), and to Edward Said's that Gramsci was right in prioritizing "territory" for cultural analysis because it is there that "discrepant realities" are "work[ed] . . . out . . . physically, on the ground" (Said 1993, 13). It is true that *umma*s (motherlands) as well as "fatherlands" require the convention-abiding choreography of "the journey between times, statuses, and places, as a meaning-creating experience," as Benedict Anderson observed, paraphrasing the anthropologist Victor Turner: but the scripts Muslim and Christian rulers deployed in "realiz[ing]" polities "(in the stagecraft sense)"—of encouraging their internal and external audiences to see them as real "imagined communities" (Anderson 1991, 53–54)—diverged dialectically. And nothing brings home a "somatization of the sign" or creates the desired "optimal confusion of the real and the imagined" quite as effectively as a tombstone, as Jean-Didier Urbain once remarked (1978, 148).

Future research can explore how such transliminal scaping also functioned contrapuntally between coreligionaries within Islamdom and Christendom. In any case, the territorializing titles of Christian rulers ultimately succumbed to a nationalism that, in the 1700s, rejected rulers' claims to owning lands—or the peoples within them. In the 1800s imported versions of that nationalism began to interact with Muslim thinking about the duty of the ulama to police rulers' invocations of orthodoxy. And both of these transliminally reflective re-scapings of the polis had trajectories that are currently being played out on the world's stage.

## NOTES

1. I use the term *convivencia* with caution, along the lines of Ruiz 2007, 139–63.

2. See my forthcoming *Transliminality in Transnational, Non-national, and Global Histories*.

3. In *ius commune* legal reasoning, "absolute power" refers to supreme sovereignty, which, by definition, must be *freed from the law* (Lat. *legibus absolutus*) at the precise moment when it *changes* it. This is what Castile's Queen Isabel was referring to in her will when she spoke of "poderío Real absoluto" (transcribed in Ballesteros Gaibrois 1964, 240), and it remains the strict understanding in more Anglo-American legal discourse, as in Chief Justice Marshall's observation in *Schooner Exchange v. M'Fadden*, 11 U.S. (7 Cranch) 116, 136 that "the jurisdiction of the nation within its own territory is necessarily exclusive and absolute. It is susceptible of no limitation not imposed by itself" (quoted in Raustiala 2006, 224). For a short history of the modern stereotype, see Henshall 1992.

4. *Mālik* was widely understood as ranking below *sulṭān* (Broadbridge 2008, 151 and n60).

5. There is an added diachronic transliminality here. In the original titles in Ibn al-Khaṭīb's copies of the diplomatic correspondence of Muslim rulers, geographical ascriptions, if mentioned, usually appear as emir *in* "x" or "y" place, whereas the modern editor glosses these same individuals as "emir" or "king" *of* this or that place (Ibn al-Khaṭīb 1966, passim).

6. The exception is the epitaph of al-Zahrā, a wife of a late eighteenth-century ʿAlawite sultan (*MPSM*, 1:6), which describes him as "the glory of the kings of the West [*fakhr mulūk al-gharb*]," an oblique territorial identification that was not politically congruent with any jurisdictional entity. On "West" as an Arabic politonym, see López Lázaro 2013.

7. Gómez-Moreno 1946, 15, 21–24, 27–29, 30–31, 53, 59, 65 and plates XXXI, XL, LVII, LIX, LXIII, LXIV, LXVI, LXXIV-LXXVII, XCIV, CXIV, CXV; cf. Herrero Calletero 1988; Yarza Luaces et al. 2005.

8. For three well-documented fourteenth-century examples, see Mas Latrie 1964, 1:278–84.

9. E.g., the treaties between Jaume I and Abū al-Ḥassān ʿAlī (1339), Pisa and Abū Isḥāq Ibrāhīm (1353), and Pisa and Abū-Fāris ʿAbd-al-ʿAzīz (1397) (Mas Latrie 1964, 2:55, 71, 193).

## REFERENCES

About, Ilsen, James Brown, and Gayle Lonergan, eds. 2013. *Identification and Registration Practices in Transnational Perspective*. New York: Palgrave Macmillan.

Acién, Almansa, Manuel and María Paz Torres Palomo, eds. 1995. *Estudios sobre cementerios islámicos andalusíes*. Málaga: Universidad de Málaga.

Aktürk, Şener. 2012. *Regimes of Ethnicity and Nationhood in Germany, Russia, and Turkey*. Cambridge: Cambridge University Press.

Aldeeb Abu-Sahlieh, Sami. 2002. *Cimetière musulman en Occident: Normes juives, chrétiennes et musulmanes*. Paris: L'Harmattan.

Amador de los Ríos, Rodrigo. 1896. "Epigrafía arábiga: Monumentos sepulcrales de Palma de Mallorca, el cementerio del real de la Almudayna de Gomera." *Boletín de la Sociedad Arqueológica Luliana* 6:357–80.

——. 1906. "Epigrafía hispano-musulmana." *Revista de archivos, bibliotecas y museos* 15:95–106.

——. 1910. "Epigrafía arábigo-española." *Revista de archivos, bibliotecas y museos* 22:418–21.

Anderson, Benedict. 1991. *Imagined Communities*. London: Verso.

Appadurai, Arjun. 1990. "Disjuncture and Difference in the Global Cultural Economy." *Theory, Culture, Society* 7:295–310.

Arco, Ricardo del. 1954. *Sepulcros de la Casa Real de Castilla.* Madrid: Consejo Superior de Investigaciones Científicas.

Bacqué-Grammont, Jean Louis, and Aksel Tibet, eds. 1996. *Cimetières et traditions funéraires dans le monde islamique.* 2 vols. Ankara: Türk Tarih Kurumu (cited in references as *CTF*).

Bagherzadeh, Firouz. 1996. "Survivance d'un motif funéraire de l'Iran ancien dans les illustrations de tragédies du *Šahnameh* aux XIVᵉ at XVᵉ siècles: Le damier." In *CTF*, 2:169–81.

Ballesteros Gaibrois, Manuel. 1964. *Isabel de Castilla, Reina Católica de España.* Madrid: Editorial Nacional.

Baydhaq, Abū Bakr ibn ʿAlī al-Ṣanhājī al-. 1928. "Les mémoires d'Al-Baidhak." In *Documents inédits d'histoire almohade*, edited by Evariste Lévi-Provençal, 75–224. Paris: Geuthner.

Bennison, Amira, 2002. *Jihad and Its Interpretations in Pre-colonial Morocco: State-Society Relations during the French Conquest of Algeria.* London: Routledge,

Bisson, Thomas N. 1989. "Some Characteristics of Mediterranean Territorial Power in the Twelfth Century." *Proceedings of the American Philosophical Society* 123:143–50.

Blore, Edward. 1826. *The Monumental Remains of Noble and Eminent Persons, Comprising the Sepulchral Antiquities of Great Britain.* London: Harding, Lepard, and Col.

Bosma, Ulbe, Gijs Kessler, and Leo Lucassen, eds. 2013. *Migration and Membership Regimes in Global and Historical Perspective: An Introduction.* Leiden: Brill.

Broadbridge, Anne. 2008. *Kingship and Ideology in the Islamic and Mongol Worlds.* Cambridge: Cambridge University Press.

Bulliett, Richard. 2004. *The Case for Islamo-Christian Civilization.* New York: Columbia University.

Burns, Robert Ignatius, SJ. 1972. "Renegades, Adventurers, and Sharp Businessmen: The Thirteenth-Century Spaniard in the Cause of Islam." *Catholic Historical Review* 58:341–66.

Cabanelas Rodríguez, Darío. 1958. "Cartas del sultán de Marruecos Aḥmad al-Manṣūr a Felipe II." *Al-Andalus* 23:19–47.

Caplan, Jane, and John Torpey, eds. 2011. *Documenting Individual Identity: The Development of State Practices in the Modern World.* Princeton, NJ: Princeton University Press.

Casciaro Ramírez, José María. 1998. "Introducción." In Lisān al-dīn Ibn al-Khaṭīb, *Historia de los reyes de la Alhambra.* Granada: Universidad de Granada.

Cohen, Mark. 1994. *Under Crescent and Cross: The Jews in the Middle Ages.* Princeton, NJ: Princeton University Press.

*CTF*: See Bacqué-Grammont et al.

Donner, Fred. 1991. "The Sources of Islamic Conceptions of War." In *Just War and Jihad*, edited by John Kelsay and James Turner Johnson, 31–70. New York: Greenwood.

Dunbar, Robin I. M. 2014. "Why Only Humans Have Language." In *Lucy to Language: The Benchmark Papers*, edited by Clive Gamble Dunbar and J. A. J. Gowlett, 427–45. Oxford: Oxford University Press.

Feliciano, María Judith. 2005. "Muslim Shrouds for Christian Kings? A Reassessment of Andalusi Textiles in Thirteenth-Century Castilian Life and Ritual." In *Under the Influence: Questioning the Comparative in Medieval Castile*, edited by Cynthia Robinson and Leyla Rouhi, 101–31. Leiden: Brill.

Fuchs, Barbara. 2009. *Exotic Nation: Maurophilia and the Construction of Early Modern Spain*. Philadelphia: University of Pennsylvania.

Futo Kennedy, Rebecca, and Molly Jones-Lewis, eds. 2016. *The Routledge Handbook of Identity and the Environment in the Classical and Medieval Worlds*. Abingdon: Routledge.

Gallego Burín, Antonio. 1961. *Granada: Guía artística e histórica de la ciudad*. Madrid: Fundación Rodríguez-Acosta.

Galve Izquierdo, Pilar. 1995. "Necrópolis islámica de la Puerta de Toledo (Zaragoza): Nuevas excavaciones." In *Estudios sobre cementerios islámicos andalusíes*, edited by Almansa Acién, Manuel and María Paz Torres Palomo, 117–36. Málaga: Universidad de Málaga.

Geary, Patrick J. 1983. "Ethnic Identity as a Situational Construct in the Early Middle Ages." *Mitteilungen der Anthropologischen Gesellschaft in Wien* 113:15–26.

Goemans, H. E. 2006. "Bounded Communities: Territoriality and Territorial Attachment, and Conflict." In *Territoriality and Conflict in an Era of Globalization*, edited by Miles Kahler and Barbara Walter, 44–56. Cambridge: Cambridge University Press.

Gómez-Moreno, Manuel. 1946. *El panteón real de las Huelgas de Burgos*. Madrid: Consejo Superior de Investigaciones Científicas.

Granqvist, Hilma. 1965. *Muslim Death and Burial: Arab Customs and Traditions Studied in a Village in Jordan*. Helsinki: Helsingfors, Societas Scientiarum Fennica.

Halevi, Leor. 2007. *Muhammad's Grave: Death Rituals and the Making of Islamic Society*. New York: Columbia University Press.

Henshall, Nicholas. 1992. *The Myth of Absolutism: Change and Continuity in Early Modern European Monarchy*. London: Longman.

Hentschel, Klaus. 2014. *Visual Cultures in Science and Technology: A Comparative History*. Oxford: Oxford University Press.

Herren, Madeleine. 2014. "The Globalisation of Death: Foreign Cemeteries in a Transnational Perspective." In *Entangled Histories: The Transcultural Past of Northeast China*, edited by Dan Ben-Canaan, Frank Grüner, and Ines Prodöhl, 59–79. Cham: Springer.

Herrero Calletero, Concha. 1988. *Museo de telas medievales: Monasterio de Santa María la Real de las Huelgas*. Madrid: Patrimonio Nacional.

Ho, Engseng. 2006. *The Graves of Tarim: Genealogy and Mobility across the Indian Ocean*. Berkeley: University of California Press.

Hyde, Carrie. 2018. *Civic Longing: The Speculative Origins of U.S. Citizenship*. Cambridge, MA: Harvard University Press.

Ibn Abī Zar', 'Alī ibn 'Abdallāh. 1999. *Rawḍ al-qirṭās*. Rabat: La Porte.

Ibn al-Khaṭīb, Lisān al-dīn. 1966. *Kunāsat al-dukkān ba'd intiqāl al-sukkān*. Edited by Muḥammad Kamāl Shabāna. Cairo: Wizārat al-Thaqāfah; Dār al-Kātib al-'Arabī.

———. 1978. *Al-Lamḥa al-badrīya fī al-dawla al-naṣrīya*. Edited by Aḥmad 'Asī. Beirut: Dār al-Āfāq al-Jadīda.

Ibn Isḥāq, Muḥammad. 1964. *The Life of Muhammad, Apostle of Allah*. London: Folio Society.

Kervran, Monik. 1996. "Cimetières islamiques de Bahrain (Ier-X[e] siècles de l'Hégire/ VIIe ou VIIIe-XVIe siècles de l'ère chrétienne." In *CTF*, 1:57–78.

Lawrence, Mark. 2017. *The Spanish Civil Wars: A Comparative History of the First Carlist War and the Conflict of the 1930s*. London: Bloomsbury.

Levine, Philippa. 2014. "Is Comparative History Possible?" *History and Theory* 53:331–47.

López Lázaro, Fabio. 2013. "The Rise and Global Significance of the First 'West': The Medieval Islamic Maghrib." *Journal of World History* 24:259–307.

López López, Manuel, Eduardo Fresneda Padilla, Isidro Toro Moyano, José Manuel Peña Rodríguez, and Encarnación Arroyo Pérez. 1995. "La necrópolis musulmana de Puerta Elvira (Granada)." In Acién et al. 1995, 135–59.

Mackay, Angus. 1977. *Spain in the Middle Ages: From Frontier to Empire, 1000–1500.* New York: St. Martin's Press.

Marcus, Abraham. 1996. "Funerary and Burial Practices in Syria, 1700–1920." In *CTF*, 2:97–104.

Martínez García, Julián, Carmen Mellado Sáez, and María del Mar Muñoz Martín. 1995. "Las necrópolis hispanomusulmanas de Almería." In Acién et al., 1995, 83–117.

Martínez Núñez, María Antonia. 2011. "Epigrafía funeraria en al-Andalus (siglos IX-XII)." *Mélanges de la Casa de Velázquez* 41:181–209.

Mas Latrie, Louis de. 1964. *Les Traités de paix et de commerce et documents divers concernant les relations des Chrétiens avec les Arabes de l'Afrique Septentrionale au Moyen Age.* 2 vols. New York: Burt Franklin.

Masulović-Marsol, Liliana. 1996. "Tombes de saints musulmans et guérison: Une approche anthropologique." In *CTF*, 2:125–34.

Mikov, Lubomir. 1996. "Monuments funéraires anthropomorphiques des musulmans en Bulgarie du nord-est." In *CTF*, 2:189–98.

Moazz, Abd al-Razzaq. 1996. "Cimetières et mausolées à Damas du XII^e au début du XVI^e siècle: Le cas du Quartier de Suwayqat Ṣārūǧā." In *CTF*, 1:57–79.

Moyn, Samuel, and Andrew Sartori, eds. 2013. *Global Intellectual History.* New York: Columbia University Press.

*MPSM (Le Mausolée des princes Saʿdiens à Marrakech).* 1925. Graphics by Gabriel-Rousseau. Arabic transcriptions and translations by Félix Arin. Preface by Edmond Doutté. Paris: Paul Geuthner.

Peral Bejarano, Carmen. 1995. "Excavación y estudio de los cementerios urbanos andalusíes: estado de la cuestión." In Acién et al., 1995: 7–10.

Raustiala, Kal. 2006. "The Evolution of Territoriality: International Relations and American Law." In *Territoriality and Conflict in an Era of Globalization*, edited by Miles Kahler and Barbara Walter, 219–50. Cambridge: Cambridge University Press.

Renaerts, Monique. 1986. *La mort, rites et valeurs dans l'Islam Maghrébin.* Brussels: Centre de Sociologie de l'Islam, Presses Universitaires de Bruxelles.

Ruiz, Teofilo. 2007. *Spain's Centuries of Crisis, 1300–1474.* Oxford: Blackwell.

Said, Edward. 1993. "An Interview with Edward W. Said." *boundary 2* 20 (1): 1–25.

Sánchez de Valladolid, Fernán. 1953. *Crónica del rey Don Alfonso Décimo.* Madrid: Atlas.

Standaert, Nicholas. 2008. *The Interweaving of Rituals: Funerals in the Cultural Exchange between China and Europe.* Seattle: University of Washington Press.

Steinmetz, George. 2014. "Comparative History and Its Critics: A Genealogy and a Possible Solution." In *A Companion to Global Historical Thought*, edited by Prasenjit Duara, Viren Murthy, and Andrew Sartori, 412–35. Malden, MA: John Wiley.

Stern, S. M. 1968. "ʿAbd al-Jabbār's Account of How Christ's Religion Was Falsified by the Adoption of Roman Customs." *Journal of Theological Studies*, n.s., 19:128–85.

Subrahmanyam, Sanjay. 2012. *Courtly Encounters: Translating Courtliness and Violence in Early Modern Eurasia.* Cambridge, MA: Harvard University Press.

Suger, Abbot. 1979. *Oeuvres complètes de Suger.* Edited by A. Lecoy de la Marche. Hildesheim: Georg Olms Verlag.

Tolan, John. 2015. "*Lex alterius*: Using Law to Construct Confessional Boundaries." *History and Anthropology* 26:55–75.

Torres Balbás, Leopoldo. 1926. "Paseos por la Alhambra: Una necrópolis nazarí, la Rauda." *Archivo español de arqueología* 2:261–85.

——. 1936. "Lápida sepulcral de Yūsuf III." *Al-Andalus* 4:155–204.

——. 1957. "Cementerios hispanomusulmanes." *Al-Andalus* 12:131–91.

Urbain, Jean-Didier. 1978. *La société de conservation: Étude sémiologique des cimetières d'Occident*. Paris: Payot.

Vatin, Nicolas, and Stéphane Yerasimos. 1996. "L'Implantation des cimetières musulmans *intra muros* à Istanbul." In *CT*, 2:37–58.

Werner, Michael, and Bénédicte Zimmermann. 2006. "Beyond Comparison: *Histoire Croisée* and the Challenge of Reflexivity." *History and Theory* 45:30–50.

Wimmer, Andreas, and Nina Glick Schiller. 2003. "Methodological Nationalism, the Social Sciences, and the Study of Migration: An Essay in Historical Epistemology." *International Migration Review* 37:576–610.

Yarza Luaces, Joaquín, José Carlos Valle Pérez, María Jesús Gómez Bárcena, Francesca Español

Bertrán, Germán Navarro Espinach, Amalia Descalzo Lorenzo, and Concha Herrero

Carretero. 2005. *Vestiduras ricas: El monasterio de las Huelgas y su época 1170–1340*. Madrid: Editorial Patrimonio Nacional.

Zahra, Tara. 2010. "Imagined Noncommunities: National Indifference as a Category of Analysis." *Slavic Review* 69:93–119.

# THE TOMB OF AL-SHADHILI
# IN MOCHA, YEMEN

Construction, Reconstruction, and Destruction

*Nancy Um*

Yemen's coffee industry is witnessing a revival, thanks to expatriates in the United States looking to improve the feeble local economy and the reputation of their war-torn homeland (Lev-Tov 2019). Of these entrepreneurs, the best known is undoubtedly Mokhtar Alkhanshali, who was profiled in a best seller by Dave Eggers (2018). After meandering through various pursuits, the protagonist eventually gains the credentials of a coffee expert and takes these hard-earned skills back to Yemen, where he advises farmers on methods to improve the quality of their beans. He then markets specialty coffee from Yemen to discriminating connoisseurs in San Francisco at sixteen dollars per cup. His efforts are disrupted, however, when Sanaa, the capital city of Yemen, is taken over by the Houthis, or Ansar Allah, causing the internationally recognized government to go into exile. A coalition headed by the Kingdom of Saudi Arabia launches a military campaign to oust the Houthis from Yemen's main cities, with support from the United States, Britain, and France. In 2015, after a harrowing journey, Alkhanshali finally manages to leave Yemen through the Red Sea port of Mocha on a boat to Djibouti.

It is fitting that Alkhanshali's final point of embarkation from Yemen is Mocha, a city enduringly linked to the local legacy of coffee, even though no coffee was ever grown there and it never served as a coffee emporium (Brouwer 2001; Um 2009, 36–47). During his brief time in that city, Alkhanshali reflects on the namesake of Eggers's book, the "monk of Mokha," his personal muse in his journey to recuperate the Yemeni coffee industry. Sheikh Shams al-Din ʿAli bin

**FIGURE 22.1.**   Rubble from the destruction of the tomb of al-Shadhili, Mocha, Yemen, in 2017. Photograph by Asmaa Waguih, 2018.

'Umar al-Qirshi al-Shadhili, the fifteenth-century patron saint of Mocha, is commonly credited with introducing the habit of coffee consumption to the world. While in Mocha, Alkhanshali visits the mosque dedicated to al-Shadhili and aspires to revitalize this once-famous port, which had declined considerably since its commercial apex in the period between the sixteenth and eighteenth centuries. Alkhanshali could not have imagined that, just a few years after his hasty departure from Yemen, al-Shadhili's tomb and resting place, located next to that mosque, would be demolished and turned into rubble (figure 22.1).

The pace of the conflict in Yemen continues today, even if it has been slowed by many fragile cease-fires, the most recent one implemented in April 2022. Yet, even when the fighting finally stops, the effects of the hunger, disease, displacement, and senseless destruction that it brought about will not be overcome quickly. Although the rising death toll is the most devastating outcome of the war, cultural heritage has also been under fire (Hollenberg and Regourd 2016). Age-old monuments have been destroyed, and precious antiquities and manuscripts have been looted. Using the destruction of the tomb of al-Shadhili as a springboard, this chapter explores the history of that famous figure and treats his burial site as a contested location, situated at the intersection of widespread coffee legends and competing visions of Islam.

# Enshrinement

The life of al-Shadhili is shrouded in colorful myths that appear in popular books about coffee and its history, of which Eggers's is one of the most widely read. Yet, these tales are quite different from the life story embedded in the local Arabic historical sources. The fifteenth-century Yemeni scholar 'Abd al-Wahhab 'Abd al-Rahman al-Burayhi (d. 904/1499) reports that al-Shadhili was born in the village of al-Qirshiyya al-Sufla, located to the north of Mocha, near the lowland city of Zabid. After traveling to the Hijaz, Jerusalem, Egypt, and Abyssinia, he established a *zawiya*, or Sufi lodge, in Mocha. According to al-Burayhi, during the sheikh's lifetime, many supplicants and followers, including well-known scholars and the Rasulid sultan al-Nasir Ahmad, flocked to the port of Mocha seeking knowledge, blessings, and intervention (al-Burayhi 1983, 263). Al-Shadhili died in Mocha on 1 Safar 828 / December 23, 1424.[1] In his panegyric account, written within forty years of al-Shadhili's death, al-Burayhi makes no mention of coffee among the Sufi's achievements or interests.[2]

After al-Shadhili's death, his tomb was built on a site that he himself had chosen, located inland from the coast (Makki 1967, 2:261). At that time, Mocha contained many modest wattle-and-daub buildings but possessed no monumental architecture. The original tomb must have appeared impressive, rising on an oblong foundation and carrying a dome; its outlines were discernible even after its later expansion (figure 22.2).

This chamber, almost cubical in its shape, was large enough to accommodate the burials of later figures, including that of al-Shadhili's son 'Abd al-Ra'uf in 857/1453 and that of a religious scholar, Faqih Ahmad b. Muhammad al-Zabidi al-Muqri in 1505 (Makki 1967, 2:261; Brouwer 1997, 34). Al-Shadhili's local prominence continued after his death. The tomb was frequented as a site for visitation and veneration, as noted by Ahmad al-Sharji, another Yemeni biographer who wrote in the late fifteenth century (Sharji 1986, 233). Like al-Burayhi, al-Sharji is silent about coffee and al-Shadhili's proposed role in promoting it.

# Tombs as Sites of Contestation

During al-Shadhili's lifetime and after his death, Mocha was a modest village dominated by the *zawiya* and local fishermen. The city rose to international significance only after 1538, when the Ottomans occupied the port and developed it as their key southern Red Sea holding. At that time, Mocha became the base for Ottoman naval activity around the Red Sea and the Indian Ocean (Casale 2010, 245). The Ottomans supported Mocha's lively trade and came to depend

**FIGURE 22.2.** A view of the tomb of al-Shadhili before its destruction, with the minaret of the neighboring mosque of al-Shadhili rising in the background. Photograph by Nancy Um, 2000.

on the revenues earned at the port. Ottoman officials would enter Yemen through Mocha, destined for inland posts, and then leave from that city after they had completed their duties in the area.

Although the first Ottoman stay in Yemen lasted less than one hundred years, early Ottoman officials contributed significantly to the local built landscape. In Mocha, they added public structures that were integral to the smooth functioning of trade and the maintenance of local urban administration (Brouwer 1997, 119–45). In the domain of religious architecture, their structural contributions linked them directly to the legacy of Mocha's patron saint. In 1590–1591, Hasan Pasha, the Ottoman governor of Yemen, ordered Ahmad Chalabi, the Syrian translator who was in charge of Mocha at the time, to enlarge and refurbish the tomb of al-Shadhili.[3] This enlargement would have constituted a significant expansion of the original single-celled form that was, by that time, more than 150 years old. Four additional chambers of varying sizes were added to accommodate later burials. The result was a multicelled Ottoman structure that stretched to the north of the original site.[4] The linkage between Ottoman authority and local sanctity was reinforced in 1607, when the Ottoman governor of Yemen, Sinan Pasha Kaykhiya, unexpectedly died at the port on his return trip to Istanbul. His son, Mehmed Bey, buried him in al-Shadhili's enlarged tomb (Soudan 1999, 80). This site was a fitting resting place for a prominent figure who had actively patronized Sufi shrines in Yemen.[5]

Saints' tombs were deeply embedded in the sectarian context of sixteenth- and seventeenth-century Ottoman Yemen. The architectural historian Barbara Finster attributes the Ottoman patronage of popular shrines in Yemen to the desire to provide a "counterbalance to the tomb cult of the Zaidi imams" (1992, 143). By encouraging local practices that catered to the Sunni population of the lowlands, the Ottomans hoped to stoke local anti-Zaydi sentiment and to emphasize the benefits of their own rule over that of their Shi'i Zaydi rivals in the mountains.[6] Similarly, they actively cultivated alliances with the Isma'ili community of Yemen, based in the region northwest of Sanaa, in order to gain leverage over the Zaydis (Blackburn 1979, 134). Through an active program of architectural sponsorship in areas dominated by Sunni communities, Ottoman officials worked to manipulate the sectarian sensibilities of Yemenis who were far removed from Zaydi authority. This Ottoman policy of encouraging the cult of saints through building projects and patronage is exemplified in the 1578 Ottoman refurbishment and expansion of the tomb of one of the most important saints of lower Yemen, Ahmad b. 'Alwan (d. 665/1267), located in the city of Yafrus on the road between Ta'izz and Mocha.[7]

The extension of al-Shadhili's tomb and the development of Ibn 'Alwan's shrine complex were carried out in the years after the death in 1572 of the Zaydi leader al-Mutahhar b. Imam Sharaf al-Din of Thula, who had seized several cities from Ottoman control in the 1560s and boldly challenged Ottoman claims to the region.[8] Al-Mutahhar's rebellion was quelled in 1569 by the wazir Koca Sinan Pasha, dubbed "the Conqueror of Yemen."[9] Against the background of this timeline, patronage at Mocha, Yafrus, and other Sufi sites must be seen as confident displays of permanence, carried out at a time when the Ottomans had access to funds and the luxury to turn to building instead of immediate defensive concerns.[10] It was also precisely during this era of relative peace that the Ottomans began to develop Yemen's coffee cultivation industry (Tuchscherer 2003, 54).

Shortly after the initial expansion of al-Shadhili's tomb in Mocha, Hasan Pasha ordered the construction of a lofty nine-domed mosque to be named after al-Shadhili (Makki 1967, 2:261).[11] He specified that the new mosque should be constructed adjacent to the tomb and that it should be used as the site for Friday prayer, thereby replacing the older and larger Great Mosque of Mocha. With the completion of the new mosque of al-Shadhili, the Ottomans had reoriented religious practice in the city. The Friday prayer was performed in the name of the Ottoman sultan and bolstered by the reputation of the city's patron saint, who was honored in two structures, recently built or rebuilt with Ottoman support.

# Coffee Legacies

None of al-Shadhili's local fifteenth-century biographers mention coffee, although they extol the Sufi's other accomplishments at length. The earliest reference to al-Shadhili as the world's first coffee drinker appears in the middle of the sixteenth century, long after his death (Hattox 1985, 18). Hence, the common characterization of Mocha's patron saint as coffee's initial proponent was clearly posthumous. As Éric Geoffroy and Ralph Hattox have noted, it is not possible to associate the beginning of coffee drinking with a single person, even if there is general agreement that the practice began in a Sufi circle somewhere in the coastal region of southwestern Yemen in the early fifteenth century. Regardless, other Sufi figures from Yemen, such as the patron saint of Aden, Abu Bakr al-'Aydarus, have been proposed as alternate originators (Geoffroy 2001, 7–8; Hattox 1985, 12–26).

It was only after coffee developed a wide following and the port of Mocha became a major international trading port that al-Shadhili came to be identified with the caffeinated drink. His reputation grew after the Qasimi imams of Shihara ousted the Ottomans and established a Zaydi imamate throughout Yemen in 1636. Following Ottoman precedent, the Qasimis promoted Mocha as their central port for overseas commerce and communication. Beginning in the late seventeenth century, European merchants began to take up continuous residence in the port. At that stage, their interest in Yemen centered on coffee, which the Ottomans had cultivated actively since the late sixteenth century, mainly for Middle Eastern consumption. Yemen was the only place in the world where coffee beans were grown and exported on a large scale, until the rise of colonial plantations in the early eighteenth century.

In fact, coffee was never Mocha's main commodity, and copious quantities of coffee were shipped through other Red Sea ports such as al-Hudayda and al-Luhayya. Indeed, the enduring connection between the port of Mocha and the coffee trade has been greatly overstated, even if it has been mobilized frequently in contemporary marketing, such as Alkhanshali's coffee brand, Port of Mokha.[12] The city of Mocha's preeminence in coffee history can be attributed largely to the Europeans, who tended to dub all coffee exported from Yemen as "Mocha," regardless of where the beans were grown. Even so, Mocha's global reputation as a coffee port and al-Shadhili's identity as coffee's illustrious inventor have been sustained to this day, repeated in popular accounts of coffee's early history and some scholarly ones as well.

Although several stories about al-Shadhili and his connection to coffee are in circulation, one tale appears frequently (Hattox 1985, 17). The German traveler Carsten Niebuhr, who spent time in Mocha in 1763, recounts his version, which he acknowledges as being "dashed with a little of the marvelous" (1968, 1:397):

Mokha is not an ancient city. It was built about four centuries since. It, like many other cities in the Tehama, owes its origin to a saint, the celebrated *Schech Schoedeli*. This Schech acquired at that period so great a reputation, that persons eagerly resorted from the most distant countries to receive his instructions. Some of his devout disciples built huts round his hermitage, which stood on the sea-side. A small village arose on this spot, and was by degrees enlarged into a city. . . . A ship bound from India to Jidda, cast anchor, one day, about 400 years since, in these latitudes. The crew observing a hut in the desert, had the curiosity to go and see it. The Schech gave those strangers a kind reception, and regaled them with coffee, of which he was very fond himself, and to which he ascribed great virtues. The Indians who were unacquainted with the use of coffee, thought that this hot liquid, might cure the master of their ship, who was ill. Schaedeli assured them, that, not only should he be cured by the efficacy of his prayers, and of the coffee, but that if they would land their cargo there, they might dispose of it to considerable advantage. Assuming at the same time the air and tone of a prophet, he told them that a city should one day, be built upon that spot, which was to become an eminent mart of the Indian trade. (1:397–98)

By aligning the diverse elements that have become associated with Mocha's history, albeit anachronistically, this story presents itself as the classic origin myth and urban legend. It gives coherence to the city's rise from its modest beginning to its status as a major international port, while assigning key roles to both al-Shadhili and coffee.

The connection between al-Shadhili and coffee also appears in later Yemeni literary sources, but with different themes. For instance, Mark Wagner cites the work of the poet 'Abd al-Rahman bin Muhammad 'Aydarus, who died in 1700–1701. 'Aydarus recounts a dream of al-Shadhili in which the Prophet appeared to him and told him to plant coffee as protection against the jinn (invisible spirits) that were kidnapping youth from Mocha. When al-Shadhili awoke, he was holding a coffee branch in his hand (Wagner 2005, 122). This episode, which involves the coffee plant rather than the beverage, is particularly fanciful given the impossibility of growing coffee in the dry, salty plain of the Red Sea coast. It also demonstrates how, by the end of the seventeenth century, al-Shadhili, the port of Mocha, and coffee had become linked in local conception, as the drink was rapidly expanding globally.[13]

Al-Shadhili's status as patron saint of Mocha increased after his death and continues to grow. His embellished biography serves as the site for the conflation of a multiplicity of legacies: the history of coffee's introduction among the

Sufis of Yemen, the rise of the international trade of the city of Mocha, and Yemen's place as the global home of the coffee bean as an export item. These legacies intersect and find tangible form in al-Shadhili's tomb in Mocha, which stood for several centuries, enduring long after the port had waned in importance. When the British took Aden in 1839, Mocha's fortunes declined. After the city's trade slowed, al-Shadhili's tomb and mosque remained as paired icons to its famous commercial past, while the surrounding city fell into ruins.

Coalition forces seized control of Mocha from the Houthis in 2017, following a devastating onslaught (Reuters 2017). According to the reporter Asmaa Waguih, who visited Mocha in November 2018, al-Shadhili's tomb was not destroyed by the damaging airstrikes that eventually led to the takeover of the city (Human Rights Watch 2015). Rather, it was deliberately razed by Salafis who were among the coalition forces that reclaimed the city and are staunchly opposed to the veneration of saints and their shrines (Waguih 2018).[14] Although I have been unable to verify or add detail to Waguih's allegation, it is clear that this tomb was directly targeted. Al-Shadhili's mosque, which was directly adjacent to the tomb, remains untouched next to the rubble of the destroyed funerary structure. Now, with the tomb decoupled from its long-standing neighbor, we have lost a building that had stood as witness to Mocha's six-hundred-year history, as well as Yemen's long record of engagement with the outside world. The tomb's first expansion in the sixteenth century was premised on the Ottoman desire to deepen the local Sunni-Shi'i fault line; its recent destruction reflects the contemporary condemnation of the popular practices of devotion encouraged by the Ottomans.

Although it is difficult to track and confirm responsibility for wartime violations to heritage in Yemen, experts agree that much of the destruction has not been accidental (Khalidi 2017, 735; Hollenberg and Regourd 2016, 158). These intentional acts can be singled out most vividly with regard to sites of veneration, which have been targeted for different ideological reasons by the various warring parties, including the Houthis, members of the coalition, Islamist groups, and others. For instance, in 2015 and 2016, respectively, the tomb of Sufyan bin 'Abdallah in al-Hawta in Lahij province and the shrine of 'Abd al-Hadi al-Sudi in Ta'izz suffered fates similar to the tomb of al-Shadhili, but neither was targeted by the coalition or forces associated with it. Both allegedly were destroyed by al-Qaeda in the Arabian Peninsula or its wing, Ansar al-Shar'ia (Hardy 2015; Mwatana for Human Rights 2018, 87–89). However, coalition airstrikes have also damaged Zaydi shrines that are of particular importance to the Houthis, such as the Great Mosque of Sa'da (Hollenberg and Regourd 2016, 167–

68; Mwatana for Human Rights 2018, 19–20, 77–80). Churches, an Isma'ili mosque, and a Hindu temple in Aden have been targeted by both the Houthis and al-Qaeda (Mwatana for Human Rights 2018, 92–99; WF-Aid 2015).[15]

As stated in a report on the destruction of heritage in Yemen, all these parties must be held accountable for their assaults on sites of historical, cultural, social, and religious significance. Coalition airstrikes have, without question, inflicted devastating damage, allegedly targeting civilian sites as well (Hollenberg and Regourd 2016, 158; Mwatana for Human Rights 2018, 49–56). The military's use of historical sites, such as the ancient city of Baraqish or the al-Qahira fortress in Ta'izz, must be condemned (Mwatana for Human Rights 2018, 32–34). It is important, however, to distinguish between the intentional destruction of sites of veneration and other types of wartime heritage casualties. Clearly, the pretense of war and its ensuing chaos have provided certain groups with the opportunity to engage in violent acts against religious practices that they deem objectionable. As for the tomb of al-Shadhili, its destruction is best understood in the context of its eventful life history, including its initial building, long veneration, opportunistic rebuilding, and legendary status.

## NOTES

1. Al-Burayhi corroborates al-Makki's death date, but al-Sharji says he died in 821/1418–1419 (Burayhi 1983, 267; Sharji 1986, 233; Makki 1967, 2:261).

2. On this point, I diverge from Hattox, who, relying on non-Yemeni sources, claims that al-Shadhili was "always immediately linked to coffee" (Hattox 1985, 20).

3. In this narrative, the tomb's expansion is referred to as "building" or "'*imāra*." It is clear, however, that this was an expansion rather than a new construction (Makki 1967, 2:261). A 1980 architectural survey confirms that the tomb's south chamber was built before the northern extension (Walls 1980, 18).

4. In total, nineteen additional graves were added to the tomb (Walls 1980, 18).

5. The linkage between Sinan Pasha and al-Shadhili was reasserted by the Ottomans when they returned in the nineteenth century, as is clear in Mustafa Hami's drawing of the tomb, above which he writes the names of both the saint and the Ottoman governor. Kreiser incorrectly identifies Sinan Pasha as Koca Sinan Pasha, the wazir, d. 1596 (Kreiser 1985, 186).

6. The Ottomans promoted their position among the lowland Sunni community in Yemen through the patronage of saints. Although the population was largely Shafi'i, the Ottomans appointed Hanafi jurists, brought in from outside of Yemen, in key sites such as Mocha (Blackburn 1979, 162).

7. The shrine was embellished by the Tahirid sultan 'Amir b. 'Abd al-Wahhab (r. 1489–1517) in the early sixteenth century (as marked by an inscription). Al-Sharji mentions active visitation of the site in the era preceding the Tahirids (1454–1517), but it is difficult to determine the initial date of the shrine's establishment (Soudan, 1999, 40, 86, 359).

8. Al-Mutahhar was technically ineligible to become imam because of a physical disability and his lack of erudition. For these reasons, he is usually cast as a "de facto imam" who served the purposes of military engagement and political leadership but was not endowed with the full remit and purview of an imam who had received the approval of the Zaydi community (Blackburn 2000).

9. The Ottomans were relieved when al-Mutahhar passed away and a clear successor failed to emerge. In 994/1585–1586, they sent four of his sons into exile in Istanbul in an effort to marginalize him and his legacy (Blackburn 2000).

10. For instance, Hasan Pasha conducted significant private trade in spices (Casale 2010, 183).

11. On the basis of stylistic evidence, Walls and Giovanna Vassallo attribute it to Rasulid patronage in the fifteenth century (Walls 1980, 14; Vasallo 1994, 213).

12. This connection between Mocha and coffee has been promoted within Yemen as well. A stamp worth 10 *buqsha*s, with the inscription "al-Yaman masdar qahwat al-Mukha" (Yemen is the source of Mocha coffee), circulated from 1926 to 1930 (Alkhanshali 2018).

13. Wagner also cites a poem, attributed to al-Shadhili, in which each Arabic letter of the word "coffee" is associated with a mystical property. Along with coffee, Wagner discusses literary interest in *qat*, the shrub that bears a leaf that is chewed recreationally across the region and is considered to be a narcotic (2005, 125).

14. Special thanks are due to Asmaa Waguih, who generously allowed me to reproduce her photograph of the ruined tomb in Mocha.

15. According to Mwatana, the Houthis destroyed the statuary of the Sheldon Church in Aden in April 2015. In July of the same year, al-Qaeda tried to blow up the structure but managed to damage only the facade. Later, in December, al-Qaeda brought down the ceiling and destroyed the church furnishings (Mwatana for Human Rights 2018, 95).

## REFERENCES

Alkhanshali, Mokhtar (@monkofmokha). 2018. "This is a rare stamp." Twitter, December 27, 2018, 11:06 p.m. https://twitter.com/monkofmokha/status/1078502534845 583360.

Blackburn, J. Richard. 1979. "The Collapse of Ottoman Authority in Yemen 968/1560-976/1568." *Die Welt des Islams* 19 (1/4): 119–76.

Blackburn, Richard. 2000. "The Era of Imam Sharaf al-Din Yahya and His Son al-Mutahhar." *Yemen Update* 42: 4–8, 74.

Brouwer, C. G. 1997. *Al-Mukha: Profile of a Yemeni Seaport as Sketched by Servants of the Dutch East India Company (VOC), 1614–1640.* Amsterdam: D'Fluyte Rarob.

——. 2001. "Al-Mukha as a Coffee Port in the Early Decades of the Seventeenth Century according to Dutch Sources." In *Le commerce du café avant l'ère des plantations coloniales: Espaces, réseaux, sociétés (XVe–XIXe siècle).* Edited by Michel Tuchscherer, 271–90. Vol. 20 of *Cahier des Annales Islamologiques.* Cairo: Institut français d'archéologie orientale.

Burayhi, 'Abd al-Wahhab b. 'Abd al-Rahman al-. 1983. *Tabaqat sulaha' al-Yaman al-ma'ruf bi-tarikh al-Burayhi.* Edited by 'Abd Allah M. al-Hibshi. Sanaa: Maktabat al-Irshad.

Casale, Giancarlo. 2010. *The Ottoman Age of Exploration.* Oxford: Oxford University Press.

Eggers, Dave. 2018. *The Monk of Mokha.* New York: Vintage.

Finster, Barbara. 1992. "An Outline of the History of Islamic Religious Architecture in Yemen." *Muqarnas* 9:124–47.

Geoffroy, Éric. 2001. "La diffusion du café au Proche-Orient arabe par l'intermédiaire des soufis: Mythe et réalité." In *Le commerce du café avant l'ère des plantations coloniales: Espaces, réseaux, sociétés (XVe–XIXe siècle).* Edited by Michel Tuchscherer, 7–15. Vol. 20 in *Cahier des Annales Islamologiques.* Cairo: Institut français d'archéologie orientale.

Hardy, Sam. 2015. "Landmark Sufi Shrine Destroyed by Islamists in Yemen." Hyperallergic, February 11, 2015. https://hyperallergic.com/181925/landmark-sufi -shrine-destroyed-by-islamists-in-yemen/.

Hattox, Ralph S. 1985. *Coffee and Coffeehouses: The Origins of a Social Beverage in the Medieval Near East*. Seattle: University of Washington Press.

Hollenberg, David, and Anne Regourd. 2016. "Manuscripts Destruction and Looting in Yemen: A Status Report." *Chroniques du manuscript au Yémen* 21 (January): 157–77.

Human Rights Watch. 2015. "Yemen: Coalition Strikes on Residence Apparent War Crime." July 27, 2015. https://www.hrw.org/news/2015/07/27/yemen-coalition-strikes-residence-apparent-war-crime.

Khalidi, Lamya. 2017. "Destruction of Yemen and Its Cultural Heritage." *International Journal of Middle East Studies* 49:735–38.

Kreiser, Klaus. 1985. "An Unpublished Ottoman Manuscript on the Yemen in 1849: Mustafa Hami's *Sevku 'l-asker 'l-cedid der 'ahd-i Sultan Mecid*." *Arabian Studies* 7:161–86.

Lev-Tov, Devorah. 2019. "This Michigan Coffee Shop Is Bringing Yemeni Coffee to the Masses." *Saveur*, January 9, 2019. https://www.saveur.com/yemeni-coffee-in-michigan?2SSjSm01u6vABiIP.03#page-5.

Makki, 'Abbas b. 'Ali al-Musawi al-. 1967. *Nuzhat al-jalis wa munyat al-adib al-anis*. Edited by Muhammad Mahdi Khurasan. 2 vols. Al-Najaf, Iraq: al-Matba'a al-Haydariyya.

Mwatana for Human Rights. 2018. "The Degradation of History: Violations Committed by the Warring Parties against Yemen's Cultural Property." Unpublished report, November.

Niebuhr, Carsten. 1968. *Travels through Arabia and Other Countries in the East*. Translated by R. Heron. 2 vols. Beirut: Librairie du Liban; Edinburgh: R. Morison and Son, [1792].

Reuters. 2017. "Gulf-Backed Yemeni Forces Capture Red Sea Coast City: Agency." February 7, 2017. https://www.reuters.com/article/us-yemen-security/gulf-backed-yemeni-forces-capture-red-sea-coast-city-agency-idUSKBN15M2FI.

Sharji, Abu al-'Abbas Ahmad al-. 1986. *Tabaqat al-khawass ahl al-sidq wa'l-ikhlas*. Edited by 'Abd Allah M. al-Hibshi. Sanaa: al-Dar al-Yamaniyya.

Soudan, Frédérique. 1999. *Le Yémen ottoman, d'après la chronique d'al-Mawza'i*. Cairo: Institut français d'archéologie orientale.

Tuchscherer, Michel. 2003. "Coffee in the Red Sea Area from the Sixteenth to the Nineteenth Century." In *The Global Coffee Economy in Africa, Asia, and Latin America, 1500–1989*, edited by W. G. Clarence-Smith and S. Topik, 50–66. Cambridge: Cambridge University Press.

Um, Nancy. 2009. *The Merchant Houses of Mocha: Trade and Architecture in an Indian Ocean Port*. Seattle: University of Washington Press.

Vasallo, Giovanna Ventrone. 1994. "The Al-Farawi Mosque in Yemen." *Proceedings of the Seminar for Arabian Studies* 24:209–30.

Wagner, Mark. 2005. "The Debate between Coffee and Qāt in Yemeni Literature." *Middle Eastern Literatures* 8 (2): 121–49.

Waguih, Asmaa. 2018. "This Yemeni Town Went from Coffee King to Smuggler's Haven." *Daily Beast*, November 30, 2018. https://www.thedailybeast.com/this-yemeni-town-went-from-coffee-king-to-smugglers-haven.

Walls, Archibald. 1980. *Preservation of Monuments and Sites: Architectural Survey of Mocha*. Paris: UNESCO.

WF-Aid. 2015. "Destruction of Khoja Shia Ithna-asheri Mosque in Aden, Yemen." July 18, 2015. https://wfaid.org/destruction-of-khoja-shia-ithnaasheri-mosque-in-aden-yemen/.

# Acknowledgments

We wish to thank all of the people who were involved in the production of this book, first and foremost our chapter authors. These twenty-two scholars are members of a group of approximately two hundred colleagues who have visited Cornell since the academic year 2000–2001 to make presentations to the Comparative Muslim Societies Program. Although we would have liked to include essays by more of our colleagues in this group, considerations of space made this impossible. The twenty-two contributors worked with us over a period of three years to prepare the manuscript under the shadow of the COVID-19 pandemic. Their efforts are very much appreciated. We also thank the staff at Cornell University Press, especially Jim Lance (senior editor) and Clare Jones (associate editor), for their support and guidance. Finally, we thank our wives and children for their love, support, and patience.

David S. Powers and Eric Tagliacozzo

July 19, 2022

# Contributors

**Patricio N. Abinales** is professor of Asian Studies at the University of Hawaii-Manoa. His research focuses on Islamic politics in the southern Philippine island of Mindanao in the late twentieth century. He is the coauthor of *State and Society in the Philippines* and the author of *Orthodoxy and History of the Muslim Mindanao Narrative* and *Modern Philippines*. His current research is on rodent infestation and political crisis.

**Angela Andersen** teaches art and architectural history at the university and high school levels. Her research examines minority practices in the Islamic context based on architectural site studies and oral history fieldwork. She is the guest editor of a special issue of the *International Journal of Islamic Architecture* devoted to marginalized communities, and she has published articles and book chapters on inter- and intrareligious interactions as reflected in architecture, architectural allegory in spiritual poetry, and communal memory and sites of worship.

**David G. Atwill** is professor of history at Penn State University. He is the author of *The Chinese Sultanate, Islamic Shangri-la*, and coauthor of *Sources in Chinese History*. Most recently, his research has focused on Tibetan Muslims, Qing official Lin Zexu, and twentieth-century High Asia.

**Anindita Banerjee** is associate professor of comparative literature and chair of environmental humanities in the Environment and Sustainability Program at Cornell University. Her latest book is *South of the Future: Marketing Care and Speculating Life in South Asia and the Americas*, coedited with Debra Castillo.

**Benjamin Claude Brower** is associate professor of history at the University of Texas at Austin. His research deals with nineteenth- and twentieth-century North Africa, focusing on colonialism in Algeria and the history of violence in the Middle East, Europe, and Africa. Some of his recent work has appeared in *L'Année du Maghreb, History and Theory*, and *The Cambridge World History of Violence*.

**Ian Coller** is professor of history at the University of California, Irvine. He studies relations between Europe and the Muslim world in the early modern period, chiefly during the revolutionary era. He is the author of *Arab France: Islam and the Making of Modern Europe, Muslims and Citizens: Islam, Politics and the French Revolution*, and articles in journals such as *French Historical Studies, Journal of World History*, and *Modern Intellectual History*.

**Mehmet Darakcioglu** is assistant dean for global programs and associate faculty at Gallatin School of Individualized Study at New York University. He studies the institutional, intellectual, and social history of the Ottoman Empire in the nineteenth century. He completed his PhD at Princeton University, where he wrote a dissertation titled "Rebuilding the Tower of Babel: Language Divide, Employment of Translators, and the Translation Bureau in the Ottoman Empire." He oversees short- and long-term study-abroad opportunities, serves as administrative director of several fellowship and scholarship programs, and teaches courses on the Ottoman Empire and the Islamicate world.

**Elena Frangakis-Syrett** is professor of history at Queens College and the Graduate Center of the City University of New York. Her research focuses on the economic history of the Ottoman Empire between 1700 and the 1920s. She is the author of *The Port-City in the Ottoman Middle East at the Age of Imperialism* and articles in journals such as *International Journal of Turkish Studies, Oriente Moderno, Perspectives on Global Development and Technology, New Perspectives on Turkey, Mediterranean Historical Review*, and *International Journal of Maritime History*. She is currently panel chair of the PSC-CUNY Research Awards in History for the City University of New York.

**Annika Marlen Hinze** is associate professor of political science and director of the Urban Studies Program at Fordham University in New York City. She specializes in urban and comparative politics, and democratic theory. She is also interested in immigration and immigrant incorporation in the United States, Canada, Germany, and Turkey. She is the author of *Turkish Berlin: Integration Policy and Urban Space*, coauthor of the two most recent editions of *City Politics: Cities and Suburbs in 21st Century America*, and articles in journals such as the *Journal of Ethnic and Migration Studies, PS: Political Science and Politics*, and *Urban Research and Practice*.

**Amr Kamal** is associate professor of French and Arabic at the City University of New York. His research focuses on Arabic and French cultures and literatures from the late nineteenth century to the present, with an emphasis on urban and material history. He is the author of articles in journals such as the *International Journal of Middle East Studies, Dibur*, and *Romanic Review*.

**Fabio López Lázaro** is associate professor of history at the University of Hawaii. His research focuses on medieval Christian-Muslim interactions in the western Mediterranean and on early modern maritime law and globalization. He is the author of *The Misfortunes of Alonso Ramírez: The True Adventures of a Spanish American with Seventeenth-Century Pirates* and articles in journals such as the *Journal of World History, Law and History Review, International Journal of Maritime History*, and the *Anuario de estudios americanos*. Since 2013 he has served as director of the Center for Research in World History at the University of Hawaii.

**Mandana Limbert** is associate professor of anthropology at Queens College and the Graduate Center of the City University of New York. Her research focuses on the politics of history, religion, and modern state building in twentieth- and twenty-first-century Oman. She is the author of *In the Time of Oil: Piety, Memory, and Social Life in an Omani Town* and articles in journals such as *Social Text, Journal of the Royal Anthropological Institute*, and *Comparative Studies of South Asia, Africa and the Middle East*.

**Rachel Fell McDermott** is professor of Asian and Middle Eastern cultures at Barnard College, Columbia University. She is the author of several books on the Hindu goddesses of Bengal, most recently, *Revelry, Rivalry, and Longing for the Goddesses of Bengal*. Currently her research and writing focus on the dual lives of the poet Kazi Nazrul Islam in India and Bangladesh.

**Farina Mir** is associate professor of South Asian history at the University of Michigan. She studies religious and cultural history in late-colonial India. She is the author of *The Social Space of Language: Vernacular Culture in British Colonial Punjab* and articles in journals such as *Comparative Studies in Society and History* and the *Indian Economic and Social History Review*.

**James Pickett** is associate professor of history at the University of Pittsburgh. He studies religion in Central Asia between the eighteenth and early twentieth centuries. He is the author of *Polymaths of Islam* and articles in journals such as the *American Historical Review, International Journal of Middle East Studies*, and *Studia Islamica*.

**David S. Powers** is professor of Islamic studies at Cornell University. He studies early Islamic history and Islamic law. He is the author of *Muḥammad Is Not the Father of Any of Your Men: The Making of the Last Prophet* and *Zayd*, and he is founding editor of the journal *Islamic Law and Society*.

**Jeremy Prestholdt** is professor of history at the University of California, San Diego. He is the author of *Domesticating the World: African Consumerism and the Genealogies of Globalization* and *Icons of Dissent: The Global Resonance of Che, Marley, Tupac, and Bin Laden*.

**Carina Ray** is the A. M. and H. P. Bentley Associate Professor of History at the University of Michigan, Ann Arbor. A scholar of race and sexuality, comparative colonialisms and nationalisms, print cultures, and bodily aesthetics, Ray focuses on Ghana and its diasporas. She is the author of *Crossing the Color Line: Race, Sex, and the Contested Politics of Colonialism in Ghana* and articles in journals such as the *American Historical Review*, *Journal of West African History*, and *PMLA*. She is series coeditor of New African Histories and of African Identities: Past and Present.

**Nerina Rustomji** is associate professor of history at St. John's University. She studies Islamic intellectual, cultural, and material history. She is the author of *The Garden and the Fire: Heaven and Hell in Islamic Culture* and *The Beauty of the Houri: Heavenly Virgins, Feminine Ideals*. She is currently chair of the history department at St. John's University.

**Eric Tagliacozzo** is John Stambaugh Professor of History at Cornell University. He is the author of monographs on the history of smuggling and on the history of the Hajj; his current focus is on the history of the sea. He is also the editor or coeditor of ten other books, including two on Islamic themes. He is (with Joshua Barker) coeditor of the journal *Indonesia*.

**Megan C. Thomas** is associate professor of politics at the University of California, Santa Cruz. She studies eighteenth- and nineteenth-century Philippine history. She is the author of *Orientalists, Propagandists, Ilustrados: Filipino Scholarship and the End of Spanish Colonialism* and articles in journals such as *Philippine Studies*, *Comparative Studies in Society and History*, and *Review of Politics*.

**Nancy Um** is professor of art history and associate dean for faculty development and inclusion at Harpur College of Arts and Sciences, Binghamton University. Her research explores the Islamic world from the perspective of the coast, with a focus on material, visual, and built culture on the Arabian Peninsula and along the rims of the Red Sea and the Indian Ocean. She is the author of *The Merchant Houses of Mocha: Trade and Architecture in an Indian Ocean Port* and *Shipped but Not Sold: Material Culture and the Social Protocols of Trade during Yemen's Age of Coffee*, in addition to studies on trade, art, diplomacy, and gift exchange along the early modern Indian Ocean rim.

**Mary Youssef** is associate professor of Arabic studies at Binghamton University, State University of New York. She studies modern Arabic literature and Arab diasporic literature. She is the author of *Minorities in the Contemporary Egyptian Novel* and articles in journals such as *Alif: Journal of Comparative Poetics* and *JALA, Journal of the African Literature Association*.

**Travis Zadeh** is associate professor in the Department of Religious Studies at Yale University, where he currently heads the Yale Program in Iranian Studies. He has written widely on Islamic intellectual and social history and is the author of *Mapping Frontiers across Medieval Islam: Geography, Translation and the ʿAbbasid Empire*; *The Vernacular Qurʾan: Translation and the Rise of Persian Exegesis*; and *Wonders and Rarities: The Marvelous Book That Traveled the World and Mapped the Cosmos*.

# Index

Note: Figures and tables are indicated by page numbers in *italics*.